American Drama
Criticism

American Drama Criticism

Supplement III
to the
Second Edition

COMPILED BY

FLOYD EUGENE EDDLEMAN

The Shoe String Press Inc
HAMDEN, CONNECTICUT
1992

First Edition 1967
Supplement I published 1970
Supplement II published 1976
Second Edition published 1979
Supplement I to the Second Edition published 1984
Supplement II to the Second Edition published 1989
Supplement III to the Second Edition published 1992

Printed in the United States of America

The paper used in this publication meets the
minimum requirements of American National Standard
for Information Sciences—Permanence of Paper for
Printed Library Materials, ANSI Z39.48-1984. ∞

Library of Congress Cataloging-in-Publication Data

American drama criticism : supplement III to the second edition /
compiled by Floyd Eugene Eddleman.
p.   cm. — (Drama explication series)
Includes bibliographical references and indexes.
1. American drama—History and criticism—Bibliography.
2. Dramatic criticism—United States—Bibliography.
3. Theater—United States—Reviews—Bibliography.
I. Eddleman, Floyd Eugene.
II. Eddleman, Floyd Eugene. American drama criticism.   III. Series.
Z1231.D7P3   1979 Suppl. 3
[PS332]   016.812009—dc20   92-3977
ISBN 0-208-02270-8

CONTENTS

For
two more truly grand grandnieces:

Calli Michele Verkamp
and
Alyssa Leigh Verkamp,

and for
these former students and long-time friends:

George Errol Smith,
Michael Wayne Adams,
Rodney Adam Houghton,
and
Stephen Charles Overman

PREFACE

This Third Supplement to the Second Edition of *American Drama Criticism* lists references to American plays published in books, periodicals, and monographs through 1990. Interest in early American plays and in Canadian drama continues. This supplement is longer than the earlier ones, although it covers fewer years, mainly because of the appearance in late 1987 of the weekly magazine *TheaterWeek* and because of the large number of articles and books examining plays through feminist criticism. Interest also continues in plays by or about Black Americans, Chinese Americans, and Hispanic Americans. Several special studies look at Jews, Native Americans, immigrants, and gays and lesbians, as well as women, in American drama. The quality of the articles was not considered; the only criterion was that a particular play was mentioned in a particular book or article.

An exhaustive search cannot be claimed, but, in addition to books and periodicals not listed in indexes, these indexes were examined: *ACCESS: The Supplementary Index to Periodicals, Bulletin Signalétique, Dramatic Index, Essay and General Literature Index, Humanities Index, Internationale Bibliographie der Zeitschriftenliteratur, MLA International Bibliography, Popular Periodical Index,* and *Reader's Guide to Periodical Literature.*

To avoid duplication and to conserve space, the full names of authors of books and the subtitles of books are provided only in the List of Books Indexed, and the full names of critics are provided only in the Index of Critics. Subtitles of journals appear in the List of Journals Indexed.

Articles of a general nature are listed immediately below the playwright's name, followed by those on specific works. Listed first will be items by or about the playwright—interviews, poems, short stories—and articles about the playwright's work in general.

The arrangement is like that of the preceding editions—alphabetical by playwright, with the plays alphabetized under the playwright's name. If known, dates of premières, often not in New York City, have been included. References in books and journals are then alphabetized by author or, if anonymous, by title. A listing of references in periodicals, alphabetized by the name of the periodical, follows, including volume number (and, at times, issue number), page or pages, and date.

Every effort has been made to prevent and to correct errors and omissions. Several corrections of errors in previous supplements appear herein. If some mistakes have escaped detection, both the compiler and the publisher will be grateful to have them brought to their attention.

I wish to express my thanks to the members of the staffs of the Texas Tech University Library and of the various libraries of The University of Texas at Austin who provided assistance in locating materials.

Floyd Eugene Eddleman
Professor Emeritus

Texas Tech University
Lubbock, Texas
September 1991

KIRK AANES

Intuition, 1990
  TheaterWeek, 4:44, 17 Sept. 1990

GEORGE ABBOTT

Hirsch, F., "The Abbott Touch," pp. 22–39 in Hirsch's *Harold Prince and the American Musical Theater*
Ilson, C., "Broadway Novice Meets Broadway Legend: Harold Prince & George Abbott," pp. 5–11 in Ilson's *Harold Prince*
TheaterWeek, 1:59–60, 20 June 1988

GEORGE ABBOTT and PHILIP DUNNING

Broadway, 1926
  Theatre Journal, 40:119–121, Mar. 1988

GEORGE ABBOTT and ROBERT MERRILL

New Girl in Town (musical version of E. O'Neill's play *Anna Christie*), 1957
  Green, S., *Broadway Musicals,* p. 173

GEORGE ABBOTT, RICHARD RODGERS, and LORENZ HART

The Boys from Syracuse (adaptation of Shakespeare's *The Comedy of Errors*), 1938
  Green, S., *Broadway Musicals,* pp. 106–107

GEORGE ABBOTT, JOSEPH TURRIN, and GLORIA NISSENSON

Frankie ("operatic" version of M. W. Shelley's *Frankenstein*), 1989
  Mandelbaum, K., "Welcome Back, Mr. Abbott!" *TheaterWeek,* 3:36–39, 16 Oct. 1989
  Mathis, S., "It's Alive: George Abbott Resurrects Frankenstein" (interview with Turrin), *TheaterWeek,* 2:25–27, 10 July 1989
  TheaterWeek, 2:8 + , 31 July 1989
  TheaterWeek, 3:8, 2 Oct. 1989
  TheaterWeek, 3:40, 23 Oct. 1989

ALSO SEE DANA BURNET and GEORGE ABBOTT

REZA ABDOH and MIRA-LANI OGLESBY

Father Was a Peculiar Man, 1990
  Playbill, 8:24, 31 Aug. 1990

Minimata, 1989
  American Theatre, 6:6–7, June 1989
  Time, 133:73, 12 June 1989

MARILYN ABRAMS and BRUCE JORDAN

Shear Madness (adaptation of the Swiss play *Scherenschnitt*), 1980
  Filichia, P., "A Letter from Boston," *TheaterWeek,* 3:8, 12 Mar. 1990
  Chicago, 37:123–125, June 1988
  Kansas City Monthly, 14:44–45, Sept. 1989
  Playbill, 8:31, 30 Apr. 1990
  TheaterWeek, 3:6, 29 Jan. 1990
  TheaterWeek, 3:12, 19 Feb. 1990

FRANÇOIS ABU SALEM
SEE JACKI LUBECK and FRANÇOIS ABU SALEM

JOAN ACKERMANN-BLOUNT

Zara Spook and Other Lures, 1990
  London, T., "6 Humana Plays Take the Woman's-Eye View," *American Theatre,* 7:37–38, June 1990
  TheaterWeek, 3:33, 30 Apr. 1990

LEE ADAMS
SEE LESLIE LEE, CHARLES STROUSE, and LEE ADAMS
AND CLIFFORD ODETS, WILLIAM GIBSON, CHARLES STROUSE, and LEE ADAMS

THOMAS ADDISON

Meyer & Son, 1909
  Harap, L., *Dramatic Encounters,* p. 76

LYNN AHRENS and STEPHEN FLAHERTY

Lucky Stiff, 1988
  Village Voice, 33:108, 17 May 1988

Once on This Island, 1990
  Filichia, P., "*Once* on This Recording Session," *TheaterWeek,* 4:12–13, 29 Oct. 1990
  Haun, H., "*Once on This Island,*" *Playbill,* 8:22, 24, 30 Sept. 1990
  Raymond, G., "Why We Tell the Story," *TheaterWeek,* 4:27–29, 5 Nov. 1990
  Commonweal, 117:757, 21 Dec. 1990
  Dance Magazine, 64:15, Oct. 1990
  Nation, 250:834, 11 June 1990
  Newsweek, 116:79, 5 Nov 1990
  New York, 23:79, 21 May 1990

New York, 23:126, 5 Nov. 1990
New Yorker, 66:101, 28 May 1990
Playbill, 8:16, 30 Sept. 1990
TheaterWeek, 3:13, 21 May 1990
TheaterWeek, 3:40–41, 21 May 1990
TheaterWeek, 4:27, 13 Aug. 1990
Time, 136:88, 12 Nov. 1990
Vogue, 180:428+, Sept. 1990

GEORGE L. AIKEN

Uncle Tom's Cabin (dramatization of novel by H. B. Stowe), 1852
    Ito, A., "Early American Drama, III: The Flattering of an Age," *Language and Culture,* 5:1–25, 1984
    Rainey, K. T., "Race and Reunion in Nineteenth-Century Reconciliation Drama," *American Transcendental Quarterly,* 2(2):155–169, June 1988

JoANNE AKALAITIS

Confino, B., "JoAnne Akalaitis's Passport to Innovation," *TheaterWeek,* 1:24–28, 4 July 1988
Greene, A., "Mabou Mines Turns Twenty," *TheaterWeek,* 3:10–14, 29 Jan. 1990
Polisner, P., "Papp's People," *TheaterWeek,* 3:12–13, 11 June 1990
Solomon, A., "Doubly Marginalized: Women in the Avant-Garde," pp. 363–371 in H. K. Chinoy and L. W. Jenkins, eds., *Women in American Theatre,* rev. and enl. ed. (new to this ed.)

Green Card, 1986
    New Yorker, 64:66, 18 July 1988
    Village Voice, 33:121–122, 28 June 1988

Leon & Lena (and Lenz) (based on G. Buchner's play *Leonce und Lena* and short prose work *Lenz*), 1987
    American Theatre, 4:7, Jan. 1988

ZOË AKINS

Bradley, J., "Zoë Akins and the Age of Excess: Broadway Melodrama in the 1920s," pp. 86–96 in J. Schlueter, ed., *Modern American Drama*

The Old Maid (dramatization of novelette by E. Wharton), 1935
    Stephens, J. L., "Women in Pulitzer Prize Plays, 1918–1949," pp. 245–253 in H. K. Chinoy and L. W. Jenkins, eds., *Women in American Theatre,* rev. and enl. ed. (pp. 243–251 in 1981 ed.)

MICHAEL ALASA and DAVID WELCH

Studio (second part of a trilogy; the first is *Salon,* 1987; the third is untitled and not yet written), 1988
  Shirakawa, S. H., "Beyond the Ghetto Mentality," *TheaterWeek,* 1:32–37, 16 May 1988

EDWARD ALBEE

Abbott, A. S., "Edward Albee," pp. 171–185 in Abbott's *The Vital Lie*
Albee, E., "Remembering Richard Barr," *Playbill,* 7:44, 31 Mar. 1989
Bigsby, C. W. E., comp., *Edward Albee*
Bloom, H., ed., *Edward Albee*
Buckley, M., "An Interview with Colleen Dewhurst," *TheaterWeek,* 3:34–38, 2 Oct. 1989
Croyden, M., "Backward Glances," *TheaterWeek,* 4:21–24, 20 Aug. 1990
Frank, G., "Albee's Play Children," *Mid-Hudson Language Studies,* 12(1): 81–88, 1989
Gilbert, S. M., and S. Gubar, *The War of the Words,* pp. 55–56, 130, 157–158
Heldreth, L. G., "The Dead Child as Fantasy in Albee's Plays," pp. 203–208 in D. Palumbo, ed., *Spectrum of the Fantastic*
Kerjan, L., "Pure and Simple: The Recent Plays of Edward Albee," pp. 99–110 in G. Debusscher, H. I. Schvey, and M. Maufort, eds., *New Essays on American Drama*
King, K., "Edward Albee," pp. 1–108 in King's *Ten Modern American Playwrights*
Kolin, P. C., ed., *Conversations with Edward Albee*
———, "Edward Albee Manuscript Materials in the HRHRC Collections," *Library Chronicle,* 20(3):94–95, Fall 1990
Myers, L., "Critic, Cornered: Michael Feingold Speaks Out" (interview), *TheaterWeek,* 1:28–34, 11 Jan. 1988
Paolucci, A., and H. Paolucci, "Edward Albee 1928– ," pp. 3–47 in M. C. Roudané, ed., *Contemporary Authors Bibliographical Series*
Patrachkova, C., "L'illusion en tant qu'autodefense (dans quelques Pieces d'Eugene O'Neill, de Tennessee Williams et d'Edward Albee)," *Literaturna Misul,* 31(9):73–78, 1987
Przemecka, I., "European Influence on the Theatre of Edward Albee, Arthur Kopit and Sam Shepard," pp. 491–495 in M. Jurak, ed., *Cross-Cultural Studies*
Roudané, M. C., "Edward Albee (28 March 1928–)," pp. 1–27 in P. C. Kolin, ed., *American Playwrights since 1945*
———, "Thematic Unity in the Theater of Edward Albee," *Publications of the Mississippi Philological Association,* 93–100, 1986
———, *Understanding Edward Albee*
Savran, D., *Danger,* n. pag.
Simard, R., "Harold Pinter and Edward Albee: The First Postmoderns," pp. 25–47 in Simard's *Postmodern Drama*
Playbill, 6:66 +, June 1988
TheaterWeek, 1:39, 7 Mar. 1988
TheaterWeek, 4:12–13, 1 Oct. 1990

W, 18:24, 2 Oct. 1989

The American Dream, 1961
 Leverett, J., "Avant and After," *American Theatre,* 7:24–29 + , Apr. 1990
 Pearlman, M., "What's New at the Zoo?: Rereading Edward Albee's *American Dream*(s) and Nightmares," pp. 183–191 in J. Schlueter, ed., *Feminist Rereadings in Modern American Drama*
 Sterling, E., "Albee's Satirization of Societal Sterility in America," *Studies in Contemporary Satire,* 15:30–39, 1987
 TheaterWeek, 3:17, 23 Apr. 1990

A Delicate Balance, 1966
 Nilsen, H. N., "Responsibility, Adulthood and the Void: A Comment on Edward Albee's *A Delicate Balance," Neophilogus,* 73(1):150–157, Jan. 1989
 Plunka, G. A., Edward Albee's *A Delicate Balance*: A Rite of Passage from Sterility to Tranquility," *Journal of Evolutionary Psychology,* 91(1–2):87–95, Mar. 1988
 American Theatre, 7:13, May 1990

The Lady from Dubuque, 1980
 Giantvalley, S., "Albee's Titles," *Explicator,* 46(2):46–47, Winter 1988

The Man Who Had Three Arms, 1982
 Giantvalley, S., "Albee's Titles," *Explicator,* 46(2):46–47, Winter 1988
 Theatre Journal, 41:407–410, Oct. 1989

Marriage Play, 1987
 TheaterWeek, 3:24, 4 Sept. 1989
 Theatre Journal, 40:108–110, Mar. 1988

The Sandbox, 1960
 Leverett, J., "Avant and After," *American Theatre,* 7:24–29 + , Apr. 1990
 TheaterWeek, 3:15, 23 Apr. 1990

Tiny Alice, 1963
 Liebler, N. C., "Magnified and Sanctified: *Tiny Alice* Reconsidered," pp. 192–210 in J. Schlueter, ed., *Feminist Rereadings in Modern American Drama*
 TheaterWeek, 4:10–11, 13 Aug. 1990

Who's Afraid of Virginia Woolf?, 1962
 Bentz, D., "*Die Zimmerschlacht* et *Who's Afraid of Virginia Woolf?" Etudes Littéraires,* 18(1):97–104, Spring–Summer 1985
 Berry, D. W., "Albee and the Iceman: O'Neill's Influence on *Who's Afraid of Virginia Woolf?" Eugene O'Neill Newsletter,* 11(3):18–21, Winter 1987
 Bordewijk, C., "Simultaneity or Separation: Edward Albee's *Who's Afraid of Virginia Woolf?* on Stage and Screen," pp. 112–126 in G. Debusscher, H. I. Schvey, and M. Maufort, eds., *New Essays on American Drama*

Coe, R., "Love Star over Lithuania," *American Theatre,* 7:22–27, Sept. 1990

Gilbert, S., "Closet Plays: An Exclusive Dramaturgy at Work," *Canadian Theatre Review,* 59:55–58, Summer 1989

Griffin, P. F., "Saying 'No' in Three Modern Dramas," *Comparatist,* 12:67–78, May 1988

Kastely, J., "Some Things Are Sad, Though: Accident in *Who's Afraid of Virginia Woolf?*" *Essays in Theatre,* 7(1):43–57, Nov. 1988

Luere, J., "A British Parallel for Edward Albee's Imaginary Child: 'A Dedicated Man' and *Who's Afraid of Virginia Woolf?*" *Studies in American Drama 1945–Present,* 3:65–78, 1988

Nelson, T. G. A., *Comedy,* pp. 3, 51–52, 72

Robertson, C. W., "An Analysis of *Who's Afraid of Virginia Woolf?*" *Publications of the Mississippi Philological Association,* 112–120, 1986

Roudané, M. C., *Who's Afraid of Virginia Woolf?: Necessary Fictions, Terrifying Realities*

Sagal, P., "Albee Directs Albee in Los Angeles," *TheaterWeek,* 3:16–19, 23 Oct. 1989

Newsweek, 114:66, 16 Oct. 1989

Los Angeles, 34:238 + , Nov. 1989

TheaterWeek, 3:24, 4 Sept. 1989

Theatre Journal, 42:372–373, Oct. 1990

The Zoo Story, 1959

Kolin, P. C., "From the Zoo to the Funnyhouse: A Comparison of Edward Albee's *The Zoo Story* with Adrienne Kennedy's *Funnyhouse of a Negro,*" *Theatre Southwest,* 8–16, Apr. 1989

——, "The London Premier of *The Zoo Story*: Edward Albee and the British Press," *Library Chronicle,* 20(3):75–93, Fall 1990

Leverett, J., "Avant and After," *American Theatre,* 7:24–29 + , Apr. 1990

Pearlman, M., "What's New at the Zoo?: Rereading Edward Albee's *American Dream*(s) and Nightmares," pp. 183–191 in J. Schlueter, ed., *Feminist Rereadings in Modern American Drama*

Sterling, E., "Albee's Satirization of Societal Sterility in America," *Studies in Contemporary Satire,* 15:30–39, 1987

ROSANNA YAMAGIWA ALFARO

Mishima, 1988
American Theatre, 5:9, June 1988

WILLIAM ALFRED

Beber, N., "Dramatis Instructus," *American Theatre,* 6:23–24, Jan. 1990

GENE ALLAN
SEE STEPHEN GLASSMAN, RON DANTE, and GENE ALLAN

JANET ALLARD

Painted Rain, 1989
  Chansky, D., "Younger than Springtime . . . Sharp as Tacks," *TheaterWeek,*
    3:29–33, 25 Sept. 1989
  TheaterWeek, 3:42, 9 Oct. 1989

BROOKE ALLEN
SEE JAY PRESSON ALLEN and BROOKE ALLEN

JAY PRESSON ALLEN

Tru (about Truman Capote), 1989
  Buckley, M., "Answered Prayers," *TheaterWeek,* 3:16–20, 12 Feb. 1990
  Horwitz, S., "Beating the *Times,*" *TheaterWeek,* 3:17–21, 28 May 1990
  Riedel, M., "Too Good to be *Tru,*" *TheaterWeek,* 3:43, 1 Jan. 1990
  America, 162:154, 17 Feb. 1990
  Mirabella, 1:76 + , Nov. 1989
  New York, 23:48–53, 5 Feb. 1990
  New Yorker, 65:63, 1 Jan. 1990
  Newsweek, 115:58, 18 June 1990
  People Weekly, 33:69–70, 15 Jan. 1990
  Playbill, 8:56–57, 31 Mar. 1990
  TheaterWeek, 3:23, 4 Sept. 1989
  TheaterWeek, 3:10, 2 Oct. 1989
  Vanity Fair, 52:165, Nov. 1989
  Village Voice, 35:96, 2 Jan. 1990

JAY PRESSON ALLEN and BROOKE ALLEN

The Big Love (based on a book by F. Aadland and T. Thomey), 1988
  Shirakawa, S. H., "Strange Romances," *TheaterWeek,* 1:20–27, 25 Apr.
    1988
  Playbill, 6:33, May 1988
  Playbill, 9:39, 31 Dec. 1990
  TheaterWeek, 1:6, 14 Mar. 1988
  TheaterWeek, 4:8, 29 Oct. 1990
  TheaterWeek, 4:8, 19 Nov. 1990

PETER ALLEN
SEE HARVEY FIERSTEIN, CHARLES SUPPON, and PETER ALLEN

WOODY ALLEN

Bell, P. K., "Woody Allen, Cultural Phenomenon: The 'Schlemiel' as Intellec-
  tual," *Encounter,* 71:72–75, June 1988
Roeder-Zerndt, M., "Unterhaltungskunst und Lachkultur: Überlegungen zur
  Situation der Amerianischen Komödie am Beispiel Woody Allens und Neil
  Simons," *Anglistik & Englischunterricht,* 35:39–59, 1988

RENÉ R. ALOMA

A Little Something to Ease the Pain, 1986
 TheaterWeek, 1:7, 18 Apr. 1988
 Village Voice, 32:86, 10 Feb. 1987

ARTHUR ALSBERG
SEE ROBERT FISHER and ARTHUR ALSBERG

LYNNE ALVAREZ

The Guitarrón, 1983
 Osborn, M. E., ed., *On New Ground,* pp. vi–viii (Preface), 1–6, 7–43 (text
 of play)

DIANA AMSTERDAM

Fast Girls, 1988
 TheaterWeek, 1:4, 1 Feb. 1988

GARLAND ANDERSON

Patterson, L., "Backward Glances: Broadway's First Black Playwright," *Playbill,*
 7:80, 82, 31 Oct. 1988

JANE ANDERSON

The Baby Dance, 1989
 American Theatre, 7:12, Sept. 1990
 TheaterWeek, 3:14, 19 Mar. 1990

The Pink Studio, 1990
 London, T., "6 Humana Plays Take the Woman's-Eye View," *American
 Theatre,* 7:37–38, June 1990
 TheaterWeek, 3:35, 30 Apr. 1990

LAURIE ANDERSON

Brustein, R., "The Premature Death of Modernism," pp. 119–123 in Brustein's
 Who Needs Theatre (rpt. of *New Republic,* 190:25–26, 28 May 1984)
Forte, J., "Women's Performance Art: Feminism and Postmodernism," pp. 251–
 269 in S.-E. Case, ed., *Performing Feminisms* (rpt. of *Theatre Journal,*
 40(2):217–235, May 1988)
Prinz, J., "Always Two Things Switching: Laurie Anderson's Alterity," pp. 150–
 174 in M. Perloff's *Postmodern Genres*

United States, I–IV, 1983 (parts performed under the title *Americans on the Move,*
 1979)
 Anderson, L., *United States* (text and photographs)

Champagne, L., ed., *Out from Under,* pp. ix-xiv (Introduction), 46–48, 49–53 (excerpts from the text of this performance piece)

Gordon, M., "Laurie Anderson: Performance Artist," *The Drama Review,* 24(4):112–115, Dec. 1980 (about Part II only)

Melville, S., "Between Art and Criticism: Mapping the Frame in *United States,*" *Theatre Journal,* 37(1):31–43, Mar. 1985

MAXWELL ANDERSON

Harap, L., *Dramatic Encounters,* pp. 106–107

Rogoff, G., "Anniversary Schmaltz," *Village Voice,* 34:83–84, 10 Jan. 1989

American Theatre, 5:44, Nov. 1988

Both Your Houses, 1933

Stephens, J. L., "Women in Pulitzer Prize Plays, 1918–1949," pp. 245–253 in H. K. Chinoy and L. W. Jenkins, eds., *Women in American Theatre,* rev. and enl. ed. (pp. 243–251 in 1981 ed.)

Key Largo, 1939

Counts, M. L., *Coming Home,* pp. 88, 92–93, 168, 175–77

Marcuson, L. R., *The Stage Immigrant,* pp. 140–143

Truckline Café, 1946

Counts, M. L., *Coming Home,* pp. 95, 156–157, 159–160, 202

Kazan, E., *Elia Kazan,* pp. 300–301, 341, 342

Winterset, 1935

Marcuson, L. R., *The Stage Immigrant,* pp. 65–69

Playbill, 8:54–55, 31 Jan. 1990

MAXWELL ANDERSON and HAROLD HICKERSON

Gods of the Lightning, 1928

Marcuson, L. R., *The Stage Immigrant,* pp. 62–65

MAXWELL ANDERSON and LAURENCE STALLINGS

What Price Glory?, 1924

Playbill, 8:51, 31 Jan. 1990

MAXWELL ANDERSON and KURT WEILL

Knickerbocker Holiday, 1938

Green, S., *Broadway Musicals,* p. 104

Lost in the Stars (musical based on A. Paton's novel *Cry, the Beloved Country*), 1949

Green, S., *Broadway Musicals,* pp. 144–145

Woll, A., *Black Musical Theatre,* pp. 193, 206–207, 226

Opera News, 52:41, June 1988
TheaterWeek, 1:9, 28 Mar. 1988

ROBERT ANDERSON

Adler, T. P., "Robert Anderson (28 April 1917–)," pp. 28–41 in P. C. Kolin, ed., *American Playwrights since 1945*
Bryer, J. R., "An Interview with Robert Anderson," *Studies in American Drama, 1945–Present,* 3:100–121, 1988
Kazan, E., *Elia Kazan,* pp. 27, 219, 495, 503–504, 506, 610, 746, 803

Silent Night, Lonely Night, 1959
      Playbill, 7:28, 30 Nov. 1988

Tea and Sympathy, 1953
      Cohen, E. M., *Working on a New Play,* pp. 13–14
      Curtin, K., *"We Can Always Call Them Bulgarians,"* pp. 297–299
      Kazan, E., *Elia Kazan,* pp. 301, 488, 489, 499–507, 719

You Know I Can't Hear You When the Water's Running (four plays: *The Shock of Recognition, The Footsteps of Doves, I'll Be Home for Christmas,* and *I'm Herbert*), 1967
      Filichia, P., "The Naked Truth," *TheaterWeek,* 1:46–51, 25 Apr. 1988

BENNY ANDERSSON
SEE RICHARD NELSON, TIM RICE, BENNY ANDERSSON, and BJÖRN ULVAEUS

MAYA ANGELOU

Redmond, E. B., "Boldness of Language and Breadth: An Interview with Maya Angelou," *Black American Literature Forum,* 22(2):156–157, Summer 1988

ALSO SEE RON MILNER, RICHARD BLACKFORD, and MAYA ANGELOU

ANONYMOUS

Catherine Brown, the Converted Cherokee, published 1819
      Jones, E. H., *Native Americans as Shown on the Stage,* pp. 48–50

ANONYMOUS

Montain Meadow Massacre, 1877
      Jones, E. H., *Native Americans as Shown on the Stage,* p. 114

ANONYMOUS

Nootka Sound; or, The Adventures of Captain Douglas, 1794
      Jones, E. H., *Native Americans as Shown on the Stage,* pp. 13–14, 29, 165

ANONYMOUS

The Paxton Boys, 1764
    Jones, E. H., *Native Americans as Shown on the Stage,* pp. 10–11

ANONYMOUS

The Prairie Waif, 1886
    Jones, E. H., *Native Americans as Shown on the Stage,* pp. 114–115

ANONYMOUS

The Snow Fiend; or, the Far, Far West, 1837
    Jones, E. H., *Native Americans as Shown on the Stage,* pp. 73–74

ANONYMOUS

The Wept of the Wish-Ton-Wish (dramatization of novel by J. F. Cooper), published 1850s
    Jones, E. H., *Native Americans as Shown on the Stage,* p. 70

TERRELL ANTHONY

Quiet on the Set, 1990
    New Yorker, 66:91, 17 Sept. 1990
    TheaterWeek, 3:12, 6 Aug. 1990
    TheaterWeek, 4:38, 3 Sept. 1990

NATHAN APPLETON

Centennial Movement, 1876, 1876
    Jones, E. H., *Native Americans as Shown on the Stage,* p. 131

H. A. ARCHIBALD

Feet on the Ground, 1936
    Kazacoff, G., *Dangerous Theatre,* pp. 183–187

ROBERT ARDREY

Kazan, E., *Elia Kazan,* pp. 168, 170, 182, 213, 214, 238, 296, 301

Jeb, 1945
    Counts, M. L., *Coming Home,* pp. 73, 75, 96–97, 111, 140, 141, 150, 164–165, 195, 196

ARTHUR ARENT

Power, 1937
    Duffy, S., and B. K. Duffy, "Theatrical Responses to Technology during the Depression: Three Federal Theatre Project Plays," *Theatre History Studies,* 6:142–164, 1986

HAROLD ARLEN

Woll, A., *Black Musical Theatre,* pp. 149, 193, 197, 200–201, 204–205, 244, 250

ALSO SEE TRUMAN CAPOTE and HAROLD ARLEN

J. V. ARLINGTON

The Red Right Hand; or, Buffalo Bill's First Scalp for Custer, 1876
Jones, E. H., *Native Americans as Shown on the Stage,* p. 114

WALTER ARMITAGE
SEE GLADYS UNGER and WALTER ARMITAGE

TOBY ARMOUR

Fanon's People: Aftershocks of a War of Independence (based on F. Fanon's book
Les damnés de la terre, translated into English as *The Wretched of the Earth*),
1988
TheaterWeek, 1:5, 4 Apr. 1988
Village Voice, 33:106, 19 Apr. 1988
Is This 24 Lily Pond Lane?, 1989
American Theatre, 6:10, Sept. 1989

OWEN G. ARNO

Once for the Asking (originally titled *Along Came a Blackbird*), 1963
Leonard, W. T., *Once Was Enough,* pp. 142–144

LARRY ARRICK

Unlikely Heroes (dramatization of three stories by P. Roth: *Defender of the Faith,*
Epstein, and *Eli, the Fanatic*), 1971
Cohen, E. M., *Working on a New Play,* pp. 110–114

JOHN ASHBERY

Auslander, P., *The New York School of Poets as Playwrights*
Tranter, J., "An Interview with John Ashbery," *Scripsi,* 4(1):93–102, July 1986

SANDRA FENICHEL ASHER

A Woman Called Truth, 1990
American Theatre, 6:11, Feb. 1990

PHILIP ATLAKSON

Norm Rex, winner of the 1988 Stanley Drama Award
American Theatre, 6:109, Oct. 1989

LARRY ATLAS

Total Abandon, 1982
   Leonard, W. T., *Once Was Enough,* pp. 195–197

W. H. AUDEN

Marchetti, P., "W. H. Auden: Teatro e Dramma Musicale," *Aevum,* 62(3):507 +,
   1988
Mendelson, E., ed., *Plays and Other Dramatic Writings, 1928–1938*

Dance of Death, 1934 (retitled *Come Out into the Sun* for first U.S. production,
   1935)
   Bentley, J., *Hallie Flanagan,* pp. 180–182
   Kazacoff, G., *Dangerous Theatre,* pp. 157–160
   Leeming, G., *Poetic Drama,* pp. 140 +

W. H. AUDEN and CHRISTOPHER ISHERWOOD

The Ascent of F6, 1937
   Leeming, G., *Poetic Drama,* pp. 144 +

The Dog Beneath the Skin; or, Where Is Francis?, 1936 (revised 1937)
   Gutwillig, S., "A Look Back in Anguish," *TheaterWeek,* 3:33–38, 25 Dec.
      1989
   Leeming, G., *Poetic Drama,* pp. 143 +

On the Frontier, 1938
   Leeming, G., *Poetic Drama,* pp. 148 +

ROBERT ALAN AURTHUR

A Very Special Baby, 1956
   Counts, M. L., *Coming Home,* pp. 68–69, 80, 136, 182

MARK AUSTIN

The White Rose, 1988
   Village Voice, 33:103 +, 5 Apr. 1988

MARY AUSTIN

The Arrow Maker, 1911
   Jones, E. H., *Native Americans as Shown on the Stage,* pp. 157–158 and
      elsewhere
   Langlois, K. S., "Mary Austin and the New Theatre: The 1911 Production
      of *The Arrow Maker,*" *Theatre History Studies,* 8:71–87, 1988

BOBBI AUSUBEL

Focus on Me!, 1974
 Natalle, E. J., *Feminist Theatre,* pp. 64–66 and elsewhere

Tell Me a Riddle (dramatization of a short story by T. Olsen), published 1977
 Natalle, E. J., *Feminist Theatre,* pp. 82–84 and elsewhere

BOBBI AUSUBEL and STAN EDELSON

How to Make a Woman, 1967
 Natalle, E. J., *Feminist Theatre,* pp. 50–51 and elsewhere

FAUSTO AVENDAÑO

El corrido de California, published 1979
 Miguelez, A., "Aproximaciones al nuevo teatro chicano de autor único,"
 Explicación de Textos Literarios, 15(2):8–18, 1986–1987

GEORGE AXELROD

Rapf, J. E., "*Bus Stop* as Self-Reflexive Parody: George Axelrod on Its Adaptation," pp. 59–68 in W. Aycock and M. Schoenecke, eds., *Film and Literature*

THOMAS BABE

Myers, L., "Taken with Playwriting," *TheaterWeek,* 2:52–56, 26 Sept. 1988

ALSO SEE ALAN JAY LERNER and KURT WEILL

ASSURBANIPAL BABILLA

Grand Central Paradise, 1989
 TheaterWeek, 2:9, 6 Mar. 1989

MARCUS BACH

Mister Jim, 1938
 Kazacoff, G., *Dangerous Theatre,* pp. 232–233

Within These Walls, 1936
 Kazacoff, G., *Dangerous Theatre,* pp. 226–227

DON BACHARDY
SEE CHRISTOPHER ISHERWOOD and DON BACHARDY

JON ROBIN BAITZ

Gholson, C., "Jon Robin Baitz" (interview), *BOMB,* 26:16, Winter 1988–1989
Elle, 4:170 +, Oct. 1988

The Film Society, 1988
  Nation, 250:395, 19 Mar. 1990
  New York, 21:48–49, 1 Aug. 1988
  New Yorker, 64:65–66, 8 Aug. 1988
  Village Voice, 33:91 + , 2 Aug. 1988

The Substance of Fire, written 1989–1990 (to be performed 1991)
  American Theatre, 6:108, Oct. 1989
  TheaterWeek, 4:11, 10 Sept. 1990

DORIS BAIZLEY

Mrs. California, 1985 (revised 1988)
  American Theatre, 4:8, Mar. 1988
  Los Angeles, 31:46 + , June 1986

DON BAKER

EarRings (dramatization of L. Smith's novel *Oral History*), 1987
  Theatre Journal, 40:421–422, Oct. 1988

DON BAKER and DUDLEY COCKE

Red Fox/Second Hangin', 1977
  French, W. W., "Don Baker and a Theater That Makes Sense for Southern
    Appalachia," *Southern Quarterly,* 25(4):49–63, Summer 1987
  Village Voice, 22:89, 30 May 1977

GEORGE M. BAKER

*The Peddler of Very Nice, Burlesque of the Trial Scene in the "Merchant of
  Venice,"* 1866
  Harap, L., *The Image of the Jew in American Literature,* p. 213

JOHN BALDERSTON and J. C. SQUIRE

Berkeley Square, 1926
  Journal of Canadian Studies, 24:165, Winter 1989/1990

JAMES BALDWIN

Alexis, F., "A Tribute/Hommage," *Présence Africaine,* 145:182–187, 1988
Baraka, A., "We Carry Him as Us," *Présence Africaine,* 145:188–190, 1988
Brown-Guillory, E., *Their Place on the Stage,* pp. 27, 34, 108, 111
Furukawa, H., "James Baldwin no Kunô to Eikô," *Eigo Seinen,* 134:65–67, n.d.
Holloway, C. G., "When a Pariah Becomes a Celebrity: An Interview with James
  Baldwin," *Xavier Review,* 7(1):1–10, 1987
Kazan, E., *Elia Kazan,* pp. 43, 582–583, 702–703, 704–705, 709, 711, 747
Kunda, T., "Tribute to James Baldwin" (poem), *Présence Africaine,* 145:193–
  194, 1988

Nicols, L., transcriber, "In Memoriam: James Baldwin: Achebe and Baldwin: The 1980 ALA Dialogue," *African Literature Association Bulletin,* 14(1):2–6, Winter 1988

Phillips, C., "A Good Man and an Honest Writer," *Présence Africaine,* 145:191–192, 1988

Porter, H., *Stealing the Fire*

Roberts, D. H., "James Baldwin (2 August 1924–1 December 1987," pp. 42–50 in P. C. Kolin, ed., *American Playwrights since 1945*

Standley, F. L., "James Baldwin as Dramatist," pp. 298–302 in Standley and N. V. Burt, eds., *Critical Essays on James Baldwin* (rpt. of J. MacNicholas, ed., *Dictionary of Literary Biography,* 7:45–49)

Standley, F. L., and N. V. Burt, eds., *Critical Essays on James Baldwin*

Standley, F. L., and L. H. Pratt, eds., *Conversations with James Baldwin*

Weatherby, W. J., *James Baldwin*

The Amen Corner, 1965
> Clurman, H., *The Amen Corner,* pp. 296–297 in F. L. Standley and N. V. Burt, eds., *Critical Essays on James Baldwin* (rpt. of *Nation,* 200:514–515, 10 May 1965)
> Cook, W., "Mom, Dad and God: Values in Black Theater," pp. 168–184 in E. Hill, ed., *The Theater of Black Americans,* Vol. 1 of two vols., rptd. as one in 1987, same pagination in both eds.

Blues for Mister Charlie, 1964
> Driver, T. F., "The Review That Was Too True to Be Published," pp. 291–295 in F. L. Standley and N. V. Burt, eds., *Critical Essays on James Baldwin* (rpt. of *Negro Digest,* 13:34–40, 1964)

RICK BALIAN

An Outpost of Progress (dramatization of story by J. Conrad), 1990
> *Village Voice,* 35:110, 3 Apr. 1990

STEPHAN BALINT

Andy Warhol's Interview, 17:31, Feb. 1987

L Train to El Dorado, 1987
> *Village Voice,* 32:134, 22 Dec. 1987

H. WESLEY BALK

The Dramatization of 365 Days, 1972
> Zinman, T. S., "Search and Destroy: The Drama of the Vietnam War," *Theatre Journal,* 42:5–26, Mar. 1990

IMAMU AMIRI BARAKA
SEE LeROI JONES

LOUIS S. BARDOLY

The Sunday Man (adaptation of F. Dunai's *A Nadrag* [*The Trousers*]), 1964
(produced earlier as *The Importance of Being Dressed*)
Leonard, W. T., *Once Was Enough,* pp. 188–189

MARJORIE BARKENTIN and PADRAIC COLUM

Ulysses in Nighttown (dramatization of J. Joyce's novel *Ulysses*), 1958
Nation, 248:247–248, 20 Feb. 1989

ALBERT W. BARKER and EDWIN L. BARKER

American Holiday, 1936
Kazacoff, G., *Dangerous Theatre,* pp. 53–54

JAMES NELSON BARKER

Grimsted, D., *Melodrama Unveiled,* pp. 61, 141, 143, 146, 151, 155
Mates, J., *America's Musical Stage,* pp. 25, 59, 69, 102, 165
Richardson, G. A., "In the Shadow of the Bard: James Nelson Barker's Republican Drama and the Shakespearean Legacy," pp. 123–36 in J. L. Fisher and S. Watt, eds., *When They Weren't Doing Shakespeare*

The Armourer's Escape; or, Three Years at Nootka Sound, 1817
Jones, E. H., *Native Americans as Shown on the Stage,* pp. 29–30, 38–39

JAMES NELSON BARKER and JOHN BRAY

The Indian Princess; or, La Belle Sauvage, 1808
Jones, E. H., *Native Americans as Shown on the Stage,* pp. 51–52

DJUNA BARNES

Larabee, A. E., "'Meeting the Outside Face to Face': Susan Glaspell, Djuna Barnes, and O'Neill's *The Emperor Jones,*" pp. 77–85 in J. Schlueter, ed., *Modern American Drama*

LYNDA BARRY

The Good Times are Killing Me (dramatization of her novel), 1989
Chase, A., "Letter from Chicago," *TheaterWeek,* 3:14–15, 18 Sept. 1989
American Theatre, 6:12, Dec. 1989

P. J. BARRY

Getting the Gold, 1988
American Theatre, 5:9, June 1988

PHILIP BARRY

Harap, L., *Dramatic Encounters*, pp. 108–109

Foolish Notion, 1945
Counts, M. L., *Coming Home*, p. 165

The Philadelphia Story, 1939
Green, G. L., "The Author behind the Author: George Cukor and the
Adaptation of *The Philadelphia Story*," pp. 69–79 in W. Aycock and M.
Schoenecke, eds., *Film and Literature*
TheaterWeek, 1:40, 28 Mar. 1988

RAYMOND J. BARRY

Once in Doubt, 1989
American Theatre, 6:11, Sept. 1989
Los Angeles, 35:182 + , Jan. 1990

WILLIAM BASCOM

Euba, F., *Archetypes, Imprecators, and Victims of Fate*, pp. 20–21, 28, 32, 39,
60, 83, 91

MRS. SIDNEY BATEMAN

The Golden Calf, 1857
Miller, T. L., "The Image of Fashionable Society in American Comedy,
1840–1870," pp. 243–252 in J. L. Fisher and S. Watt, eds., *When They
Weren't Doing Shakespeare*

Self, 1856
Abramson, D., " 'The New Path': Nineteenth-Century American Women
Playwrights," pp. 38–51 in J. Schlueter, ed., *Modern American Drama*
Miller, T. L., "The Image of Fashionable Society in American Comedy,
1840–1870," pp. 243–252 in J. L. Fisher and S. Watt, eds., *When They
Weren't Doing Shakespeare*

TERRY BAUM
SEE CAROLYN MEYERS and TERRY BAUM

RUTH BECKFORD and RON STACKER THOMPSON

'Tis the Morning of My Life, 1989
TheaterWeek, 2:10, 9 Jan. 1989

S. N. BEHRMAN

Harap, L., *Dramatic Encounters*, pp. 96–98
Kazan, E., *Elia Kazan*, pp. 71, 239–240, 241, 264, 272, 276, 296–298, 690–691,
692, 822

The Cold Wind and the Warm (based on his autobiographical book *The Worcester Account*), 1958
Marcuson, L. R., *The Stage Immigrant,* pp. 275–280

S. N. BEHRMAN, JOSHUA LOGAN, and HAROLD ROME

Fanny (musical based on M. Pagnol's trilogy *Marius*), 1954
   Green, S., *Broadway Musicals,* p. 164
   Mandelbaum, K., "Roman Holiday," *TheaterWeek,* 3:38, 23 Apr. 1990
   New York, 23:104, 23 Apr. 1990

HENRY BEISSEL

Inook and the Sun, 1974
   Glaap, A.-R., "*Der Goldene Westen* und *Die Sonne des Nordens*: Zeitgenössische Dramen aus den USA und Kanada für die gymnasiale Oberstufe," *Die Neueren Sprachen,* 86(5):370–383, Oct. 1987

DAVID BELASCO

Kauffmann, S., "Two Vulgar Geniuses: Augustin Daly and David Belasco," *Yale Review,* 76(4):496–513, Summer 1987
Murphy, B., "*Beyond the Horizon*'s Narrative Sentence: An American Intertext for O'Neill," *Theatre Annual,* 41:49–62, 1986
Winter, W., *The Life of David Belasco*

The Girl of the Golden West, 1905
   TheaterWeek, 1:5, 25 Jan. 1988

The Heart of Maryland, 1895
   Rainey, K. T., "Race and Reunion in Nineteenth-Century Reconciliation Drama," *American Transcendental Quarterly,* 2(2):155–169, June 1988

DAVID BELASCO and FRANKLIN FYLES

The Girl I Left Behind, 1893
   Jones, E. H., *Native Americans as Shown on the Stage,* pp. 123–126, 161

ALSO SEE HENRY CHURCHILL De MILLE and DAVID BELASCO
AND GEORGE SCARBOROUGH and DAVID BELASCO

BERNETT BELGRAIER

Lobotomy Stew, 1988
   TheaterWeek, 1:5, 11 Apr. 1988

Walking Through, 1985
   Village Voice, 30:78–79, 9 July 1985

NEAL BELL

Ragged Dick, 1990
   American Theatre, 6:11, Mar. 1990

Ready for the River, 1990
   Backalenick, I., "In the Shadow of O'Neill," *TheaterWeek,* 3:28–31, 21 Aug.
   1989
   Coe, R. L., "A Quartet Debuts in Denver," *American Theatre,* 7:86, Oct.
   1990

Sleeping Dogs, 1989
   TheaterWeek, 2:7, 13 Mar. 1989
   Village Voice, 34:81–82, 4 Apr. 1989

EDWARD BELLING

Made in Heaven, 1990
   TheaterWeek, 3:10, 23 Apr. 1990
   TheaterWeek, 3:41, 21 may 1990

SAUL BELLOW

The Last Analysis, 1964
   Aharoni, A., "*The Last Analysis*: Drama and Introspection," *Saul Bellow
   Journal,* 6(2):36–46, Summer 1987
   Stasio, M., "On *The Last Analysis,*" pp. 238–261 in Stasio's *Broadway's
   Beautiful Losers* (text of play on pp. 177–237)

PETER BELLWOOD, STANLEY LEBOWSKY, and FRED TOBIAS

Gantry (musical version of S. Lewis's novel *Elmer Gantry*), 1970
   Leonard, W. T., *Once Was Enough,* pp. 58–61
   New Yorker, 46:62 + , 21 Feb. 1970
   Saturday Review, 53:61, 28 Feb. 1970

ERIC BENTLEY

Bentley, E., "Büchner's Pornography" (letter to editor), *TheaterWeek,* 4:6, 12
Nov. 1990
Bentley, J., *Hallie Flanagan,* pp. 399–404
Bertin, M., "Bentley Uncensored" (interview), *American Theatre,* 5:38–40,
Apr. 1988
Myers, L., "An Interview with Eric Bentley and Judith Malina of the Living
Theater," *TheaterWeek,* 3:26–33, 2 Oct. 1989

Are You Now or Have You Ever Been?, 1972
   TheaterWeek, 4:34–35, 10 Dec. 1990
   TheaterWeek, 4:38, 17 Dec. 1990

German Requiem (written 1985; a "variation" of *The Schroffenstein Family* by
H. von Kleist), 1990

Bell, J., and M. Bertin, "Two Views of Bentley's *German Requiem*," *TheaterWeek*, 3:41, 18 June 1990

Bentley, E., "A Kleist Heist" (letter to editor), *TheaterWeek*, 3:6, 6 Aug. 1990

Chamberlain, T. J., "Kleistgeist: The Living Theater and Eric Bentley Adapt a German Classic," *TheaterWeek*, 3:23–25, 23 July 1990

Robinson, M., "Eric Bentley on Kleist," *American Theatre*, 7:55–56, July/Aug. 1990 (also considers Bentley's three other "variations" on Kleist: *The Fall of the Amazons* [*Penthesilea*], *Wannsee* [*The Broken Jug*], and *Concord* [*Kätchen von Heilbronn*])

Village Voice, 35:106, 22 May 1990

GERTRUDE BERG

Me and Molly (dramatization of her radio sketches), 1948
Harap, L., *Dramatic Encounters*, p. 133

RALPH BERKEY
SEE HENRY DENKER and RALPH BERKEY

LEN BERKMAN

Keyssar, H., "Nooks, Crannies and New Directions: Collective Scripts, Gay Drama, Feminist Dramas by Men and the Example of Wendy Kesselman," pp. 167–184 in Keyssar's *Feminist Theatre* (Berkman's *'Til the Beatles Reunite* and *Voila: Rape in Technicolor* considered)

IRVING BERLIN

Bergreen, L., *As Thousands Cheer* (excerpt rptd. in *Playbill*, 9:S1–S16, 31 Oct. 1990)

Bordman, G., "Irving Berlin Remembered," *TheaterWeek*, 3:14–16, 9 Oct. 1989

Buckley, M., "An Irving Berlin Theater Chronology," *TheaterWeek*, 3:18–23, 9 Oct. 1989

Mates, J., *America's Musical Stage*, pp. 148, 149, 150, 152, 178, 182, 183, 187, 189, 190, 191

Walsh, M., "America's Master Songwriter," *Time*, 134:84, 2 Oct. 1989

TheaterWeek, 1:58, 23 May 1988

ALSO SEE GEORGE S. KAUFMAN and IRVING BERLIN

KENNETH BERNARD

How We Danced While We Burned, 1973
Skloot, R., *The Darkness We Carry*, pp. 60–63

LAWRENCE J. BERNARD

Lars Killed His Son, 1937
Kazacoff, G., *Dangerous Theatre*, pp. 260–261

MITCHELL BERNARD
SEE CHAIM POTOK, PHILIP SPRINGER, and MITCHELL BERNARD

JULIE BERNS and IRVING ELMAN

Uncle Willie, 1956
    Marcuson, L. R., *The Stage Immigrant,* pp. 262–269

LEONARD BERNSTEIN

Hirsch, F., *Harold Prince and the American Musical Theater,* pp. 14, 15, 74, 76–77, 147–150, 154
Mandelbaum, K., "The Musical Theater of Leonard Bernstein," *TheaterWeek,* 4:17–23, 29 Oct. 1990
Mates, J., *America's Musical Stage,* pp. 37, 51, 64, 131, 190, 192–193
Swed, M., "Music Theater," *Opera News,* 53:60–61, Nov. 1988
Walsh, M., "The Best and the Brightest," *Time,* 136:18, 29 Oct. 1990
TheaterWeek, 4:7, 31 Dec. 1990

ALSO SEE JOSEPH FIELDS, JEROME CHODOROV,
LEONARD BERNSTEIN, BETTY COMDEN, and ADOLPH GREEN
AND ARTHUR LAURENTS, LEONARD BERNSTEIN, and STEPHEN SONDHEIM
AND HUGH WHEELER, LEONARD BERNSTEIN, RICHARD WILBUR, JOHN LATOUCHE, and STEPHEN SONDHEIM

DANIEL BERRIGAN

True, M., ed., *Daniel Berrigan*

The Trial of the Catonsville Nine, 1969
    Bartow, A., "Controversy and Gordon Davidson" (interview), *American Theatre,* 5:24–30, 54–55, May 1988
    Gustainis, J. J., "Crime as Rhetoric: *The Trial of the Catonsville Nine,*" pp. 164–178 in R. Hariman, ed., *Popular Trials*
    Kiralyfalvi, B., "The Catonsville 'Trilogy': History, Testimony and Art," *Theatre History Studies,* 6:132–141, 1986

KATHLEEN BETSKO

Betsko, K., and R. Koenig, *Interviews with Contemporary Women Playwrights,* pp. 47–61

WILLIAM BEYER

I Confess, 1936
    Kazacoff, G., *Dangerous Theatre,* pp. 236–238

SANDRA BIANO

A Place beyond the Clouds, 1990
 TheaterWeek, 4:7, 5 Nov. 1990

ARTHUR BICKNELL

Moose Murders, 1983
 Leonard, W. T., *Once Was Enough,* pp. 128–130

STEPHEN BILL

Curtains, 1988
 Komar, M., "Dobra śmierć," *Dialog,* 33(7[382]):104–106, July 1988
 Encounter, 70:76, May 1988

C. E. BINGHAM

The Oatman Family, 1857
 Jones, E. H., *Native Americans as Shown on the Stage,* pp. 105–106

ROBERT MONTGOMERY BIRD

Grimsted, D., *Melodrama Unveiled,* pp. 56–57, 145, 151, 165, 167–169

Broker of Bogata, 1834
 Harap, L., *The Image of the Jew in American Literature,* pp. 200–201

The Gladiator, 1831
 McConachie, B. A., "The Theatre of Edwin Forrest and Jacksonian Hero
 Worship," pp. 3–18 in J. L. Fisher and S. Watt, eds., *When They Weren't
 Doing Shakespeare*

DAVID BIRNEY

The Diaries of Adam and Eve (dramatization of story by M. Twain), 1990
 TheaterWeek, 4:8, 26 Nov. 1990

CONRAD BISHOP and ELIZABETH FULLER

Mine Alone, 1990
 Coe, R. L., "A Quartet Debuts in Denver," *American Theatre,* 7:86, Oct.
 1990

JOHN BISHOP

Charlotte, S., "Strained Interludes" (interview), *Playbill,* 7:53, 28 Feb. 1989
Myers, L., "John Bishop Exposed" (interview), *TheaterWeek,* 2:34–36, 26 June
 1989

Borderlines (two one-acts: *Borderline* and *Keepin' an Eye on Louie*), 1988
  Shirakawa, S. H., "Strange Romances," *TheaterWeek,* 1:20–27, 25 Apr.
    1988
  American Theatre, 5:9, Apr. 1988
  New York, 21:98–99, 18 Apr. 1988
  New Yorker, 64:103–104, 25 Apr. 1988
  TheaterWeek, 1:8, 28 Mar. 1988

The Great Grandson of Jedediah Kohler, 1982 (revised 1990)
  TheaterWeek, 4:11, 19 Nov. 1990

The Musical Comedy Murders of 1940, 1985
  Godfrey, T., "Foul Play on Broadway," *Armchair Detective,* 21(1):5–14,
    Winter 1988

JOHN BISHOP, MEL MARVIN, and ROBERT SATULOFF

Elmer Gantry (musical version of novel by S. Lewis), 1988
  Oklahoma Observer, 20:12, 25 May 1988
  Playbill, 6:19, Feb. 1988
  Playbill, 7:24, 30 June 1989
  TheaterWeek, 1:4, 25 Jan. 1988
  TheaterWeek, 1:6, 14 Mar. 1988
  TheaterWeek, 1:5, 30 May 1988
  Time, 131:91, 14 Mar. 1988

SHEM BITTERMAN

Beijing Legends, 1990
  American Theatre, 6:57, Sept. 1989

FRANK L. BIXBY

Little Boss, 1901
  Harap, L., *The Image of the Jew in American Literature,* pp. 228–229

RICHARD BLACKFORD
SEE RON MILNER, RICHARD BLACKFORD, and MAYA ANGELOU

RALPH BLANE
SEE HUGH WHEELER, HUGH MARTIN, and RALPH BLANE

MICHAEL BLANKFORT
SEE MICHAEL GOLD and MICHAEL BLANKFORT

HILARY BLEECHER

Brightness Falling, 1989
  Village Voice, 34:96, 28 Mar. 1989

LEE BLESSING

Filichia, P., "What a Blessing" (interview), *TheaterWeek*, 2:14–16, 29 May 1989
Elle, 3:60, Mar. 1988

Cobb (about Ty Cobb), 1989
    Henry, W. A., III, "Myth, Ambition and Anger," *Time*, 136:78, 23 July
      1990
    American Theatre, 6:7, June 1989
    Connecticut, 52:14, Mar. 1989
    Time, 136:54, 31 Dec. 1990

Down the Road, 1989
    American Theatre, 6:12, Oct. 1989

Eleemosynary, 1989
    Hudson Review, 42:465–466, Autumn 1989
    New York, 22:74+, 22 May 1989
    Playbill, 7:37+, 31 May 1989
    TheaterWeek, 2:7, 17 Apr. 1989
    TheaterWeek, 2:3, 8 May 1989
    Time, 133:110, 22 May 1989

Independence, 1984
    TheaterWeek, 4:11, 5 Nov. 1990

Two Rooms, 1988
    American Theatre, 5:12, Sept. 1988
    San Diego Magazine, 40:34+, Aug. 1988

A Walk in the Woods, 1987
    Backalenick, I., "Broadway Sees Red: *A Walk in the Woods* in Moscow,"
      TheaterWeek, 2:22–25, 3 July 1989
    Shirakawa, S. H., "Check Mates," *TheaterWeek*, 1:37–42, 23 May 1988
    ———, "Theater Trends: Political Action Plays," *TheaterWeek*, 1:13–15, 21
      Mar. 1988
    America, 158:306, 19 Mar. 1988
    Commonweal, 115:181–182, 25 Mar. 1988
    Georgia Review, 42:594–595, Fall 1988
    Journal of Dramatic Theory and Criticism, 3:204–207, Spring 1989
    Massachusetts Review, 29:95–96, Spring 1988
    Nation, 246:510–511, 9 Apr. 1988
    New Leader, 71:23, 21 Mar. 1988
    New Republic, 198:25–26, 4 Apr. 1988
    New York, 21:70+, 14 Mar. 1988
    New Yorker, 64:80, 14 Mar. 1988
    San Diego Magazine, 40:48, Mar. 1988
    TheaterWeek, 1:56, 30 May 1988
    Theatre Crafts, 23:20, Oct. 1989
    Time, 131:91, 14 Mar. 1988

Village Voice, 33:102, 8 Mar. 1988
Village Voice, 33:109, 31 May 1988
W Supplement, 17:1–8, 27 June 1988

MARC BLITZSTEIN

Gordon, E. A., *Mark the Music*
Mates, J., *America's Musical Stage,* pp. 37, 51, 64, 131, 190, 192–193
Paller, M., "Political Provocation," *TheaterWeek,* 2:30–35, 3 Oct. 1988

The Cradle Will Rock, 1937
    Bentley, J., *Hallie Flanagan,* pp. 260–264
    Green, S., *Broadway Musicals,* p. 101
    San Diego Magazine, 40:60 + , Sept. 1988

Regina (musical version of L. Hellman's play *The Little Foxes*), 1949
    Fitzgerald, G., and P. O'Connor, "Vivat *Regina!*" *Opera News,* 52:40–41,
    June 1988
    Gordon E. A., "A Night at the Opera," *Opera News,* 53:67, Sept. 1988
    American Theatre, 5:4–5, June 1988

FRITZ BLOCKI

Money Mad (revision of his and W. Howard's *Bet Your Life,* which see), 1937
    Leonard, W. T., *Once Was Enough,* pp. 121–123

FRITZ BLOCKI and WILLIE HOWARD

Bet Your Life, 1937
    Leonard, W. T., *Once Was Enough,* pp. 121–123

DAN BLUE

Three in Time, 1988
    TheaterWeek, 1:5, 11 Apr. 1988

EDWIN HARVEY BLUM

Backwash, 1936
    Kazacoff, G., *Dangerous Theatre,* pp. 79–80

SAM BOBRICK and RON CLARK

No Hard Feelings, 1973
    Leonard, W. T., *Once Was Enough,* pp. 138–140

JERRY BOCK
SEE JOSEPH STEIN, JERRY BOCK, and SHELDON HARNICK

MARTHA BOESING

Greeley, L., "Martha Boesing: Playwright of Performance," *Text and Performance Quarterly,* 9(3):207–215, July 1989

Love Song for an Amazon, 1976
> Natalle, E. J., *Feminist Theatre,* pp. 62–63 and elsewhere

River Journal, published 1979
> Natalle, E. J., *Feminist Theatre,* pp. 80–82
> Stephens, J. L., "Subverting the Demon-Angel Dichotomy: Innovation and Feminist Intervention in Twentieth-Century Drama," *Text and Performance Quarterly,* 9(1):53–64, Jan. 1989

The Story of a Mother (a collaborative effort), created 1977/1978, published 1981 (revised as *The Story of a Mother II,* 1987)
> Boesing, M., "*The Story of a Mother,* a Ritual Drama" (outline of the original version of the play), pp. 44–50 in H. K. Chinoy and L. W. Jenkins, eds., *Women in American Theatre,* rev. and enl. ed. (same pagination in both eds.)
> Collins, R., "A Feminist Theatre in Transition," *American Theatre,* 4:32–34, Feb. 1988
> Natalle, E. J., *Feminist Theatre,* pp. 84–85 and elsewhere

The Web, published 1981
> Natalle, E. J., *Feminist Theatre,* pp. 66–68 and elsewhere

MARTHA BOESING, ALBERT GREENBERG, and HELEN STOLTZFUS

Heart of the World, 1989
> *American Theatre,* 6:13, May 1989
> *American Theatre,* 6:11–12, Dec. 1989

ERIC BOGOSIAN

Carter, E. G., "Talkman," *Connoisseur,* 217:166–169, Nov. 1987
Gentile, J. S., *Cast of One,* pp. 175–179
Giessen, N., "Sex, Drugs, and Eric Bogosian," *TheaterWeek,* 2:50–53, 22 Aug. 1988
Siegle, R., "Condensed Book: Performance Art and Fiction," pp. 250–272 in Siegle's *Suburban Ambush*
Playbill, 7:30, 31 Aug. 1989

Sex, Drugs, Rock & Roll, 1990
> Botto, L., "One Man in Fourteen," *Playbill,* 8:40, 43–45, 31 Mar. 1990
> Rosenberg, S., "Sex and the Solo Artist," *Mother Jones,* 15:49–50, Jan. 1990
> "Talking 'bout Degeneration," *Rolling Stone,* p. 19, 22 Feb. 1990
> *New York,* 23:62, 19 Feb. 1990
> *New Yorker,* 66:98, 26 Feb. 1990
> *TheaterWeek,* 3:9, 15 Jan. 1990
> *TheaterWeek,* 3:41, 19 Feb. 1990
> *Time,* 136:54, 31 Dec. 1990
> *Village Voice,* 35:107, 20 Feb. 1990

Talk Radio, 1985
  Village Voice, 32:87, 9 June 1987

GARY BOHLKE

Doublecross, 1983
  TheaterWeek, 4:8, 17 Sept. 1990

GEORGE HENRY BOKER

Francesca da Rimini, 1853
  TheaterWeek, 4:26, 3 Sept. 1990

WILLIAM BOLCOM

Bolcom, W., "Trouble in the Music World," *Michigan Quarterly Review,* 27:541–
  557, Fall 1988
Friedrich, O., "Where the Old Joins the New," *Time,* 135:77, 29 Jan. 1990

ALSO SEE ARNOLD WEINSTEIN and WILLIAM BOLCOM

JONATHAN BOLT

The Whore and the h'Empress (dramatization of H. Mayhew's four-volume 1861
  work *London Labour and the London Poor*), 1988
  American Theatre, 5:9–10, Nov. 1988

JONATHAN BOLT, THOMAS TIERNEY, and JOHN FORSTER

Eleanor, 1990
  American Theatre, 7:11, May 1990

GUY BOLTON and GEORGE MIDDLETON

The Light of the World, 1920
  Harap, L., *Dramatic Encounters,* p. 114

GARY BONASORTE

The Aunts, 1989
  Popkin, H., "Review," *TheaterWeek,* 3:42, 16 Oct. 1989
  New York, 22:107, 16 Oct. 1989
  New Yorker, 65:111, 16 Oct. 1989
  TheaterWeek, 3:8, 11 Sept. 1989

TONY BONDI
SEE RICHARD IORIO, TONY BONDI, and SAL PIRO

MARK BOONE, JR.
SEE STEVE BUSCEMI and MARK BOONE, JR.

ERIC STEPHEN BOOTH

Metamorphosis, 1990
   TheaterWeek, 3:8, 28 May 1990

JOHN HUNTER BOOTH

Created Equal, 1938
   Kazacoff, G., *Dangerous Theatre,* pp. 176–180

CLARE BOOTH

Margin for Error, 1939
   Marcuson, L. R., *The Stage Immigrant,* pp. 135–140

The Women, 1936
   Carlson, S. L., "Comic Textures and Female Communities 1937 and 1977:
   Clare Booth and Wendy Wasserstein," pp. 207–217 in J. Schlueter, ed.,
   Modern American Drama (rpt. of *Modern Drama,* 27:564–573, Dec.
   1984)
   Harap, L., *Dramatic Encounters,* p. 118

ALSO SEE CLARE BOOTH LUCE

GLYNN BORDERS
SEE JAN TORI EVANS and GLYNN BORDERS

ALLEN BORETZ
SEE JOHN MURRAY and ALLEN BORETZ

NANCY BORGENICHT and MICHAEL BUTTARS

Saturday's Voyeur: The Tenth Anniversary Roadshow, 1977 (updated by Ed
   Gryska, 1987)
   American Theatre, 4:9, Jan. 1988

ALEXANDER BORODIN
SEE CHARLES LEDERER, LUTHER DAVIS, ROBERT WRIGHT,
GEORGE FORREST, and ALEXANDER BORODIN

JOHN BORUFF

The Loud Red Patrick (dramatization of book by R. McKenny), 1956
   Marcuson, L. R., *The Stage Immigrant,* pp. 252–256

Timber House, 1936
   Leonard, W. T., *Once Was Enough,* pp. 192–193

PHIL BOSAKOWSKI

Crossin' the Line, 1989
   Paller, M., *"Crossin'* Crashes," *TheaterWeek,* 2:40, 29 May 1989
   TheaterWeek, 2:6, 1 May 1989
   Village Voice, 34:101, 6 June 1989

Wheel and Deal, 1988
   Village Voice, 33:97–98, 21 June 1988

JAMES BOSLEY

Fun, 1988
   Ouderkirk, C., " 'A Rock and Roll Sensibility,' " *TheaterWeek,* 2:24–30, 31
   Oct. 1988

DION BOUCICAULT

Basta, S., "The French Influence on Dion Boucicault's Sensation Drama,"
   2:199–206 in W. Zach and H. Kosok, eds., *Literary Interrelations*
Cave, R. A., "The Presentation of English and Irish Characters in Boucicault's
   Irish Melodrama," 3:115–123 in W. Zach and H. Kosok, eds., *Literary Inter-
   relations*
Hurt, J., "Dion Boucicault's Comic Myths," pp. 253–265 in J. L. Fisher and S.
   Watt, eds., *When They Weren't Doing Shakespeare*
Kosok, H., "Dion Boucicault's 'American' Plays: Considerations on Defining
   National Literatures in English," pp. 81–97 in R. Welch and S. B. Bushrui,
   eds., *Literature and the Art of Creation*
Moore, S., "An Actor's Diary," *Drama,* no. 169:53–54, 1988
Murphy, B., "Literary Stepchildren: Nineteenth-Century Dramatists," *Review,*
   8:197–204, 1986
Stowell, S., "Actors as Dramatic Personae: Nell Gwynne, Peg Woffington and
   David Garrick on the Victorian Stage, *Theatre History Studies,* 8:117–136,
   1988

After Dark, a Drama of London Life in 1868, 1868
   Harap, L., *The Image of the Jew in American Literature,* p. 215

Belle Lamar, 1874
   Rainey, K. T., "Race and Reunion in Nineteenth-Century Reconciliation
   Drama," *American Transcendental Quarterly,* 2(2):155–169, June 1988

Flying Scud, 1867
   Harap, L., *The Image of the Jew in American Literature,* pp. 214–215

Forbidden Fruit, 1876
   TheaterWeek, 4:26–27, 3 Sept. 1990

The Octoroon; or, Life in Louisiana, 1859
   Fletcher, W. L., "Who Put the 'Tragic' in the Tragic Mulatto?" pp. 262–

268 in H. K. Chinoy and L. W. Jenkins, eds., *Women in American Theatre,* rev. and enl. ed. (pp. 260–266 in 1981 ed.)
Jones, E. H., *Native Americans as Shown on the Stage,* pp. 95–97 and elsewhere

The Shaughraum, 1874
Gargano, J. W., "Tableaux of Renunciation: Wharton's Use of *The Shaughran* in *The Age of Innocence,*" *Studies in American Fiction,* 15(1):1–11, 1987
Playbill, 6:66, July/Aug. 1990
TheaterWeek, 4:24, 3 Sept. 1990
Theatre Crafts, 23:10, Jan. 1989

Used Up, 1844
Stanton, M., "Charles Dickens: *Used Up,*" *Dickensian,* 84(3[416]):143–152, Autumn 1988

JULIE BOVASSO

Keyssar, H., "A Network of Playwrights," pp. 102–125 in Keyssar's *Feminist Theatre*

JANE BOWLES

In the Summer House (dramatization of her story "Two Serious Ladies"), 1953
Austin, G., *Feminist Theories for Dramatic Criticism,* pp. 67–72

ALAN BOWNE

American Theatre, 6:45, Feb. 1990
Andy Warhol's Interview, 17:67+, Aug. 1987

Beirut, 1987
Ouderkirk, C., "'A Rock and Roll Sensibility,'" *TheaterWeek,* 2:24–30, 31 Oct. 1988
Village Voice, 32:93–94, 16 June 1987

Sharon and Billy, 1988
Ouderkirk, C., "'A Rock and Roll Sensibility,'" *TheaterWeek,* 2:24–30, 31 Oct. 1988

NEITH BOYCE

Winter's Night, 1916
France, R., "Apropos of Women and the Folk Play," pp. 145–152 in H. K. Chinoy and L. W. Jenkins, eds., *Women in American Theatre,* rev. and enl. ed. (same pagination in 1981 ed.)

BILL BOZZONE

The Inuit, 1990
    American Theatre, 7:12–13, May 1990

The Second Coming, 1990
    American Theatre, 7:13, May 1990

RAY BRADBURY

Mogen, D., *Ray Bradbury*

RAY BRADBURY, JOSÉ FELICIANO, and SUSAN FELICIANO

The Wonderful Ice Cream Suit (based on one of Bradbury's short stories), 1990
    Doph, D., "We All Scream for *Ice Cream,*" *TheaterWeek,* 4:32–35, 24 Sept.
    1990

MICHAEL BRADY

To Gillian on Her 34th Birthday, 1983
    Cohen, E. M., *Working on a New Play,* pp. 12, 42–43, 113–114, 118, 144–
    145, 160–161, 170, 177, 192, 194

MARK BRAMBLE
SEE MICHAEL STEWART, MARK BRAMBLE, and JERRY HERMAN

WILLIAM BRANCH

Brown-Guillory, E., *Their Place on the Stage,* pp. 26, 37, 108

JOHN BRAY
SEE JAMES NELSON BARKER and JOHN BRAY

JIMMY BRESLIN

The Queen of the Leaky Roof Circuit, 1988
    Breslin, J., "TKO in Louisville," *American Theatre,* 5:25–27, 57, June 1988
    American Theatre, 4:10–11, Feb. 1988

BESSIE BREUER

Sundown Beach, 1948
    Counts, M. L., *Coming Home,* pp. 95, 115–116, 160–161

LEE BREUER (Asher Leopold Breuer)

Breuer, L., "How Tall Was Coriolanus," *American Theatre,* 5:22, May 1988
Cody, G., "Lee Breuer on Interculturalism" (interview), *Performing Arts Journal,* 11(3)/12(1):59–66, 1988/1989

Greene, A., "Mabou Mines Turns Twenty," *TheaterWeek*, 3:10–14, 29 Jan. 1990
Levy, E., "Inspiration in Its Roots: The Place of Poetry in the Theater of Lee Breuer," *Theater*, 18(2):66–68, Spring 1987
Neely, K., "Lee Breuer's Theatrical Technique: From *The Animations* to *Gospel at Colonus*," *Journal of Dramatic Theory and Criticism*, 3(2):181–190, Spring 1989
Savran, D., "Lee Breuer," pp. 3–17 in Savran's *In Their Own Words*
Wetzsteon, R., "Wild Man of the Theater," *Village Voice*, 32:19–26, 19 May 1987 and 32:33–36, 26 May 1987

B. Beaver (Part II of *Animations*), 1972 (later revised)
    TheaterWeek, 3:41, 11 June 1990
    Village Voice, 35:91, 5 June 1990

Lear (based on Shakespeare's tragedy *King Lear*), 1988
    Holmberg, A., "The Liberation of Lear," *American Theatre*, 5:12–19, July/Aug. 1988
    Popkin, H., "Southern Fried *Lear*," *TheaterWeek*, 3:40, 12 Feb. 1990
    Spillane, M., "Gender-Bending *Lear*," *TheaterWeek*, 3:16–19, 29 Jan. 1990
    New York, 23:84–85, 5 Feb. 1990
    TheaterWeek, 3:33, 2 Apr. 1990
    Theatre Journal, 42:481–484, Dec. 1990
    Village Voice, 35:39–42, 30 Jan. 1990
    Village Voice, 35:95+, 6 Feb. 1990 (Erika Munk)
    Village Voice, 35:95+, 6 Feb. 1990 (Michael Feingold)

The Warrior Ant (Part IV of *Animations*), 1986
    Philadelphia Magazine, 79:71–72, June 1988
    Village Voice, 33:103, 1 Nov. 1988

LEE BREUER and BOB TELSON

The Gospel at Colonus (based on Sophocles's play *Oedipus at Colonus*), 1983
    Pacheco, P., "The Gospel Musical," *Playbill*, 6:10, 12, 14, 16, May 1988
    Scher, H., "Center Stage: The *Gospel* According to Lee Breuer," *TheaterWeek*, 1:6–11, 4 Apr. 1988
    America, 158:433, 23 Apr. 1988
    Christianity Today, 31:58–60, 10 July 1987
    Connoisseur, 218:128–129, May 1988
    High Fidelity (Musical America Edition), 36:MA27–MA29, Apr. 1986
    Los Angeles, 31:52+, Feb. 1986
    Nation, 246:690, 14 May 1988
    New Leader, 71:23, 18 Apr. 1988
    New Republic, 198:28, 25 Apr. 1988
    New York, 21:96, 18 Apr. 1988
    New Yorker, 64:72–74, 4 Apr. 1988
    Newsweek, 102:105+, 21 Nov. 1983
    Newsweek, 111:75, 4 Apr. 1988
    Vanity Fair, 51:88, Apr. 1988
    Village Voice, 33:103+, 5 Apr. 1988

MARTY BRILL
SEE HY KRAFT, ALBERT HAGUE, and MARTY BRILL

BARBARA BRINSON-PINEDA and ANTONIO CURIEL

Tongues of Fire, 1981
Yarbro-Bejarano, Y., "The Female Subject in Chicano Theatre: Sexuality, 'Race,' and Class," pp. 131–149 in S.-E. Case, ed., *Performing Feminisms* (rpt. of *Theatre Journal,* 38(4):389–407, Dec. 1986)

DANIEL GARRISON BRINTON

Maria Candelaria: An Historic Drama from American Aboriginal Life, published 1897
Jones, E. H., *Native Americans as Shown on the Stage,* p. 135

W. DAINGERFIELD BRISTOL

Reprise, 1934
Leonard, W. T., *Once Was Enough,* pp. 160–161

ROBERT BRITTAN
SEE ROBERT NEMIROFF, CHARLOTTE ZALTZBERG, JUDD WOLDIN, and ROBERT BRITTAN

MICHAEL BRODSKY

Dose Center, 1990
TheaterWeek, 3:43, 12 Mar. 1990
Village Voice, 35:106, 6 Mar. 1990

ALAN BRODY

Invention for Fathers and Sons, 1989
TheaterWeek, 2:40, 26 Sept. 1988

LESLIE BRODY

Cohen, E. M., *Working on a New Play,* pp. 67–68 (Brody's *Emma Rothstein* considered)

Harriet the Spy (dramatization of book by L. Fitzhugh), 1988
American Theatre, 4:10, Mar. 1988

ERIK BROGGER

A Normal Life (based on three autobiographical short stories by D. Schwartz), 1990
American Theatre, 7:12, July/Aug. 1990

CONRAD BROMBERG

Dream of a Blacklisted Actor, 1975
  Village Voice, 31:128, 23 Dec. 1986

CHANDLER BROSSARD

Landesman, J., "Notes on Chandler Brossard as Playwright," *Review of Contemporary Fiction,* 7(1):132–135, Spring 1987

JOHN BROUGHAM

Columbus el Filibustero, 1857
  Harap, L., *The Image of the Jew in American Literature,* p. 212

The Game of Life, 1856
  Miller, T. L., "The Image of Fashionable Society in American Comedy, 1840–1870," pp. 243–252 in J. L. Fisher and S. Watt, eds., *When They Weren't Doing Shakespeare*

The Great Tragic Revival, 1858
  Harap, L., *The Image of the Jew in American Literature,* p. 212

Lottery of Life, a Story of New York, 1867
  Harap, L., *The Image of the Jew in American Literature,* p. 212

Metamora; or, The Last of the Pollywogs, 1847
  Jones, E. H., *Native Americans as Shown on the Stage,* pp. 89–90

Much Ado About a Merchant of Venice, 1868
  Harap, L., *The Image of the Jew in American Literature,* pp. 212–213

ALICE BROWN

France, R., "Apropos of Women and the Folk Play," pp. 145–152 in H. K. Chinoy and L. W. Jenkins, eds., *Women in American Theatre,* rev. and enl. ed. (same pagination in 1981 ed.)

DANIEL R. BROWN
SEE DANIEL CURZON

DELOSS BROWN

Heart of a Dog (dramatization of novella by M. Bulgakov), 1990
  Village Voice, 35:100, 27 Mar. 1990

HARRY BROWN

A Sound of Hunting, 1945
  Marcuson, L. R., *The Stage Immigrant,* pp. 151–154

KENNETH BROWN

The Brig, 1963
Copeland, R., "Imagination after the Fact," *American Theatre,* 6:54–57, 123–125, Oct. 1989
Shank, T., *American Alternative Theater,* pp. 11–13

KENT R. BROWN

Dancing in Box Step, 1990
Weiner, B., "Dramaturgy in Denver," *TheaterWeek,* 3:31–32, 25 June 1990

MICHAEL HENRY BROWN

Generations of the Dead in the Abyss of Coney Island Madness, 1990
American Theatre, 7:11–12, Dec. 1990
TheaterWeek, 4:10, 5 Nov. 1990

MURRAY BROWN

Fickle Women, 1937
Leonard, W. T., *Once Was Enough,* pp. 49–50

TRISHA BROWN

Kertess, K., "Dancing with Carmen," *Art in America,* 75:180–185 +, Apr. 1987

TRISHA BROWN and DONALD JUDD

Newark, 1987
Artforum, 26:136, Nov. 1987

WILLIAM WELLS BROWN

Brown-Guillory, E., *Their Place on the Stage,* pp. 2, 108

The Escape; or, a Leap for Freedom, published 1858
Alexander, L., "A Letter from Iowa," *TheaterWeek,* 3:19, 19 Mar. 1990
Miller, J.-M. A., "Black Women in Plays by Black Playwrights," pp. 256–262 in H. K. Chinoy and L. W. Jenkins, eds., *Women in American Theatre,* rev. and enl. ed. (pp. 254–260 in 1981 ed.)

IRVING BROWNE

Our Best Society, 1868
Miller, T. L., "The Image of Fashionable Sociey in American Comedy, 1840–1870," pp. 243–252 in J. L. Fisher and S. Watt, eds., *When They Weren't Doing Shakespeare*

STUART BROWNE

Angel, 1990
   Village Voice, 35:104, 24 Apr. 1990

JOHN HERBERT BRUNDAGE
SEE JOHN HERBERT

ANTHONY BRUNO

Soul Survivor, 1989
   Portantiere, M., "Carrying the Torch," *TheaterWeek,* 2:33–37, 10 July 1989
   TheaterWeek, 2:6–7, 24 July 1989
   TheaterWeek, 3:8, 11 Sept. 1989
   Village Voice, 34:108, 3 Oct. 1989

NANCY BUCHANAN

Deer/Dear, 1978
   Forte, J., "Women's Performance Art: Feminism and Postmodernism,"
   pp. 251–269 in S.-E. Case, ed., *Performing Feminisms* (rpt. of *Theatre
   Journal,* 40(2):217–235, May 1988)

THOMPSON BUCHANAN

Civilian Clothes, 1919
   Counts, M. L., *Coming Home,* pp. 165–166

ALSO SEE PATRICK KEARNEY

HAROLD BUCHMAN
SEE LOUIS SOLOMON and HAROLD BUCHMAN

WILLIAM F. BUCKLEY, JR.

Stained Glass (dramatization of his novel), 1989
   Time, 133:71, 17 Apr. 1989

DAVID BUCKNAM
SEE LISA PETERSON and DAVID BUCKNAM

JORDAN BUDDE

Heaven's Hard, 1989
   Theatre Journal, 41:542–543, Dec. 1989

ED BULLINS

Brown-Guillory, E., *Their Place on the Stage,* pp. 18, 27–28, 108, 118
Elder, A. A., "Ed Bullins: Black Theatre as Ritual," pp. 101–109 in E. S. Nelson, ed., *Connections*

Harap, L., *Dramatic Encounters*, pp. 16–17
Hay, S. A., "Structural Elements in Ed Bullins' Plays," pp. 185–191 in E. Hill,
    ed., *The Theater of Black Americans*, Vol. 1 of two vols. rptd. as one in 1987;
    same pagination in both eds. (rpt. of *Black World*, 23(6):20–26, Apr. 1974)
King, K., "Ed Bullins," pp. 137–154 in King's *Ten Modern American Playwrights*
Sanders, L., "'Dialect Determinism': Ed Bullins' Critique of the Rhetoric of
    the Black Power Movement," pp. 161–175 in J. Weixlmann and C. J. Fon-
    tenot, eds., *Belief vs. Theory in Black American Literary Criticism*
————, "Ed Bullins (2 July 1935–)," pp. 66–79 in P. C. Kolin, ed., *American
    Playwrights since 1945*
Sanders, L. C., "'Like Niggers': Ed Bullins' Theater of Reality," pp. 176–228
    in Sanders's *The Development of Black Theater in America*

Clara's Ole Man, 1965
    Lahr, J., "Black Theatre: The American Tragic Voice," *Evergreen Review*,
        13:55–63, Aug. 1969

The Duplex, 1970
    Hay, S. A., "Structural Elements in Ed Bullins' Plays," pp. 185–191 in E.
        Hill, ed., *The Theater of Black Americans*, Vol. 1 of two vols. rptd. as
        one in 1987; same pagination in both eds. (rpt. of *Black World*, 23(6):20–
        26, Apr. 1974)

In the Wine Time, 1968
    Cook, W., "Mom, Dad and God: Values in Black Theater," pp. 168–184 in
        E. Hill, ed., *The Theater of Black Americans*, Vol. 1 of two vols. rptd.
        as one in 1987, same pagination in both eds.

VICTOR BUMBALO

Adam and the Experts, 1989
    Gutwillig, S., "A Look Back in Anguish," *TheaterWeek*, 3:33–38, 25 Dec.
        1989
————, "Gay Theater's Second Wave," *TheaterWeek*, 3:34–36, 5 Feb. 1990

NED BUNTLINE and FRED G. MEADER

The Scouts of the Prairie; or, Red Deviltry as It Is, 1872
    Jones, E. H., *Native Americans as Shown on the Stage*, pp. 111–114

NICOLE BURDETTE

Chelsea Walls, 1990
    TheaterWeek, 3:7, 11 June 1990

LARRY BURKE

Da Caravaggio, 1988
    TheaterWeek, 1:6, 27 June 1988

DANA BURNET and GEORGE ABBOTT

Four Walls, 1927
  Harap, L., *Dramatic Encounters,* pp. 115–116

MARY BURRILL

Brown-Guillory, E., *Their Place on the Stage,* pp. 4, 5, 9–10, 12

ABE BURROWS, JO SWERLING, and FRANK LOESSER

Guys and Dolls (musical based on stories by D. Runyon), 1950
  Green, S., *Broadway Musicals,* pp. 148–149

ABE BURROWS, JACK WEINSTOCK, WILLIE GILBERT, and FRANK LOESSER

How to Succeed in Business without Really Trying (musical version of novel by
  S. Mead), 1961
  Green, S., *Broadway Musicals,* p. 196

STEVE BUSCEMI and MARK BOONE, JR.

Dead Reckoning, 1987
  Village Voice, 32:94, 19 May 1987

Yap Thaw, 1987
  Village Voice, 32:94, 19 May 1987

CHARLES BUSCH

Chansky, D., "Busch in the Bush Era," *TheaterWeek,* 2:32–37, 7 Aug. 1989
Essman, J., "Big Wigs in the Mainstream," *TheaterWeek,* 3:19–22, 23 Apr. 1990
Giessen, N., "The Actor in Question: Charles Busch," *TheaterWeek,* 2:48–55,
  28 Nov. 1988
American Theatre, 7:50, Oct. 1990

The Lady in Question, 1988
  Botto, L., "The Lady Is a Camp," *Playbill,* 8:56, 59–61, 31 Oct. 1989
  Ledford, L. S., "The Lady and the Camp," *TheaterWeek,* 3:41, 14 Aug.
    1989
  Connoisseur, 219:44+, Nov. 1989
  New York, 22:44, 7 Aug. 1989
  Playbill, 7:32, 31 Jan. 1989
  Playbill, 7:29+, 31 Aug. 1989
  TheaterWeek, 2:6, 1 May 1989
  TheaterWeek, 2:5, 17 July 1989
  Village Voice, 34:93, 1 Aug. 1989

Psycho Beach Party, 1987
  Botto, L., "Bedlam on the Beach," *Playbill,* 6:44, 47, 48–49, Apr. 1988

Vampire Lesbians of Sodom, 1982
    Connoisseur, 219:62 + , Sept. 1989
    Playbill, 8:38, 30 Sept. 1990
    TheaterWeek, 2:5, 28 Nov. 1988
    TheaterWeek, 3:9, 13 Nov. 1989
    TheaterWeek, 3:19, 2 Apr. 1990
    TheaterWeek, 3:8, 14 May 1990
    TheaterWeek, 3:9, 21 May 1990

MICHAEL BUTTARS
SEE NANCY BORGENICHT and MICHAEL BUTTARS

JAN BUTTRAM

East Texas, 1990
    Playbill, 9:34, 31 Oct. 1990
    TheaterWeek, 4:7, 20 Aug. 1990
    TheaterWeek, 4:9, 17 Sept. 1990

SAMUEL H. M. BYERS

Pocahontas, published 1875
    Jones, E. H., *Native Americans as Shown on the Stage,* pp. 137–138

DAVID BYRNE
SEE ROBERT WILSON and DAVID BYRNE

DOLLY BYRNE
SEE GILDA VARESI and DOLLY BYRNE

JOE CACACI

Old Business, 1987
    Forbes, D., "Dirty Dealing," *American Theatre,* 4:12–18, Feb. 1988
    Village Voice, 32:109, 18 Nov. 1987

ED CACHIANES

Everybody Knows Your Name, 1990
    TheaterWeek, 3:8, 21 May 1990

BILL CAIN

Stand-Up Tragedy, 1988
    Dickman, K., "Asphalt Jungle," *TheaterWeek,* 4:20–23 + , 8 Oct. 1990
    Harris, J., "Playwright Bill Cain" (interview), *TheaterWeek,* 4:23, 8 Oct.
      1990
    America, 163:351, 10 Nov. 1990
    American Theatre, 6:8, July/Aug. 1989
    Christian Century, 107:1139–1142, 5 Dec. 1990

New York, 23:91–92, 15 Oct. 1990
Playbill, 8:15, 31 Aug. 1990
Playbill, 8:12, 30 Sept. 1990
TheaterWeek, 3:7, 1 Jan. 1990
TheaterWeek, 3:10, 8 Jan. 1990
TheaterWeek, 4:7, 20 Aug. 1990
TheaterWeek, 4:41, 22 Oct. 1990

BEN R. CALDWELL
SEE ROGER GUENVEUR SMITH and BEN R. CALDWELL

RICHARD CALIBAN

Homo Sapien Shuffle, 1989
Village Voice, 34:119 + , 20 June 1989

Rodents and Radios, 1990
Village Voice, 35:116 + , 1 May 1990

BARTLEY CAMPBELL

The White Slave, 1882
Fletcher, W. L., "Who Put the 'Tragic' in the Tragic Mulatto?" pp. 262–268 in H. K. Chinoy and L. W. Jenkins, eds., *Women in American Theatre,* rev. and enl. ed. (pp. 260–266 in 1981 ed.)

ANTOINE CAMPO

Ophelie Song, 1989
Village Voice, 34:99 + , 4 July 1989

NORMAND CANAC-MARQUIS

The Cezanne Syndrome, 1989
TheaterWeek, 2:10, 9 Jan. 1989
Village Voice, 34:90, 7 Feb. 1989

JACK CANNON

Le Club Hotzy Totzy, 1989
American Theatre, 5:10, Jan. 1989

ROSE CANO

Case, S.-E., *Feminism and Theatre,* pp. 108–109 (Cano's *Self-Portrait* considered)

LOREN-PAUL CAPLIN

A Subject of Childhood, 1988
　　Nation, 246:512, 9 Apr. 1988
　　TheaterWeek, 1:5, 15 Feb. 1988

TRUMAN CAPOTE

Garson, H. L., *Truman Capote*
Windham, D., *Lost Friendships*

TRUMAN CAPOTE and HAROLD ARLEN

House of Flowers (musical version of Capote's short story), 1954
　　Driscoll, T., "Forgotten Musicals: *House of Flowers," TheaterWeek,* 1:36–
　　40, 18 Jan. 1988
　　Green, S., *Broadway Musicals,* p. 165

VINCENT CARDINAL

The Colorado Catechism, 1990
　　New York, 23:126–127, 5 Nov. 1990
　　Playbill, 9:48, 30 Nov. 1990
　　TheaterWeek, 4:7, 24 Sept. 1990

DAVE CARLEY

Carley, D., "A Canada Nobody Knows," *American Theatre,* 4:46–47, Feb. 1988

LAURIE CARLOS, JESSICA HAGEDORN, and ROBBIE McCAULEY

Teenytown, 1988
　　Champagne, L., ed., *Out from Under,* pp. ix–xiv (Introduction), 90–94, 95–
　　117 (text of performance piece)

AL CARMINES

The Journey of Snow White, 1971
　　Village Voice, 35:103, 22 May 1990

ALSO SEE LEON KATZ and AL CARMINES
AND GERTRUDE STEIN and AL CARMINES

MATTHEW CARNAHAN

Velvet Elvis, 1990
　　American Theatre, 7:13, July/Aug. 1990

CRAIG CARNELIA

TheaterWeek, 3:15, 12 Feb. 1990

ALSO SEE CRAIG LUCAS and CRAIG CARNELIA

EDWARD CHILDS CARPENTER
SEE LAURENCE GROSS and EDWARD CHILDS CARPENTER

ALEXANDER CARR

The Wooden Soldier, 1931
  Counts, M. L., *Coming Home,* pp. 78, 120, 194, 197

BAIKIDA CARROLL
SEE NTOZAKE SHANGE, EMILY MANN, and BAIKIDA CARROLL

JO CARSON

Lutenbacher, C., " 'So Much More Than Just Myself': Women Theatre Artists in the South," pp. 380–382 in H. K. Chinoy and L. W. Jenkins, eds., *Women in American Theatre,* rev. and enl. ed. (new to this ed.; excerpted from a paper Lutenbacher presented at the 1987 Themes in Drama Conference in Riverside, CA, later printed in J. Redmond, ed., *Women in Theatre,* pp. 253–263)

Daytrips, 1989
  Mitchell, S., "Eavesdropper Jo Carson Spins a Personal Story," *American Theatre,* 6:56–57, Jan. 1990
  America, 163:453, 8 Dec. 1990
  American Theatre, 6:57, Nov. 1989
  Playbill, 9:45, 30 Nov. 1990
  TheaterWeek, 4:7, 22 Oct. 1990
  TheaterWeek, 4:32, 19 Nov. 1990

ARTHUR P. CARTER

The Number, 1951
  Marcuson, L. R., *The Stage Immigrant,* pp. 168–172

LONNIE CARTER

Gulliver (suggested by J. Swift's *Gulliver's Travels*), 1989
  Backalenick, I., "In the Shadow of O'Neill," *TheaterWeek,* 3:28–31, 21 Aug. 1989

WILFRED CARTEY

Spirit Time (adapted from his poetry), 1989
  TheaterWeek, 2:5, 17 July 1989
  Village Voice, 34:93, 18 July 1989

CHRISTOPHER CARTMILL

Incorruptible, 1989
  TheaterWeek, 3:15, 18 Sept. 1989

RAYMOND E. CARVER

TheaterWeek, 2:60, 15 Aug. 1988

Ain't Nobody Loves You like a Mama but Your Mama, 1988
  TheaterWeek, 1:6, 1 Aug. 1988

W. F. CARVER
SEE WILLIAM F. CODY, W. F. CARVER, and OTHERS

JOAN CASADEMONT

Maids of Honor, 1990
  Hoag, P., "Female Bonding Off-Broadway," *TheaterWeek,* 3:15–17, 2 July
    1990
  TheaterWeek, 3:8, 11 June 1990
  TheaterWeek, 3:40, 9 July 1990

ANTHONY CASARETTI

Little Caesar, 1988
  American Theatre, 5:8, Sept. 1988

ANNA THERESA CASCIO

June 8, 1968, 1988
  Ouderkirk, C., "'A Rock and Roll Sensibility,'" *TheaterWeek,* 2:24–30, 31
    Oct. 1988

MOLLY CASTELLOE

Night Cries for a Mirror Memory, 1989
  TheaterWeek, 2:6, 15 May 1989

HARRY CAULEY
SEE LEONORA THUNA and HARRY CAULEY

KENNETH CAVANDER

The Legend of Oedipus (based on, among other things, certain plays of Sophocles
  and Euripides), 1988
  American Theatre, 5:10–11, July/Aug. 1988

ROBERT BOODEY CAVERLY

Battle of the Bush (a five-part "dramatic epic": *Last Night of a Nation, Miantonimoh, King Philip, The Regicides,* and *Chocurua in the Mountain*), published 1884
Jones, E. H., *Native Americans as Shown on the Stage,* pp. 131–132

JOSEPH CHAIKIN

Daniels, B., ed., *Joseph Chaikin and Sam Shepard*

ALSO SEE JEAN-CLAUDE van ITALLIE and JOSEPH CHAIKIN
AND SAM SHEPARD and JOSEPH CHAIKIN

MARISHA CHAMBERLAIN

The Angels of Warsaw, 1987 (revised 1990)
Sumption, C., "Solidarity's Spirit," *American Theatre,* 7:9–10, Apr. 1990

JANE CHAMBERS

Dolan, J., " 'Lesbian' Subjectivism in Realism: Dragging at the Margins of Structure and Ideology," pp. 40–53 in S.-E. Case, ed., *Performing Feminisms* (Chambers's *A Late Show, Last Summer at Bluefish Cove,* and *The Quintessential Image* considered)
Village Voice, 34:93, 15 Aug. 1989

Last Summer at Bluefish Cove, 1979
Case, S.-E., *Feminism and Theatre,* pp. 77–78
Dolan, J., *The Feminist Spectator as Critic,* pp. 109–110
American Theatre, 6:53, July/Aug. 1989

A Late Show (revision of her screenplay for the stage), 1974
Natalle, E. J., *Feminist Theatre,* pp. 72–73 and elsewhere

The Quintessential Image, 1989 (written 1983)
Case, S.-E., *Feminism and the Theatre,* pp. 78–79
Chansky, D., "Chamber Pieces," *TheaterWeek,* 2:40, 7 Aug. 1989
Portantiere, M., "Carrying the Torch," *TheaterWeek,* 2:33–37, 10 July 1989
New York, 22:77–78, 14 Aug. 1989
TheaterWeek, 2:5, 17 July 1989
Village Voice, 34:98, 11 Apr. 1989

LENORA CHAMPAGNE

Getting Over Tom, 1987
Champagne, L., ed., *Out from Under,* pp. ix–xiv (Introduction), 154–156, 157–164 (text of performance piece)

BRUCE CHARLESWORTH

Mpls/St Paul, 15:52+, May 1987

F. E. CHASE

The Great Umbrella Case, 1881
  Harap, L., *The Image of the Jew in American Literature,* p. 225

In the Trenches, 1898
  Harap, L., *The Image of the Jew in American Literature,* pp. 226–227

A Ready-Made Suit, 1885
  Harap, L., *The Image of the Jew in American Literature,* pp. 225–226

MARY CHASE

Wertheim, A., "The Comic Muse of Mary Chase," pp. 163–170 in H. K. Chinoy
  and L. W. Jenkins, eds., *Women in American Theatre,* rev. and enl. ed. (same
  pagination in 1981 ed.)

Harvey, 1944
  Stephens, J. L., "Women in Pulitzer Prize Plays, 1918–1949," pp. 245–253
  in H. K. Chinoy and L. W. Jenkins, eds., *Women in American Theatre,*
  rev. and enl. ed. (pp. 243–251 in 1981 ed.)

Me Third (later retitled *Now You've Done It*), 1936
  Kazacoff, G., *Dangerous Theatre,* pp. 248–250

DENISE CHÁVEZ

Gray, L., "Interview with Denise Chavez," *Short Story Review,* 5(4):2–4, Fall
  1988
Heard, M. E., "The Theatre of Denise Chávez: Interior Landscapes with 'sabor
  nuevomexicano,'" *Americas Review,* 16(2):83–91, Summer 1988

PADDY CHAYEFSKY

Goff, D. H., "Paddy Chayefsky (29 January 1923–1 August 1981)," pp. 80–90
  in P. C. Kolin, ed., *American Playwrights since 1945*
Harap, L., *Dramatic Encounters,* pp. 136–138

Middle of the Night, 1956
  Marcuson, L. R., *The Stage Immigrant,* pp. 226–232

The Tenth Man (originally titled *The Dybbuk from Woodhaven*), 1959
  Backalenick, I., "Making a Quorum Leap," *TheaterWeek,* 3:20–25, 11 Dec.
  1989
  Harris, J., "Chayefsky's Dybbuk," *TheaterWeek,* 3:42, 1 Jan. 1990
  Marcuson, L. R., *The Stage Immigrant,* pp. 232–244

America, 162:66, 27 Jan. 1990
Nation, 250:142–143, 29 Jan. 1990
New Republic, 202:27–28, 29 Jan. 1990
New Yorker, 65:63, 1 Jan. 1990
TheaterWeek, 3:23, 4 Sept. 1989
TheaterWeek, 3:10, 30 Oct. 1989
Village Voice, 34:115–116, 19 Dec. 1989

ROBERT CHESLEY

Deutsch, N., "Robert Chesley, Playwright," *TheaterWeek,* 4:36, 24 Dec. 1990
Village Voice, 33:22+, 28 June 1988 (interview)

Jerker, the Helping Hand: A Pornographic Elegy with Redeeming Social Value and a Hymn to the Queer Men of San Francisco in Twenty Telephone Calls, Many of Them Dirty, 1987
    Gutwillig, S., "A Look Back in Anguish," *TheaterWeek,* 3:33–38, 25 Dec. 1989
    Hall, R., "Eleven Different Directions," *American Theatre,* 5:32–33, Dec. 1988
    Shewey, D., "Gay Theatre Grows Up," *American Theatre,* 5:10–17, 52–53, May 1988
    Village Voice, 32:85–86, 20 Jan. 1987

PAUL CHIHARA
SEE JOHN DRIVER and PAUL CHIHARA

ALICE CHILDRESS

Austin, G., "Alice Childress: Black Woman Playwright as Feminist Critic," *Southern Quarterly,* 25(3):53–62, Spring 1987
Betsko, K., and R. Koenig, *Interviews with Contemporary Women Playwrights,* pp. 62–74
Brown-Guillory, E., "Alice Childress: A Pioneering Spirit" (interview), *Sage,* 4(1):66–68, Spring 1987
——, "Alice Childress, Lorraine Hansberry, Ntozake Shange: Carving a Place for Themselves on the American Stage," pp. 25–49 in Brown-Guillory's *Their Place on the Stage*
——, "Black Women Playwrights: Exorcising Myths," *Phylon,* 48(3): 229–239, Fall 1987
——, "The African Continuum: The Progeny in the New World," pp. 135–150 in Brown-Guillory's *Their Place on the Stage*
Case, S.-E., *Feminism and Theatre,* p. 101 (Childress's *Florence* and *Trouble in Mind* considered)
Keyssar, H., "Foothills: Precursors of Feminist Drama," pp. 22–52 in Keyssar's *Feminist Theatre*
Miller, J.-M. A., "Black Women in Plays by Black Playwrights," pp. 256–262 in H. K. Chinoy and L. W. Jenkins, eds., *Women in American Theatre,* rev. and enl. ed. (pp. 254–260 in 1981 ed.)

Wedding Band: A Love/Hate Story in Black and White, 1966

    Dillon, J., "Alice Childress's *Wedding Band* at the Milwaukee Repertory Theater: A Photo Essay," *Studies in American Drama, 1945–Present,* 4:129–141, 1989

    Holliday, P., "I Remember Alice Childress," *Southern Quarterly,* 25(3):63–65, Spring 1987

    Moore, H., "Woman Alone, Women Together," pp. 186–191 in H. K. Chinoy and L. W. Jenkins, eds., *Women in American Theatre,* rev. and enl. ed. (pp. 186–191 in 1981 ed.)

    Wiley, C., "Whose Name, Whose Protection: Reading Alice Childress's *Wedding Band,*" pp. 184–197 in J. Schlueter, ed., *Modern American Drama*

    Wilkerson, M. B., "Music as Metaphor: New Plays of Black Women," pp. 61–75 in L. Hart, ed., *Making a Spectacle*

American Theatre, 6:11, May 1989

Wine in the Wilderness, televised 1969, produced on stage 1976

    Austin, G., *Feminist Theories for Dramatic Criticism,* pp. 88–91

    Keyssar, H., "Rites and Responsibilities: The Drama of Black American Women," pp. 226–240 in E. Brater, ed., *Feminine Focus*

FRANK CHIN

Berson, M., "Between Worlds," *American Theatre,* 6:20–25, Mar. 1990 (based on Berson's Introduction to *Between Worlds*)

EDWARD CHODOROV

Common Ground, 1945

    Marcuson, L. R., *The Stage Immigrant,* pp. 147–151

Signor Chicago (based on the H. and H. Granville-Barker version of a play by S. and J. Alvarez-Quintero, *The Women Have Their Way*), 1949

    Leonard, W. T., *Once Was Enough,* pp. 207, 208

JEROME CHODOROV, JACK LAWRENCE, and STAN FREEMAN

I Had a Ball, 1964

    Rubin, M. H., "The *Ball* Bounces Back," *TheaterWeek,* 1:50–53, 16 May 1988

ALSO SEE JOSEPH FIELDS, JEROME CHODOROV, LEONARD BERNSTEIN, BETTY COMDEN, and ADOLPH GREEN

PING CHONG

Berson, M., "Between Worlds," *American Theatre,* 6:20–25, Mar. 1990 (based on Berson's Introduction to *Between Worlds*)

Sandla, R., "Practical Visionary: Ping Chong," *TheaterWeek,* 2:26–35, 30 Jan. 1989

American Theatre, 7:50, Oct. 1990
Village Voice, 31:83–84, 11 Nov. 1986

The Angels of Swedenborg, 1985
    Pittsburgh, 14 Nov. 1986
    Village Voice, 31:100, 4 Nov. 1986

Brightness, 1989
    Jacobson, L., "Chong and Dance," *American Theatre,* 6:10–11, Dec. 1989
    Theatre Journal, 42:491–493 +, Dec. 1990
    Village Voice, 34:122, 28 Nov. 1989

Elephant Memories, 1990
    Bell, J., "Pachyderm Memoria," *TheaterWeek,* 4:36–37, 12 Nov. 1990
    TheaterWeek, 4:9, 22 Oct. 1990
    TheaterWeek, 4:34–35, 26 Nov. 1990

Lazarus, 1978
    Anderson, J., "*Lazarus,* a Multimedia Event," pp. 218–219 in Anderson's
    Choreography Observed

Maraya—Acts of Nature in Geological Time, 1988
    American Theatre, 4:12, Jan. 1988
    TheaterWeek, 1:29, 18 Jan. 1988

Noiresque: The Fallen Angel, 1989
    American Theatre, 6:10, June 1989
    TheaterWeek, 2:8, 17 Apr. 1989
    TheaterWeek, 2:2, 15 May 1989
    Village Voice, 34:100, 16 May 1989

Snow, 1988
    American Theatre, 5:10, July/Aug. 1988
    American Theatre, 6:56, Mar. 1990
    Theatre Journal, 41:234–235, May 1989

PING CHONG and OTHERS

4 A.M. America, 1990
    Robinson, M., "Storm King Odd Couple Creates Pungent *4 A.M.,*" *American Theatre,* 7:96–98, Oct. 1990

Nuit Blanche: A Select View of Earthlings, 1981
    Berson, M., ed., *Between Worlds,* pp. ix-xiv (Introduction), 1–6, 7–28 (text of performance piece)

CHARLES CISSEL

Home Sweet Home/Crack, 1988
    TheaterWeek, 1:7, 30 May 1988

JACK CLARK
SEE BOB MEYER and JACK CLARK

RON CLARK
SEE SAM BOBRICK and RON CLARK

HAROLD CLARKE and MAXWELL NURNBERG

Chalk Dust, 1936
  Kazacoff, G., *Dangerous Theatre,* pp. 87–91

JOSEPH I. C. CLARKE

Luck, published 1877
  Jones, E. H., *Native Americans as Shown on the Stage,* pp. 117–118

MARTHA CLARKE

Backalenick, I., "Sneak Preview: Richard Foreman and Martha Clarke,"
  TheaterWeek, 3:25–29, 30 July 1990
Bartow, A., "Images from the Id" (interview), *American Theatre,* 5:10–17, 55–
  57, June 1988 (adapted from Bartow's *The Director's Voice*)
Copeland, R., "Master of the Body," *American Theatre,* 5:14–15, June 1988
Madotti, M., "What Becomes of the Brokenhearted," *Artforum,* 27:117–121,
  Sept. 1988

MARTHA CLARKE, RICHARD COE, RICHARD PEASLEE, and STANLEY WALDEN

Endangered Species, 1990
  Anderson, P., "Wild Kingdom," *TheaterWeek,* 4:18–24, 15 Oct. 1990
  American Theatre, 7:12, July/Aug. 1990
  Commonweal, 117:654–655, 9 Nov. 1990
  Dance Magazine, 64:46–49, Oct. 1990
  National Review, 42:56–57, 3 Dec. 1990
  New Republic, 203:26–28, 19 Nov. 1990
  TheaterWeek, 3:20, 26 Mar. 1990
  TheaterWeek, 4:40+, 22 Oct. 1990
  Theatre Crafts, 24:39, Nov. 1990

MARTHA CLARKE, RICHARD GREENBERG, and RICHARD PEASLEE

The Hunger Artist (based on the life and work of F. Kafka), 1987
  Vanity Fair, 50:138, Mar. 1987
  Village Voice, 32:81–82, 10 Mar. 1987
  Village Voice, 32:89, 10 Mar. 1987

MARTHA CLARKE, CHARLES L. MEE, JR., and RICHARD PEASLEE

Vienna: Lusthaus, 1986
> Brustein, R., "Vienna Dreams," pp. 148–150 in Brustein's *Who Needs Theatre* (rpt. of *New Republic,* 194:28–29, 26 May 1986)
> Mee, C. L., Jr., and A. Smith, "*Vienna: Lusthaus*: Play Text and Photo Essay," *The Drama Review,* 31:42–58, Fall 1987

MARTHA CLARKE and RICHARD PEASLEE

The Garden of Earthly Delights (based on the painting of H. Bosch), 1983
> Brustein, R., "Theaterphobia," pp. 127–131 in Brustein's *Who Needs Theatre*
> *Journal of Dramatic Theory and Criticism,* 3:120–125, Fall 1988
> *Mpls/St Paul,* 15:68+, Dec. 1987

Miracolo d'Amore (inspired by the drawings of Tiepolo and the sketches of Grandville), 1988
> *New Yorker,* 64:77, 11 July 1988
> *TheaterWeek,* 1:6, 27 June 1988
> *Vanity Fair,* 51:50, July 1988
> *Village Voice,* 33:29+, 21 June 1988
> *Village Voice,* 33:91–92, 12 July 1988

MARY CARR CLARKE

Benevolent Lawyer; or, Villainy Detected, 1823
> Harap, L., *The Image of the Jew in American Literature,* p. 210

ANTHONY CLARVOE

Pick Up Ax, 1990
> *American Theatre,* 7:69, May 1990

PEARL CLEAGE

Lutenbacher, C., "'So Much More Than Just Myself': Women Theatre Artists in the South," pp. 380–382 in H. K. Chinoy and L. W. Jenkins, eds., *Women in American Theatre,* rev. and enl. ed. (new to this ed.; excerpted from a paper Lutenbacher presented at the 1987 Themes in Drama Conference in Riverside, CA, later printed in J. Redmond, ed., *Women in Theatre,* pp. 253–263)

COLIN CLEMENTS
SEE FLORENCE RYERSON and COLIN CLEMENTS

RICK CLEVELAND

Chicago, 37:34, July 1988

MARGARET ELLEN CLIFFORD
SEE HALLIE FLANAGAN and MARGARET ELLEN CLIFFORD

MYLA JO CLOSSER and HOMER LITTLE

Raw Meat, 1933
    Leonard, W. T., *Once Was Enough,* pp. 159–160

DARRAH CLOUD

The Mud Angel, 1987
    TheaterWeek, 4:9, 29 Oct. 1990
    Village Voice, 32:97–98, 23 June 1987

O Pioneers! (dramatization of novel by W. Cather), 1990
    Savage, J., "Go West, Young Woman," *American Theatre,* 6:8–9, Mar. 1990

The Obscene Bird of Night (dramatization of novel by J. Donoso), 1989
    American Theatre, 6:13, May 1989

GEORGE COATES

Right Mind (based on C. Dodgson and his works), 1989
    Perry, D., "The Cheshire Coates," *American Theatre,* 6:16–20, 22–23, Dec.
        1989

MARY L. COBB

Home, 1873
    Jones, E. H., *Native Americans as Shown on the Stage,* p. 131

D. L. COBURN

The Gin Game, 1977
    Clarke, G., "Two Lives, One Ambition," *Time,* 135:62–64, 2 Apr. 1990

DUDLEY COCKE
SEE DON BAKER and DUDLEY COCKE

WILLIAM F. CODY, W. F. CARVER, and OTHERS

Wild West, Rocky Mountain and Prairie Exhibition, 1883
    Jones, E. H., *Native Americans as Shown on the Stage,* pp. 115–117

RICHARD COE
SEE MARTHA CLARKE, RICHARD COE, RICHARD PEASLEE,
and STANLEY WALDEN

ROBERT COE
SEE RICHARD NELSON, TIM RICE, BENNY ANDERSSON, and
BJÖRN ULVAEUS

LENORE COFFEE and JOYCE COWAN

Family Portrait, 1939
    Harap, L., *Dramatic Encounters,* p. 115

GEORGE M. COHAN

Mates, J., *America's Musical Stage,* pp. 150, 166, 172, 174, 177–179, 183
TheaterWeek, 1:59–60, 27 June 1988

Little Johnny Jones, 1904
    Green, S., *Broadway Musicals,* p. 10

ALICE EVE COHEN

Cohen, A. E., "Staples and Tears," *American Theatre,* 6:7, Jan. 1990

BELLA COHEN and SAMUEL SPEWACK

Poppa, 1928
    Harap, L., *Dramatic Encounters,* p. 114

ALSO SEE BELLA SPEWACK and SAMUEL SPEWACK

LAWRENCE D. COHEN, MICHAEL GORE, and DEAN PITCHFORD

Carrie (musical version of novel by S. King), 1988
    Henry, W. A., III, "The Biggest All-Time Flop Ever," *Time,* 131:65, 30
        May 1988
    New Yorker, 64:85, 23 May 1988
    TheaterWeek, 1:7, 29 Feb. 1988
    TheaterWeek, 1:56, 30 May 1988
    Time, 131:80, 23 May 1988
    Village Voice, 33:115, 24 May 1988 (Michael Feingold)
    Village Voice, 33:115, 24 May 1988 (Melanie Pitts)

MICHAEL COHEN
SEE ENID FUTTERMAN and MICHAEL COHEN

R. JEFFREY COHEN

Anderson, W., "House Seats: Artist's Oasis: The RAPP Arts Center,"
    TheaterWeek, 1:12–15, 7 Mar. 1988

As You Like It—Fresh! (suggested by Shakespeare's play), 1990
    TheaterWeek, 4:43–44, 10 Sept. 1990

The Seagull: The Hamptons, 1990 (adaptation of Chekhov's play *The Seagull*),
   1988 (later revised)
   Bell, J., "Chekhov Updated," *TheaterWeek,* 4:31–33, 31 Dec. 1990
   New Yorker, 66:4, 10 Dec. 1990
   TheaterWeek, 4:10, 19 Nov. 1990

TOM COLE

About Time, 1990
   America, 163:350, 10 Nov. 1990
   New York, 23:150–151, 22 Oct. 1990
   New Yorker, 66:109, 22 Oct. 1990

The Eighties, 1983 (revised 1989)
   Ledford, L. S., "Eightysomething," *TheaterWeek,* 2:26–30, 20 Feb. 1989
   American Theatre, 7:11, May 1990
   Los Angeles, 34:256+, Dec. 1989

Medal of Honor Rag, 1975
   Counts, M. L., *Coming Home,* pp. 75–76, 117–118, 139, 147, 163–164, 195,
      196, 198
   Zinman, T. S., "Search and Destroy: The Drama of the Vietnam War,"
      Theatre Journal, 42:5–26, Mar. 1990

CY COLEMAN

Haun, H., "Broadway Music Maker," *Playbill,* 8:18, 20, 22, 31 Dec. 1989

ALSO SEE BETTY COMDEN, ADOLPH GREEN, and CY COLEMAN
AND LARRY GELBART, CY COLEMAN, and DAVID ZIPPEL

JOHN J. COLEMAN

Help Yourself (adaptation of play by P. Vilpius), 1934
   Kazacoff, G., *Dangerous Theatre,* pp. 61–63

LONNIE COLEMAN

A Warm Body, 1967
   Leonard, W. T., *Once Was Enough,* pp. 202–204

KATHLEEN COLLINS

Village Voice, 33:69, 11 Oct. 1988

PADRAIC COLUM
SEE MARJORIE BARKENTIN and PADRAIC COLUM

BETTY COMDEN

Chase, A., "Comden and Green: A Hell of a Team," *TheaterWeek*, 2:22–27, 26
    June 1989
Playbill, 7:52, 28 Feb. 1989 (interview)

BETTY COMDEN and ADOLPH GREEN

A Doll's Life (musical sequel to Ibsen's *A Doll's House*), 1982
    Ilson, C., *Harold Prince*, pp. 314–323

BETTY COMDEN, ADOLPH GREEN, and CY COLEMAN

On the Twentieth Century (musical version of *Twentieth Century*, play by B. Hecht
    and C. MacArthur, adapted from a play by C. B. Milholland), 1978
    Green, S., *Broadway Musicals*, p. 249
    Ilson, C., *Harold Prince*, pp. 249–259

ALSO SEE JOSEPH FIELDS, JEROME CHODOROV, LEONARD
    BERNSTEIN, BETTY COMDEN, and ADOLPH GREEN

ANNE COMMIRE

Betsko, K., and R. Koenig, *Interviews with Contemporary Women Playwrights*,
    pp. 85–93

Starting Monday, 1990
    TheaterWeek, 3:41, 23 Apr. 1990
    Village Voice, 35:114, 24 Apr. 1990

CONSTANCE CONGDON

Booth, S. V., "Dramaturg in Search of an Axis," *American Theatre*, 7:62–63,
    Sept. 1990
Klementowski, N., and S. Kuftinec, "An Interview with Constance Congdon,"
    Studies in American Drama, 1945–Present, 4:203–221, 1989
London, T., "Opening a Door Up Left," *American Theatre*, 5:38–41, Mar. 1989

Tales of the Lost Formicans, 1988
    American Theatre, 5:47, Dec. 1988
    American Theatre, 6:n. pag., May 1989 (text of play)
    TheaterWeek, 3:10, 16 Apr. 1990
    Time, 133:70–71, 17 Apr. 1989
    Village Voice, 35:116, 1 May 1990
    Village Voice, 35:101, 8 May 1990

CONSTANCE CONGDON and MARK STRAND

Rembrandt Takes a Walk (dramatization of a book by Strand), 1989
    American Theatre, 5:12–14, Mar. 1989

E. P. CONKLE

Prologue to Glory, 1938
    Kazacoff, G., *Dangerous Theatre,* pp. 65–68

WILLY CONLEY

Broken Spokes, 1990
    Village Voice, 35:102, 30 Jan. 1990

MARC CONNELLY

The Green Pastures (dramatization of tales by R. Bradford), 1930
    Woll, A., *Black Musical Theatre,* pp. 137–141, 144, 150, 156–157, 193, 223

ALSO SEE ARNOLD SUNDGAARD and MARC CONNELLY

CHARLOTTE BARNES CONNER

The Forest Princess; or, Two Centuries Ago, 1848
    Jones, E. H., *Native Americans as Shown on the Stage,* pp. 57–58

ROBERT T. CONRAD

Jack Cade, 1835
    McConachie, B. A., "The Theatre of Edwin Forrest and Jacksonian Hero
    Worship," pp. 3–18 in J. L. Fisher and S. Watt, eds., *When They Weren't
    Doing Shakespeare*

H. J. CONWAY

Guiscard the Guerilla, 1844
    Harap, L., *The Image of the Jew in American Literature,* pp. 202–203

GEORGE CRAM COOK and SUSAN GLASPELL

Suppressed Desires, 1914
    Kolin, P. C., "Therapists in Susan Glaspell's *Suppressed Desires* and David
    Rabe's *In the Boom Boom Room,*" *Notes on Contemporary Literature,*
    18(5):2–3, Nov. 1988

ROSE TERRY COOKE

Makosky, D. R., "Rose Terry Cooke's *Matred and Tamar, a Drama,*" *Resources
for American Literary Study,* 14(1–2):1–58, Spring-Autumn 1984 (includes text
of play)

IRVING COOPER

Have I Got a Girl for You! (based on a story by H. Cooper), 1963
    Leonard, W. T., *Once Was Enough,* pp. 74–75

SUSAN COOPER
SEE HUME CRONYN and SUSAN COOPER

JOHN CORBIN

Husband, 1910
    Harap, L., *Dramatic Encounters,* p. 78

HAL CORLEY

Finding Donis Anne, 1989
    TheaterWeek, 2:7, 24 Apr. 1989

BARTLETT CORMACK

The Racket, 1927
    Harap, L., *Dramatic Encounters,* p. 116
    Village Voice, 32:134, 22 Dec. 1987

ROGER CORNISH

Offshore Signals, 1989
    American Theatre, 5:7, Jan. 1989
    TheaterWeek, 2:40, 26 Sept. 1988

Rocky and Diego, 1989
    American Theatre, 6:12, May 1989

WALTER CORWIN

Future Tense (three short plays with music), 1990
    TheaterWeek, 3:10, 11 June 1990

CLARE COSS

Horwitz, S., "Roberta Sklar and Clare Coss," *TheaterWeek,* 2:17–21, 29 May
    1989

The Blessing, 1989
    TheaterWeek, 2:6, 8 May 1989
    Village Voice, 34:92 + , 6 June 1989

CLARE COSS, SONDRA SEGAL, and ROBERTA SKLAR

Electra Speaks (Part III of their trilogy *The Daughters Cycle*), published 1980
    Natalle, E. J., *Feminist Theatre,* pp. 68–71 and elsewhere

RANDY COURTS
SEE MARK ST. GERMAIN and RANDY COURTS

NORMAN COUSINS, JEROME LAWRENCE, and ROBERT E. LEE

Whisper in the Mind, 1990
  Playbill, 9:27, 31 Oct. 1990

JOYCE COWAN
SEE LENORE COFFEE and JOYCE COWAN

MARIA M. COXE

If Ye Break Faith, 1938
  Kazacoff, G., *Dangerous Theatre*, pp. 200–203

TOM CREAMER

Sister Carrie (dramatization of novel by T. Dreiser), 1990
  American Theatre, 7:11, May 1990

LUIGI CREATORE

The Man Who Shot Lincoln, 1989
  TheaterWeek, 3:11, 21 Aug. 1989
  TheaterWeek, 3:13, 2 Oct. 1989

KID CREOLE
SEE AUGUST DARNELL

HARRY CREWS

Blood Issue, 1989
  Time, 133:71, 17 Apr. 1989

MICHAEL CRISTOFER (Michael Procassion)

Ice, 1976
  Shrager, S., *Scatology in Modern Drama*, p. 36

The Lady and the Clarinet, 1980
  American Theatre, 7:13, July/Aug. 1990

Love Me or Leave Me (based on the life of R. Etting), 1989
  TheaterWeek, 2:7, 7 Aug. 1989

The Shadow Box, 1975
  Kelley, M. A., "Life near Death: Art of Dying in Recent American Drama," pp. 117–127 in K. Hartigan, ed., *Text and Presentation*

HUME CRONYN and SUSAN COOPER

Foxfire (developed from the magazine of this title), 1982
  Clarke, G., "Two Lives, One Ambition," *Time,* 135:62–64, 2 Apr. 1990

JOSEPH CROSWELL

A New World Planted; or, The Adventures of The Forefathers of New England,
  published 1802
  Jones, E. H., *Native Americans as Shown on the Stage,* pp. 23–24, 28, 38,
  46–47

RACHEL CROTHERS

Abramson, D., "Rachel Crothers: Broadway's Feminist," pp. 55–65 in J.
  Schlueter, ed., *Modern American Drama*
Gottlieb, L., "Looking to Women: Rachel Crothers and the Feminist Heroine,"
  pp. 137–145 in H. K. Chinoy and L. W. Jenkins, eds., *Women in American
  Theatre,* rev. and enl. ed. (same pagination in 1981 ed.)

Everyday, 1921
  Counts, M. L., *Coming Home,* pp. 77, 113

He and She (originally titled *The Herfords*), 1911
  Stephens, J. L., "Gender Ideology and Dramatic Convention in Progressive
  Era Plays, 1890–1920," pp. 283–293 in S.-E. Case, ed., *Performing Fem-
  inisms* (rpt. of *Theatre Journal,* 41(1):45–55, Mar. 1989)

A Little Journey, 1918
  Harap, L., *Dramatic Encounters,* p. 78

A Man's World, 1909
  Stephens, J. L., "Gender Ideology and Dramatic Convention in Progressive
  Era Plays, 1890–1920," pp. 283–293 in S.-E. Case, ed., *Performing Fem-
  inisms* (rpt. of *Theatre Journal,* 41(1):45–55, Mar. 1989)

RUSSEL CROUSE
SEE HOWARD LINDSAY and RUSSEL CROUSE
AND HOWARD LINDSAY, RUSSEL CROUSE,
OSCAR HAMMERSTEIN II, and RICHARD RODGERS

MART CROWLEY

The Boys in the Band, 1968
  Curtin, K., *"We Can Always Call Them Bulgarians,"* pp. 327–329
  Shewey, D., "Gay Theatre Grows Up," *American Theatre,* 5:10–17, 52–53,
  May 1988

OWEN CRUMP

The Sixth Floor, 1989
  Playbill, 7:56, 30 Nov. 1989

MIGDALIA CRUZ

Miriam's Flowers (second play of a trilogy, the first being *Lillian,* the third
  unwritten), 1990
    Greene, A., "South Bronx Memoirs: Migdalia Cruz Explores Her Urban
    Roots," *American Theatre,* 7:58, June 1990
    American Theatre, 7:66, Nov. 1990
    TheaterWeek, 3:8, 18 June 1990

GRETCHEN CRYER

Betsko, K., and R. Koenig, *Interviews with Contemporary Women Playwrights,*
  pp. 94–108

G. D. CUMMINGS

Geronimo's Summer Campaign of 1885, published 1890
  Jones, E. H., *Native Americans as Shown on the Stage,* pp. 144–145

PAT CUMPER

The Rapist, 1981
    Fido, E., "Radical Woman: Woman and Theatre in the Anglophone Carib-
    bean," pp. 33–45 in E. S. Smilowitz and R. Q. Knowles, eds., *Critical
    Issues in West Indian Literature*

FRED CURCHACK

Greene, A., "A One-Man Tempest," *TheaterWeek,* 3:36–39, 6 Nov. 1989

Sexual Mythology, Part One: The Underworld (first part of a trilogy), 1989
    American Theatre, 6:10, July/Aug. 1989

Sexual Mythology, Part Two: Purgatory (second part of a trilogy), 1990
    Darrah, J. L., "'Twixt Heaven and Hell," *American Theatre,* 7:9–10, Sept.
    1990

ANTONIO CURIEL
SEE BARBARA BRINSON-PINEDA and ANTONIO CURIEL

KEITH CURRAN

Horwitz, S., "Keith Curran: Playwright as Skeptic," *TheaterWeek,* 2:50–53, 13
  Mar. 1989

Dalton's Back, 1989
  New York, 22:72–73, 20 Feb. 1989
  New Yorker, 65:89, 20 Feb. 1989
  Village Voice, 34:79–80, 28 Feb. 1989

LEIGH CURRAN

The Lunch Girls, 1977
  Moore, H., "Woman Alone, Women Together," pp. 186–191 in H. K. Chinoy and L. W. Jenkins, eds., *Women in American Theatre,* rev. and enl. ed. (pp. 184–190 in 1981 ed.)

DANIEL CURZON (Daniel R. Brown)

My Unknown Son, 1988
  TheaterWeek, 2:8, 10 Oct. 1988

SARAH ANNE CURZON

Laura Secord, the Heroine of 1812, 1887
  Jones, E. H., *Native Americans as Shown on the Stage,* pp. 135–136
  Jones, H., "Feminism and Nationalism in Domestic Melodramas: Gender, Genre, and Canadian Identity," *Essays in Theatre,* 8(1):5–14, Nov. 1989

TOM CUSHING

Grin and Bare It!, written 1929; see Ken Mcguire
  Filichia, P., "The Naked Truth," *TheaterWeek,* 1:46–51, 25 Apr. 1988

GEORGE WASHINGTON PARKE CUSTIS

The Indian Prophecy, 1825
  Jones, E. H., *Native Americans as Shown on the Stage,* pp. 31–32

W. B. DAILEY

Saratoga, a Dramatic Romance of the Revolution, published 1848
  Jones, E. H., *Native Americans as Shown on the Stage,* p. 88

AUGUSTIN DALY

Kauffmann, S., "Two Vulgar Geniuses: Augustin Daly and David Belasco," *Yale Review,* 76(4):496–513, Summer 1987
Murphy, B., "Literary Stepchildren: Nineteenth-Century Dramatists," *Review,* 8:197–204, 1986

Horizon, 1871
  Jones, E. H., *Native Americans as Shown on the Stage,* pp. 121–123

Leah, the Forsaken (adaptation of S. H. von Mosenthal's play *Deborah*), 1862
    Harap, L., *The Image of the Jew in American Literature,* pp. 216–220

Roughing It (dramatization of book by M. Twain), 1873
    Jones, E. H., *Native Americans as Shown on the Stage,* p. 109

HENRY JACKSON WELLS DAM

The Shop Girl, 1894
    Degen, J. A., "The Evolution of *The Shop Girl* and the Birth of 'Musical
    Comedy,'" *Theatre History Studies,* 7:40–50, 1987

BARBARA DAMASHEK

Writer's Digest, 68:6–9, Aug. 1988

DARIO D'AMBROSI

Enemy of Mine, 1988
    TheaterWeek, 1:5, 11 Apr. 1988

GRACIELA DANIELE, JIM LEWIS, WILLIAM FINN, and
ASTOR PIAZZOLLA

Dangerous Games (two parts: *Tango* and *Orfeo*), 1989
    Chansky, D., "sex, lies, and *Dangerous Games,*" *TheaterWeek,* 3:20–22, 23
    Oct. 1989
    TheaterWeek, 3:10, 4 Sept. 1989
    TheaterWeek, 3:15, 6 Nov. 1989
    TheaterWeek, 3:40, 15 Jan. 1990
    TheaterWeek, 3:23 + , 30 July 1990

NICOLAS DANTE (Conrado Morales)
SEE JAMES KIRKWOOD, NICOLAS DANTE, MARVIN HAMLISCH, and EDWARD KLEBAN

RON DANTE
SEE STEPHEN GLASSMAN, RON DANTE, and GENE ALLAN

JOE DARION
SEE DALE WASSERMAN, MITCH LEIGH, and JOE DARION

AUGUST DARNELL (also known as Kid Creole)
SEE ERIC OVERMYER and AUGUST DARNELL

N. R. DAVIDSON, JR.

El Hajj Malik (based on the speeches and autobiography of Malcolm X), 1971
    Shirakawa, S. H., "Theater Trends: Political Action Plays," *TheaterWeek,*
    1:13–15, 21 Mar. 1988

ROBERTSON DAVIES

Davis, J. M., ed., *Conversations with Robertson Davies*
Peterman, M., *Robertson Davies*

ALLAN DAVIS

The Promised Land, 1908
   Harap, L., *Dramatic Encounters,* p. 75

BILL C. DAVIS

Mass Appeal, 1981
   Sheehan, R. L., "*Get Thee Behind Me!* and *Mass Appeal*: A Case of Parallel
   Genesis," *Estreno,* 14(2):10–13, Fall 1988

CHRISTOPHER DAVIS

A Peep into the Twentieth Century (dramatization of his novel), 1988
   American Theatre, 6:56, Mar. 1990
   Georgia Review, 43:579–580, Fall 1989

GUY DAVIS

The Trial, 1990
   TheaterWeek, 3:12, 30 July 1990

LUTHER DAVIS, ROBERT WRIGHT, GEORGE FORREST, and
MAURY YESTON

Grand Hotel: The Musical (musical version of V. Baum's novel; revision of Davis,
   Wright, and Forrest's 1958 musical *At the Grand*), 1989
   Akers, K., "Life at the *Grand Hotel* [Part I]," *TheaterWeek,* 3: 22–33, 20
   Nov. 1989; "Life at the *Grand Hotel*: Part II," *TheaterWeek,* 3:26–30, 11
   Dec. 1989
   Flatow, S., "Ain't It Grand!" *Playbill,* 8, 10, 12, 28 Feb. 1990
   Gottfried, M., "The Big Three," *TheaterWeek,* 3:14–19, 4 June 1990
   Mandelbaum, K., "Auteur! Auteur! Tommy Tune Talks about *Grand Ho-
   tel*" (interview), *TheaterWeek,* 3:14–16, 18, 20, 20 Nov. 1989
   ———, "Room Service," *TheaterWeek,* 3:41, 4 Dec. 1989
   Willison, W., "Return to *Grand Hotel*," *TheaterWeek,* 4:19–25, 13 Aug.
   1990
   America, 161:453, 16 Dec. 1989
   Commonweal, 117:52–54, 26 Jan. 1990
   Dance Magazine, 64:64–65, Mar. 1990
   Elle, 5:220, Nov. 1989
   Fame, 2:102–103, Nov. 1989
   Harper's Bazaar, 122:180 + , Oct. 1989
   Nation, 250:67–68, 8–15 Jan. 1990
   New York, 22:99, 27 Nov. 1989
   New Yorker, 65:101, 27 Nov. 1989

Newsweek, 114:79 + , 4 Dec. 1989
TheaterWeek, 3:8, 4 Sept. 1989
TheaterWeek, 3:10, 2 Oct. 1989
TheaterWeek, 3:8, 23 Oct. 1989
TheaterWeek, 3:13, 30 Oct. 1989
TheaterWeek, 3:40, 15 Jan. 1990
Theatre Crafts, 24:42–45 + , Jan. 1990
Time, 134:87, 27 Nov. 1989
Village Voice, 34:114 + , 21 Nov. 1989

ALSO SEE CHARLES LEDERER, LUTHER DAVIS, ROBERT WRIGHT,
GEORGE FORREST, and ALEXANDER BORODIN

MATTHEW DAVIS

Waiting for Stanislavsky, 1989
TheaterWeek, 3:6, 16 Oct. 1989

OSSIE DAVIS

Bigsby, C. W. E., "Three Black Playwrights: Loften Mitchell, Ossie Davis,
Douglas Turner Ward," pp. 148–167 in E. Hill, ed., *The Theatre of Black
Americans,* Vol. 1 of two vols. rptd. as one in 1987; same pagination in both
eds. (rpt. of Bigsby, ed., *The Black American Writer,* 2:137–155)
Woll, A., *Black Musical Theatre,* pp. 251, 256–257, 259

The Last Dance of Sibyl, 1990
American Theatre, 7:10–11, May 1990

Purlie Victorious, 1961
Woll, A., *Black Musical Theatre,* pp. 226, 256–257, 261, 263

OSSIE DAVIS, PETER UDELL, PHILIP ROSE, and GARY GELD

Purlie (musical version of Davis's *Purlie Victorious*), 1970
Green, S., *Broadway Musicals,* p. 228
Woll, A., *Black Musical Theatre,* pp. xiv, 249, 256–259, 261

OWEN DAVIS

The Detour, 1921
Harap, L., *Dramatic Encounters,* p. 115

Icebound, 1923
Stephens, J. L., "Women in Pulitzer Prize Plays, 1918–1949," pp. 245–253
in H. K. Chinoy and L. W. Jenkins, eds., *Women in American Theatre,*
rev. and enl. ed. (pp. 243–251 in 1981 ed.)

PHILLIP HAYES DEAN

Paul Robeson, 1978
  Drake, P., "Black Arts Draw upon Folklore," *American Theatre,* 7:84, Oct.
    1990
  Kahn, S., "Avery Brooks, 'Theater Artist'" (interview), *TheaterWeek,*
    2:10–15, 10 Oct. 1988
  New Yorker, 64:84, 10 Oct. 1988
  TheaterWeek, 2:63, 19 Sept. 1988
  TheaterWeek, 2:7, 26 Sept. 1988
  Village Voice, 33:87–88, 30 Aug. 1988

ANGELYN DeBORD

Lutenbacher, C., "'So Much More Than Just Myself': Women Theatre Artists
  in the South," pp. 380–382 in H. K. Chinoy and L. W. Jenkins, eds., *Women
  in American Theatre,* rev. and enl. ed. (new to this ed.; excerpted from a
  paper Lutenbacher presented at the 1987 Themes in Drama Conference in
  Riverside, CA, later printed in J. Redmond, ed., *Women in Theatre,* pp. 253–
  263)

SANDRA DEER

Hulbert, D., "Actors Are the Spark for Atlanta's Writers," *American Theatre,*
  7:44–45, June 1990

So Long on Lonely Street, 1985
  Hubert, L. L., "Humor and Heritage in Sandra Deer's *So Long on Lonely
    Street,*" *Southern Quarterly,* 25(3):105–115, Spring 1987
  San Diego Magazine, 41:58+, Nov. 1988

3-Point Shot, 1990
  American Theatre, 7:12, Dec. 1990

A Wrinkle in Time (dramatization of book by M. L'Engle), 1987
  American Theatre, 4:8–9, Jan. 1988

NATHANIEL DEERING

Carabasset; or, The Last of the Norridgewocks, 1831
  Jones, E. H., *Native Americans as Shown on the Stage,* pp. 25–26

LEWIS DEFFEBACH

Oolaita, or the Indian Heroine, 1821
  Jones, E. H., *Native Americans as Shown on the Stage,* pp. 42–44

JOHN de GROOT

Papa (about Ernest Hemingway), 1988
  Warren, S., "Peppard as Papa," *TheaterWeek,* 2:42–45, 14 Nov. 1988

CONSTANCE DeJONG
SEE PHILIP GLASS and CONSTANCE DeJONG

DON DeLILLO

Arensberg, A., "Seven Seconds" (interview), *Vogue,* 178:336–339+, Aug. 1988
Bryant, P., "Don DeLillo: An Annotated Bibliography and Critical Secondary
   Bibliography, 1977–1986," *Bulletin of Bibliography,* 45(3):208–212, Sept. 1988
DeCurtis, A., "Matters of Fact and Fiction," *Rolling Stone,* p. 113+, 17 Nov.
   1988
Goldstein, W., "*PW* Interviews," *Publishers Weekly,* 234:55–56, 19 Aug. 1988

The Day Room, 1986
   Shirakawa, S. H., "Theater Trends: Dramatic Disabilities," *TheaterWeek,*
      1:24–27, 11 Jan. 1988
   New York, 21:45, 4 Jan. 1988
   New Yorker, 63:74–75, 11 Jan. 1988

Rapture of the Athlete Assumed into Heaven (a "one-minute play"), 1990
   Carpenter, B., "Just Add Water . . . ," *TheaterWeek,* 3:32–33, 28 May 1990

DONNA de MATTEO

Betsko, K., and R. Koenig, *Interviews with Contemporary Women Playwrights,*
   pp. 109–124

HENRY CHURCHILL De MILLE and DAVID BELASCO

Men and Women, 1890
   Harap, L., *The Image of the Jew in American Literature,* pp. 235–237

WILLIAM CHURCHILL De MILLE

Strongheart, 1905
   Jones, E. H., *Native Americans as Shown on the Stage,* pp. 149–153 and
   elsewhere

HENRY DENKER

Something Old, Something New (originally titled *Second Time Around*), 1976
   Leonard, W. T., *Once Was Enough,* pp. 170–172

HENRY DENKER and RALPH BERKEY

Time Limit!, 1956
   Counts, M. L., *Coming Home,* pp. 64–66, 161–162, 180

PATRICK DENNIS and MURRAY GRAND

Good Good Friends, unproduced
Playbill, 6:36, 30 Sept. 1988
TheaterWeek, 1:61, 8 Aug. 1988

PHILIP DePOY, LEVI LEE, and REBECCA WACKLER

Saving Grace (originally titled *Sluts*), 1988
American Theatre, 5:11, Nov. 1988

ALEXIS DeVEAUX

The Tapestry: A Play Woven in 2, 1975
Wilkerson, M. B., "Music as Metaphor: New Plays of Black Women,"
pp. 61–75 in L. Hart, ed., *Making a Spectacle*

JOHN HUNTER DEWAR

De Roberval, 1888
Jones, E. H., *Native Americans as Shown on the Stage,* p. 136

DAVID DIAMOND

No`Xya:, 1987
Maclean's, 101:67, 9 May 1988

THOMAS H. DICKINSON

Winter Bound, 1929
Curtin, K., "Getting Even with Sappho in Overalls in 1929," pp. 140–153
in Curtin's *"We Can Always Call Them Bulgarians," Commonweal,*
11:144–145, 4 Dec. 1929

PIETRO Di DONATO

von Huene-Greenberg, D., "A MELUS Interview: Pietro Di Donato," *MELUS,*
14(3–4):33–52, Fall-Winter 1987

Christ in Concrete (dramatization of his autobiographical novel), unpublished
Beranger, J., "De la mort Pere au Dieu retrouve: Mentalities italiennes et
crise religieuse dans les romans autobiographiques de Pietro di Donato,"
pp. 43–58 in Beranger and P. Guillaume, eds., *Le Facteur religieux en
Amérique du Nord,* No. 7
Coles, N., "Mantraps: Men at Work in Pietro Di Donato's *Christ in Con-
crete* and Thomas Bell's *Out of This Furnace," MELUS,* 14(3–4):23–32,
Fall-Winter 1987

HOWARD DIETZ
SEE FAY KANIN, MICHAEL KANIN, HOWARD DIETZ, and ARTHUR
SCHWARTZ

STEVEN DIETZ

Dietz, S., "Doom Eager: Writing What We Need to Know," *American Theatre*,
7:58–59, July/Aug. 1990

God's Country, 1988
  American Theatre, 5:6–7, Sept. 1988

More Fun than Bowling, 1989
  American Theatre, 5:14, Feb. 1989

STEVEN DIETZ and ERIC PELTONIEMI

Happenstance, 1989
  American Theatre, 6:8–9, Sept. 1989

JOHN DiFUSCO and OTHERS

Tracers, 1980
  Zinman, T. S., "Search and Destroy: The Drama of the Vietnam War,"
  Theatre Journal, 42:5–26, Mar. 1990

ELIZABETH DIGGS

Nightingale (originally titled *Saint Florence*; based on the life of Florence Night-
ingale), 1988
  American Theatre, 5:7, Dec. 1988
  New York, 23:85–86, 17 Dec. 1990
  New Yorker, 66:111, 17 Dec. 1990
  Playbill, 9:45, 30 Nov. 1990
  TheaterWeek, 1:5, 30 May 1988
  TheaterWeek, 2:4, 17 Oct. 1988
  TheaterWeek, 4:8, 15 Oct. 1990

INA DILLAYE

Ramona (dramatization of novel by H. H. Jackson), published 1887
  Jones, E. H., *Native Americans as Shown on the Stage*, pp. 141–143 and
  elsewhere

THOMAS M. DISCH

Lehman, D., "A Conversation with Tom Disch," *Southwest Review*, 73:220–231,
Spring 1988

The Audition, 1990
  TheaterWeek, 3:9, 21 May 1990
  TheaterWeek, 3:40–41, 11 June 1990

Ben-Hur (suggested by the novel by L. Wallace), 1989
  Filichia, P., "Letter from Baltimore," *TheaterWeek,* 3:11, 11 Sept. 1989
  American Theatre, 6:11, Oct. 1989
  Playbill, 7:26, 31 July 1989
  TheaterWeek, 3:11, 16 Oct. 1989

The Cardinal Detoxes, 1990
  Disch, T. M., "Disching the Church," *TheaterWeek,* 4:4–5, 15 Oct. 1990
    (letter, also printed in *Nation,* which see)
  Harris, J., "RAPP Rapped by Church," *TheaterWeek,* 4:16–17, 8 Oct. 1990
  Christian Century, 107:961, 24 Oct. 1990
  Nation, 251:405, 15 Oct. 1990
  TheaterWeek, 3:9, 21 May 1990
  TheaterWeek, 3:40–41, 11 June 1990

RON DOBSON

Under the Surface, 1989
  TheaterWeek, 3:11, 18 Sept. 1989

E. L. DOCTOROW

Moyers, B., *Bill Moyers' World of Ideas,* ed. B. S. Flowers, pp. 83–95 (interview on PBS, 1988)

JOSEPH DODDRIDGE

Logan, the Last of the Race of Shikellemus, Chief of the Cayuga Nation, 1821
  Jones, E. H., *Native Americans as Shown on the Stage,* pp. 30–31

OWEN DODSON

Hatch, J. V., "Owen Dodson: Excerpts from a Biography in Progress," *Massachusetts Review,* 28:627–641, Winter 1987

TOM DONAGHY

The Weather Outside, 1990
  TheaterWeek, 3:9, 1 Jan. 1990
  Village Voice, 35:96, 6 Feb. 1990

HILDA DOOLITTLE

Hippolytus Temporizes, 1927
  Bann, S., "The Mission of Ion," *Agenda,* 25(3–4):191–196, Autumn-Winter 1987–1988

JEFF DORCHEN and OTHERS

The Slow and Painful Death of Sam Shepard, 1988
    Theatre Journal, 41:538–539, Dec. 1989

JOHN DOS PASSOS

Airways, Inc., 1929
    Harap, L., *Dramatic Encounters*, pp. 111–112

Fortune Heights, written 1933
    Harap, L., *Dramatic Encounters*, pp. 111–112

MARJORY STONEMAN DOUGLAS

Gallows Gate, 1937
    Kazacoff, G., *Dangerous Theatre*, pp. 193–195

ROGER DOWNEY

Downey, R., "Empowering the Players," *American Theatre*, 7:40–42, 124–126,
    Oct. 1990

Lulu (adaptation of F. Wedekind's *Monster-Tragedy* and parts of *Earth Spirit*
    and *Pandora's Box*), 1988
    New York, 21:141–142, 22 Aug. 1988
    Village Voice, 34–104, 31 Oct. 1989

SARAH DREHER

Case, S.-E., *Feminism and Theatre*, p. 77 (Dreher's *8x10 Glossy* considered)

THEODORE DREISER

The Hand of the Potter, 1918
    Harap, L., *Creative Awakening*, pp. 128–132
    ———, *Dramatic Encounters*, pp. 78–79

RICHARD DRESSER

Elle, 4:170+, Oct. 1988

The Downside, 1987
    Forbes, D., "Dirty Dealing," *American Theatre*, 4:12–18, Feb. 1988

ROSALYN DREXLER

Betsko, K., and R. Koenig, *Interviews with Contemporary Women Playwrights*,
    pp. 125–138

Keyssar, H., "A Network of Playwrights," pp. 102–125 in Keyssar's *Feminist Theatre*

The Heart That Eats Itself (based on F. Kafka's story "A Hunger Artist"), 1987
   Village Voice, 32:89, 21 Apr. 1987

DONALD DRIVER

Status Quo Vadis, 1971
   Leonard, W. T., *Once Was Enough,* pp. 178–181

JOHN DRIVER and PAUL CHIHARA

James Clavell's Shōgun: The Musical (musical version of novel by J. Clavell), 1990
   Harris, J., "Born to Be Much Better: *Shōgun* Composer Paul Chihara Speaks Out against the Show," *TheaterWeek,* 4:36–37, 31 Dec. 1990
   Henry, W. A., III, "Sailing through the Storms," *Time,* 136:104, 26 Nov. 1990
   Hurley, J., "Putting the Show in *Shōgun*: Profiles of the Author, Director, Set Designer, and Star," *TheaterWeek,* 23–31, 19 Nov. 1990
   Business Week, p. 74+, 22 Oct. 1990
   New York, 23:38–39, 10 Sept. 1990
   New York, 23:83, 26 Nov. 1990
   New Yorker, 66:162–163, 3 Dec. 1990
   Newsweek, 116:83, 26 Nov. 1990
   Playbill, 8:12, 16, 30 Sept. 1990
   TheaterWeek, 3:9, 30 Apr. 1990
   TheaterWeek, 4:10, 13 Aug. 1990
   TheaterWeek, 4:29, 13 Aug. 1990
   TheaterWeek, 4:9, 3 Sept. 1990
   TheaterWeek, 4:41, 3 Dec. 1990
   TheaterWeek, 4:15, 10 Dec. 1990
   Theatre Crafts, 24:10–11, Dec. 1990

JOHN DRIVER and JEFFREY HADDOW

Scrambled Feet, 1981
   New Jersey Monthly, 15:18, Dec. 1989

KITTY DUBIN

Detroit Monthly, 12:18, May 1989

W. E. B. Du BOIS

Brown-Guillory, E., *Their Place on the Stage,* pp. 2, 4–5, 9, 18, 42, 98, 107–108, 143

The Star of Ethiopia, 1915
    Scott, F. L., *"The Star of Ethiopia*: A Contribution toward the Development
    of Black Drama and Theater in the Harlem Renaissance," pp. 257–269
    in A. Singh, W. S. Shiver, and S. Brodwin, eds., *The Harlem Renaissance*

LAWRENCE JOSEPH DUGAN

Once upon a Time, 1939
    Leonard, W. T., *Once Was Enough,* pp. 146–147

TOM DULACK

Breaking Legs, 1989
    Crowley, D., "The Director: Necessary Evil or Source of Inspiration?"
    (interview with Dulack and John Tillinger, the director of *Breaking Legs*),
    TheaterWeek, 3:36–38, 23 July 1990
    San Diego Magazine, 42:54+ , Nov. 1989
    TheaterWeek, 2:7, 17 July 1989
    TheaterWeek, 3:11, 23 July 1990

Incommunicado (about Ezra Pound), 1989
    Zinman, T. S. "Pound in a Cage," *American Theatre,* 5:10–11, Mar. 1989
    Georgia Review, 43:580–581, Fall 1989
    Theatre Journal, 42:505–506, Dec. 1990
    Village Voice, 34:97–98, 18 Apr. 1989

WILLIAM DUMARESQ and GALT MacDERMOT

The Human Comedy (musical version of novel by W. Saroyan), 1984
    Chicago, 38:89–91, Aug. 1989
    TheaterWeek, 3:21, 25 Dec. 1989

FRANK DUMONT

The Girl from the Klondike; or, Wide Awake Nell, published 1898
    Jones, E. H., *Native Americans as Shown on the Stage,* pp. 145–146

Society Acting, published 1898
    Jones, E. H., *Native Americans as Shown on the Stage,* p. 141

ALICE DUNBAR-NELSON

Brown-Guillory, E., *Their Place on the Stage,* pp. 4–5, 8–9, 11

WILLIAM DUNLAP

Grimsted, D., "William Dunlap: The Corruption of an Enlightened Age,"
    pp. 1–21 in Grimsted's *Melodrama Unveiled* (also see pp. 22–23, 87, 91, 108,
    110, 141, 144, 154, 165–166, 184, 187, 211, 214, 250, 254)
Mates, J., *America's Musical Stage,* pp. 25, 30, 67–68, 99, 108

Bonaparte in England, 1803
    Harap, L., *The Image of the Jew in American Literature,* pp. 206–207

TOM DUNN

In Pursuit of the Song of Hydrogen, 1989
    TheaterWeek, 3:11, 27 Nov. 1989

PHILIP DUNNING
SEE GEORGE ABBOTT and PHILIP DUNNING

TOM DUPREE
SEE JOHN MAXWELL and TOM DUPREE

HERVÉ DUPUIS

Return of the Young Hippolytus (tr. Jean Vigneault), 1988
    Temerson, C., and F. Kourilsky, Preface (n. pag.), *Gay Plays,* pp. 251–326
    (text of play)

CHRISTOPHER DURANG

Botto, L., "Christopher Durang Explains It All for You," *Playbill,* 6:98–101,
    Jan. 1988
Demastes, W. W., "Christopher Durang (2 January 1949–)," pp. 91–101 in P. C.
    Kolin, ed., *American Playwrights since 1945*
Popkin, H., "Life Is a Cabaret," *TheaterWeek,* 3:25–27, 16 Oct. 1989
Savran, D., "Christopher Durang," pp. 18–34 in Savran's *In Their Own Words*
American Theatre, 5:10, July/Aug. 1988
TheaterWeek, 3:13, 9 Oct. 1989

The Actor's Nightmare, 1981
    McKenzie, M., "Theatre Three Times Two," *TheaterWeek,* 2:54–58, 30 Jan.
    1989

Entertaining Mr. Helms (a "one-minute play"), 1990
    TheaterWeek, 4:32–34, 22 Oct. 1990 (text of play)

Laughing Wild, 1987
    Village Voice, 32:105–106, 24 Nov. 1987

The Marriage of Bette and Boo, 1973 (revised 1979)
    Brustein, R., "Combating Amnesia," pp. 79–83 in Brustein's *Who Needs*
    Theatre (rpt. of *New Republic,* 193:28–29, 1 July 1985)

The Vietnamization of New Jersey (An American Tragedy), 1977
    Counts, M. L., *Coming Home,* pp. 82–83, 169–170, 194–195, 202
    Zinman, T. S., "Search and Destroy: The Drama of the Vietnam War,"
    Theatre Journal, 42:5–26, Mar. 1990

The Visit, 1989
McKenzie, M., "Theatre Three Times Two," *TheaterWeek,* 2:54–58, 30 Jan. 1989

GEORGE DURNING

Night Hostess, 1928
Harap, L., *Dramatic Encounters,* p. 116

ARNAUD d'USSEAU
SEE JAMES GOW and ARNAUD d'USSEAU
AND DOROTHY PARKER and ARNAUD d'USSEAU

RALPH DYAR

Girl Wants Glamour, 1936
Kazacoff, G., *Dangerous Theatre,* pp. 282–283

AL EATON

M.L.K. . . . We Are the Dream, 1990
American Theatre, 6:11, Feb. 1990

FRED EBB

Ledford, L. S., "The World Goes Round . . . with Kander and Ebb," *TheaterWeek,* 2:10–14, 12 June 1989
TheaterWeek, 1:33, 4 Apr. 1988

ALSO SEE JOE MASTEROFF, JOHN KANDER, and FRED EBB
AND TERRENCE McNALLY, JOHN KANDER, and FRED EBB

ARTHUR EBENHACK

Marilyn's Affairs (originally titled *Cinderella's Brothers*), 1933
Leonard, W. T., *Once Was Enough,* pp. 114–115

ALLAN W. ECKERT

Tecumseh!, 1874
Jones, E. H., *Native Americans as Shown on the Stage,* p. 35

STAN EDELSON
SEE BOBBI AUSUBEL and STAN EDELSON

RANDOLPH EDMONDS

Sanders, L. C., "'How Shall the Negro Be Portrayed?': Willis Richardson and Randolph Edmonds, the Pioneers," pp. 19–61 in Sanders's *The Development of Black Theater in America*

GUS EDWARDS

Lifetimes on the Streets, 1990
   New Yorker, 66:88, 23 Apr. 1990
   Village Voice, 35:119, 17 Apr. 1990

T. J. EDWARDS

Washingtonian, 22:48, June 1987

ELIZABETH EGLOFF

Phaedra and Hippolytus (suggested by the Hippolytus myth, especially Euripides's *Hippolytus* and Racine's *Phèdre*), 1989
   Theatre Journal, 41:546–548, Dec. 1989

The Swan, 1988 (revised 1990)
   London, T., "6 Humana Plays Take the Woman's-Eye View," *American
      Theatre,* 7:37–38, June 1990
   American Theatre, 7:59, Dec. 1990
   TheaterWeek, 3:33, 30 Apr. 1990

Wolf-Man, 1989
   TheaterWeek, 3:6, 25 Sept. 1989
   TheaterWeek, 3:11 + , 30 Oct. 1989

ETHYL EICHELBERGER (James Roy Eichelberger)

Jeffreys, J. E., "Ethyl Eichelberger, 1945–1990," *TheaterWeek,* 4:42–43, 27 Aug.
   1990
Smith, R., "Ethyl Eichelberger," *Theatre Crafts,* 23:28–33 + , Jan. 1989
New Yorker, 64:20, 22 Aug. 1988
Time, 136:67, 27 Aug. 1990

Ariadne Obnoxious, 1988
   Village Voice, 33:125 + , 6 Dec. 1988

Herd of Buffalo, 1989
   Village Voice, 34:91 + , 18 July 1989

NED EISENBERG

Soulful Scream of a Chosen Son, 1990
   TheaterWeek, 4:13, 27 Aug. 1990

LONNE ELDER III

Ceremonies in Dark Old Men, 1965 (revised 1969)
   Brown-Guillory, E., *Their Place on the Stage,* pp. 27–28
   Lahr, J., "Black Theatre: The American Tragic Voice," *Evergreen Review,*
      13:55–63, Aug. 1969

Splendid Mummer, 1988
> Frank, G., "Setting the Record Straight," *TheaterWeek,* 1:26–30, 16 May
> 1988
> *American Theatre,* 5:8, June 1988
> *Nation,* 246:689–690, 14 May 1988
> *TheaterWeek,* 1:5, 11 Apr. 1988
> *Village Voice,* 33:105–106, 10 May 1988

ALSO SEE RON MILNER, RICHARD BLACKFORD,
and MAYA ANGELOU

RUDOLPH ELIE
SEE BARBARA RING and RUDOLPH ELIE

JAMES ELLISON

American Captive, 1812
> Harap, L., *The Image of the Jew in American Literature,* pp. 208–209

IRVING ELMAN
SEE JULIE BERNS and IRVING ELMAN

KENWARD ELMSLIE and CLAIBE RICHARDSON

The Grass Harp (musical version of T. Capote's novel and play), 1971
> Filichia, P., "*The Grass Harp* Plays On," *TheaterWeek,* 2:36–45, 30 Jan.
> 1989

AMBROSE ELWELL, JR. (Norman H. White, Jr.)

Reunion, 1938
> Leonard, W. T., *Once Was Enough,* pp. 161–162

JOHN EMERSON and ANITA LOOS

The Whole Town's Talking, 1926
> Harap, L., *Dramatic Encounters,* p. 115

CAROLINE EMMONS

Cohen, E. M., *Working on a New Play,* pp. 118–119 (Emmons's *When Petulia
Comes* considered)

RICHARD EMMONS

Tecumseh; or, The Battle of the Thames, 1836
> Jones, E. H., *Native Americans as Shown on the Stage,* pp. 34–35

THOMAS DUNN ENGLISH

The Mormons; or, Life at Salt Lake City, 1858
　　Jones, E. H., *Native Americans as Shown on the Stage,* pp. 106–108

EVE ENSLER and JOSHUA SCHNEIDER

Ladies, 1989
　　American Theatre, 5:15, Mar. 1989
　　TheaterWeek, 2:3, 17 Apr. 1989
　　Village Voice, 34:97, 11 Apr. 1989

HENRY EPHRON *SEE NEXT ENTRY*

PHOEBE EPHRON and HENRY EPHRON

Take Her, She's Mine (originally titled *Age of Consent*), 1961
　　Ilson, C., *Harold Prince,* pp. 67–69

RICHARD EPP

Intimate Admiration, 1986
　　Journal of Canadian Studies, 22:125, Winter 1987/1988

MARTIN EPSTEIN

Beber, N., "Dramatis Instructus," *American Theatre,* 6:22–23, 25, Jan. 1990

BILL ERVOLINO

The Lights on Walden Court, 1988
　　TheaterWeek, 1:4, 39, 25 Jan. 1988

CHRISTOPHER ESCHENBACH
SEE ROBERT WILSON, HEINER MÜLLER, CHRISTOPHER
ESCHENBACH, and MARTIN PERLMAN

JOSÉ LUIS RAMOS ESCOBAR

Indocumentados, 1990
　　Bensussen, M., "Whose Language Is It?" *American Theatre,* 7:82–83, Oct.
　　1990

JEFFREY ESSMAN

Ward, A., "Jeffrey Essman in Triplicate" (interview), *TheaterWeek,* 2:44–56, 20
Feb. 1989

Triplets in Uniform, 1989
　　Village Voice, 34:103, 21 Feb. 1989

HUGH ESTEN

All My Three Sons, 1987
   Village Voice, 32:88, 25 Aug. 1987

Elmo Dunkle: Soldier of Fortune, 1987
   Village Voice, 32:88, 25 Aug. 1987

GARLAND ETHEL

In His Image, 1936
   Kazacoff, G., *Dangerous Theatre,* pp. 285–286

JAN TORI EVANS and GLYNN BORDERS

The Dark Star from Harlem (about Josephine Baker), 1990
   Playbill, 9:46, 30 Nov. 1990
   TheaterWeek, 4:44, 8 Oct. 1990

SHARON EVANS

Girls, Girls, Girls, Live on Stage, Totally Rude, 1990
   Williams, A., "Stripper in Training," *American Theatre,* 7:8–9, Nov. 1990

BERNARD EVSLIN

Step on a Crack, 1962
   Leonard, W. T., *Once Was Enough,* pp. 181–183

TOM EYEN and HENRY KRIEGER

Dangerous Music, 1988
   TheaterWeek, 2:42, 26 Sept. 1988
   TheaterWeek, 2:61, 28 Nov. 1988

Dreamgirls, 1981
   Brustein, R., "Arguing with a Tank," pp. 162–164 in Brustein's *Who Needs
      Theatre* (rpt. of *New Republic,* 186:25–26, 27 Jan. 1982)
   Green, S., *Broadway Musicals,* p. 261
   TheaterWeek, 3:19, 25 Dec. 1989
   Time, 135:100, 1 Jan. 1990

JONATHAN FALLA

Topokana Martyr's Day, 1985
   Village Voice, 32:100, 10 Mar. 1987

LAURA FARABOUGH

Betsko, K., and R. Koenig, *Interviews with Contemporary Women Playwrights,*
   pp. 139–153

WILLIAM FAULKNER

Dardis, T., "Faulkner: 'Civilization Begins with Distillation,'" pp. 23–95 in Dardis's *The Thirsty Muse*
Goodwin, D. W., "Faulkner: The Count No'Count Who Went to Stockholm," pp. 100–122 in Goodwin's *Alcohol and the Writer*
Kawin, B. F., ed., *Faulkner's MGM Screenplays*
———, "*War Birds* and the Politics of Refusal," pp. 274–289 in A. Kinney, ed., *Critical Essays on William Faulkner*
Phillips, G. D., *Fiction, Film, and Faulkner*

The Marionettes, 1920
   Hönnighausen, L., "The Poetic Play," pp. 117–153 in Hönnighausen's *William Faulkner*

JULES FEIFFER

Horwitz, S., "Jules Feiffer's People," *TheaterWeek,* 3:14–17, 9 July 1990
Chicago, 37:32, Apr. 1988

Anthony Rose, 1989
   Commonweal, 116:676, 1 Dec. 1989
   Playbill, 8:48, 30 Nov. 1989
   TheaterWeek, 3:8, 13 Nov. 1989

Carnal Knowledge, 1988 (written 1971)
   Dickmann, K., "Gregory Harrison: Primed and Waiting," *TheaterWeek,* 2:32–39, 26 Dec. 1988
   Horwitz, S., "Brat Packers Go through the Sexual Revolution: Four Young Actors Talk about Their Roles in *Carnal Knowledge,*" *TheaterWeek,* 4:20–27, 26 Nov. 1990
   American Theatre, 5:4, Apr. 1988
   New York, 23:148+, 3 Dec. 1990
   New Yorker, 66:138–139, 10 Dec. 1990
   Playbill, 9:40, 30 Nov. 1990
   TheaterWeek, 4:10, 22 Oct. 1990

Elliot Loves, 1990
   Sneerwell, R., "Who's Afraid of Jules Feiffer?" *TheaterWeek,* 3:39, 25 June 1990
   Commonweal, 117:455–456, 10 Aug. 1990
   New York, 23:63–64, 18 June 1990
   New Yorker, 66:67, 18 June 1990
   Newsweek, 115:58, 18 June 1990
   TheaterWeek, 3:7, 11 June 1990
   Time, 135:85, 18 June 1990

Feiffer's America, 1988
   American Theatre, 5:5, Apr. 1988
   Chicago, 37:32, Apr. 1988

Grownups, 1981
    Kakutani, M., "Jules Feiffer," pp. 157–160 in Kakutani's *The Poet at the Piano* (rpt. of *The New York Times,* Dec. 1981)

Little Murders, 1966
    Village Voice, 32:92, 19 May 1987

JULES FEIFFER, DAN GREENBURG, LEONARD MELFI, SAM SHEPARD, and OTHERS

Oh! Calcutta!, 1969
    Filichia, P., "The Bare Necessities: *Oh! Calcutta!* Throws in the Towel after 5,959 Performances," *TheaterWeek,* 3:34–36, 4 Sept. 1989
    ———, "The Naked Truth," *TheaterWeek,* 1:46–51, 25 Apr. 1988
    TheaterWeek, 1:58–59, 13 June 1988
    TheaterWeek, 1:4, 8 Aug. 1988

JANET FEINDEL

A Particular Class of Women, 1988
    Feindel, J., "Developing *A Particular Class of Women,*" *Canadian Theatre Review,* 59:38–41, Summer 1989

DAVID FELDSHUH

American Theatre, 6:62, Mar. 1990 (letter)

Miss Evers' Boys (suggested by, among other things, the book *Bad Blood* by J. H. Jones), 1989
    Bannon, B. M., "Letter from Sundance," *TheaterWeek,* 3:15–16, 18 Sept. 1989
    Greer, A., "Harsh Medicine," *American Theatre,* 6:10–12, Jan. 1990
    American Theatre, 6:57, Sept. 1989
    American Theatre, 7:1–18, Nov. 1990 (text of play; special pull-out section)
    New York, 23:62+, 17 Sept. 1990

JOSÉ FELICIANO
SEE RAY BRADBURY, JOSÉ FELICIANO, and SUSAN FELICIANO

SUSAN FELICIANO
SEE RAY BRADBURY, JOSÉ FELICIANO, and SUSAN FELICIANO

MARILYN FELT

Acts of Faith, 1987
    Shirakawa, S. H., "Theater Trends: Two for the Road," *TheaterWeek,* 1:20–23, 4 Jan. 1988
    Village Voice, 33:100, 19 Jan. 1988

EDNA FERBER
SEE GEORGE S. KAUFMAN and EDNA FERBER

ERNEST FERLITA

Black Medea (based on Euripides's play *Medea*), 1990
    Playbill, 8:52, 31 May 1990
    TheaterWeek, 3:12–13, 5 Mar. 1990
    Village Voice, 35:106, 20 Mar. 1990

CHUCK FERRERO

Love Song for Chairman Mao, 1989
    TheaterWeek, 3:10–11, 9 Oct. 1989

BARBARA FIELD

Frankenstein—Playing with Fire (dramatization of novel by M. W. Shelley), 1988
    Henry, W. A., III, "Heartland Heartiness," *Time,* 132:83–84, 12 Sept. 1988
    American Theatre, 4:11, Jan. 1988

JOSEPH FIELDS, JEROME CHODOROV, LEONARD BERNSTEIN BETTY COMDEN, and ADOLPH GREEN

Wonderful Town (musical version of *My Sister Eileen* by Fields and Chodorov, based on the stories of R. McKenney), 1953
    Green, S., *Broadway Musicals,* p. 155
    Nation, 249:611, 20 Nov. 1989

HARVEY FIERSTEIN

Elle, 2:106, May 1987

Forget Him, 1988
    Hall, R., "Eleven Different Directions," *American Theatre,* 5:32–33, Dec. 1988

Safe Sex (three one-acts: *Manny and Jake, Safe Sex,* and *On Tidy Endings*), 1987 (later revised)
    Village Voice, 32:95–96, 14 Apr. 1987

Torch Song Trilogy (three plays: *The International Stud, Fugue in a Nursery,* and *Children First!*), 1981
    Curtin, K., *"We Can Always Call Them Bulgarians,"* pp. 329–330
    Portantiere, M., "Carry the Torch," *TheaterWeek,* 2:33–37, 10 July 1989
    Shewey, D., "Gay Theatre Grows Up," *American Theatre,* 5:10–17, 52–53, May 1988
    Playbill, 6:74, June 1988

HARVEY FIERSTEIN and JERRY HERMAN

La Cage aux Folles (musical version of J. Poiret's play), 1983
    Brustein, R., "Musicalized Propaganda," pp. 167–170 in Brustein's *Who
      Needs Theatre* (rpt. of *New Republic*, 189:26–27, 19–26, Sept. 1983)
    Curtin, K., *"We Can Always Call Them Bulgarians,"* pp. 330–331
    Green, S., *Broadway Musicals*, pp. 266–267
    Shewey, D., "Gay Theatre Grows Up," *American Theatre*, 5:10–17, 52–53,
      May 1988
    TheaterWeek, 3:20–21, 25 Dec. 1989

HARVEY FIERSTEIN, CHARLES SUPPON, and PETER ALLEN

Legs Diamond, 1988
    Grubb, K., *"Legs Diamond* Comes to Broadway: Give 'em the Old Razzle-
      dazzle," *Dance Magazine*, 63:40–44, Jan. 1989
    Haun, H., "Peter Allen's Musical," *Playbill*, 7:8, 10, 31 Oct. 1988
    Henry, W. A., III, *"Legs Diamond* Shoots Blanks," *Time*, 133:67, 9 Jan.
      1989
    Mandelbaum, K., "Anatomy of a Musical: *Legs Diamond,*" *TheaterWeek*,
      2:12–25, 2 Jan. 1989
    New York, 21:48–49, 12 Sept. 1988
    New York, 22:56–57, 9 Jan. 1989
    New Yorker, 64:26–28, 31 Oct. 1988
    New Yorker, 64:82–83, 9 Jan. 1989
    TheaterWeek, 2:6–7, 21 Nov. 1988
    TheaterWeek, 2:61, 28 Nov. 1988
    TheaterWeek, 2:60–61, 9 Jan. 1989
    Village Voice, 34:89, 3 Jan. 1989

KAREN FINLEY

Carr, C., "Karen Finley," *Artforum*, 27:148, Nov. 1988
Dolan, J., *The Feminist Spectator as Critic*, pp. 65–67
Erickson, J., "Appropriation and Transgression in Contemporary American Per-
    formance: The Wooster Group, Holly Hughes, and Karen Finley,' *Theatre
    Journal*, 42:225–236, May 1990
Finley, K., "In [My] Own Words," *TheaterWeek*, 3:19–21, 16 July 1990
Forte, J., "Women's Performance Art: Feminism and Postmodernism," pp. 251–
    269 in S.-E. Case, ed., *Performing Feminisms* (rpt. of *Theatre Journal*,
    40(2):217–235, May 1988)
Schechner, R., "Karen Finley: A Constant State of Becoming" (interview), *The
    Drama Review*, 32 (1):152–158, Spring 1988
Simon, J., "Art Failure: Karen Finley and the Absurdity of Performance Art,"
    TheaterWeek, 4:19–21, 27 Aug. 1990
Span, P., and C. Hall, "At Home with the NEA 4," *American Theatre*, 7:14–
    20, Sept. 1990

The Constant State of Desire, 1986
> Champagne, L., ed., *Out from Under,* pp. ix–xiv (Introduction), 56–58, 59–70 (text of performance piece)
> Finley, K., "The Constant State of Desire" (text of play), *The Drama Review,* 32:139–151, Spring 1988
> Schuler, C., "Spectator Response and Comprehension: The Problem of Karen Finley's *Constant State of Desire,*" *The Drama Review,* 34:131–145, Spring 1990

The Theory of Total Blame, 1988
> Reidel, B., "All in the Family," *TheaterWeek,* 2:42, 3 July 1989
> *Village Voice,* 33:119–120, 13 Dec. 1988

We Keep Our Victims Ready, 1989
> *Theatre Journal,* 42:495–497, Dec. 1990
> *Village Voice,* 35:118, 1 May 1990

HENRY J. FINN and JAMES H. HACKETT

The Indian Wife; or, The Falls of Montmorency (revision of Finn's 1825 play *Montgomery; or, The Falls of Montmorency*), 1830
> Jones, E. H., *Native Americans as Shown on the Stage,* p. 47

WILLIAM FINN

Filichia, P., "Finnland: Composer/Lyricist William Finn's Tales of the City," *TheaterWeek,* 4:12–15, 24 Sept. 1990

America Kicks Up Its Heels, 1982 (also see Richard Greenberg and Finn's *Romance in Hard Times*)
> *TheaterWeek,* 2:4, 28 Nov. 1988

In Trousers (first play of *Marvin's Trilogy*; the second is *March of the Falsettos,* which see; the third is *Falsettoland,* by James Lapine and Finn, which see), 1985
> Cohen, E. M., *Working on a New Play,* pp. 9, 10, 93

March of the Falsettos (second play of *Marvin's Trilogy*; the first is *In Trousers,* which see; the third is *Falsettoland,* by James Lapine and Finn, which see), 1981
> Cohen, E. M., *Working on a New Play,* pp. 9, 20, 87, 88, 189, 196
> Shewey, D., "Gay Theatre Grows Up," *American Theatre,* 5:10–17, 52–53, May 1988

ALSO SEE GRACIELA DANIELE, JIM LEWIS, WILLIAM FINN,
and ASTOR PIAZZOLLA
AND RICHARD GREENBERG and WILLIAM FINN
AND JAMES LAPINE and WILLIAM FINN

RICHARD FIRE
SEE JUNE SHELLENE and RICHARD FIRE

ROBERT FISHER and ARTHUR ALSBERG

Happiness Is Just a Little Thing Called a Rolls-Royce, 1968
Leonard, W. T., *Once Was Enough,* pp. 73–74

ALSO SEE ARTHUR MARX and ROBERT FISHER

CLYDE FITCH

Harap, L., *Dramatic Encounters,* p. 74

Barbara Frietchie, 1899
Rainey, K. T., "Race and Reunion in Nineteenth-Century Reconciliation
Drama," *American Transcendental Quarterly,* 2(2):155–169, June 1988

Beau Brummel, 1890
Harap, L., *The Image of the Jew in American Literature,* pp. 215–216

The Woman in the Case, 1906
Stephens, J. L., "Subverting the Demon-Angel Dichotomy: Innovation and
Feminist Intervention in Twentieth-Century Drama," *Text and Perfor-
mance Quarterly,* 9(1):53–64, Jan. 1989

F. SCOTT FITZGERALD

Dardis, T., "Fitzgerald: 'Blue Skies Somewhere,'" pp. 97–153 in Dardis's *The
Thirsty Muse*
Goodwin, D. W., "Fitzgerald: 'I'm F. Scott Fitzgerald, the Well-Known Alco-
holic,'" pp. 36–49 in Goodwin's *Alcohol and the Writer*

KIT FITZGERALD and PETER GORDON

Spectaccalo, 1987
Artforum, 26:119–120, Dec. 1987

STEPHEN FLAHERTY
SEE LYNN AHRENS and STEPHEN FLAHERTY

HALLIE FLANAGAN

The Curtain (dramatization of her story), 1922
Bentley, J., *Hallie Flanagan,* p. 35

The Garden of Wishes, 1922
    Bentley, J., *Hallie Flanagan,* pp. 32–33

The Lost Aphrodite, written 1934 (never produced or published)
    Bentley, J., *Hallie Flanagan,* pp. 165–166

HALLIE FLANAGAN and MARGARET ELLEN CLIFFORD

Can You Hear Their Voices? (dramatization of an article by W. Chambers), 1931
    Bentley, J., *Hallie Flanagan,* pp. 120–122

HALLIE FLANAGAN and JANET HARTMANN

The Sky Will Be Lit Up, 1928/1929
    Bentley, J., *Hallie Flanagan,* pp. 107–110

MARTIN FLAVIN

Achilles Had a Heel, 1935
    Counts, M. L., *Coming Home,* pp. 66–67, 71–72, 96, 120, 195, 198, 226

Around the Corner, 1936
    Kazacoff, G., *Dangerous Theatre,* pp. 259–260

Criminal Code, 1925
    Harap, L., *Dramatic Encounters,* p. 115

Lady of the Rose, 1925
    Harap, L., *Dramatic Encounters,* p. 115

Tapestry in Gray, 1935
    Counts, M. L., *Coming Home,* pp. 112, 197

JOHN FLECK

Fleck, J., "In [My] Own Words," *TheaterWeek,* 3:24–25, 16 July 1990

RUDD FLEMING
SEE EZRA POUND and RUDD FLEMING

HORTON FOOTE

Davis, R. L., "Roots in Parched Ground: An Interview with Horton Foote," *Southwest Review,* 73:298–318, Summer 1988
Edgerton, G., "A Visit to the Imaginary Landscape of Harrison, Texas: Sketching the Film Career of Horton Foote," *Literature/Film Quarterly,* 17(1):2–12, 1989
Foote, H., "Writing for Film," pp. 5–20 in W. Aycock and M. Schoenecke, eds., *Film and Literature*

Dividing the Estate, 1989 (revised 1990)
    American Theatre, 7:13, May 1990
    Playbill, 9:48, 30 Nov. 1990

The Habitation of Dragons, 1988
    American Theatre, 5:13, Oct. 1988
    American Theatre, 5:12, Nov. 1988
    TheaterWeek, 2:6, 10 Oct. 1988

Talking Pictures, 1990
    Anderson, P., "Silent No More," *American Theatre,* 7:9–10, May 1990
    Playbill, 8:52, 31 May 1990
    TheaterWeek, 3:14–15, 2 Apr. 1990

HORTON FOOTE and HAROLD ROME

Gone with the Wind (musical version of novel by M. Mitchell), 1973
    Driscoll, T., "Forgotten Musicals: *Gone with the Wind,*" *TheaterWeek,* 1:28–30, 11 Apr. 1988

JAMES FORBES

The Famous Mrs. Fair, 1919
    Counts, M. L., *Coming Home,* pp. 70–71, 73, 93, 150

The Show Shop, 1914
    Harap, L., *Dramatic Encounters,* p. 78
    TheaterWeek, 4:28–29, 3 Sept. 1990

RICHARD FOREMAN

Backalenick, I., "Sneak Preview: Richard Foreman and Martha Clarke," *TheaterWeek,* 3:25–29, 30 July 1990
Confino, B., "Theatrical Wavelengths: Richard Foreman," *TheaterWeek,* 1:35–43, 2 May 1988
Dolan, J., *The Feminist Spectator as Critic,* pp. 12, 15, 48–58
Hertz, U., "Interview with Richard Foreman," *Third Rail,* 6:57–59, 1984
Kalb, J., "The Iconoclast and the Underdog," *American Theatre,* 7:22–27, 71–72, May 1990
Savran, D., "Richard Foreman," pp. 35–50 in Savran's *In Their Own Words*
———, "Richard Foreman (10 July 1937–)," pp. 102–110 in P. C. Kolin, ed., *American Playwrights since 1945*
Schechner, R., "Richard Foreman on Richard Foreman" (interview), *The Drama Review,* 31 (4[116]):125–135, Winter 1987
———, "Talking with Kate Manheim: Unpeeling a Few Layers" (interview), *The Drama Review,* 31:136–142, Winter 1987
Shank, T., "Richard Foreman: The Ontological-Hysteric Theatre," pp. 159–170 in Shank's *American Alternative Theater*

Film Is Evil: Radio is Good, 1987
>Foreman, R., "Film Is Evil: Radio Is Good" (text of play), *The Drama Review,* 31:149–176, Winter 1987
>*The Drama Review,* 31:143–148, Winter 1987
>*Village Voice,* 32:91, 19 May 1987

Lava, 1989
>*Village Voice,* 34:115–116, 19 Dec. 1989

Symphony of Rats, 1988
>Shirakawa, S. H., "Audience Notes: Alternating Currents," *TheaterWeek,* 1:36–38, 29 Feb. 1988
>*American Theatre,* 4:9–10, Jan. 1988
>*Artforum,* 26:145, Apr. 1988
>*Nation,* 246:174–175, 6 Feb. 1988
>*TheaterWeek,* 1:28, 4 Jan. 1988
>*Village Voice,* 33:99–100, 19 Jan. 1988

What Did He See?, 1988
>Ward, A., "What Did They See?" *TheaterWeek,* 2:22–31, 26 Dec. 1988
>*TheaterWeek,* 2:7, 10 Oct. 1988
>*Village Voice,* 33:103, 25 Oct. 1988
>*Village Voice,* 33:101, 15 Nov. 1988

RICHARD FOREMAN and STANLEY SILVERMAN

Love and Science, 1990
>Yohalem, J., "Music of the Cosmos," *American Theatre,* 7:10–11, Oct. 1990
>*American Theatre,* 7:12, July/Aug. 1990

MARÍA IRENE FORNÉS

Austin, G., "The Madwoman in the Spotlight: Plays of Maria Irene Fornes," pp. 76–85 in L. Hart, ed., *Making a Spectacle*

Beber, N., "Dramatis Instructus," *American Theatre,* 6:22–25, Jan. 1990

Betsko, K., and R. Koenig, *Interviews with Contemporary Women Playwrights,* pp. 154–167

Cummings, S. T., "Maria Irene Fornes (14 May 1930–)," pp. 111–123 in P. C. Kolin, ed., *American Playwrights since 1945*

Dolan, J., *The Feminist Spectator as Critic,* pp. 101, 108–110

Geis, D. R., "Wordscapes of the Body: Performative Language as *Gestus* in Maria Irene Fornes's Plays," *Theatre Journal,* 42:291–307, Oct. 1990

Gray, A., "The Big If," *American Theatre,* 6:18–21, 56, June 1989

Keyssar, H., "A Network of Playwrights," pp. 102–125 in Keyssar's *Feminist Theatre*

O'Malley, L. D., "Pressing Clothes/Snapping Beans/Reading Books: Maria Irene Fornés's Women's Work," *Studies in American Drama, 1945–Present,* 4:103–117, 1989

Savran, D., "Maria Irene Fornes," pp. 51–69 in Savran's *In Their Own Words*

Schuler, C. A., "Gender Perspective and Violence in the Plays of Maria Irene

Fornes and Sam Shepard," pp. 218–228 in J. Schlueter, ed., *Modern American Drama*
Worthen, W. B., *"Still Playing Games*: Ideology and Performance in the Theater of Maria Irene Fornes," pp. 167–185 in E. Brater, ed., *Feminine Focus*
Zinman, T. S., "Hen in a Foxhouse: The Absurdist Plays of Maria Irene Fornes," pp. 203–220 in E. Brater and R. Cohn, eds., *Around the Absurd*
Chicago, 36:93–94, Apr. 1987

Abingdon Square, 1987
   American Theatre, 4:n. pag., Feb. 1988 (text of play, special pull-out section)
   Theatre Journal, 40:264–266, May 1988
   Village Voice, 32:112, 27 Oct. 1987

And What of the Night? (four parts: *Charlie, Lust, Springtime,* and *Hunger*), 1989
   American Theatre, 5:14–15, Mar. 1989
   TheaterWeek, 3:18, 25 June 1990

The Conduct of Life, 1985
   Osborn, M. E., ed., *On New Ground,* pp. vi–viii (Preface), 45–50, 51–72 (text of play)

The Danube, 1982
   American Theatre, 5:9, Apr. 1988

Fefu and Her Friends, 1977
   Arnold, S. K., "Multiple Spaces, Simultaneous Action and Illusion," pp. 259–269 in J. Redmond, ed., *The Theatrical Space*
   Pevitts, B. B., *"Fefu and Her Friends,"* pp. 314–317 in H. K. Chinoy and L. W. Jenkins, eds., *Women in American Theatre,* rev. and enl. ed. (pp. 316–320 in 1981 ed.)

Uncle Vanya (adaptation of Marian Fell's tr. of Chekhov's play), 1988
   New Yorker, 63:59, 4 Jan. 1988

GEORGE FORREST
SEE LUTHER DAVIS, ROBERT WRIGHT, GEORGE FORREST, and MAURY YESTON
AND CHARLES LEDERER, LUTHER DAVIS, ROBERT WRIGHT, GEORGE FORREST, and ALEXANDER BORODIN

JOHN FORSTER
SEE JONATHAN BOLT, THOMAS TIERNEY, and JOHN FORSTER

GENE FOWLER
SEE BEN HECHT and GENE FOWLER

TERRY CURTIS FOX

Justice, 1979
   TheaterWeek, 2:8, 24 Apr. 1989

VERONICA FRANCIS

Siren Tears (based on Shakespeare's sonnets), 1989
  TheaterWeek, 3:13, 6 Nov. 1989

CAROLINE FRANCKE
SEE FLORENCE LOWE and CAROLINE FRANCKE

ROSE FRANKEN

Another Language, 1932
  Harap, L., *Dramatic Encounters,* p. 119

Outrageous Fortune, 1943
  Curtin, K., *"We Can Always Call Them Bulgarians,"* pp. 255–263

Soldier's Wife, 1944
  Counts, M. L., *Coming Home,* pp. 77–78, 138, 150, 152, 154–155, 195, 199

BRAD FRASER

Unidentified Human Remains and the Nature of Love, 1990
  Kucherawy, D., "Letter from Toronto," *TheaterWeek,* 3:13, 2 July 1990

KERMIT FRAZIER and JOHN LEICHT

An American Journey, 1987
  Milwaukee, 12:82–84, Feb. 1987

DONALD FREED

Alfred and Victoria: A Life (about Alfred Bloomingdale and Vicki Morgan),
  1987
  Commonweal, 117:29, 20 Apr. 1990
  Los Angeles, 32:60 + , Jan. 1987
  Playbill, 8:30, 31 Jan. 1990

Circe and Bravo, 1984
  Chicago, 36:26 + , May 1987

Is He Still Dead?, 1990
  Shapiro, B., "The Dubliners," *TheaterWeek,* 3:36, 11 June 1990
  American Theatre, 6:108, Oct. 1990
  TheaterWeek, 3:13, 7 May 1990

The Last Hero (based on the life of Charles Lindbergh), 1987
  American Theatre, 4:44, Feb. 1988

Veteran's Day, 1988
  American Theatre, 5:56, Feb. 1989

STAN FREEMAN
SEE JEROME CHODOROV, JACK LAWRENCE, and STAN FREEMAN

BRUCE JAY FRIEDMAN

Scuba Duba: A Tense Comedy, 1967
   Harap, L., *Dramatic Encounters,* pp. 20–21

KEN FRIEDMAN

Claptrap, 1987
   Village Voice, 32:86, 7 July 1987

STEVE FRIEDMAN

Animal Nation, 1989
   American Theatre, 6:12, Dec. 1989

ROBIN FULFORD

Steel Kiss, 1990
   TheaterWeek, 4:24, 20 Aug. 1990

CHARLES FULLER

Harriott, E., "Charles Fuller: The Quest for Justice," pp. 101–111, and "Interview with Charles Fuller," pp. 112–125, in Harriott's *American Voices*
Kucherawy, D., "Charles Fuller: Haunted by History," *TheaterWeek,* 2:8–17, 12 Dec. 1988
Savran, D., "Charles Fuller," pp. 70–83 in Savran's *In Their Own Words*

Burner's Frolic (fourth play in the cycle *We*), 1990
   New Yorker, 66:99, 19 Mar. 1990

Jonquil (third play in the cycle *We*), 1990
   American Theatre, 6:9, Mar. 1990
   New Yorker, 65:83, 29 Jan. 1990
   Village Voice, 35:100, 30 Jan. 1990

Prince (second play in the cycle *We*), 1988
   Hudson Review, 42:283–286, Summer 1989
   New York, 22:57, 9 Jan. 1989
   New Yorker, 64:82, 9 Jan. 1989

Sally (first play in the cycle *We*), 1988
   Hulbert, D., "Atlanta Makes a Bid as New Hub of Black Arts," *American Theatre,* 5:78–80, Oct. 1988
   Hudson Review, 42:283–286, Summer 1989
   New York, 22:57, 9 Jan. 1989
   New Yorker, 64:82, 9 Jan. 1989

Theatre Journal, 41:541, Dec. 1988
Village Voice, 33:104, 27 Dec. 1988

A Soldier's Play, 1981
    Demastes, W. W., "Charles Fuller and *A Soldier's Play,*" pp. 126–136 in
    Demastes's *Beyond Naturalism* (rpt. of *Studies in American Drama,*
    1945–Present, 2:43–56, 1987, with the title "Charles Fuller and *A Sol-*
    dier's Play: Attacking Prejudice, Challenging Form")

ELIZABETH FULLER
SEE CONRAD BISHOP and ELIZABETH FULLER

ALFRED A. FURMAN

Philip of Pokanoket, published 1894
    Jones, E. H., *Native Americans as Shown on the Stage,* p. 134

GEORGE FURTH and STEPHEN SONDHEIM

Company (musical version of some short plays by Furth), 1970
    Green, S., *Broadway Musicals,* p. 229
    Ilson, C., *Harold Prince,* pp. 160–177
    TheaterWeek, 1:6, 29 Feb. 1988
    TheaterWeek, 1:58–59, 25 Apr. 1988

Merrily We Roll Along (revision of Furth and Sondheim's 1981 musical version
    of play by M. Hart and G. S. Kaufman), 1983
    Ilson, C., *Harold Prince,* pp. 299–314
    Mandelbaum, K., "How Did You Get to Be Here, Mr. Sondheim?"
    TheaterWeek, 3:16–22, 26 Feb. 1990
    Maslon, L., "Rolling 'Merrily' Along," *American Theatre,* 7:14–21, May
    1990

ENID FUTTERMAN and MICHAEL COHEN

Yours, Anne (musical adaptation of *Anne Frank: The Diary of a Young Girl* and
    of the F. Goodrich-A. Hackett play *The Diary of Anne Frank*), 1985
    Filichia, P., "Only 175 Minutes from Broadway," *TheaterWeek,* 2:16–23, 23
    Jan. 1989
    New York, 18:98+, 28 Oct. 1985
    New Yorker, 61:82, 28 Oct. 1985

FRANKLIN FYLES
SEE DAVID BELASCO and FRANKLIN FYLES

FRANK GAGLIANO

Croyden, M., "Backward Glances," *TheaterWeek,* 4:21–24, 20 Aug. 1990

RUTH ADA GAINES-SHELTON

The Church Fight, 1926
    Brown-Guillory, E., *Their Place on the Stage,* pp. 4, 16–17
    Walker, E. P., "Krigwa, a Theatre by, for, and about Black People," *Theatre Journal,* 40:347–356, Oct. 1988

FRANK GALATI

Galati, F., "The Wrath of Frank Galati: A Broadway Director on the NEA," *TheaterWeek,* 3:32–33, 9 July 1990
London, T., "Chicago Impromptu," *American Theatre,* 7:14–23, 60–64, July/ Aug. 1990

The Grapes of Wrath (dramatization of novel by J. Steinbeck), 1988
    Abarbanel, J., "Steppenwolf in Steinbeck Country," *American Theatre,* 6:22–28, June 1989
    Buckley, M., "Ma Joad on the Road," *TheaterWeek,* 3:29–32, 19 Mar. 1990
    Chase, T., "The Group behind *The Grapes,*" *TheaterWeek,* 3:24–27, 19 Mar. 1990
    Gutwillig, S., "The Grapes of Math," *TheaterWeek,* 3:28, 19 Mar. 1990
    Haun, H., "*The Grapes of Wrath,*" *Playbill,* 8:8, 12, 30 Apr. 1990
    MacNamara, T., "Oakies at the Tonys," *TheaterWeek,* 3:34–35, 25 June 1990
    Stevens, L., "Steppenwolf Goes West with *The Grapes of Wrath,*" *TheaterWeek,* 2:20–25, 12 June 1989
    Wilson, L., "Grape Performances," *Mirabella,* 1:48–50, Apr. 1990
    America, 162:382, 14 Apr. 1990
    American Theatre, 5:11–12, Oct. 1988
    American Theatre, 6:12–13, Mar. 1990
    Chicago, 38:77–79, Jan. 1989
    Commonweal, 117:294 + , 4 May 1990
    Hudson Review, 43:470–471, Autumn 1990
    Nation, 250:610, 30 Apr. 1990
    National Review, 42:58 + , 11 June 1990
    New Republic, 202:30–31, 7 May 1990
    New York, 23:93, 2 Apr. 1990
    New Yorker, 66:87–88, 2 Apr. 1990
    Newsweek, 115:55, 2 Apr. 1990
    Progressive, 54:10, Oct. 1990
    San Diego Magazine, 41:44 + , July 1989
    TheaterWeek, 3:21–22, 4 Sept. 1989
    TheaterWeek, 3:39, 2 Apr. 1990
    TheaterWeek, 3:26–27, 2 July 1990
    Time, 133:102, 2 Jan. 1989
    Time, 135:71, 2 Apr. 1990
    Village Voice, 35:101 + , 3 Apr. 1990

She Always Said, Pablo (based on the work of G. Stein), 1987
    American Theatre, 4:4–5, Apr. 1987
    Chicago, 36:16, Mar. 1987

ZONA GALE

Maxwell, W., "Zona Gale," *Yale Review*, 76(2):221–225, Winter 1987

Miss Lulu Bett, 1920
    Stephens, J. L., "Women in Pulitzer Prize Plays, 1918–1949," pp. 245–253
    in H. K. Chinoy and L. W. Jenkins, eds., *Women in American Theatre*,
    rev. and enl. ed. (pp. 243–251 in 1981 ed.)

The Neighbors, 1912
    France, R., "Apropos of Women and the Folk Play," pp. 145–152 in H. K.
    Chinoy and L. W. Jenkins, eds., *Women in Contemporary Theatre*, rev.
    and enl. ed. (same pagination in 1981 ed.)

MARY GALLAGHER

Betsko, K., and R. Koenig, *Interviews with Contemporary Playwrights*, pp. 168–
183

¿De Donde?, 1988
    Horwitz, S., "Stranger in Our Strange Land," *TheaterWeek*, 4:34–37, 13
    Aug. 1990
    Hulser, K., "Gallagher Listens on Location," *American Theatre*, 6:55–56,
    Nov. 1989
    American Theatre, 6:31, July/Aug. 1989
    American Theatre, 6:1–20, Nov. 1989 (text of play, special pull-out section)
    American Theatre, 7:63, Sept. 1990
    Commonweal, 117:549, 28 Sept. 1990
    New York, 23:120, 20 Aug. 1990
    TheaterWeek, 4:37, 20 Aug. 1990

How to Say Goodbye, 1986
    Village Voice, 31:128, 16 Dec. 1986

ANTHONY GARCIA

Serafin, 1990
    Bensussen, M., "Whose Language Is It?" *American Theatre*, 7:82–82, Oct.
    1990

MANUEL PEREIRAS GARCIA

Santiago, 1990
    American Theatre, 7:9, June 1990
    American Theatre, 7:11, July/Aug. 1990

SERGIO GARCIA-MARRUIZ
SEE EDUARDO MACHADO and SERGIO GARCIA-MARRUIZ

HERB GARDNER

Conversations with My Father, 1990
    Playbill, 8:37, 30 Sept. 1990

The Goodbye People, 1968
    Leonard, W. T., *Once Was Enough,* pp. 68–69

I'm Not Rappoport, 1985
    San Diego Magazine, 41:42 + , Mar. 1989
    Westways, 79:6, June 1987

HERSCHEL GARFEIN
SEE RUTH MALECZECH and HERSCHEL GARFEIN

HAMLIN GARLAND

The Rise of Boomtown, an incomplete, unpublished play, written 1889
    Rocha, M. W., "Hamlin Garland's Temperance Play," *American Literary Realism, 1870–1910,* 21(3):67–71, Spring 1989

JIMMY GARRETT

And We Own the Night: A Play of Blackness, 1968
    Kaufman, M. W., "The Delicate World of Reprobation: A Note on the Black Revolutionary Theatre," pp. 192–209 in E. Hill, ed., *The Theater of Black Americans,* Vol. 1 of two vols. rptd. as one in 1987, same pagination in both eds.
    The Drama Review, 12(4):62–69, Summer 1968 (text of play)

NANCY FALES GARRETT

Some Sweet Day, 1989
    Playbill, 7:40, 31 Mar. 1989

OLIVER H. P. GARRETT

Waltz in Goose Step, 1938
    Curtin, K., *"We Can Always Call Them Bulgarians,"* pp. 233–237

SHELLY GARRETT

Beauty Shop, 1990
    TheaterWeek, 3:12, 26 Feb. 1990
    TheaterWeek, 3:12, 26 Mar. 1990

BARBARA GARSON

MacBird!, 1966
Ahrens, R., "Political History and Satire in William Shakespeare's *Macbeth* and Barbara Garson's *MacBird!*" pp. 7–25 in J. E. Peters and T. M. Stein, eds., *Scholastic Midwifery*

JULIET GARSON

Tiny Mommy, 1987
Village Voice, 32:101+, 6 Oct. 1987

MICHAEL V. GAZZO

A Hatful of Rain, 1955
Counts, M. L., *Coming Home,* pp. 62–63, 161–162
Paller, M., "The Actors Studio Changes Direction under Frank Corsaro," *TheaterWork,* 3:22–27, 11 Sept. 1989
American Theatre, 5:8, Apr. 1988

VIRGIL GEDDES

Native Ground, 1937
Kazacoff, G., *Dangerous Theatre,* pp. 86, 98–105

BARBARA GELB

My Gene (includes excerpts from five plays of E. O'Neill), 1987
Theatre Journal, 40:123, Mar. 1988

LARRY GELBART

Rubin, T., "Mastermind of *Mastergate,*" *Playbill,* 8:24, 26, 28, 31 Oct. 1989
Playbill, 7:34, 30 Sept. 1989
Playbill, 8:48, 30 Nov. 1989
TheaterWeek, 2:35, 27 Feb. 1989

Feats of Clay, 1990
Playbill, 8:30, 31 July 1990

Mastergate, 1989
Horwitz, S., "*Mastergate* Potshots," *TheaterWeek,* 3:18–24, 16 Oct. 1989
"*Mastergate*—The Scandal Continues," *Nation,* 249:528–530, 6 Nov. 1989 (includes excerpts from the play)
Riedel, M., "Gate Crashing," *TheaterWeek,* 3:43, 23 Oct. 1989
Rothstein, M., "Is There Life after 'M*A*S*H?'" *New York Times Magazine,* pp. 53–56+, 8 Oct. 1989
America, 161:321, 11 Nov. 1989
American Theatre, 5:14, Feb. 1989
American Theatre, 6:7, Apr. 1989

American Theatre, 6:52–53, Sept. 1989
Commonweal, 117:18–19, 12 Jan. 1990
Connoisseur, 220:39, Jan. 1990
New York, 22:165–166, 23 Oct. 1989
New Yorker, 65:131, 23 Oct. 1989
Newsweek, 114:74, 30 Oct. 1989
Playbill, 8:73, 31 Oct. 1989
TheaterWeek, 3:22, 4 Sept. 1989
TheaterWeek, 3:6, 18 Sept. 1989
TheaterWeek, 3:24, 25 Dec. 1989
TheaterWeek, 3:38, 15 Jan. 1990
TheaterWeek, 3:24, 30 July 1990
Village Voice, 34:103 + , 24 Oct. 1989

The Sly Fox (adaptation of B. Jonson's play *Volpone*), 1976
TheaterWeek, 2:11, 27 Mar. 1989

LARRY GELBART, CY COLEMAN, and DAVID ZIPPEL

City of Angels (originally titled *Death Is for Suckers* and *Double Exposure*), 1989
Filichia, P., "Death Is for Suckers," *TheaterWeek,* 3:14–18, 18 Dec. 1989
————, "One of the Good Guys," *TheaterWeek,* 3:27–29, 28 May 1990
Gottfried, M., "The Big Three," *TheaterWeek,* 3:14–19, 4 June 1990
Mandelbaum, K., "Musical Noir," *TheaterWeek,* 3:40, 1 Jan. 1990
Morehouse, R., "A Name to Reckon With," *Playbill,* 8:8, 10, 31 Aug. 1990
America, 162:66, 27 Jan. 1990
Commonweal, 117:150, 9 Mar. 1990
Nation, 250:141–142, 29 Jan. 1990
New York, 23:56–57, 8 Jan. 1990
New York, 23:52–53, 30 Apr. 1990
New Yorker, 65:77, 25 Dec. 1989
Newsweek, 115:62–63, 8 Jan. 1990
TheaterWeek, 1:5, 11 Apr. 1988
TheaterWeek, 2:5, 10 July 1989
TheaterWeek, 2:8, 17 July 1989
TheaterWeek, 3:11, 21 Aug. 1989
TheaterWeek, 3:8, 30 Oct. 1989
TheaterWeek, 3:8, 25 June 1990
Time, 134:92, 25 Dec. 1989
Village Voice, 34:115–116, 19 Dec. 1989

LARRY GELBART and MAURY YESTON

One Two Three Four Five, 1989
American Theatre, 5:14, Feb. 1989

JACK GELBER

Gale, S. H., "Jack Gelber: An Annotated Bibliography," *Bulletin of Bibliography,* 44(2):102–110, June 1987

King, K., "Jack Gelber," pp. 155–165 in King's *Ten Modern American Playwrights*
Petronella, V. F., "Jack Gelber (12 October 1925–)," pp. 133–141 in P. C. Kolin, ed., *American Playwrights since 1945*

The Connection, 1959
    Harap, L., *Dramatic Encounters*, p. 138

The Cuban Thing, 1968
    Leonard, W. T., *Once Was Enough*, pp. 33–35

Sleep, 1972
    Grabes, H., "Myth and Myth Destruction in American Plays of the 60s and Early 70s," *Amerikastudien*, 32(1):39–48, 1987

GARY GELD
SEE OSSIE DAVIS, PETER UDELL, PHILIP ROSE, and GARY GELD

GRATIEN GÉLINAS

The Passion of Narcisse Mondoux, 1986
    TheaterWeek, 2:6, 5 June 1989

JIM GEOGHAN

Botto, L., "Look Who's Kidding," *Playbill*, 7:40, 43–45, 31 Aug. 1989

Only Kidding!, 1988
    Horwitz, S., "Jim Geoghan's *Only Kidding*—A Splenetic Look at the World of the Stand-up Comic as Metaphor," *TheaterWeek*, 3:24–28, 9 Oct. 1989
    Commonweal, 116:503–504, 22 Sept. 1989
    New Yorker, 65:97, 29 May 1989
    Playbill, 7:37, 31 May 1989
    Playbill, 8:46, 31 Oct. 1989
    TheaterWeek, 2:60, 12 Dec. 1988
    TheaterWeek, 2:3, 24 Apr. 1989
    TheaterWeek, 2:6, 24 Apr. 1989

GEORGE GERSHWIN

Hirsch, F., *Harold Prince and the American Musical Theater*, pp. 2, 11–14
Kendall, A., *George Gershwin*
Mates, J., *America's Musical Stage*, pp. 37, 51, 64, 150, 152, 182, 183, 186, 198
Woll, A., *Black Musical Theatre*, pp. 94, 146, 148, 154, 160–175, 189, 194

ALSO SEE DOROTHY HEYWARD, DuBOSE HEYWARD,
GEORGE GERSHWIN, and IRA GERSHWIN
AND GEORGE S. KAUFMAN, MORRIE RYSKIND,
GEORGE GERSHWIN, and IRA GERSHWIN

IRA GERSHWIN
SEE DOROTHY HEYWARD, DuBOSE HEYWARD,
GEORGE GERSHWIN, and IRA GERSHWIN
AND GEORGE S. KAUFMAN, MORRIE RYSKIND,
GEORGE GERSHWIN, and IRA GERSHWIN

JOEL GERSMANN

The Hangwoman (dramatization of novel by P. Kohout), published 1989
Auerbach, L., and E. J. Czerwinski, eds., "Pavel Kohout's *The Hang-woman*: A Dramatization by Joel Gersmann," *Slavic and East European Arts,* 6(1):Spring 1989 (monograph issue, includes an interview)

CRAIG GHOLSON

Andy Warhol's Interview, 19:24, Dec. 1989

VICTOR GIALANELLA

Frankenstein (dramatization of M. W. Shelley's novel), 1981
Leonard, W. T., *Once Was Enough,* pp. 54–58

WOLCOTT GIBBS

Season in the Sun, 1950
Curtin, K., *"We Can Always Call Them Bulgarians,"* pp. 293–294

P. J. GIBSON

Brown Silk and Magenta Sunsets, 1985
Wilkerson, M. B., "Music as Metaphor: New Plays of Black Women," pp. 61–75 in L. Hart, ed., *Making a Spectacle*

WILLIAM GIBSON

Handy Dandy, 1984
America, 163:350, 10 Nov. 1990
New Yorker, 66:120, 5 Nov. 1990
Playbill, 8:49, 31 May 1990
TheaterWeek, 3:15, 2 Apr. 1990
TheaterWeek, 3:41, 7 May 1990

WILLIAM GIBSON and JOE RAPOSO

Raggedy Ann, 1984
Lutskaya, E., "Albany—Moscow," *Soviet Literature,* 2[467]:174–175, 1987

ALSO SEE CLIFFORD ODETS, WILLIAM GIBSON,
CHARLES STROUSE, and LEE ADAMS

SKY GILBERT

Drag Queens on Trial, 1985
Taylor, P., "Canadians React to 'Tampering,'" *American Theatre,* 6:32,
Mar. 1990

WILLIE GILBERT
SEE ABE BURROWS, JACK WEINSTOCK, WILLIE GILBERT,
and FRANK LOESSER

WILLIAM GILLETTE

Held by the Enemy, 1886
Rainey, K. T., "Race and Reunion in Nineteenth-Century Reconciliation
Drama," *American Transcendental Quarterly,* 2(2):155–169, June 1988

Secret Service, 1895
Rainey, K. T., "Race and Reunion in Nineteenth-Century Reconciliation
Drama," *American Transcendental Quarterly,* 2(2)155–169, June 1988

FRANK GILROY

Playbill, 6:71–72, June 1988

Match Point, 1990
American Theatre, 7:13, May 1990

The Subject Was Roses, 1964
Counts, M. L., *Coming Home,* pp. 127–128, 133
Playbill, 7:30, 31 Jan. 1989
TheaterWeek, 1:56, 23 May 1988

Who'll Save the Plowboy?, 1962
Counts, M. L., *Coming Home,* pp. 67–68, 106–107

ALLEN GINSBERG

Kaddish (dramatization of his 1961 poem), 1988
Istel, J., "The Faces of Paranoia," *American Theatre,* 5:4–5, May 1988
Art in America, 76:183–184, Sept. 1988

ALLEN GINSBERG and PHILIP GLASS

Hydrogen Jukebox, 1990
Stearns, D. P., "Glass of 1990: *Hydrogen Jukebox,*" *TheaterWeek,* 3:27–29,
9 July 1990

ARTHUR GIRON

Edith Stein, 1969 (revised 1979, 1987, 1988)
    Cummings, S. T., "Mysteries of Faith," *American Theatre,* 5:9–10, Oct. 1988
    Christian Century, 105:1144–1145, 14 Dec. 1988

SUSAN GLASPELL

Ben-Zvi, L., "Susan Glaspell's Contributions to Contemporary Women Playwrights," pp. 147–166 in E. Brater, ed., *Feminine Focus*

Dymkowski, C., "On the Edge: The Plays of Susan Glaspell," *Modern Drama,* 31(1):91–105, Mar. 1988

Larabee, A., "Death in Delphi: Susan Glaspell and the Compassionate Marriage," *Mid-American Review,* 7(2):93–106, 1987

Larabee, A. E., "'Meeting the Outside Face to Face': Susan Glaspell, Djuna Barnes, and O'Neill's *The Emperor Jones,*" pp. 77–85 in J. Schlueter, ed., *Modern American Drama*

Ozieblo, B., "Rebellion and Rejection: The Plays of Susan Glaspell," pp. 66–76 in J. Schlueter, ed., *Modern American Drama*

Shafer, Y., "Susan Glaspell: German Influence, American Playwright," *Zeitschrift für Anglistik und Amerikanistic,* 36(4):333ff., 1988

Alison's House, 1930
    Gilbert, S. M., and S. Gubar, *The War of the Words,* p. 209 (Vol. 1 of their *No Man's Land*)
    Helle, A. P., "Re-Presenting Women Writers Onstage: A Retrospective to the Present," pp. 195–208 in L. Hart, ed., *Making a Spectacle*
    Stephens, J. L., "Women in Pulitzer Prize Plays, 1918–1949," pp. 245–253 in H. K. Chinoy and L. W. Jenkins, eds., *Women in American Theatre,* rev. and enl. ed. (pp. 243–251 in 1981 ed.)

Trifles, 1916
    France, R., "Apropos of Women and the Folk Play," pp. 145–152 in H. K. Chinoy and L. W. Jenkins, eds., *Women in American Theatre,* rev. and enl. ed. (same pagination in 1981 ed.)
    Gilbert, S. M., and S. Gubar, *The War of the Words,* pp. 90–91, 114 (Vol. 1 of their *No Man's Land*)
    Keyssar, H., "Foothills: Precursors of Feminist Drama," pp. 22–52 in Keyssar's *Feminist Theatre*
    Mael, P., "*Trifles*: The Path to Sisterhood," *Literature/Film Quarterly,* 17(4):281–284, 1989
    Stein, K. F., "The Women's World of Glaspell's *Trifles,*" pp. 253–256 in H. K. Chinoy and L. W. Jenkins, eds., *Women in American Theatre,* rev. and enl. ed. (pp. 251–254 in 1981 ed.)
    Stephens, J. L., "Gender Ideology and Dramatic Convention in Progressive Era Plays, 1890–1920," pp. 283–293 in S.-E. Case, ed., *Performing Feminisms* (rpt. of *Theatre Journal,* 41(1):45–55, Mar. 1989)

The Verge, 1921
>   Rajkowska, B. O., "Discovering and Reading the American Woman," *Revista Alicantina de Estudios Ingleses,* 2:119–125, Nov. 1989

ALSO SEE GEORGE CRAM COOK and SUSAN GLASPELL

JOANNA GLASS

Canadian Gothic, 1972
>   Filichia, P., "New Directions," *TheaterWeek,* 3:42–43, 22 Jan. 1990

Play Memory, 1984
>   Ilson, C., *Harold Prince,* pp. 324–327

Yesteryear, 1989
>   *Maclean's,* 102:47, 23 Jan. 1989

PHILIP GLASS

Berg, C. M., "Philip Glass on Composing for Film and Other Forms: The Case of *Koyaanisqatsi*" (interview), *Journal of Dramatic Theory and Criticism,* 4(2):300–322, Spring 1990
Croce, A., "Reflections on Glass," pp. 125–128 in Croce's *Sight Lines*
Glass, P., *Music by Philip Glass,* ed. R. T. Jones
Horwitz, S., "Papp's Controversial *Cymbeline,*" *TheaterWeek,* 2:31–36, 19 June 1989
Page, T., "Glass," *Opera News,* 52:8–10 + , June 1988
Sandow, G., "The Composer and Performer and Other Matters: A Panel Discussion with Virgil Thomson and Philip Glass," ed. J. B. Clark, *American Music,* 7:181–204, Summer 1989
Village Voice, 35:94, 20 Feb. 1990

PHILIP GLASS and CONSTANCE DeJONG

Satyagrapha (adapted from the *Bhagavad Gita*), 1988
>   *Opera News,* 52:27, May 1988

ALSO SEE ALLEN GINSBERG and PHILIP GLASS
AND DAVID HENRY HWANG, PHILIP GLASS, and JEROME SIRLIN
AND ROBERT WILSON and PHILIP GLASS
AND ARTHUR YORINKS and PHILIP GLASS

STEPHEN GLASSMAN, RON DANTE, and GENE ALLAN

Billy (musical version of novella by H. Melville, *Billy Budd*), 1969
>   Leonard, W. T., *Once Was Enough,* pp. 11–14

BENJAMIN F. GLAZER
SEE OSCAR HAMMERSTEIN II, BENJAMIN F. GLAZER,
and RICHARD RODGERS

JOHN GLINES

Men of Manhattan (Scenes of New York City Gay Life), 1990
TheaterWeek, 3:8, 2 July 1990

FREDERIC GLOVER

The Return, 1990
TheaterWeek, 3:8, 8 Jan. 1990
Village Voice, 35:97, 23 Jan. 1990

STEPHEN GLOVER (attributed to)

The Last of the Mohicans (unpublished dramatization of novel by J. F. Cooper),
written 1820s or 1830s
Jones, E. H., *Native Americans as Shown on the Stage,* p. 70

JANUSZ GLOWACKI

Hunting Cockroaches (tr. Jadwiga Kosicka), 1987
Vanity Fair, 50:104, Feb. 1987
Village Voice, 32:90 + , 10 Mar. 1987

THOMAS GODFREY

The Prince of Parthia, 1767
Egri, P., "The Shadow of Shakespeare across the Atlantic: The Shakespear-
ean Tradition in Early American Tragedy," *Acta Litteraria Academiae
Scientiarum Hungaricae,* 28(3–4):345–363, 1986

AUGUSTUS GOETZ and RUTH GOETZ

The Heiress (dramatization of novel by H. James, *Washington Square*), 1947
Playbill, 7:26, 31 July 1989

The Immoralist (dramatization of novel by A. Gide), 1954
Curtin, K., *"We Can Always Call Them Bulgarians,"* pp. 291–293, 303–316

JOHN PATRICK GOGGAN
SEE JOHN PATRICK

MICHAEL GOLD
(pseudonym of Itzok Isaac Granich; also known as Irwin Granich)
Folsom, M., ed., *Mike Gold*

MICHAEL GOLD and MICHAEL BLANKFORT

Battle Hymn, 1936
Kazacoff, G., *Dangerous Theatre,* pp. 91–94

MOSES GOLDBERG

A Wrinkle in Time (dramatization of book by M. L'Engle), 1988
    American Theatre, 4:8–9, Jan. 1988

WHOOPI GOLDBERG (Caryn Johnson)

Whoopi Goldberg, 1984
    Gentile, J. S., *Cast of One,* pp. 172–175

ROSE LEIMAN GOLDEMBERG

Letters Home (dramatization of S. Plath's letters to her mother), 1979
    Helle, A. P., "Re-Presenting Women Writers Onstage: A Retrospective to
    the Present," pp. 195–208 in L. Hart, ed., *Making a Spectacle*

JORGE GOLDENBERG

Knepp, 1988
    Village Voice, 33:84, 9 Aug. 1988

SIDNEY GOLDFARB

Music Rescue Service, 1990
    Village Voice, 35:80, 29 May 1990

ANDREW GOLDMAN

Fast, 1989
    American Theatre, 6:109, Oct. 1989

JAMES GOLDMAN

They Might Be Giants, 1961
    Ilson, C., *Harold Prince,* pp. 61–64

JEFF GOLDSMITH

McCarthy (about Senator Joe McCarthy), 1988
    American Theatre, 5:7–8, July/Aug. 1988
    Los Angeles, 33:196+, Sept. 1988
    Theatre Journal, 42:506–508, Dec. 1990

OLIVER GOLDSTICK

Snow White Falling, 1988
    TheaterWeek, 1:6, 27 June 1988

BRYAN GOLUBOFF

One Hundred Bucks a Tooth, 1990
  TheaterWeek, 3:13, 9 Apr. 1990

GUILLERMO GÓMEZ-PEÑA

Border Brujo, 1990
  Theatre Journal, 42:495–497, Dec. 1990

GEORGE GONNEAU and NORMAN ROSE

Monsieur Amilcar (adaptation of play by Y. Jamiaque), 1980
  TheaterWeek, 1:6, 23 May 1988

REUBEN GONZALEZ

The Boiler Room, 1987
  American Theatre, 4:7, Feb. 1988

ARTHUR GOODMAN and A. WASHINGTON PEZET

In Heaven and Earth, 1936
  Kazacoff, G., *Dangerous Theatre,* pp. 77–79

PAUL GOODMAN

Jonah, 1966
  Village Voice, 35:102, 3 Apr. 1990

Stop-Light (five Noh plays), published 1941
  Bell, J., "Paul Goodman's Noh Plays," *TheaterWeek,* 4:31, 31 Dec. 1990

FRANCES GOODRICH and ALBERT HACKETT

The Diary of Anne Frank (dramatization of A. Frank's *Diary*), 1955
  Harap, L., *Dramatic Encounters,* p. 132
  Thurman, J., "Not Even a Nice Girl," *New Yorker,* 65:116–120, 18 Dec.
  1989

AIN GORDON

30 Stories, 1990
  Village Voice, 35:119, 17 Apr. 1990

ALEX GORDON, ROBERT WALDMAN, and ALFRED UHRY

Here's Where I Belong (musical version of J. Steinbeck's novel *East of Eden*),
  1968
  Leonard, W. T., *Once Was Enough,* pp. 77–80
  New Yorker, 44:132, 9 Mar. 1968

CHARLES GORDON
SEE OyamO

PETER GORDON
SEE KIT FITZGERALD and PETER GORDON

STEVE GORDON

Tough to Get Help, 1972
    Leonard, W. T., *Once Was Enough,* pp. 197–198

STUART GORDON

London, T., "Chicago Impromptu," *American Theatre,* 7:14–23, 60–64, July/
    Aug. 1990

CHARLES GORDONE

Smith, S. H., "An Interview with Charles Gordone," *Studies in American
    Drama, 1945–Present,* 3:122–132, 1988
———, "Charles Gordone (12 October 1925–)," pp. 133–141 in P. C. Kolin,
    ed., *American Playwrights since 1945*

No Place to Be Somebody: A Black-Black Comedy, 1967
    Los Angeles, 32:244+, Oct. 1987

MICHAEL GORE
SEE LAWRENCE D. COHEN, MICHAEL GORE, and DEAN PITCHFORD

PHILIP KAN GOTANDA

Berson, M., "Between Worlds," *American Theatre,* 6:20–25, Mar. 1990 (based
    on her Introduction to *Between Worlds*)
———, "Gotanda's Plays Explore Lives of Asian-Americans," *American
    Theatre,* 5:54–55, Sept. 1988
Booth, S. V., "Dramaturg in Search of an Axis," *American Theatre,* 7:62–63,
    Sept. 1990
Gray, A., "The Big If," *American Theatre,* 6:18–21, 56, June 1989

The Wash, 1987
    Berson, M., ed., *Between Worlds,* pp. ix–xiv (Introduction), 29–35, 37–73
        (text of play)
    New Yorker, 66:119, 19 Nov. 1990
    Playbill, 9:48, 31 Dec. 1990
    TheaterWeek, 4:9, 13 Aug. 1990
    TheaterWeek, 4:10, 8 Oct. 1990

Yankee Dawg You Die, 1988
    Horwitz, S., "'Nix "Nip" Clichés,' Urge Stars of *Yankee Dawg You Die,*"
        TheaterWeek, 2:31–34, 12 June 1989

Moy, J. S., "David Henry Hwang's *M. Butterfly* and Philip Kan Gotanda's *Yankee Dawg You Die*: Repositioning Chinese American Marginality on the American Stage," *Theatre Journal*, 42:48–56, Mar. 1990
Hudson Review, 42:463, Autumn 1989
New Yorker, 65:97–98, 29 May 1989
Village Voice, 34:98, 25 May 1989

JAMES GOW and ARNAUD D'USSEAU

Deep Are the Roots, 1945
Counts, M. L., *Coming Home*, pp. 73–75
Kazan, E., *Elia Kazan*, pp. 293–295
Press, M., "Black Man-White Woman: The 'Lynch Pattern' as Morality Play," pp. 157–168 in K. Hartigan, ed., *Text and Presentation*

Tomorrow the World, 1943
Harap, L., *Dramatic Encounters*, p. 132
Marcuson, L. R., *The Stage Immigrant*, pp. 143–147

CHRISTOPHER GRABOWSKI

A Forest in Arden (adaptation of Shakespeare's *As You Like It*), 1990
TheaterWeek, 3:9, 29 Jan. 1990
TheaterWeek, 3:41–42, 19 Feb. 1990
Village Voice, 35:110, 20 Feb. 1990

ED GRACZYK

Come Back to the 5 & Dime, Jimmy Dean, Jimmy Dean, 1982
Kazan, E., *Elia Kazan*, pp. 800, 805, 806–807

A Murder of Crows, 1987
TheaterWeek, 2:7, 29 Aug. 1988
Village Voice, 33:104, 27 Sept. 1988

TODD GRAFF

The Grandma Plays, 1988
TheaterWeek, 1:7, 18 Apr. 1988
TheaterWeek, 1:6, 2 May 1988
Village Voice, 33:104, 11 Oct. 1988

BRUCE GRAHAM

Belmont Avenue Social Club, 1990
TheaterWeek, 3:26–27, 7 May 1990

Early One Evening at the Rainbow Bar and Grille, 1989
Harris, J., "Apocalyptic Blues," *TheaterWeek*, 2:38–39, 1 May 1989
New Yorker, 65:82, 24 Apr. 1989

JUDY GRAHN

The Queen of Swords, published 1987
    Case, S.-E., "Judy Grahn's Gynopoetics: *The Queen of Swords,"* *Studies in the Literary Imagination,* 21(2):47–67, Fall 1988

MURRAY GRAND
SEE PATRICK DENNIS and MURRAY GRAND

IRWIN GRANICH
SEE MICHAEL GOLD

ITZOK ISAAC GRANICH
SEE MICHAEL GOLD

AMLIN GRAY

Gray, A., "The Big If," *American Theatre,* 6:18–21, 56, June 1989

How I Got That Story, 1980
    Zinman, T. S., "Search and Destroy: The Drama of the Vietnam War," *Theatre Journal,* 42:5–26, Mar. 1990

DAMIEN GRAY

The Florentine, 1989
    TheaterWeek, 3:11, 4 Dec. 1989

JOHN GRAY

Bessai, D., "Discovering the Popular Audience," *Canadian Literature,* 118:7–28, Autumn 1988

JOHN GRAY and ERIC PETERSON

Billy Bishop Goes to War, 1978
    Miller, M. J., "*Billy Bishop Goes to War* and *Maggie and Pierre*: A Matched Set," *Theatre History in Canada,* 10(2):188–198, Fall 1989

SPALDING GRAY

Gentile, J. S., *Cast of One,* pp. 148–152
Horwitz, S., "Exercising Demons: Spalding Gray Mines His Past for Your Amusement," *TheaterWeek,* 4:16–23, 3 Dec. 1990
Jenkins, R., *Acrobats of the Soul,* pp. 123–41
Shank, T., "Spalding Gray and Elizabeth LeCompte: The Wooster Group," pp. 170–179 in Shank's *American Alternative Theater*
Siegle, R., "Condensed Book: Performance Art and Fiction," pp. 250–272 in Siegle's *Suburban Ambush*

India and After (America), 1979 (the introduction to *Three Places in Rhode Island* by Elizabeth LeCompte and others, which see)
    Savran, D., "From the Rhode Island Trilogy to *Hula*: Simple Demonstrations of the Law of Physics," pp. 47–167 in Savran's *The Wooster Group*

Monster in a Box, 1990
    American Theatre, 7:12–13, Apr. 1990
    New York, 23:109, 10 Dec. 1990
    TheaterWeek, 4:6, 17 Sept. 1990
    TheaterWeek, 4:34, 26 Nov. 1990

Swimming to Cambodia, 1984
    Demastes, W. W., "Spalding Gray's *Swimming to Cambodia* and the Evolution of an Ironic Presence," *Theatre Journal,* 41:75–94, Mar. 1989
    Phelan, P., "Spalding Gray's *Swimming to Cambodia*: The Article," *Critical Texts,* 5(1):27–30, 1988

ADOLPH GREEN

Chase, A., "Comden and Green: A Hell of a Team," *TheaterWeek,* 2:22–27, 26 June 1989

ALSO SEE BETTY COMDEN and ADOLPH GREEN
AND BETTY COMDEN, ADOLPH GREEN, and CY COLEMAN
AND JOSEPH FIELDS, JEROME CHODOROV, LEONARD BERNSTEIN, BETTY COMDEN, and ADOLPH GREEN

PAUL GREEN

Coates, A., "Paul Green—A Total Human Being," *Pembroke Magazine,* 10:64–65, 1978
Daniels, J., "American Antaeus," *Pembroke Magazine,* 10:11–14, 1978
Lowery, R., "Paul Green as Screenwriter," *Pembroke Magazine,* 10:50–53, 1978
"Paul Green: The South's Greatest Playwright," *Pembroke Magazine,* 10:1–86, 1978 [Special Issue]
Ragan, S., M. W. Wellman, W. Spearman, and T. Sanford, "History: A Night for Paul Green," *Pembroke Magazine,* 10:79–86, 1978
Spearman, W., "Paul Green, the Teacher," *Pembroke Magazine,* 10:66, 1978
Spence, J. P., "Paul Green, Son of Harnett County," *Pembroke Magazine,* 10:14–26, 1978
Stem, T., Jr., "Paul Green, Rassie McLeon, and Friends," *Pembroke Magazine,* 10:67–76, 1978
Walser, R., "Paul Green Undergraduate," *Pembroke Magazine,* 10:29–38, 1978
Walters, T. N., "Some Reflections of Paul Green: A Play, a Visit," *Pembroke Magazine,* 10:41–42, 1978

Hymn to the Rising Sun, 1936
    Kazacoff, G., *Dangerous Theatre,* pp. 108–109

In Abraham's Bosom, 1926
  Atkinson, B., "Paul Green—Part of the Glory of Our Civilization," *Pembroke Magazine,* 10:39, 1978
  Stephens, J. L., "Women in Pulitzer Prize Plays, 1918–1949," pp. 245–253 in H. K. Chinoy and L. W. Jenkins, eds., *Women in American Theatre,* rev. and enl. ed. (pp. 243–251 in 1981 ed.)
  Walters, T. N., "Mournful Songs and Flying Sparks: Paul Green's *In Abraham's Bosom,*" *Pembroke Magazine,* 10:42–50, 1978

The Lost Colony, 1937
  Bentley, J., *Hallie Flanagan,* pp. 230–231

Unto Such Glory, 1936
  Kazacoff, G., *Dangerous Theatre,* pp. 108–109

PAUL GREEN and KURT WEILL

Johnny Johnson: The Biography of a Common Man, 1936 (revised 1972)
  Counts, M. L., *Coming Home,* pp. 86, 118–119, 134–135, 197
  Harap, L., *Dramatic Encounters,* p. 113
  Leonard, W. T., *Once Was Enough,* pp. 90–94
  New Yorker, 65:98, 23 Oct. 1989

PAUL GREEN and RICHARD WRIGHT

Native Son (dramatization of Wright's novel), 1941 (revised 1980)
  TheaterWeek, 1:38, 21 Mar. 1988

VANALYNE GREEN

Trick or Drink, 1984
  Case, S.-E., *Feminism and Theatre,* pp. 59–60
  Forte, J., "Women's Performance Art: Feminism and Postmodernism," pp. 251–269 in S.-E. Case, ed., *Performing Feminisms* (rpt. of *Theatre Journal,* 40(2):217–235, May 1988)

ALBERT GREENBERG
SEE MARTHA BOESING, ALBERT GREENBERG, and HELEN STOLTZFUS

RICHARD GREENBERG

Gholson, C., "Richard Greenberg" (interview), *BOMB,* 21:36–39, Fall 1987
Hubbard, K., "A New, Young Playwright Risks Success for His Art," *People Weekly,* 31:125–126, 13 Feb. 1989
Raymond, G., "Richard Greenberg: *Eastern Standard* Time," *TheaterWeek,* 2:42–47, 31 Oct. 1988
Szentgyorgyi, T., "Richard Greenberg: Uncomfortably Yours," *TheaterWeek,* 4:18–21, 31 Dec. 1990

The American Plan (originally titled *Refugees*), 1990
   New Yorker, 66:83, 31 Dec. 1990
   TheaterWeek, 3:11, 22 Jan. 1990
   TheaterWeek, 4:9, 13 Aug. 1990
   TheaterWeek, 4:10, 19 Nov. 1990
   TheaterWeek, 4:34, 31 Dec. 1990

Eastern Standard, 1988
   Haun, H., "The Meara Image," *Playbill,* 7:8, 12, 14, 28 Feb. 1989
   Sandla, R., "Tales of the City," *TheaterWeek,* 2:10–19, 16 Jan. 1989
   America, 160:248, 18 Mar. 1989
   American Theatre, 5:8–9, June 1988
   Commonweal, 116:210–212, 7 Apr. 1989
   Connoisseur, 219:42, Apr. 1989
   Georgia Review, 43:575–576, Fall 1989
   Hudson Review, 42:287–289, Summer 1989
   Massachusetts Review, 30:129–130, Spring 1989
   Nation, 247:663, 12 Dec. 1988
   New Republic, 199:33–34, 21 Nov. 1988
   New York, 22:79, 16 Jan. 1989
   New Yorker, 64:121, 14 Nov. 1988
   Time, 133:102, 2 Jan. 1989
   Village Voice, 33:99, 8 Nov. 1988
   Vogue, 179:266B, Mar. 1989

The Maderati, 1987
   Village Voice, 32:88+, 3 Mar. 1987

Neptune's Hips, 1988
   New Yorker, 64:75, 25 July 1988

RICHARD GREENBERG and WILLIAM FINN

Romance in Hard Times (revision of Finn's *America Kicks Up Its Heels,* which see), 1988
   TheaterWeek, 2:5–6, 3 Apr. 1989
   TheaterWeek, 2:4, 12 June 1989
   TheaterWeek, 2:8–9, 10 July 1989
   TheaterWeek, 2:6, 31 July 1989
   TheaterWeek, 3:4, 25 Dec. 1989
   Village Voice, 35:95+, 9 Jan. 1990

ALSO SEE MARTHA CLARKE, RICHARD GREENBERG, and RICHARD PEASLEE

STANLEY R. GREENBERG

Feathers: Variations on Aristophanes' "The Birds", 1988
   American Theatre, 5:8, May 1988
   American Theatre, 5:7, June 1988

DAN GREENBURG
SEE JULES FEIFFER, DAN GREENBURG, LEONARD MELFI,
SAM SHEPARD, and OTHERS

FRANCES NIMMO GREENE and ROBERT HARVEY GREENE

The Last Enemy, 1937
Kazacoff, G., *Dangerous Theatre,* pp. 213–214

DAVID GREENSPAN

Dig a Hole and Bury Your Father, 1989
Village Voice, 34:89–90, 31 Jan. 1989

The Horizontal and the Vertical, 1989
Village Voice, 34:89–90, 31 Jan. 1989

Principia, 1988
Village Voice, 33:98+, 3 May 1988

2 Samuel 11, Etc., 1989
American Theatre, 7:9, June 1990
TheaterWeek, 3:43, 18 June 1990
Village Voice, 34:107+, 10 Oct. 1989

JESS GREGG

A Swim in the Sea (originally titled *The Sea Shell*), 1958
Ilson, C., *Harold Prince,* pp. 45–46

SUSAN GREGG

Saint Joan (revision of G. B. Shaw's abandoned screenplay), 1989
American Theatre, 5:16, Mar. 1989

SUSAN GRIFFIN

Case, S.-E., *Feminism and Theatre,* p. 70

Voices, televised 1974, produced on stage 1975
Mael, P., "A Rainbow of Voices," pp. 317–321 in H. K. Chinoy and L. W. Jenkins, eds., *Women in American Theatre,* rev. and enl. ed. (pp. 320–324 in 1981 ed.)
Moore, H., "Woman Alone, Women Together," pp. 186–191 in H. K. Chinoy and L. W. Jenkins, eds., *Women in American Theatre,* rev. and enl. ed. (pp. 184–190 in 1981 ed.)

TOM GRIFFIN

Amateurs, 1990
    Playbill, 8:29, 31 July 1990

The Boys Next Door, 1987
    Hersh, A., "Audience Notes: Where the *Boys* Are," *TheaterWeek,* 1:10–
        11, 15 Feb. 1988
    Shirakawa, S. H., "Theater Trends: Dramatic Disabilities," *TheaterWeek,*
        1:24–26, 11 Jan. 1988
    New Yorker, 64:96, 22 Feb. 1988
    Village Voice, 32:87–88, 18 Aug. 1987
    Village Voice, 33:102, 9 Feb. 1988

LINDA GRIFFITHS

Maggie and Pierre, 1980
    Miller, M. J., "*Billy Bishop Goes to War* and *Maggie and Pierre*: A Matched
        Set," *Theatre History in Canada,* 10(2):188–198, Fall 1989

ANGELINA WELD GRIMKÉ

Graybill, R., "The Abolitionist-Millerite Connection," pp. 139–152 in R. L.
    Numbers and J. M. Butler, eds., *The Disappointed*

Rachel, 1920
    Brown-Guillory, E., *Their Place on the Stage,* pp. 4–7, 9, 12, 18–19
    Keyssar, H., "Rites and Responsibilities: The Drama of Black American
        Women," pp. 226–240 in E. Brater, ed., *Feminine Focus*
    Miller, J.-M. A., "Black Women in Plays by Black Playwrights," pp. 256–
        262 in H. K. Chinoy and L. W. Jenkins, eds., *Women in American
        Theatre,* rev. and enl. ed. (pp. 254–260 in 1981 ed.)

JIM GRIMSLEY

Hulbert, D., "Actors Are the Spark for Atlanta's Writers," *American Theatre,*
    7:44–45, June 1990
Atlanta, 28:18, Mar. 1989 (interview)
TheaterWeek, 1:6, 9 May 1988

Mr. Universe, 1987
    American Theatre, 5:8, May 1988
    TheaterWeek, 1:4, 4 Apr. 1988
    Village Voice, 33:98+, 3 May 1988

DOUG GRISSOM

Tocoi Light, 1988
    American Theatre, 4:55, Nov. 1987

CHARLES GRODIN

Grodin, C., "Breakthrough," *Playbill,* 8:S1–S12, 31 Aug. 1990 (excerpt from Grodin's autobiography, *It Would Be So Nice If You Weren't Here*)
Playbill, 8:85–86, 30 Nov. 1989

Price of Fame, 1990
>   Botto, L., "Show Biz Four-Letter Man," *Playbill,* 8:40, 43–45, 30 June 1990
>   Filichia, P., "Writing Is the Best Revenge," *TheaterWeek,* 3:20, 22–23, 25 June 1990
>   Sneerwell, R., "Celebrity Hangups," *TheaterWeek,* 3:41, 2 July 1990
>   *New York,* 23:58–59, 25 June 1990
>   *New Yorker,* 66:71, 25 June 1990
>   *TheaterWeek,* 3:24, 4 Sept. 1989

KATHRYN GRODY

A Mom's Life, 1990
>   *Village Voice,* 35:100+, 27 Mar. 1990

LAURENCE GROSS and EDWARD CHILDS CARPENTER

Whistling in the Dark, 1932
>   Harap, L., *Dramatic Encounters,* p. 199

ED GRYSKA
SEE NANCY BORGENICHT and MICHAEL BUTTARS

JOHN GUARE

Guare, J., "Setting the Scene," *House & Garden,* 162:72+, Nov. 1990
Guare, J., and B. Branson, "Radical Descent," *Andy Warhol's Interview,* 19:72–73, Oct. 1989 (review of T. Williams's *Orpheus Descending*)
Michener, C., "The Bard of Jackson Heights," *New York,* 23:84–85, 24–31 Dec. 1990
Savran, D., "John Guare," pp. 84–99 in Savran's *In Their Own Words*
Wilmeth, D. B., "John Guare (5 February 1938–)," pp. 142–154 in P. C. Kolin, ed., *American Playwrights since 1945*
Chicago, 37:32, Mar. 1988
Playbill, 6:72, June 1988

Gardenia, 1982
>   *TheaterWeek,* 2:5, 24 Apr. 1989

The House of Blue Leaves, 1971
>   Brustein, R., "A Shaggy Dog Story," pp. 95–98 in Brustein's *Who Needs Theatre* (rpt. of *New Republic,* 194:27–29, 5 May 1986)
>   *Playbill,* 7:64–65, 31 Dec. 1988

Landscape of the Body, 1977
    Chicago, 37:32, Mar. 1988

Muzeeka, 1967
    Zinman, T. S., "Search and Destroy: The Drama of the Vietnam War,"
    Theatre Journal, 42:5–26, Mar. 1990

Six Degrees of Separation, 1990
    Burns, N., "*Separation* Anxiety" (interview), *TheaterWeek,* 3:23, 11 June
    1990
    Leslie, G., "Trivial Pursuits," *TheaterWeek,* 3:38, 25 June 1990
    Raymond, G., "Behind the Scenes at *Six Degrees of Separation*" (interview
    with director Jerry Zaks), *TheaterWeek,* 3:17–21, 11 June 1990
    Simpson, J. C., "Back to Broadway: Courtney B. Vance Stars in *Six De-
    grees of Separation,*" *TheaterWeek,* 4:24–27, 12 Nov. 1990
    American Theatre, 7:13, July/Aug. 1990
    Nation, 251:783, 17 Dec. 1990
    New Republic, 203:34 + , 9–16 July 1990
    New York, 23:58, 25 June 1990
    New Yorker, 66:71–72, 25 June 1990
    Newsweek, 115:54, 25 June 1990
    Playbill, 8:16, 20, 30 Sept. 1990
    TheaterWeek, 3:9, 14 May 1990
    TheaterWeek, 3:7, 2 July 1990
    Time, 135:77, 25 June 1990
    Time, 136:54, 31 Dec. 1990

BILL GUNN

Village Voice, 34:98 + , 25 Apr. 1989

The Forbidden City, 1989
    Ledford, L. S., "Gloria Foster: The Informer" (interview with Foster),
    2:26–31, 8 May 1989
    American Theatre, 6:56, Mar. 1990
    New York, 22:80–81, 17 Apr. 1989
    New Yorker, 65:111–112, 17 Apr. 1989
    Village Voice, 34:97–98, 18 Apr. 1989

ROBERT GURIK

Le Procès de Jean-baptiste M., 1972
    Grace, S., "The Expressionist Legacy in the Canadian Theatre: George
    Ryga and Robert Gurik," *Canadian Literature,* 118:47–58, Autumn 1988

A. R. GURNEY, JR.

Barbour, D., "Scenes from American Life: A Conversation with Playwright A.
R. Gurney" (interview), *TheaterWeek,* 2:18–25, 12 Dec. 1988
"Conversation Piece," *Newsweek,* 113:10–11, 26 June 1989

"The Dinner Party," *American Heritage,* 39:69–71, Sept./Oct. 1988
Playbill, 7:51, 28 Feb. 1989 (interview)
Playbill, 9:51, 31 Oct. 1990
TheaterWeek, 2:5, 1 May 1989
W, 18:19, 1 May 1989

Another Antigone, 1987
    Shirakawa, S. H., "Theater Trends: The Greeks Had Words for It,"
        TheaterWeek, 1:16–19, 8 Feb. 1988
    Nation, 246:174, 6 Feb. 1988
    New York, 21:71–72, 25 Jan. 1988
    New Yorker, 63:85, 25 Jan. 1988
    San Diego Magazine, 39:72+, May 1987
    Village Voice, 33:88+, 26 Jan. 1988

The Cocktail Hour, 1988
    Botto, L., "Cocktails with Nancy Marchand," *Playbill,* 7:40, 43–45, 31 Jan.
        1989
    Freeman, P., "Playwright A. R. Gurney, Jr.'s *Cocktail Hour* Leaves His
        Genteel Family Shaken, Not Stirred," *People Weekly,* 31:103–104, 23 Jan.
        1989
    Marowitz, C., "Turgenev in Buffalo: *Love Letters* and *The Cocktail Hour,*"
        TheaterWeek, 3:15–16, 11 June 1990
    America, 160:378, 22 Apr. 1989
    Commonweal, 116:280, 5 May 1989
    Connoisseur, 219:42, Apr. 1989
    Georgia Review, 43:578, Fall 1989
    Hudson Review, 42:122–124, Spring 1989
    Nation, 247:661–662, 12 Dec. 1988
    New York, 21:105–106, 31 Oct. 1988
    New Yorker, 64:134, 7 Nov. 1988
    Playbill, 7:74, 31 Mar. 1989
    San Diego Magazine, 40:34+, Aug. 1988
    TheaterWeek, 2:5–6, 3 Oct. 1988
    Time, 132:85, 31 Oct. 1988
    Time, 133:102, 2 Jan. 1989
    Village Voice, 33:99, 8 Nov. 1988

The Dining Room, 1982
    Cohen, E. M., *Working on a New Play,* pp. 3, 12–14, 20–24, 27, 50–51, 63,
        68–70, 76, 104, 116–118, 122, 132–133, 162–163, 178, 185–187, 189, 192,
        197, 198, 199–200

Love Letters, 1989
    Helbing, T., "To Whom It May Concern," *TheaterWeek,* 3:41, 2 Oct. 1989
    Marowitz, C., "Turgenev in Buffalo: *Love Letters* and *The Cocktail Party,*"
        TheaterWeek, 3:15–16, 11 June 1990
    Morehouse, R., "*Love Letters,*" *Playbill,* 8:8, 10, 12, 31 Jan. 1990
    American Theatre, 6:41, June 1989
    Georgia Review, 43:578–579, Fall 1989

New York, 22:64, 18 Sept. 1989
Playbill, 7:16, 30 June 1989
Playbill, 8:85, 31 Oct. 1989
TheaterWeek, 2:3, 17 Apr. 1989
TheaterWeek, 2:8, 17 Apr. 1989
TheaterWeek, 3:10, 20 Nov. 1989
TheaterWeek, 3:8, 11 June 1990
TheaterWeek, 3:12, 2 July 1990
TheaterWeek, 3:24, 30 July 1990
TheaterWeek, 4:10, 10 Dec. 1990
Time, 134:78, 11 Sept. 1989
Time, 135:100, 1 Jan. 1990
Village Voice, 34:89–90, 12 Sept. 1989
Village Voice, 34:90, 12 Sept. 1989 (excerpt of play)

The Perfect Party, 1986
   San Diego Magazine, 41:46 + , Apr. 1989

Show Me the Way to Go Home, 1988
   TheaterWeek, 1:4, 2 May 1988

The Snow Ball, to be produced in 1991
   Playbill, 9:30, 31 Oct. 1990
   TheaterWeek, 4:6, 1 Oct. 1990

Sweet Sue, 1987
   Village Voice, 32:88, 3 Feb. 1987

ALBERT HACKETT
SEE FRANCES GOODRICH and ALBERT HACKETT

JAMES H. HACKETT
SEE HENRY J. FINN and JAMES H. HACKETT

JEFFREY HADDOW
SEE JOHN DRIVER and JEFFREY HADDOW

JENNIFER HADLEY, MICHAEL HADLEY, and
THEODORE ROSENGARTEN

All God's Dangers (based on a book by Rosengarten, *All God's Dangers: The Life of Nate Shaw*), 1989
   Ledford, L., "The Life of a Sharecropper," *TheaterWeek,* 3:27–30, 30 Oct. 1989
   American Theatre, 6:7–8, June 1989
   American Theatre, 6:9, Sept. 1989
   New Yorker, 65:110, 30 Oct. 1989
   TheaterWeek, 3:43, 6 Nov. 1989

JEFF HAGEDORN

TheaterWeek, 2:5, 5 Sept. 1988

JESSICA HAGEDORN

Berson, M., "Between Worlds," *American Theatre*, 6:20–25, Mar. 1990 (based on her Introduction to *Between Worlds*)

Evangelista, S., "Jessica Hagedorn: Pinay Poet," *Philippine Studies*, 35(4):475–487, 1987

Tenement Lover: no palm trees / in new york city (expansion of her song "Tenement Lover"), 1981
    Berson, M., ed., *Between Worlds*, pp. ix–xiv (Introduction), 75–80, 81–90 (text of performance piece)

ALSO SEE LAURIE CARLOS, JESSICA HAGEDORN, and ROBBIE McCAULEY

ALBERT HAGUE
SEE HY KRAFT, ALBERT HAGUE, and MARTY BRILL

ELIZABETH FORSYTHE HAILEY

A Woman of Independent Means (based on her novel), 1984
    Gillenwater, S. K., "Grand Dame at the Deane," *San Diego Magazine*, 39:42, June 1987

OLIVER HAILEY

Father's Day, 1970
    Leonard, W. T., *Once Was Enough*, pp. 47–49

ADRIAN HALL

Coe, R., "The Once and Future Trinity," *American Theatre*, 7:12–21, 59–63, June 1990

"'Juggling Act' Ends as Dallas Ousts Adrian Hall," *American Theatre*, 6:48–49, July/Aug. 1989

Hope of the Heart (dramatization of the fourth chapter of R. P. Warren's novel *All the King's Men*, originally titled *Prologue to All the King's Men*), 1990
    American Theatre, 7:14–15, Oct. 1990

CAROL HALL
SEE LARRY L. KING and CAROL HALL
AND LARRY L. KING, PETER MASTERSON, and CAROL HALL

HOLWORTHY HALL and ROBERT MIDDLEMASS

The Valiant, 1920
    Counts, M. L., *Coming Home*, pp. 61, 117, 206

JOHN T. HALL

Dash, 1988
  TheaterWeek, 1:7, 23 May 1988

VICKI HALL

Ominous Operation, 1971
  Forte, J., "Women's Performance Art: Feminism and Postmodernism,"
  pp. 251–269 in S.-E. Case, ed., *Performing Feminisms* (rpt. of *Theatre
  Journal,* 40(2):217–235, May 1988)

ANDY HALLIDAY

Sex Slaves of the Lost Kingdom, 1988
  TheaterWeek, 1:58, 18 July 1988

THOMAS HALL-ROGERS

Altars of Steel, 1937
  Kazacoff, G., *Dangerous Theatre,* pp. 196–200

OSCAR SAUL HALPERN and HOFFMAN R. HAYS

Medicine Show, 1940
  Duffy, S., and B. K. Duffy, "Theatrical Responses to Technology during
  the Depression: Three Federal Theatre Project Plays," *Theatre History
  Studies,* 6:142–164, 1986

FRANCIS HAMIT

Marlowe: An Elizabethan Tragedy (about Christopher Marlowe), 1988
  TheaterWeek, 1:4, 11 Apr. 1988

MARVIN HAMLISCH
SEE JAMES KIRKWOOD, NICOLAS DANTE, MARVIN HAMLISCH, and EDWARD KLEBAN

OSCAR HAMMERSTEIN II

Chapin, T. S., comp. and pref., *Rodgers and Hammerstein Rediscovered*
Filichia, P., "Rodgers and Hammerstein: Many a New Day Will Dawn,"
  TheaterWeek, 2:20–28, 3 Oct. 1988
Hirsch, F., *Harold Prince and the American Musical Theater,* pp. 10, 18, 19–21,
  74
Mates, J., *America's Musical Stage,* pp. 36, 121, 162, 184, 189–190, 192, 193,
  197
Woll, A., *Black Musical Theatre,* pp. 164, 184, 186, 188–189, 193, 195, 244
American Heritage, 41:20+, Sept./Oct. 1990

OSCAR HAMMERSTEIN II, BENJAMIN F. GLAZER, and RICHARD RODGERS

Carousel (musical version of F. Molnar's *Liliom*), 1945
  Green, S., *Broadway Musicals,* p. 127

OSCAR HAMMERSTEIN II and JEROME KERN

Show Boat (musical version of E. Ferber's novel), 1927
  Green, S., *Broadway Musicals,* pp. 60–61, 128
  Korte, S., "*Show Boat* Just Keeps Rolling Along," *TheaterWeek,* 2:34–39, 12 Sept. 1988
  Kreuger, M., Show Boat: *The Story of a Classic American Musical*
  Mandelbaum, K., "*Show Boat*: Complete, Unexpurgated, Nothing Left Out," *TheaterWeek,* 2:56–60, 31 Oct. 1988
  Mordden, E., "A Critic at Large: *Show Boat* Crosses Over," *New Yorker,* 65:79–94, 3 July 1989
  Walsh, M., "Here Comes the Show Boat!" *Time,* 132:114, 7 Nov. 1988
  New Jersey Monthly, 14:21, Oct. 1989
  Playbill, 8:70, 31 Oct. 1989
  Playbill, 9:73, 31 Oct. 1990

OSCAR HAMMERSTEIN II, JOSHUA LOGAN, and RICHARD RODGERS

South Pacific (musical version of J. A. Michener's *Tales of the South Pacific*), 1949
Green, S., *Broadway Musicals,* pp. 142–143
McGhee, P. O., "*South Pacific* Revisited: Were We Carefully Taught or Reinforced?" *Journal of Ethnic Studies,* 15(4):125–130, Winter 1988
Playbill, 6:73, Apr. 1988
TheaterWeek, 2:58, 26 Sept. 1988

OSCAR HAMMERSTEIN II and RICHARD RODGERS

The King and I (musical version of M. Landon's novel *Anna and the King of Siam*), 1951
  Brynner, R., "Broadway King," *Playbill,* 8:S1–S16, 30 June 1990 (excerpt from Brynner's *Yul*)
  Filichia, P., "Pacific Overtures," *TheaterWeek,* 3:33–35, 21 Aug. 1989
  Green, S., *Broadway Musicals,* pp. 150–151, 248
  Detroit Monthly, 14:31, Jan. 1990
  TheaterWeek, 1:40, 28 Mar. 1988
  TheaterWeek, 3:10, 2 Oct. 1989
  Village Voice, 34:53, 24 Oct. 1989

Oklahoma! (musical version of L. Riggs's play *Green Grow the Lilacs*), 1943
  Donovan, T. P., "Oh, What a Beautiful Mornin': The Musical *Oklahoma!* and the Popular Mind in 1943," *Journal of Popular Culture,* 8:477–488, Winter 1974
  Green, S., *Broadway Musicals,* pp. 118–119, 255
  TheaterWeek, 1:40, 28 Mar. 1988

ALSO SEE HOWARD LINDSAY, RUSSEL CROUSE,
OSCAR HAMMERSTEIN II, and RICHARD RODGERS

WENDY HAMMOND

The Ghostman, 1990
  TheaterWeek, 3:8, 29 Jan. 1990
  Village Voice, 35:106, 22 May 1990

Jersey City, 1990
  New York, 23:53–54, 23 July 1990
  Playbill, 8:29, 31 July 1990
  TheaterWeek, 3:43, 23 July 1990

C. W. HANCOCK

Down on the Farm, 1906
  Harap, L., *Dramatic Encounters,* p. 74

BERNARD HANIGHEN
SEE SIDNEY HOWARD, WILL IRWIN, RAYMOND SCOTT,
and BERNARD HANIGHEN

WILLIAM HANLEY

Mrs. Dally Has a Lover, 1962 (revised 1988)
  TheaterWeek, 1:4, 16 May 1988

LORRAINE HANSBERRY

Ashley, L. R. N., "Lorraine Hansberry and the Great Black Way," pp. 151–160
  in J. Schlueter, ed., *Modern American Drama*
Brown-Guillory, E., "Alice Childress, Lorraine Hansberry, Ntozake Shange,"
  pp. 25–49 in Brown-Guillory's *Their Place on the Stage*
———, "The African Continuum: The Progeny in the New World," pp. 135–
  150 in Brown-Guillory's *Their Place on the Stage*
Dedmond, F., "Lorraine Hansberry (19 May 1930–12 January 1965)," pp. 155–
  168 in P. C. Kolin, ed., *American Playwrights since 1945*
Friedman, S., "Lorraine Hansberry 1930–1965," pp. 69–89 in M. C. Roudané,
  ed., *Contemporary Authors Bibliographical Series*
Fuchs, E. "Rethinking Lorraine Hansberry," *Village Voice,* 33:93+, 15 Mar.
  1988
Harap, L., *Dramatic Encounters,* pp. 7–8
Keyssar, H., "Foothills: Precursors of Feminist Drama," pp. 22–52 in Keyssar's
  Feminist Theatre
Miller, J.-M. A., "Black Women in Plays by Black Playwrights," pp. 256–262
  in H. K. Chinoy and L. W. Jenkins, eds., *Women in American Theatre,* rev.
  and enl. ed. (pp. 254–260 in 1981 ed.)
———, "Lorraine Hansberry: Feminist, Realist," *Theatre News,* 12(7): 2, Apr.
  1980 (correction of entry in Suppl. I to 2nd Ed.)

Wilkerson, M. "Lorraine Hansberry: Artist, Activist, Feminist," pp. 180–185 in H. K. Chinoy and L. W. Jenkins, eds., *Women in American Theatre,* rev. and enl. ed. (new to this ed.)

Wilkerson, M. B., "Music as Metaphor: New Plays of Black Women," pp. 61–75 in L. Hart, ed., *Making a Spectacle*

————, "The Dark Vision of Lorraine Hansberry: Excerpts from a Literary Biography," *Massachusetts Review,* 28(4):642–650, Winter 1987

Woll, A., *Black Musical Theatre,* pp. 229, 251, 261–262

Les Blancs, 1970
> *American Theatre,* 5:5–6, Apr. 1988
> *Village Voice,* 32:94+, 2 June 1987
> *Village Voice,* 33:93+, 15 Mar. 1988

The Drinking Gourd, written 1960
> Brown-Guillory, E., "Black Women Playwrights: Exorcising Myths," *Phylon,* 48(3):229–239, Fall 1987
>> ————, "Lorraine Hansberry: The Politics of the Politics Surrounding *The Drinking Gourd,*" *Griot,* 4(1–2):18–28, Winter-Summer 1985

A Raisin in the Sun, 1959
> Barthelemy, A., "Mother, Sister, Wife: A Dramatic Perspective," *Southern Review,* 21(3):770–789, 1985
> Berrian, B., "The Afro-American-West African Marriage Question: Its Literary and Historical Contexts," *African Literature Today,* 15:152–159, 1987
> Cook, W., "Mom, Dad and God: Values in Black Theater," pp. 168–184 in E. Hill, ed., *The Theater of Black Americans,* Vol. 1 of two vols. rptd. as one in 1987; same pagination in both eds.
> Euba, F., *Archetypes, Imprecators, and Victims of Fate,* pp. 142–143
> Keyssar, H., "Rites and Responsibilities: The Drama of Black American Women," pp. 226–240 in E. Brater, ed., *Feminine Focus*
> Washington, J. C., "*A Raisin in the Sun* Revisited," *Black American Literature Forum,* 22(1):109–124, Spring 1988
> Wilkerson, M. B., "*A Raisin in the Sun*: Anniversary of a Classic," pp. 119–130 in S.-E. Case, ed., *Performing Feminisms* (rpt. of *Theatre Journal,* 38(4):441–452, Dec. 1986)
> Wilt, J., "Black Maternity: 'A Need for Someone to Want the Black Baby to Live,'" pp. 132–166 in Wilt's *Abortion, Choice, and Contemporary Fiction*
> *American Theatre,* 5:37–38, Nov. 1988
> *TheaterWeek,* 1:39, 7 Mar. 1988

The Sign in Sidney Brustein's Window, 1964
> Carter, S. R. (and reply by H. MacLam), "Inter-Ethnic Issues in Lorraine Hansberry's *The Sign in Sidney Brustein's Window,*" *Explorations in Ethnic Studies,* 11(2):1–13, July 1988

Toussaint, an unfinished work, one scene of which was presented on NET in 1961 and an excerpt of which was published in 1986

Carter, S. R., "Lorraine Hansberry's *Toussaint*," *Black American Literature Forum*, 23(1):139–148, Spring 1989

WALDEMAR HANSEN

The Garden of Sweets, 1961
  Leonard, W. T., *Once Was Enough*, pp. 64–65

ISAAC HARBY

Grimsted, D., *Melodrama Unveiled*, pp. 100, 145, 151, 154n, 223

CHRIS HARDMAN

Etiquette of the Undercaste, 1989
  Mother Jones, 14:55, Apr. 1989

MARK HARELIK

Houston City Magazine, 11:76, Mar. 1987

The Immigrant: A Hamilton County Album, 1985
  TheaterWeek, 2:9, 16 Jan. 1989
  Village Voice, 34:79–80, 28 Feb. 1989

ROBERT HARLING

Steel Magnolias, 1987
  Helbing, T., "The Hair Doctor," *TheaterWeek*, 2:35–38, 24 Apr. 1989
  Hubbard, K., "Robert Harling, Author of a Hit Comedy Based on a Family Tragedy," *People Weekly*, 29:86+, 25 Jan. 1988
  Levy, L. M., "*Driving Miss Daisy* with Eddie Murphy and Bette Midler. . .?" *TheaterWeek*, 3:26–30, 4 Sept. 1989
  Chicago, 38:79–80, Feb. 1989
  Connoisseur, 219:24–25, Aug. 1989
  Playbill, 7:80, 31 May 1989
  TheaterWeek, 2:30, 17 Oct. 1988
  TheaterWeek, 2:37, 3 July 1989
  TheaterWeek, 3:6, 2 Oct. 1989
  Theatre Crafts, 24:58–61+, Feb. 1990
  Village Voice, 32:86–87, 7 Apr. 1987

SHELDON HARNICK

TheaterWeek, 1:60, 25 Apr. 1988
TheaterWeek, 2:34, 27 Feb. 1989

ALSO SEE JOSEPH STEIN, JERRY BOCK, and SHELDON HARNICK

LESLIE HARRELL

Death Quilt, staged reading in 1989
  Bannon, B. M., "Letter from Sundance," *TheaterWeek,* 3:15–16, 18 Sept.
  1989

EDWARD HARRIGAN

The Leather Patch, 1886
  Harap, L., *The Image of the Jew in American Literature,* p. 223

Mordecai Lyons, 1882
  Harap, L., *The Image of the Jew in American Literature,* pp. 223–224

The Mulligan Guard Ball, 1879
  Harap, L., *The Image of the Jew in American Literature,* p. 223

BILL HARRIS

Coda, 1990
  TheaterWeek, 3:10, 14 May 1990

CHRISTOPHER HARRIS

The Pixie Led (loosely based on N. Gogol's stories "Diary of a Madman" and
  "The Nose"), 1989
  Coen, S., "A Lead Balloon," *TheaterWeek,* 2:41, 7 Aug. 1989
  TheaterWeek, 2:6, 24 July 1989

PAUL CARTER HARRISON

Brown-Guillory, E., *Their Place on the Stage,* pp. 1, 140–141
Harrison, P. C., "Black Theatre in the African Continuum: Word/Song as
  Method," Introduction in Harrison, ed., *Totem Voices*
———, "The (R)evolution of Black Theatre," *American Theatre,* 6:30–32, 116–
118, Oct. 1989

PAUL CARTER HARRISON and JULIUS HEMPHILL

Anchorman, 1988
  TheaterWeek, 1:33, 15 Feb. 1988

PAUL CARTER HARRISON and COLERIDGE-TAYLOR PERKINSON

The Great MacDaddy, 1974
  Elder, A. A., "Paul Carter Harrison and Amos Tutuola: The Vitality of
    the African Continuum," *World Literature Written in English,* 28(2):171–
    178, Autumn 1988

JOE HART

The People Who Could Fly, 1990
    TheaterWeek, 4:9, 24 Dec. 1990

LORENZ HART

TheaterWeek, 1:57, 2 May 1988

ALSO SEE GEORGE ABBOTT, RICHARD RODGERS, and
LORENZ HART

MOSS HART

Light Up the Sky, 1948
    New York, 23:51, 3 Sept. 1990
    New Yorker, 66:91–92, 17 Sept. 1990
    TheaterWeek, 4:43, 10 Sept. 1990

MOSS HART and GEORGE S. KAUFMAN

The Fabulous Invalid, 1938
    Playbill, 8:60, 31 May 1990

George Washington Slept Here, 1940
    Shirakawa, S. H., "A Non-Traditional *George Washington," TheaterWeek,*
    1:52–55, 1 Aug. 1988
    Playbill, 8:29, 31 Jan. 1990

The Man Who Came to Dinner, 1939
    Playbill, 7:30, 30 Nov. 1988

Once in a Lifetime, 1930
    American Theatre, 5:6, July/Aug. 1988
    San Diego Magazine, 40:48 + , July 1988
    Journal of Canadian Studies, 23:126, Winter 1988/1989

ALSO SEE GEORGE S. KAUFMAN and MOSS HART

STANLEY HART

Some of My Best Friends, 1977
    Ilson, C., *Harold Prince,* pp. 245–248

LINDA HARTINIAN

Flow My Tears, the Policeman Said (dramatization of novel by P. K. Dick), 1985
    Village Voice, 33:122, 28 June 1988

JAN HARTMAN

K: The Mind and Imagination of Franz Kafka, 1988
    Village Voice, 33:100 + , 9 Feb. 1988

JANET HARTMANN
SEE HALLIE FLANAGAN and JANET HARTMANN

M. M. A. HARTNEDY

Christopher Columbus, 1892
    Jones, E. H., *Native Americans as Shown on the Stage,* pp. 136–137

MILO HASTINGS
SEE ORRIE LASHIN and MILO HASTINGS

NANCY HASTY

Florida Girls, 1990
    Loyd, B., "Florida Women: Playwright/Performer Nancy Hasty Stakes out
        Her Turf," *TheaterWeek,* 4:36–38, 24 Sept. 1990
    TheaterWeek, 3:40–41, 25 June 1990

JEFFREY HATCHER

Neddy, 1987
    TheaterWeek, 3:41–42, 16 Apr. 1990

WILLIAM HAUPTMAN

Gillette, 1986 (revision of his 1985 play)
    American Theatre, 4:8, Feb. 1988

WILLIAM HAUPTMAN and ROGER MILLER

Big River (musical version of M. Twain's *The Adventures of Huckleberry Finn*),
    1984
    Green, S., *Broadway Musicals,* p. 270
    TheaterWeek, 2:4, 26 Sept. 1988
    Time, 135:100, 1 Jan. 1990

DOUG HAVERTY

Aftershocks, 1989
    American Theatre, 6:7–8, Apr. 1989

ALLAN HAVIS

A Daring Bride, 1990
    Playbill, 8:32, 31 Mar. 1990
    TheaterWeek, 3:6, 8 Jan. 1990

Hospitality, 1988
  Georgia Review, 42:595–596, Fall 1988

Morocco, 1985
  Hersh, A., "Caught in the Arabesque with Gordana Rashovich,"
    TheaterWeek, 1:40–44, 8 Aug. 1988
  TheaterWeek, 1:4, 25 July 1988
  Village Voice, 33:96, 19 July 1988

JUNE HAVOC

Marathon '33 (dramatization of her book *Early Havoc*), 1963
  Journal of Canadian Studies, 22:136–137, Winter 1987/1988

EDGAR HAYES

Rhapsody in Two Flats, 1937
  Kazacoff, G., *Dangerous Theatre,* p. 193

LYNN HAYES

Playground, 1989
  Village Voice, 34:98+, 13 June 1989

HOFFMAN R. HAYS

The Ballad of Davy Crockett, 1936
  Kazacoff, G., *Dangerous Theatre,* pp. 162–164

ALSO SEE OSCAR SAUL HALPERN and HOFFMAN R. HAYS

JOHN E. HAZARD
SEE WINCHELL SMITH and JOHN E. HAZARD

BEN HECHT

A Jew in Love, 1931
  Harap, L., *Dramatic Encounters,* p. 119

BEN HECHT and GENE FOWLER

The Great Magoo, 1932
  Harap, L., *Dramatic Encounters,* p. 119

BEN HECHT and CHARLES MacARTHUR

The Front Page, 1928
  Harap, L., *Dramatic Encounters,* p. 119
  American Theatre, 5:52, Jan. 1989
  TheaterWeek, 2:6, 5 Dec. 1988

ROGER HEDDEN

Bodies, Rest, and Motion, 1986
  Village Voice, 31:125–126, 23 Dec. 1986

PETER HEDGES

Imagining Brad (two "playlets": *The Valerie of Now* and *Imagining Brad*), 1990
  Popkin, H., "A Perfect Man," *TheaterWeek,* 3:43, 19 Feb. 1990
  New York, 23:62+, 19 Feb. 1990
  New Yorker, 66:99, 26 Feb. 1990
  TheaterWeek, 3:7–8, 29 Jan. 1990
  Village Voice, 35:107, 20 Feb. 1990

KEVIN HEELAN

Right behind the Flag, 1988
  Barbour, D., "The Actor as Daredevil: Kevin Spacey," *TheaterWeek,* 1:32–38, 27 June 1988
  New Yorker, 64:60, 4 July 1988
  Village Voice, 33:88, 5 July 1988

FORBES HEERMANS

Down the Black Canyon, 1890
  Harap, L., *The Image of the Jew in American Literature,* p. 227

JOSEPH HELLER

Moyers, B., *Bill Moyers' World of Ideas,* ed. B. S. Flowers, pp. 28–38 (interview on PBS 1988)

LILLIAN HELLMAN

Barranger, M. S., "Lillian Hellman: Standing in the Minefields," *New Orleans Review,* 15(1):62–68, Spring 1988
Brustein, R., "Lillian Hellman: Epilogue to Anger," pp. 43–47 in Brustein's *Who Needs Theatre*
Ervin, P. T., "Lillian Hellman: Light on A Dark Road," *Chu-Shikoku Studies in American Literature,* 24:59–65, June 1988
———, "Lillian Hellman: The Finished Woman," *Chu-Shikoku Studies in American Literature,* 22:98–109, June 1986
Estrin, M. W., ed., *Critical Essays on Lillian Hellman*
Feibleman, P. S., *Lilly*
Goodman, C., "The Fox's Cubs: Lillian Hellman, Arthur Miller, and Tennessee Williams," pp. 130–142 in J. Schlueter, ed., *Modern American Drama*
Griffin, J., "Hellman, Williams, Hemingway and Cowley: Views and Interviews," *Canadian Review of American Studies,* 18(4):519–525, Winter 1987
Harap, L., *Dramatic Encounters,* pp. 98–99
Hirsch, F., *Harold Prince and the American Musical Theater,* pp. 147–149

Holditch, W. K., "Another Part of the Country: Lillian Hellman as Southern Playwright," *Southern Quarterly,* 25(3):11–35, Spring 1987
Johnson, D. (tr. Carlos Losilla), "Hammett: Una biografía difícil," *Quimera,* 50:38–45, n.d.
Johnson, P., "Lies Damned Lies and Lillian Hellman," pp. 288–305 in Johnson's *Intellectuals*
Kazan, E., *Elia Kazan,* pp. 136, 294, 319, 324–325, 382–383, 441–442, 472, 592
Keyssar, H., "Foothills: Precursors of Feminist Drama," pp. 22–52 in Keyssar's *Feminist Theatre*
Lederer, K., *Lillian Hellman*
"Lillian Hellman Talks about Women," pp. 174–180 in H. K. Chinoy and L. W. Jenkins, eds., *Women in American Theatre,* rev. and enl. ed. (new to this ed.; portions of interviews taken from Jackson R. Bryer, ed., *Conversations with Lillian Hellman,* Jackson: Univ. Pr. of Mississippi, 1986)
Newman, R. P., *The Cold War Romance of Lillian Hellman and John Melby*
Norman, M., "So Much Rage," *American Theatre,* 5:17–18, Jan. 1989
Rollyson, C., Jr., *Lillian Hellman*
Schneiderman, L., "Lillian Hellman: The Uses of Rage," *American Journal of Psychoanalysis,* 47(1):72, 1987
Wright, W., *Lillian Hellman*
Andy Warhol's Interview, 18:72–77, July 1988

Another Part of the Forest, 1946
Austin, G., *Feminist Theories for Dramatic Criticism,* pp. 51–55
————, "The Exchange of Women and Male Homosocial Desire in Arthur Miller's *Death of a Salesman* and Lillian Hellman's *Another Part of the Forest,*" pp. 59–66 in J. Schlueter, ed., *Feminist Rereadings of Modern American Drama*

The Children's Hour, 1934
Curtin, K., "A Most Revolutionary Play and a Commissioner of Licenses on the Prowl," pp. 191–209 in Curtin's *"We Can Always Call Them Bulgarians";* also see pp. 295–297 and elsewhere
Dolan, J., " 'Lesbian' Subjectivism in Realism: Dragging at the Margins of Structure and Ideology," pp. 40–53 in S.-E. Case, ed., *Performing Feminisms*
Hart, L., "Canonizing Lesbians?" pp. 275–292 in J. Schlueter, ed., *Modern American Drama*

The Lark (adaptation of J. Anouilh's Play *L'Alouette*), 1955
Playbill, 7:30, 30 June 1989
TheaterWeek, 2:6, 29 May 1989

The Little Foxes, 1939
Feibleman, P., "Lilly and Liz," *Playbill,* 7:n. pag., 28 Feb. 1989 (excerpt from Feibleman's *Lilly*)
D Magazine, 15:15, Mar. 1988

The Searching Wind, 1944
Counts, M. L., *Coming Home,* pp. 94, 110, 130–132, 199

Watch on the Rhine, 1941
> Patraka, V. M., "Lillian Hellman's *Watch on the Rhine*: Realism, Gender, and Historical Crisis," *Modern Drama,* 32(1):128–145, Mar. 1989

JESSE HELMS

Jesse Helms Speaks (Helms's own words taken from the *Congressional Record*; presented with Larry Kramer's *Reports from the Holocaust,* which see, under the title *Indecent Materials*), 1990
> *Playbill,* 9:34, 31 Oct. 1990
> *TheaterWeek,* 4:15, 3 Sept. 1990
> *TheaterWeek,* 4:44, 10 Sept. 1990

ERNEST HEMINGWAY

Dardis, T., "Hemingway: 'I'm No Rummy,'" pp. 155–209 in Dardis's *The Thirsty Muse*

Goodwin, D. W., "Hemingway: Scenes from New York and Havana," pp. 50–02 in Goodwin's *Alcohol and the Writer*

Griffin, J., "Hellman, Williams, Hemingway and Cowley: Views and Interviews," *Canadian Review of American Studies,* 18(4):519–525, Winter 1987

The Fifth Column, 1940 (revised 1990 by A. E. Hotchner)
> Conlon, R., "*The Fifth Column*: A Political Morality Play," *Hemingway Review,* 6(2):11–16, Spring 1987
> *Playbill,* 9:48, 31 Dec. 1990

HILARY HEMINGWAY

South Florida, 39:26–27, Sept. 1987

JULIUS HEMPHILL
SEE PAUL CARTER HARRISON and JULIUS HEMPHILL

WELLAND HENDRICKS

Pocahontas, published 1886
> Jones, E. H., *Native Americans as Shown on the Stage,* pp. 138–140

BETH HENLEY

Betsko, K., and R. Koenig, *Interviews with Contemporary Women Playwrights,* pp. 211–222

Guerra, J., "Beth Henley: Female Quest and the Family-Play Tradition," pp. 118–130 in L. Hart, ed., *Making a Spectacle*

Harbin, B. J., "Familial Bonds in the Plays of Beth Henley," *Southern Quarterly,* 25(3):81–94, Spring 1987

Jaehne, K., "Beth's Beauties," *Film Comment,* 25:9–12 + , May/June 1989

Kullman, C. H., and M. Neuringer, "Beth Henley (8 May 1952–)," pp. 169–178 in P. C. Kolin, ed., *American Playwrights since 1945*

McDonnell, L. J., "Beth Henley 1952– ," pp. 91–107 in M. C. Roudané, ed., *Contemporary Authors Bibliographical Series*

———, "Diverse Similitude: Beth Henley and Marsha Norman," *Southern Quarterly,* 25(3):95–104, Spring 1987

Elle, 4:100+, Apr. 1989

Savvy Woman, 8:66–67, Jan. 1987

Abundance, 1989

Buckley, M., "Mail-Order Brides," *TheaterWeek,* 4:24–26, 5 Nov. 1990

America, 163:453–454, 8 Dec. 1990

American Theatre, 6:11, Apr. 1989

New Republic, 203:28–29, 17 Dec. 1990

New York, 23:92–93, 12 Nov. 1990

New Yorker, 66:105–106, 12 Nov. 1990

Playbill, 8:30, 31 July 1990

Playbill, 9:33, 31 Oct. 1990

TheaterWeek, 4:9, 13 Aug. 1990

TheaterWeek, 4:8, 1 Oct. 1990

TheaterWeek, 4:40–41, 12 Nov. 1990

Time, 133:73, 12 June 1989

Crimes of the Heart, 1979

Demastes, W. W., "New Voices Using New Realism: Fuller, Henley, and Norman," pp. 125–154 in Demastes's *Beyond Naturalism* (the part of the chapter dealing with this play is titled "Beth Henley and *Crimes of the Heart*," pp. 136–144)

Dolan, J., "Bending Gender to Fit the Canon: The Politics of Production," pp. 318–344 in L. Hart, ed., *Making a Spectacle*

———, *The Feminist Spectator as Critic,* pp. 25–26, 35

Gagen, J., "'Most Resembling Unlikeness, and Most Unlike Resemblances': Beth Henley's *Crimes of the Heart* and Chekhov's *Three Sisters*," *Studies in American Drama, 1945–Present,* 4:119–128, 1989

Karpinski, J. B., "The Ghosts of Chekhov's *Three Sisters* Haunt Beth Henley's *Crimes of the Heart,*" pp. 229–245 in J. Schlueter, ed., *Modern American Drama*

Keyssar, H., "Success and Its Limits: Mary O'Malley, Wendy Wasserstein, Nell Dunn, Beth Henley, Catherine Hayes, Marsha Norman," pp. 148–166 in Keyssar's *Feminist Theatre*

Laughlin, K. L., "Criminality, Desire, and Community: A Feminist Approach to Beth Henley's *Crimes of the Heart,*" *Women & Performance,* 3(1[5]):35–51, 1986

Morrow, L., "Orality and Identity in *'night, Mother* and *Crimes of the Heart,*" *Studies in American Drama, 1945–Present,* 3:23–39, 1988

Nelson, T. G. A., *Comedy,* pp. 12–13

Nischik, R. M., "'Look Back in Gender': Beziehungskonstellationen in Dramen von Beth Henley und Marsha Norman—einige Grundzüge des zeitgenössischen feministischen Theaters in den USA," *Anglistik & Englischunterricht,* 35:61–89, 1988

Porter, L. R., "Women Re-Conceived: Changing Perceptions of Women in

Contemporary American Drama," *Conference of College Teachers of English Studies,* 54:53–59, Sept. 1989
TheaterWeek, 1:4, 8 Aug. 1988

The Lucky Spot, 1987
Village Voice, 32:99+, 12 May 1987

The Miss Firecracker Contest, 1982
Levy, L. M., *"Driving Miss Daisy* with Eddie Murphy and Bette Midler . . .?"* TheaterWeek, 3:26–30, 4 Sept. 1989

CAROLINE LEE HENTZ

Lamorah; or, The Western Wild, 1832
Jones, E. H., *Native Americans as Shown on the Stage,* p. 50

F. HUGH HERBERT

The Moon Is Blue, 1951
TheaterWeek, 1:38, 7 Mar. 1988

JOHN HERBERT (John Herbert Brundage)

Fortune and Men's Eyes, 1967
Village Voice, 32:104, 10 Nov. 1987

JERRY HERMAN

Filichia, P., "Hello, Jerry!" *TheaterWeek,* 3:35–37, 30 Oct. 1989
Playbill, 6:71, June 1988
Playbill, 6:12, 30 Sept. 1988

ALSO SEE HARVEY FIERSTEIN and JERRY HERMAN
AND JEROME LAWRENCE, ROBERT E. LEE, and JERRY HERMAN
AND MICHAEL STEWART, MARK BRAMBLE, and JERRY HERMAN
AND MICHAEL STEWART and JERRY HERMAN

ALFONSO HERNÁNDEZ

The False Advent of Mary's Child, 1979
Miguelez, A., "Aproximaciones al nuevo teatro chicano de autor único," *Explicación de Textos Literarios,* 15(2):8–18, 1986–1987

JAMES A. HERNE

Demastes, W. W., *Beyond Naturalism,* pp. 18–19
Murphy, B., *"Beyond the Horison*'s Narrative Sentence: An American Intertext for O'Neill," *Theatre Annual,* 41:49–62, 1986

Margaret Fleming, 1891
Stephens, J. L., "Gender Ideology and Dramatic Convention in Progressive

Era Plays, 1890–1920," pp. 283–293 in S.-E. Case, ed., *Performing Feminisms* (rpt. of *Theatre Journal*, 41(1):45–55, Mar. 1989)

The Minute Men of 1774–1775, 1886
Jones, E. H., *Native Americans as Shown on the Stage,* pp. 143–144

The Reverend Griffith Davenport (dramatization of novel by H. Gardner, *An Unofficial Patriot*), 1899
Rainey, K. T., "Race and Reunion in Nineteenth-Century Reconciliation Drama," *American Transcendental Quarterly,* 2(2):155–169, June 1988

Sag Harbor, 1899
Stephens, J. L., "Gender Ideology and Dramatic Convention in Progressive Era Plays, 1890–1920," pp. 283–293 in S.-E. Case, ed., *Performing Feminisms* (rpt. of *Theatre Journal,* 41(1):45–55, Mar. 1989)

ELIZABETH HERRING

Dodger Blue, 1988
TheaterWeek, 2:5, 19 Sept. 1988

LEE HEUERMANN

Lutenbacher, C., "'So Much More Than Just Myself': Women Theatre Artists in the South," pp. 380–382 in H. K. Chinoy and L. W. Jenkins, eds., *Women in American Theatre,* rev. and enl. ed. (new to this ed.; excerpted from a paper Lutenbacher presented at the 1987 Themes in Drama Conference in Riverside, CA, later printed in J. Redmond, ed., *Women in Theatre,* pp. 253–263)

JOHN HILL HEWITT

Watson, C. S., "Confederate Drama: The Plays of John Hill Hewitt and James Dabney McCabe," *Southern Literary Journal,* 22[21]:100–112, Spring 1989

DOROTHY HEYWARD

Woll, A., *Black Musical Theatre,* pp. 154, 160, 162, 164–165, 172, 195

DOROTHY HEYWARD and DuBOSE HEYWARD

Porgy (their dramatization of his novel), 1927
Woll, A., *Black Musical Theatre,* pp. 139, 160, 162–166, 171, 177, 194

DOROTHY HEYWARD, DuBOSE HEYWARD, GEORGE GERSHWIN, and IRA GERSHWIN

Porgy and Bess (musical version of the Heywards' *Porgy*), 1935
Alpert, H., *The Life and Times of* Porgy and Bess
Green, S., *Broadway Musicals,* pp. 90–91, 156

Hamm, C., "The Theatre Guild Production of *Porgy and Bess*," *Journal of the American Musicological Society,* 40:495–532, Fall 1987
Woll, A., *Black Musical Theatre,* pp. 31, 154, 160, 162, 165–175, 186, 189, 193–194, 199, 207, 233, 272
D Magazine, 14:16, May 1987

DuBOSE HEYWARD

Woll, A., *Black Musical Theatre,* pp. 139, 154, 160, 162, 164–165, 172, 195

DELIA A. HEYWOOD (Polly Ann Pritchard)

Kindness Softens Even Savage Hearts, published 1860
Jones, E. H., *Native Americans as Shown on the Stage,* pp. 88–89

HAROLD HICKERSON
SEE MAXWELL ANDERSON and HAROLD HICKERSON

GEORGE HIELGE

Montezuma; or, The Conquest of Mexico, 1846
Jones, E. H., *Native Americans as Shown on the Stage,* p. 37

TOMSON HIGHWAY

Carley, D., "A Canada Nobody Knows," *American Theatre,* 4:46–47, Feb. 1988

Dry Lips Oughta Move to Kapuskasing, 1989
Maclean's, 102:62, 8 May 1989

CHARLES BARTON HILL

Magnolia, 1862
Fletcher, W. L., "Who Put the 'Tragic' in the Tragic Mulatto?" pp. 262–268 in H. K. Chinoy and L. W. Jenkins, eds., *Women in American Theatre,* rev. and enl. ed. (pp. 260–266 in 1981 ed.)

DAVID J. HILL

A White Rose of Memphis, 1988
TheaterWeek, 1:4, 4 Apr. 1988

GARY LEON HILL

Soundbite, 1990
Coe, R. L., "A Quartet Debuts in Denver," *American Theatre,* 7:86, Oct. 1990

LESLIE PINCKNEY HILL

Toussaint L'Ouverture, 1928
    Ako, E. O., "Leslie Pinckney Hill's *Toussaint L'Ouverture,*" *Phylon,*
    48(3):190–195, Fall 1987

DAVID HIRSON

La Bête: A Comedy of Manners, 1990
    Playbill, 8:15, 31 Aug. 1990
    Playbill, 8:20, 30 Sept. 1990
    Playbill, 9:51, 31 Oct. 1990
    Playbill, 9:42, 30 Nov. 1990
    TheaterWeek, 4:8, 12 Nov. 1990

JANE STANTON HITCHCOCK

W, 19:19, 25 June 1990

New Listings (a one-act play presented with Carole Schweid's *On the Bench*
    under the collective title *The Bench*), 1990
    TheaterWeek, 3:8, 28 May 1990
    TheaterWeek, 3:42, 18 June 1990

PETER B. HODGES

White Collar, 1990
    TheaterWeek, 3:13, 30 Apr. 1990

A. S. HOFFMAN
SEE HARRY L. NEWTON and A. S. HOFFMAN

AARON HOFFMAN

Two Blocks Away, 1921
    Harap, L., *Dramatic Encounters,* p. 116

Welcome Stranger, 1920
    Harap, L., *Dramatic Encounters,* p. 116

WILLIAM HOFFMAN

As Is, 1985
    Cohen, E. M., *Working on a New Play,* pp. 197–198
    Gutwillig, S., "A Look Back in Anguish," *TheaterWeek,* 3:33–38, 25 Dec.
    1989
    Hall, R., "Eleven Different Directions," *American Theatre,* 5:32–33, Dec.
    1988
    Shewey, D., "Gay Theatre Grows Up," *American Theatre,* 5:10–17, 52–53,
    May 1988

San Diego Magazine, 41:46+, Apr. 1989
Village Voice, 32:99–100, 12 May 1987

JACK HOFSISS
SEE EVE MERRIAM, PAULA WAGNER, and JACK HOFSISS

JOAN HOLDEN

Gray, A., "The Big If," *American Theatre,* 6:18–21, 56, June 1989
Savran, D., "Joan Holden," pp. 100–116 in Savran's *In Their Own Words*
Van Erven, E., *Radical People's Theatre,* pp. 29, 32, 35–36, 42, 184, 185

The Independent Female; or, A Man Has His Pride, 1970
    Natalle, E. J., *Feminist Theatre,* pp. 77–80 and elsewhere

LAURENCE HOLDER

Phoenix, 22:68+, Feb. 1987

Zora Neale Hurston, 1979 (revised 1990)
    Jacobson, L., "The Mark of Zora," *American Theatre,* 7:24–30, July/Aug.
        1990
    American Theatre, 7:11, Apr. 1990
    Village Voice, 35:100, 13 Feb. 1990

ENDESHA IDA MAE HOLLAND

From the Mississippi Delta, 1987
    American Theatre, 6:11, Mar. 1990
    New Yorker, 64:89, 5 Sept. 1988
    TheaterWeek, 4:8–9, 10 Dec. 1990
    Village Voice, 32:104, 13 Oct. 1987

MARGARET HOLLINGSWORTH

Parker, D., "Alienation and Identity: The Plays of Margaret Hollingsworth,"
    Canadian Literature, 118:97–113, Autumn 1988
Saddlemyer, A., "Two Canadian Women Playwrights," pp. 251–256 in M. Jurak,
    ed., *Cross-Cultural Studies*

RUPERT HOLMES

Greene, A., "You've Gotta Have a Gimmick," *TheaterWeek,* 3:16–19, 30 Apr.
    1990
Playbill, 8:34, 30 Sept. 1990
TheaterWeek, 3:9, 30 July 1990

Accomplice, 1990
    Horwitz, S., "Beating the *Times,*" *TheaterWeek,* 3:17–21, 28 May 1990
    Sneerwell, R., "Murder, He Wrote," *TheaterWeek,* 3:39–40, 14 May 1990

America, 162:506, 19 May 1990
Nation, 250:834–835, 11 June 1990
New Yorker, 66:93, 14 May 1990
TheaterWeek, 3:20, 30 July 1990
Village Voice, 35:119, 15 May 1990

The Mystery of Edwin Drood (title later changed to *Drood: The Musical Hall Mystery*; musical based on a novel by C. Dickens), 1985
Brustein, R., "Droodling," pp. 179–182 in Brustein's *Who Needs Theatre* (rpt. of *New Republic,* 193:28–29, 14 Oct. 1985)
Godfrey, T., "Foul Play on Broadway," *Armchair Detective,* 21(1):5–14, Winter 1988
Green, S., *Broadway Musicals,* p. 271
America, 154:53, 25 Jan. 1986
American Theatre, 2:19–20, Oct. 1985
Dance Magazine, 60:78, Feb. 1986
Los Angeles, 31:40, Aug. 1986
New Leader, 68:18–19, 4–18 Nov. 1985
New York, 18:57–58, 2 Sept. 1985
New York, 18:100–101, 16 Dec. 1985
New York, 18:34, 23–30 Dec. 1985
New Yorker, 61:71, 2 Sept. 1985
New Yorker, 61:140, 16 Dec. 1985
Newsweek, 106:66, 2 Sept. 1985
Playbill, 6:74, June 1988
Plays and Players, 386:37–38, Nov. 1985
Theatre Crafts, 23:52–55 + , Apr. 1989
Time, 126:83, 16 Dec. 1985
Vanity Fair, 48:92–93, Aug. 1985
Village Voice, 30:79, 3 Sept. 1985
Village Voice, 30:122, 24 Dec. 1985
Vogue, 175:88, Dec. 1985

STEPHEN HOLT

The Casting of Kevin Christian, 1987
Village Voice, 32:105 + , 26 May 1987

WILL HOLT

A Walk on the Wild Side (musical version of novel by N. Algren), 1988
Stevens, R., "Walking the Wild Side," *TheaterWeek,* 2:42–47, 23 Jan. 1989
Los Angeles, 33:244 + , Oct. 1988
TheaterWeek, 2:9, 15 Aug. 1988

WILLY HOLTZMAN

Bovver Boys, 1987
American Theatre, 5:15, Mar. 1989
New Yorker, 66:4, 12 Mar. 1990

TheaterWeek, 3:14, 12 Feb. 1990
TheaterWeek, 3:42, 5 Mar. 1990
Village Voice, 32:87–88, 18 Aug. 1987

Inside Out, 1987
American Theatre, 5:15, Mar. 1989
American Theatre, 6:10, May 1989
Village Voice, 32:89–90, 21 July 1987

WILLY HOLTZMAN, SKIP KENNON, and MICHAEL KORIE

Blanco (adaptation of one-act play by G. B. Shaw, *The Shewing-Up of Blanco Posnet*), 1990
Playbill, 8:24, 31 Aug. 1990
Playbill, 9:34, 31 Oct. 1990

MARK HONEA

Atlanta, 27:18+, June 1987

AVERY HOPWOOD

Sharrar, J. F., *Avery Hopwood*

A. F. HORN

The Legend of Sharon Shashanovah, 1988
New York, 21:107–108, 17 Oct. 1988

CHARLES HORNER and HENRY MILES

Hook 'n Ladder, 1952
Leonard, W. T., *Once Was Enough,* pp. 84–85

ISRAEL HOROVITZ

Hartigan, P., "Horovitz's Life as a Town Bard," *American Theatre,* 6:58–59, Dec. 1989
Horovitz, I., "Never Goodbye: A Remembrance of Samuel Beckett," *TheaterWeek,* 3:17–19, 8 Jan. 1990
———, "The Legacy of O'Neill," *Eugene O'Neill Newsletter,* 11(1):3–10, Spring 1987
Jacobi, M. J., "Israel Horovitz (31 March 1939–)," pp. 179–189 in P. C. Kolin, ed., *American Playwrights since 1945*
Boston Magazine, 78:172+, Oct. 1986
Playbill, 7:39, 31 Mar. 1989

Faith (presented with T. McNally's *Hope* and L. Melfi's *Charity*), 1988
American Theatre, 5:48, Feb. 1989
TheaterWeek, 1:4–5, 8 Aug. 1988

TheaterWeek, 2:6, 5 Dec. 1988
Village Voice, 34:89–90, 3 Jan. 1989

Henry Lumpur (loosely based on Shakespeare's *Henry IV,* Parts One and Two),
    1989
    TheaterWeek, 2:6, 30 Jan. 1989

It's Called the Sugar Plum (presented with David Mamet's *The Frog Prince* under
    the collective title *Love in the Afternoon*), 1968
    TheaterWeek, 3:12, 5 Feb. 1990

Line, 1967
    Playbill, 6:55, June 1988

North Shore Fish, 1987
    TheaterWeek, 1:7, 22 Feb. 1988

Strong-Man's Weak Child, 1990
    American Theatre, 7:9, Sept. 1990
    Playbill, 8:32, 31 July 1990

The Widow's Blind Date, 1978
    Chansky, D., "Israel Horovitz's Memory Play," *TheaterWeek,* 3:24–26, 4
        Dec. 1989
    Nation, 249:766, 18 Dec. 1989
    New Yorker, 65:110, 20 Nov. 1989
    TheaterWeek, 3:5–6, 2 Oct. 1989
    Village Voice, 34:123, 21 Nov. 1989

JACK HORRIGAN

Children! Children!, 1972
    Leonard, W. T., *Once Was Enough,* pp. 31–32

MARTHA HORSTMAN

Junglebird, 1990
    TheaterWeek, 4:8, 3 Dec. 1990
    TheaterWeek, 4:35, 31 Dec. 1990

A. E. HOTCHNER
SEE ERNEST HEMINGWAY, the revision of his *The Fifth Column*

VELINA HOUSTON

Arnold, S., "Dissolving the Half Shadows: Japanese American Women Playwrights," pp. 181–194 in L. Hart, ed., *Making a Spectacle*

BRONSON HOWARD

Saratoga, 1870
>   Miller, T. L., "The Image of Fashionable Society in American Comedy, 1840–1870," pp. 243–252 in J. L. Fisher and S. Watt, eds., *When They Weren't Doing Shakespeare*

Shenandoah, 1887
>   Rainey, K. T., "Race and Reunion in Nineteenth-Century Reconciliation Drama," *American Transcendental Quarterly,* 2(2):155–169, June 1988

ELEANOR HARRIS HOWARD and HELEN McAVITY

Mating Dance, 1965
>   Leonard, W. T., *Once Was Enough,* pp. 116–118

SIDNEY HOWARD

Harap, L., *Dramatic Encounters,* pp. 107–108

Madam, Will You Walk?, 1939
>   Marcuson, L. R., *The Stage Immigrant,* pp. 52–57

They Knew What They Wanted, 1924
>   Marcuson, L. R., *The Stage Immigrant,* pp. 48–52
>   Stephens, J. L., "Women in Pulitzer Prize Plays, 1918–1949," pp. 245–253 in H. K. Chinoy and L. W. Jenkins, eds., *Women in American Theatre,* rev. and enl. ed. (pp. 243–251 in 1981 ed.)

SIDNEY HOWARD, WILL IRWIN, RAYMOND SCOTT, and BERNARD HANIGHEN

Lute Song (musical version of Howard and Irwin's play, an adaptation of *Pi-Pa-Chi* by Kao-Tsi-ch'ing), 1946
>   *American Theatre,* 6:9, Sept. 1989

WILLIE HOWARD
SEE FRITZ BLOCKI and WILLIE HOWARD

TONY HOWARTH

On the Move (three one-act plays), 1990
>   *TheaterWeek,* 3:11, 5 Mar. 1990

JULIA WARD HOWE

The World's Own, 1857
>   Harap, L., *The Image of the Jew in American Literature,* p. 211

TINA HOWE

Backes, N., "Body Art: Hunger and Satiation in the Plays of Tina Howe,"
pp. 41–60 in L. Hart, ed., *Making a Spectacle*
Barlow, J. E., "An Interview with Tina Howe," *Studies in American Drama,*
1945–Present, 4:159–175, 1989
——, "The Art of Tina Howe," pp. 241–254 in E. Brater, ed., *Feminine Focus*
Betsko, K., and R. Koenig, *Interviews with Contemporary Women Playwrights,*
pp. 223–235
Gray, A., "The Big If," *American Theatre,* 6:18–21, 56, June 1989
Russo, F., "Approaching Tina Howe," *TheaterWeek,* 2:26–30, 12 June 1989
American Theatre, 5:43–44, Nov. 1988
Art & Antiques, pp. 89–90, Jan. 1987
New York Woman, 3:100, June/July 1989
Playbill, 7:51, 28 Feb. 1989 (interview)
Vanity Fair, 52:112, May 1989

Approaching Zanzibar, 1989
   Russo, F., "Dance at a Deathbed," *TheaterWeek,* 2:40, 15 May 1989
   New York, 22:124, 15 May 1989
   New Yorker, 65:94, 15 May 1989
   TheaterWeek, 2:3, 1 May 1989
   Time, 133:87, 15 May 1989

The Art of Dining, 1979
   Moore, H., "Woman Alone, Women Together," pp. 186–191 in H. K. Chinoy and L. W. Jenkins, eds., *Women in American Theatre,* rev. and enl.
   ed. (pp. 184–190 in 1981 ed.)

Birth and After Birth, 1974
   Keyssar, H., "A Network of Playwrights," pp. 102–125 in Keyssar's *Feminist*
   Theatre

Coastal Disturbances, 1986
   Theatre Journal, 40:101–102, Mar. 1988
   Village Voice, 31:127–128, 2 Dec. 1986

GLEN HUGHES

Too Lucky, 1936
   Kazacoff, G., *Dangerous Theatre,* pp. 284–285

HATCHER HUGHES

Hell-Bent fer Heaven, 1924
   Counts, M. L., *Coming Home,* pp. 97–98, 128, 194, 199
   Stephens, J. L., "Women in Pulitzer Prize Plays, 1918–1949," pp. 245–253
   in H. K. Chinoy and L. W. Jenkins, eds., *Women in American Theatre,*
   rev. and enl. ed. (pp. 243–251 in 1981 ed.)

HOLLY HUGHES

Dolan, J., *The Feminist Spectator as Critic,* pp. 70, 107, 117, 120

Erickson, J., "Appropriation and Transgression in Contemporary American Performance: The Wooster Group, Holly Hughes, and Karen Finley," *Theatre Journal,* 42:225–236, May 1990

Gray, A., "The Big If," *American Theatre,* 6:18–21, 56, June 1989

Hughes, H., "A Case Concerning Hughes" (letter), *The Drama Review,* 33:10–17, Winter 1989

———, "In [My] Own Words," *TheaterWeek,* 3:22–23, 16 July 1990

London, T., "Taking Back the Word," *American Theatre,* 5:46–49, Jan. 1989

Schneider, R., "Holly Hughes: Polymorphous Perversity and the Lesbian Scientist" (interview), *The Drama Review,* 33:171–183, Spring 1989

Span, P., and C. Hall, "At Home with the NEA 4," *American Theatre,* 7:14–20, Sept. 1990

Westfall, S., "Holly Hughes at Beitzel," *Art in America,* 75:226–227, Apr. 1987

Village Voice, 32:32+, 19 May 1987

Village Voice, 33:22+, 28 June 1988 (interview)

Dress Suits to Hire, 1987
> Davy, K., "Reading Past the Heterosexual Imperative: *Dress Suits to Hire,*" *The Drama Review,* 33:153–170, Spring 1989
>
> Hughes, H., *Dress Suits to Hire* (text of play), *The Drama Review,* 33:132–152, Spring 1989
>
> Shirakawa, S. H., "Audience Notes: Alternating Currents," *TheaterWeek,* 1:36–38, 29 Feb. 1988
>
> *Village Voice,* 33:90, 12 Jan. 1988

The Lady Dick, 1985
> Davy, K., "Constructing the Spectator: Reception, Context, And Address in Lesbian Performance," *Performing Arts Journal,* 10(2[29]):43–52, 1986

The Well of Horniness, 1983
> Hall, R., "Eleven Different Directors," *American Theatre,* 5:32–33, Dec. 1988
>
> Hart, L., "Canonizing Lesbians?" pp. 275–292 in J. Schlueter, ed., *Modern American Drama*

World without End, 1989
> Champagne, L., ed., *Out from Under,* pp. ix–xiv (Introduction), 4–7, 9–32 (text of performance piece)
>
> *TheaterWeek,* 4:41, 29 Oct. 1990

LANGSTON HUGHES

Berry, F., *Langston Hughes*

Brown-Guillory, E., *Their Places on the Stage,* pp. 7, 14–15, 26, 35–37

Dickinson, D. C., "Remembering Langston Hughes: 'Langston Hughes—A Bibliographical Reminiscence,'" *Langston Hughes Review,* 6(1):44–46, Spring 1987

Emanuel, J. A., *Langston Hughes*
Kitamura, T., "Langston Hughes and Japan," *Langston Hughes Review,* 6(1):8–12, Spring 1987
Mikolyzk, T. A., *Langston Hughes*
Mullen, E. J., *Langston Hughes*
Rampersad, A., *The Life of Langston Hughes,* 2 vols.
Sanders, L. C., "'It'll Be Me': Langston Hughes," pp. 62–119 in Sanders's *The Development of Black Theater in America*
Turner, D. T., "Langston Hughes as Playwright," pp. 136–147 in E. Hill, ed., *The Theater of Black Americans.* Vol. 1 of two vols. rptd. as one in 1987; same pagination in both eds. (rpt. of T. B. O'Daniel, ed., *Langston Hughes, Black Genius,* pp. 81–95)
Woll, A., "Langston Hughes and the New Black Musical," pp. 229–248 in Woll's *Black Musical Theatre*

Mulatto, 1935
    Fletcher, W. L., "Who Put the 'Tragic' in the Tragic Mulatto?" pp. 262–268 in H. K. Chinoy and L. W. Jenkins, eds., *Women in American Theatre,* rev. and enl. ed. (pp. 260–266 in 1981 ed.)
    Woll, A., *Black Musical Theatre,* pp. 177, 210, 229–230, 233, 262

LANGSTON HUGHES and DAVID MARTIN

Simply Heavenly (musical version of Hughes's novel), 1957
    Woll, A., *Black Musical Theatre,* pp. 226, 235–237, 250
    Catholic World, 185:388–389, Aug. 1957
    Nation, 185:230, 5 Oct. 1957
    Saturday Review, 40:24, 7 Sept. 1957
    TheaterWeek, 3:6, 18 Sept. 1989

LANGSTON HUGHES and JAN MEYEROWITZ

The Barrier (musical version of Hughes's play *Mulatto*), 1950
    Bartow, A., "Controversy and Gordon Davidson" (interview), *American Theatre,* 5:24–30, 54–55, May 1988

ALSO SEE ZORA NEALE HURSTON, LANGSTON HUGHES,
and TAJ MAHAL
AND ELMER RICE, KURT WEILL, and LANGSTON HUGHES

DAVE HUNSAKER

Pieces of Eight, 1989
    American Theatre, 6:11, Feb. 1990

Summer Face Woman (based on myths of the Aleut people), 1988
    Village Voice, 33:102, 9 Feb. 1988

MARK HUNTER
SEE BARBARA BATES SMITH and MARK HUNTER

ROBERT HUNTER

Androboros, 1715
Davis, P. A., "Evidence of Collaboration in the Writing of Robert Hunter's *Androboros,*" *Restoration and 18th Century Theatre Research,* 3(1):20–29, Summer 1988

WILLIAM HENRY HURLBURT

American in Paris, 1858
Miller, T. L., "The Image of Fashionable Society in American Comedy, 1840–1870," pp. 243–252 in J. L. Fisher and S. Watt, eds., *When They Weren't Doing Shakespeare*

ZORA NEALE HURSTON

Jacobson, L., "The Mark of Zora," *American Theatre,* 7:24–30, July/Aug. 1990
Ryan, B. C., "Zora Neale Hurston—A Checklist of Secondary Sources," *Bulletin of Bibliography,* 45(1):33–39, Mar. 1988

The Fiery Chariot, written 1933
Newson, A. S., "*The Fiery Chariot*: A One-Act Play by Zora Neale Hurston," *Zora Neale Hurston Forum,* 1(1):32–37, Fall 1986

ZORA NEALE HURSTON, LANGSTON HUGHES, and TAJ MAHAL

Mule Bone, written by Hurston and Hughes in 1931, based on her short story "The Bone of Contention"; to be premièred in Jan. 1991 with a score by Taj Mahal
Jacobson, L., "The Mark of Zora," *American Theatre,* 7:24–30, July/Aug. 1990
Playbill, 8:16, 30 Sept. 1990

NOEL HUSTON

According to Law, 1940
Leonard, W. T., *Once Was Enough,* pp. 2–3

DAVID HENRY HWANG

Berson, M., "Between Worlds," *American Theatre,* 6:20–25, Mar. 1990 (based on Berson's Introduction to *Between Worlds*)
Gerard, J., "David Hwang: Riding on the Hyphen," *New York Times Magazine,* pp. 44–45+, 13 Mar. 1988
Horn, M., "The Mesmerizing Power of Racial Myths," *U.S. News & World Report,* 104:52–53, 28 Mar. 1988
O'Quinn, J., "Stages of History," *American Theatre,* 5:19–23, 53, Sept. 1988
Savran, D., "David Hwang," pp. 117–131 in Savran's *In Their Own Words*
Street, D., *David Henry Hwang*

Andy Warhol's Interview, 18:32, Dec. 1988
TheaterWeek, 2:60, 30 Jan. 1989

As the Crow Flies, 1986
    Berson, M., ed., *Between Worlds,* pp. ix–xiv (Introduction), 92–95, 97–108
    (text of play)

FOB, 1979
    American Theatre, 7:10–11, June 1990
    TheaterWeek, 3:14–15, 21 May 1990
    TheaterWeek, 3:39, 28 May 1990

M. Butterfly, 1988
    Cody, G., "David Hwang's *M. Butterfly*: Perpetuating the Misogynist
    Myth," *Theater,* 20(2):24–27, Spring 1989
    Colby, D., "Director's Chair: Keeping Intuition Alive: A Talk with John
    Dexter" (interview), *TheaterWeek,* 1:11–13, 11 Apr. 1988
    Demastes, W. W., *Beyond Naturalism,* p. 158
    DiGaetani, J. L., "*M. Butterfly*: An Interview with David Henry Hwang,"
    The Drama Review, 33 (3[T123]):141–153, Fall 1989
    Henderson, K., "A Rare Butterfly," *Playbill,* 6:8, 10, 12, July/Aug. 1988
    Henry, W. A., III, "When East and West Collide," *Time,* 134:62–64, 14
    Aug. 1989
    Hersh, A., "Setting the Scene: Crossed Cultures: Eiko Ishioka,"
    TheaterWeek, 1:14–17, 11 Apr. 1988
    Moy, J. S., "David Henry Hwang's *M. Butterfly* and Philip Kan Gotanda's
    Yankee Dawg You Die: Repositioning Chinese American Marginality on
    the American Stage," *Theatre Journal,* 42:48–56, Mar. 1990
    Raymond, G., "Center Stage: Smashing Stereotypes," *TheaterWeek,* 1:6–
    9, 11 Apr. 1988
    Sandla, R., "B. D. Wong: States of Desire," *TheaterWeek,* 1:21–25, 18 July
    1988
    Shirakawa, S. H., "Strange Romances," *TheaterWeek,* 1:20–27, 25 Apr.
    1988
    Skloot, R., "Breaking the Butterfly: The Politics of David Henry Hwang,"
    Modern Drama, 33:59–66, Mar. 1990
    America, 158:385, 9 Apr. 1988
    American Theatre, 5:n. pag., July/Aug. 1988 (text of play, special pull-out
    section)
    Commonweal, 115:245–247, 22 Apr. 1988
    Dance Magazine, 62:60–61, July 1988
    Georgia Review, 42:592–593, Fall 1988
    Hudson Review, 41:512–513, Autumn 1988
    Manhattan, inc., 5:144 + , June 1988
    Massachusetts Review, 30:132–136, Spring 1989
    Nation, 246:577–578, 23 Apr. 1988
    New Leader, 71:22–23, 18 Apr. 1988
    New Republic, 198:28–29, 25 Apr. 1988
    New York, 21:117–118, 11 Apr. 1988
    New York, 21:145–146, 24 Oct. 1988

New York Times Magazine, pp. 44–45 + , 13 Mar. 1988
New Yorker, 64:72, 4 Apr. 1988
Newsweek, 111:75, 4 Apr. 1988
People Weekly, 30:88–89 + , 8 Aug. 1988
Playbill, 7:64–65, 30 June 1989
TheaterWeek, 2:7, 12 June 1989
TheaterWeek, 2:36–37, 3 July 1989
Time, 131:74, 4 Apr. 1988
Time, 133:102, 2 Jan. 1989
Vanity Fair, 51:112, Mar. 1988
Village Voice, 33:115 + , 29 Mar. 1988
Vogue, 178:144, Mar. 1988
W Supplement, 17:1–8, 27 June 1988

The Sound of a Voice, 1983
Berson, M., ed., *Between Worlds*, pp. ix-xiv (Introduction), 92–95, 109–126 (text of play)

DAVID HENRY HWANG, PHILIP GLASS, and JEROME SIRLIN

1000 Airplanes on the Roof, 1988
Zinman, T. S., "Music for UFOs," *American Theatre*, 5:8–9, Oct. 1988
Chicago, 37:24, Oct. 1988
D Magazine, 15:17, Oct. 1988
Journal of Dramatic Theory and Criticism, 3:209–211, Spring 1989
Kansas City Monthly, 13:15–16, Oct. 1988
San Diego Magazine, 41:54 + , Jan. 1989
Village Voice, 33:103 + , 23 Dec. 1988

HAROLD IGOW

Ohio Doom, 1938
Kazacoff, G., *Dangerous Theatre*, pp. 235–236

MOMOKO IKO

Arnold, S., "Dissolving the Half Shadows: Japanese American Women Playwrights," pp. 181–194 in L. Hart, ed., *Making a Spectacle*

Boutique Living and Disposable Icons, 1988
TheaterWeek, 1:4–5, 13 June 1988

WILLIAM INGE

Reilinger, M., "William Inge (3 May 1913–10 June 1973)," pp. 190–208 in P. C. Kolin, ed., *American Playwrights since 1945*
Shuman, R. B., *William Inge*, rev. ed.
Voss, R. F., *A Life of William Inge*

Bus Riley's Back in Town, written in the 1950s, revised several times, published 1962

Dixon, W., "William Inge as Walter Gage: *Bus Riley's Back in Town*," *Literature/Film Quarterly,* 16(2):101–106, 1988

Bus Stop, 1955
Marowitz, C., "Los Angeles in Review," *TheaterWeek,* 4:12–13, 20 Aug. 1990
Rapf, J. E., "*Bus Stop* as Self-Reflexive Parody: George Axelrod on Its Adaptation," pp. 59–68 in W. Aycock and M. Schoenecke, eds., *Film and Literature*
American Theatre, 6:12, Dec. 1989

The Dark at the Top of the Stairs, produced in 1947 as *Farther Off from Heaven,* revised 1957
Harap, L., *Dramatic Encounters,* p. 134
Kazan, E., *Elia Kazan,* pp. 513, 572–574, 601

ANTHONY J. INGRASSIA

Fame, 1974
Leonard, W. T., *Once Was Enough,* pp. 45–47

AVRAHAM INLENDER

On an Open Roof, 1963
Leonard, W. T., *Once Was Enough,* pp. 141–142

ALBERT INNAURATO

DiGaetani, J. L., "An Interview with Albert Innaurato," *Studies in American Drama, 1945–Present,* 2:87–95, 1987
McDaniel, L. E., "Albert Innaurato (2 June 1948–)," pp. 209–216 in P. C. Kolin, ed., *American Playwrights since 1945*
Myers, L., "Albert Innaurato: Coming of Age Off-Broadway" (interview), *TheaterWeek,* 2:26–33, 20 Mar. 1989
Elle, 4:266+, Mar. 1989
Philadelphia Magazine, 79:17, Mar. 1988

Gus and Al, 1988
New York, 22:75, 13 Mar. 1989
New Yorker, 65:74, 13 Mar. 1989
Village Voice, 34:89–90, 7 Mar. 1989

Magda & Callas, 1988
American Theatre, 5:50, Mar. 1989
Philadelphia Magazine, 79:17, Mar. 1988

RICHARD IORIO, TONY BONDI, and SAL PIRO

Arrivederci Papa, 1989
Ledford, L. S., "Funerals Can Be a Drag," *TheaterWeek,* 2:43, 3 July 1989

RICHARD IRIZARRY

Ariano, 1988
  TheaterWeek, 1:29, 25 Jan. 1988
  TheaterWeek, 3:8, 15 Jan. 1990
  Village Voice, 35:98, 6 Feb. 1990

BILL IRWIN

Chansky, D., "Largely Bill Irwin," *TheaterWeek,* 2:8–14, 15 May 1989
Dalva, N. V., "The Postmodern Funny Man: Bill Irwin, Dance Clown," *Dance Magazine,* 63:40–44, Sept. 1989
Hersh, A., "Theater People: Bill Irwin: Fragments of a Clown Jigsaw," *TheaterWeek,* 1:24–26, 4 Jan. 1988
Hoban, P., "Clowning Around," *New York,* 22:28, 8 May 1989
Jenkins, R., *Acrobats of the Soul,* pp. 143–161
Towers, D., "Collaborators," *Dance Magazine,* 62:70–71, May 1988
Connoisseur, 219:24–25, Aug. 1989
Elle, 4:126, June 1989
Village Voice, 34:93–94, 16 May 1989

BILL IRWIN, DOUG SKINNER, and MICHAEL O'CONNOR

The Regard of Flight, 1982
  Village Voice, 32:93–94, 28 Apr. 1987

BILL IRWIN and OTHERS

Largely New York, 1988
  Filichia, P., "Special on Broadway," *TheaterWeek,* 2:40–41, 22 May 1989
  Connoisseur, 219:24–25, Aug. 1989
  Georgia Review, 43:582, Fall 1989
  Nation, 246:804, 4 June 1988
  New Republic, 200:26–28, 29 May 1989
  New York, 22:124, 15 May 1989
  New Yorker, 65:94–96, 15 May 1989
  Newsweek, 113:76–77, 15 May 1989
  TheaterWeek, 2:7–8, 10 Apr. 1989
  TheaterWeek, 2:41, 17 Apr. 1989
  TheaterWeek, 2:3, 1 May 1989
  TheaterWeek, 2:2, 15 May 1989
  Theatre Journal, 42:242–244, May 1990
  Time, 133:87, 15 May 1989
  Village Voice, 34:99, 16 May 1989

WILL IRWIN
SEE SIDNEY HOWARD, WILL IRWIN, RAYMOND SCOTT, and BERNARD HANIGHEN

CHRISTOPHER ISHERWOOD

Mendelson, E., ed., *Plays and Other Dramatic Writings,* 1928–1938

CHRISTOPHER ISHERWOOD and DON BACHARDY

A Meeting by the River (dramatization of Isherwood's novel), 1972
    Leonard, W. T., *Once Was Enough,* pp. 119–121

ALSO SEE W. H. AUDEN and CHRISTOPHER ISHERWOOD

DAVID IVES

Ancient History, 1989
    TheaterWeek, 2:6, 8 May 1989

Mere Mortals, 1990
    American Theatre, 7:13, May 1990

GARY IWAMOTO

Who Killed the Dragon Lady?, 1990
    Theatre Journal, 42:499–501, Dec. 1990

CORINNE JACKER

Betsko, K., and R. Koenig, *Interviews with Contemporary Women Playwrights,*
    pp. 236–245

Bits and Pieces, 1975
    Moore, H., "Woman Alone, Women Together," pp. 186–191 in H. K. Chi-
    noy and L. W. Jenkins, eds., *Women in American Theatre,* rev. and enl.
    ed. (pp. 184–190 in 1981 ed.)

MARSHA A. JACKSON

Sisters, 1988
    American Theatre, 5:10, Dec. 1988
    TheaterWeek, 3:43, 18 June 1990
    Theatre Journal, 41:541, Dec. 1988

NAGLE JACKSON

A Tale of Two Cities (dramatization of novel by C. Dickens), 1989
    Perry, D., "Double Dickens," *American Theatre,* 6:9–10, Feb. 1990

KENNETH JACOBSON
SEE PAUL OSBORN, KENNETH JACOBSON, and RHODA ROBERTS

HENRY JAMES

Edel, L., ed., *The Complete Plays of Henry James,* new ed.
Hocks, R. A., "Henry James," *American Literary Scholarship,* 1–2:93ff., 1986

JOSEPH JAMES

Simon Says . . . , 1989
    TheaterWeek, 2:6, 29 May 1989

ROBINSON JEFFERS

Brophy, R., *Robinson Jeffers*
Karman, J., *Critical Essays on Robinson Jeffers*
————, *Robinson Jeffers*

W. J. JEFFERSON

Mandy, 1927
    Walker, E. P., "Krigwa, a Theatre by, for, and about Black People," *Theatre Journal,* 40:347–356, Oct. 1988

LAWRENCE JEFFERY

Carley, D., "A Canada Nobody Knows," *American Theatre,* 4:46–47, Feb. 1988

LEN JENKIN

Beber, N., "Dramatis Instructus," *American Theatre,* 6:22–23, Jan. 1990
Robinson, M., "Don't Fence Them In," *American Theatre,* 6:28–34, Sept. 1989

American Notes, 1988
    Nation, 246:511–512, 9 Apr. 1988
    New York, 21:122, 29 Feb. 1988

A Country Doctor (dramatization of story by F. Kafka), 1985
    Nation, 248:248, 20 Feb. 1989
    TheaterWeek, 2:8, 26 Dec. 1988

Limbo Tales, 1981
    TheaterWeek, 3:8, 29 Jan. 1990

CHARLES JENKINS

The Vigil, 1989
    Nation, 248:863, 19 June 1989
    TheaterWeek, 2:11, 27 Mar. 1989
    TheaterWeek, 2:38–39, 22 May 1989

TALBOT JENNINGS

American Wing, 1938
    Kazacoff, G., *Dangerous Theatre,* pp. 174–176

GEORGE H. JESSOP

Sam'l of Rosen, 1881
  Harap, L., *The Image of the Jew in American Literature,* pp. 230–233

JOHN JESURUN

Everything That Rises Must Converge, 1990
    Theatre Journal, 42:495–497, Dec. 1990
    Village Voice, 35:103, 20 Mar. 1990

Sunspot, 1989
    Village Voice, 34:95, 28 Mar. 1989

White Water, 1986
    Osborn, M. E., ed., *On New Ground,* pp. vi–viii (Preface), 73–78, 79–142
    (text of play)

JOHN JILER

Ball (an expansion of his one-act play), 1990
    TheaterWeek, 4:11, 22 Oct. 1990

Icetown (two one-acts developed from his series of newspaper articles on the
    homeless: *Too Late* and *Early Birds*), 1989
    TheaterWeek, 2:7, 8 May 1989

BYRON JOHNS

Solo: A Life in Progress, 1990
    Village Voice, 35:118, 1 May 1990

CARYN JOHNSON
SEE WHOOPI GOLDBERG

CHARLES R. JOHNSON

Amidst the Floating Monsters, 1989
    TheaterWeek, 2:7–8, 6 Feb. 1989

CINDY LOU JOHNSON

Elle, 4:170 + , Oct. 1988

Brilliant Traces, 1989
    New York, 22:72, 20 Feb. 1989
    New Yorker, 65:89–90, 20 Feb. 1989
    TheaterWeek, 2:10, 2 Jan. 1989
    Village Voice, 34:104, 21 Feb. 1989

DALE JOHNSON

Channels, 1988
  Shirakawa, S. H., "Audience Notes: Alternating Currents," *TheaterWeek,*
    1:36–38, 29 Feb. 1988
  TheaterWeek, 1:7, 14 Mar. 1988

GEORGIA DOUGLAS JOHNSON

Brown-Guillory, E., *Their Place on the Stage,* pp. 4–7, 13–16, 33

Plumes, 1927
  Keyssar, H., "Foothills: Precursors of Feminist Drama," pp. 22–52 in Keyssar's *Feminist Theatre*

RICK JOHNSTON

Cahoots, 1989
  TheaterWeek, 3:12, 26 Feb. 1990
  TheaterWeek, 3:42–43, 19 Mar. 1990

GEORGE JONES

Tecumseh and the Prophet of the West, published 1844
  Jones, E. H., *Native Americans as Shown on the Stage,* p. 35

JEFFREY M. JONES

Robinson, M., "Don't Fence Them In," *American Theatre,* 6:28–34, Sept. 1989

The Crazy Plays, 1990
  Village Voice, 35:103–104, 20 Mar. 1990

Tomorrowland (second play of a trilogy titled *A History of Western Philosophy by W. T. Jones*; the first is *Der Inka Von Peru*; the third is *Caesar's Surf Party*), 1985
  Theatre Journal, 40:116–117, Mar. 1988

JOSEPH STEVENS JONES

The Fire Warrior, 1834
  Jones, E. H., *Native Americans as Shown on the Stage,* pp. 36, 73

The Hunter in the Far West, 1836
  Jones, E. H., *Native Americans as Shown on the Stage,* pp. 35, 73

KEN JONES

Darkside, 1989
  American Theatre, 6:10, Apr. 1989

LeROI JONES (Imamu Amiri Baraka)

Baraka, A., "Black Theater in the Sixties," pp. 225–237 in J. Weixlmann and C. J. Fontenot, eds., *Belief vs. Theory in Black American Literary Criticism*

Bonner, T., Jr., "Amiri Baraka (LeRoi Jones, 7 October 1934–)," pp. 51–65 in P. C. Kolin, ed., *American Playwrights since 1945*

Brown-Guillory, E., *Their Place on the Stage,* pp. 18, 27, 43, 108, 116–118

Dixon, M., "Trouble about My Grave: Richard Wright, Ralph Ellison, and LeRoi Jones," pp. 56–82 in Dixon's *Ride out the Wilderness*

Duval, E. I., "Reasserting and Raising Our History, an Interview with Amiri Baraka (August 27, 1987, Newark, New Jersey)," *Obsidian II,* 3(1):1–19, Spring 1988

Euba, F., *Archetypes, Imprecators, and Victims of Fate,* pp. 1, 12, 141–147

Gilbert, S. M., and S. Gubar, *The War of the Words,* pp. 53–55, 157, 158

Harap, L., *Dramatic Encounters,* p. 16

Harrison, P. C., "The (R)evolution of Black Theatre," *American Theatre,* 6:30–32, 116–118, Oct. 1989

Hodges, G., "Amiri Baraka, Sterling Plumpp and K. Curtis Lyle: An Interview by Graham Hodges," *Another Chicago Magazine,* 12:186–194, 1985

Jackson, P. K., Jr., "Amiri Baraka (LeRoi Jones) 1934– ," pp. 49–68 in M. C. Roudané, ed., *Contemporary Authors Bibliographical Series*

King, K., "Amiri Baraka," pp. 109–135 in King's *Ten Modern American Playwrights*

Pennington-Jones, P., comp., *Amiri Baraka*

Sanders, L. C., " 'No One Will Turn to That Station Again': LeRoi Jones," pp. 120–175 in Sanders's *The Development of Black Theater in America*

Shannon, S. G., "Amiri Baraka on Directing," *Black American Literature Forum,* 21(4):425–433, Winter 1987

Steele, S., "Notes on Ritual in the New Black Theater," pp. 3–44 in E. Hill, ed., *The Theater of Black Americans,* Vol. 1 of two vols. rptd. as one in 1987; same pagination in both eds. (rpt. of *Black World,* 22(8):4–13, 78–84, June 1973)

Thielemans, J., "From LeRoi Jones to Baraka and Back," pp. 127–142 in G. Debusscher, H. I. Schvey, and M. Maufort, eds., *New Essays on American Drama*

A Black Mass, 1966

    Schwank, K., "Drama as Functional Art: The Political Use of Myth in Amiri Baraka's *A Black Mass," Amerikastudien,* 32(1):81–86, 1987

Dutchman, 1964

    Cardullo, B., "Lula and the *Dutchman," Notes on Contemporary Literature,* 18(5):8–9, Nov. 1988

    Heble, A., "The Poetics of Jazz: From Symbolic to Semiotic," *Textual Practice,* 2(1):51–68, Spring 1988

    Leverett, J., "Avant and After," *American Theatre,* 7:24–29 +, Apr. 1990

    O'Sullivan, M., "*Dutchman's* Demons: Lula and Lilith," *Notes on Contemporary Literature,* 10(1):Item 4, Spring-Summer 1986

    American Theatre, 6:15, Dec. 1989

    TheaterWeek, 3:16, 23 Apr. 1990

Home on the Range, 1968
  Lahr, J., "Black Theatre: The American Tragic Voice," *Evergreen Review,* 13:55–63, Aug. 1969

Police, published 1968
  Lahr, J., "Black Theatre: The American Tragic Voice," *Evergreen Review,* 13:55–63, Aug. 1969

The Slave, 1964
  Kaufman, M. W., "The Delicate World of Reprobation: A Note on the Black Revolutionary Theatre," pp. 192–209 in E. Hill, ed., *The Theater of Black Americans,* Vol. 1 of two vols. rptd. as one in 1987; same pagination in both eds. (rpt. of *Educational Theatre Journal,* 23:446–451, Dec. 1971)

The Toilet, 1962
  Shrager, S., *Scatology in Modern Drama,* pp. 50–54, 56–61

LeROI JONES and MAX ROACH

The Life and Life of Bumpy Johnson, 1990
  Playbill, 9:46, 30 Nov. 1990
  TheaterWeek, 3:12, 5 Mar. 1990
  TheaterWeek, 4:8, 1 Oct. 1990

MARTIN JONES

West Memphis Mojo, 1988
  New Yorker, 64:82, 27 June 1988
  TheaterWeek, 3:13, 25 Sept. 1989

PRESTON JONES

McClure, C. S., "Preston Jones (7 April 1936–19 September 1979)," pp. 217–225 in P. C. Kolin, ed., *American Playwrights since 1945*

The Oldest Living Graduate (the third play of *A Texas Trilogy;* the first is *Lu Ann Hampton Laverty Oberlander,* the second is *The Last Meeting of the Knights of the White Magnolias*), 1974
  Counts, M. L., *Coming Home,* pp. 58, 95, 120, 149, 181, 194, 197

R. JONES

Wacousta; or, The Curse, 1851
  Jones, E. H., *Native Americans as Shown on the Stage,* pp. 45–46

SILAS JONES and LAURENCE MASLON

Conquest of the South Pole (dramatization of book by M. Karge), 1990
  American Theatre, 7:66, Nov. 1990

STEPHEN MACK JONES

Back in the World, 1987
    Paller, M., "Dispatches from the Front," *TheaterWeek,* 2:28–33, 21 Nov.
    1988
    Detroit, 10:42, Apr. 1987

THOMAS CADWALADER JONES

A Circle on the Cross, 1986
    American Theatre, 4:48, Feb. 1988
    TheaterWeek, 1:7, 29 Feb. 1988

TOM JONES

Hulbert, D., "Actors Are the Spark for Atlanta's Writers," *American Theatre,*
    7:44–45, June 1990
American Theatre, 7:52–53, Oct. 1990

The Wizard of Hip, 1990
    TheaterWeek, 4:11, 1 Oct. 1990

TOM JONES and HARVEY SCHMIDT

The Fantasticks (based on *Les Romanesques* by E. Rostand, as tr. by George
    Fleming), 1960
    Filichia, P., "*The Fantasticks* at 30," *TheaterWeek,* 3:12, 21 May 1990
    Green, S., *Broadway Musicals,* p. 189
    Playbill, 7:29, 30 June 1989
    Playbill, 7:52–53, 30 June 1989
    Playbill, 8:81, 30 Sept. 1990
    TheaterWeek, 3:11, 9 Apr. 1990
    TheaterWeek, 4:13, 10 Sept. 1990

Grover's Corners (musical version of T. Wilder's play *Our Town*), 1987
    Chicago, 36:24, Sept. 1987
    TheaterWeek, 1:5, 21 Mar. 1988

I Do! I Do! (musical version of J. de Hartog's play *The Fourposter*), 1966
    Green, S., *Broadway Musicals,* p. 220
    People Weekly, 31:89–90, 1 May 1989

ALSO SEE N. RICHARD NASH, TOM JONES, and HARVEY SCHMIDT

KAREN JONES-MEADOWS

Major Changes, 1989
    American Theatre, 5:50, Mar. 1989

Tapman, 1988
  New Yorker, 64:81, 14 Mar. 1988
  TheaterWeek, 1:5, 1 Feb. 1988

BRUCE JORDAN
SEE MARILYN ABRAMS and BRUCE JORDAN

ERNEST JOSELOVITZ

Washingtonian, 24:44, *July 1989*

The Devil and All His Works, 1990
  American Theatre, 6:57, Sept. 1989
  American Theatre, 7:10, July/Aug. 1990

JAMAL JOSEPH

Horwitz, S., "Turning Points: Jamal Joseph," *TheaterWeek,* 2:38–43, 20 Feb.
  1989

DONALD JUDD
SEE TRISHA BROWN and DONALD JUDD

EDWARD ZANE CARROLL JUDSON
SEE NED BUNTLINE (his pseudonym)

BARBARA KAHN

Hell's Kitchen Has a Tub in It, 1989
  TheaterWeek, 2:8, 27 Mar. 1989

NATHANIEL KAHN

Owl's Breath, 1989
  TheaterWeek, 3:11, 9 Oct. 1989

LEE KALCHEIM

Breakfast with Les and Bess, 1982
  Cohen, E. M., *Working on a New Play,* pp. 16, 38, 79, 92, 120–121, 140,
  155–156, 158, 160, 184–185, 191, 192–194, 196, 198, 199

BERT KALMAR
SEE GEORGE S. KAUFMAN, MORRIE RYSKIND, BERT KALMAR,
and HARRY RUBY

JOHN KANDER

Ledford, L. S., "The World Goes Round . . . with Kander and Ebb,"
  TheaterWeek, 2:10–14, 12 June 1989

ALSO SEE JOE MASTEROFF, JOHN KANDER, and FRED EBB
AND TERRENCE McNALLY, JOHN KANDER, and FRED EBB

FAY KANIN and MICHAEL KANIN

Rashomon (dramatization of stories by R. Akutagawa), 1959
    Currie, T., "*Rashomon*: The Enigma Returns," *TheaterWeek,* 1:34–40, 18
      Apr. 1988
    New York, 21:96–98, 18 Apr. 1988

FAY KANIN, MICHAEL KANIN, HOWARD DIETZ, and ARTHUR SCHWARTZ

The Gay Life (based on A. Schnitzler's play *Anatol*), 1961
    Driscoll, T., "Forgotten Musicals: *The Gay Life*," *TheaterWeek,* 3:36–41,
      21 Aug. 1989

GARSON KANIN

Born Yesterday, 1946
    Barbour, D., "Dawn Springs Anew: A Talk with Garson Kanin,"
      TheaterWeek, 1:26, 25 July 1988
    Chase, A., "Garson Kanin: Born Again," *TheaterWeek,* 2:10–17, 6 Feb.
      1989
    Haun, H., "Born Again," *Playbill,* 7:6, 8, 10, 12, 31 Dec. 1988
    America, 160:176, 25 Feb. 1989
    American Theatre, 4:9, Mar. 1988
    Connoisseur, 219:74+ , Mar. 1989
    Nation, 248:354–355, 13 Mar. 1989
    New York, 22:76–77, 13 Feb. 1989
    New Yorker, 64:81–82, 13 Feb. 1989
    TheaterWeek, 2:7, 9 Jan. 1989
    Time, 133:80, 6 Feb. 1989
    Village Voice, 34:96, 14 Feb. 1989

Peccadillo, 1985
    Chase, A., "Garson Kanin's New Play *Peccadillo*," *TheaterWeek,* 3:24–25,
      2 Oct. 1989
    American Theatre, 6:11, Sept. 1989
    TheaterWeek, 2:42, 8 May 1989

MICHAEL KANIN
SEE FAY KANIN and MICHAEL KANIN
AND FAY KANIN, MICHAEL KANIN, HOWARD DIETZ,
and ARTHUR SCHWARTZ

MICHAEL B. KAPLAN

Diphthong, 1988
    New Yorker, 64:73, 25 July 1988

SHIRLEY KAPLAN

Buster B and Olivia, 1988
 New Yorker, 64:75, 25 July 1988

TERRI KAPSALIS and JANE RICHLOVSKY

A Body Can Be a Worry to Anyone or a Box to Contain our Solution, 1989
 Theatre Journal, 42:118–119, Mar. 1990

HIROSHI KASHIWAGI

Laughter and False Teeth, 1989 (revised after having been written thirty years earlier)
 American Theatre, 5:15, Mar. 1989

SAM HENRY KASS

Lusting after Pipino's Wife, 1990
 TheaterWeek, 4:43, 8 Oct. 1990

LEON KATZ and AL CARMINES

The Making of Americans (musical dramatization of novel by G. Stein), 1972
 American Theatre, 7:11, 20, June 1990

JOHN KAUFFMAN

Campbell, J., "When an Artistic Director has AIDS," *American Theatre,* 6:27–30, 58–60, Mar. 1990

According to Coyote, 1987
 American Theatre, 7:12, Apr. 1990

GEORGE S. KAUFMAN

Harap, L., *Dramatic Encounters,* pp. 89–94
Hirsch, F., *Harold Prince and the American Musical Theater,* pp. 4, 11–13, 23, 26, 131–132
Jacobson, L., "Kaufman X 7" (interviews), *American Theatre,* 6:26–32, Feb. 1990
Mason, J. D., "The Fool and the Clown: The Ironic Vision of George S. Kaufman," pp. 207–217 in J. Redmond, ed., *Farce*
———, *Wise-Cracks*
Pollack, R.-G., *George S. Kaufman*

The Butter and Egg Man, 1925
 Los Angeles, 31:284+, Dec. 1986

GEORGE S. KAUFMAN and IRVING BERLIN

The Cocoanuts, 1926
Winer, L., "High Marx," *American Theatre,* 5:14–18, Sept. 1988

GEORGE S. KAUFMAN and EDNA FERBER

Dinner at Eight, 1932
Macauley, M. W., "*Dinner* Is Served," *TheaterWeek,* 2:34–39, 14 Nov. 1988
American Theatre, 5:57, Nov. 1988
Time, 132:85, 31 Oct. 1988
Time, 133:102, 2 Jan. 1989

GEORGE S. KAUFMAN and MOSS HART

You Can't Take It with You, 1936
Stephens, J. L., "Women in Pulitzer Prize Plays, 1918–1949," pp. 245–253
in H. K. Chinoy and L. W. Jenkins, eds., *Women in American Theatre,*
rev. and enl. ed. (pp. 243–251 in 1981 ed.)
California, 12:64 + , Dec. 1987

GEORGE S. KAUFMAN and LEUEEN MacGRATH

The Small Hours, 1951
Curtin, K., "*We Can Always Call Them Bulgarians,*" pp. 300–301

GEORGE S. KAUFMAN, MORRIE RYSKIND, GEORGE GERSHWIN,
and IRA GERSHWIN

Of Thee I Sing, 1931
Stephens, J. L., "Women in Pulitzer Prize Plays, 1918–1949," pp. 245–253
in H. K. Chinoy and L. W. Jenkins, eds., *Women in American Theatre,*
rev. and enl. ed. (pp. 243–251 in 1981 ed.)
Village Voice, 35:99 + , 10 Apr. 1990

GEORGE S. KAUFMAN, MORRIE RYSKIND, BERT KALMAR,
and HARRY RUBY

Animal Crackers, 1928
Winer, L., "High Marx," *American Theatre,* 5:14–18, Sept. 1988

GEORGE S. KAUFMAN and HOWARD TEICHMANN

The Solid Gold Cadillac, 1953
Playbill, 8:46, 31 Oct. 1989

ALSO SEE MOSS HART and GEORGE S. KAUFMAN

LYNNE KAUFMAN

Our Lady of the Desert, 1990
American Theatre, 7:68, May 1990

NICHOLAS KAZAN

Just Horrible, 1988
  Ouderkirk, C., " 'A Rock and Roll Sensibility,' " *TheaterWeek,* 2:24–30, 31
  Oct. 1988

PATRICK KEARNEY

Elmer Gantry (dramatization of novel by S. Lewis; with revisions by Thompson
  Buchanan), 1928
  Leonard, W. T., *Once Was Enough,* pp. 61–63

DANIEL KEENE

Silent Partner, 1990
  TheaterWeek, 3:43, 19 Mar. 1990

EDDIE KEGLEY

Sadness of a Faded Dream, 1988
  TheaterWeek, 1:5, 4 Apr. 1988

THOMAS KEITH
SEE JANE YOUNG and THOMAS KEITH

GEORGE KELLY

Behold the Bridegroom, 1927
  Harap, L., *Dramatic Encounters,* p. 115

Craig's Wife, 1925
  Stephens, J. L., "Women in Pulitzer Prize Plays, 1918–1949," pp. 245–253
  in H. K. Chinoy and L. W. Jenkins, eds., *Women in American Theatre,*
  rev. and enl. ed. (pp. 243–251 in 1981 ed.)

JOHN KELLY

"Performance Strategies," *Performing Arts Journal,* 10(3):38–41, 1987

Love of a Poet, 1990
  TheaterWeek, 4:40, 29 Oct. 1990

ADRIENNE KENNEDY

Beber, N., "Dramatis Instructus," *American Theatre,* 6:22–23, 25–26, Jan. 1990
Betsko, K., and R. Koenig, *Interviews with Contemporary Women Playwrights,*
  pp. 246–258
Binder, W., "A MELUS Interview: Adrienne Kennedy," *MELUS,* 12(3):99–108,
  Fall 1985
Blau, H., "The American Dream in American Gothic: The Plays of Sam Shep-

ard and Adrienne Kennedy," pp. 42–64 in Blau's *The Eye of Prey* (rpt. of *Modern Drama*, 27(4):520–539, Dec. 1984)

Case, S.-E., *Feminism and Theatre*, pp. 101–102 (Kennedy's *A Movie Star Has to Star in Black and White* and *The Owl Answers* considered)

Curb, R. K., " 'Lesson I Bleed': Adrienne Kennedy's Blood Rites," pp. 50–56 in H. K. Chinoy and L. W. Jenkins, eds., *Women in American Theatre*, rev. and enl. ed. (same pagination in 1981 ed.)

Diamond, E., "An Interview with Adrienne Kennedy," *Studies in American Drama, 1945–Present*, 4:143–157, 1989

Giddings, P., "Word Star," *Essence*, 19:26, Nov. 1988

Kennedy, A., *Adrienne Kennedy in One Act*

———, "Becoming a Playwright," *American Theatre*, 4:26–27, Feb. 1988

———, *The Deadly Triplets*

Keyssar, H., "A Network of Playwrights," pp. 102–125 in Keyssar's *Feminist Theatre*

Meigs, S. E., "No Place but the Funnyhouse: The Struggle for Identity in Three Adrienne Kennedy Plays," pp. 172–183 in J. Schlueter, ed., *Modern American Drama* (Kennedy's *Funnyhouse of a Negro*, *The Owl Answers*, and *A Movie Star Has to Star in Black and White* considered)

Miller, J.-M. A., "Black Women in Plays by Black Playwrights," pp. 256–262 in H. K. Chinoy and L. W. Jenkins, eds., *Women in American Theatre*, rev. and enl. ed. (pp. 254–260 in 1981 ed.)

Overbeck, L. M., "Adrienne Kennedy 1931– ," pp. 109–124 in M. C. Roudané, ed., *Contemporary Authors Bibliographical Series*

An Evening with Dead Essex, 1973

  Zinman, T. S., "Search and Destroy: The Drama of the Vietnam War," *Theatre Journal*, 42:5–26, Mar. 1990

Funnyhouse of a Negro, 1964

  Fletcher, W. L., "Who Put the 'Tragic' in the Tragic Mulatto?" pp. 262–268 in H. K. Chinoy and L. W. Jenkins, eds., *Women in American Theatre*, rev. and enl. ed. (pp. 260–266 in 1981 ed.)

  Harrison, P. C., "The (R)evolution of Black Theatre," *American Theatre*, 6:30–32, 116–118, Oct. 1989

  Kolin, P. C., "From the Zoo to the Funnyhouse: A Comparison of Edward Albee's *The Zoo Story* with Adrienne Kennedy's *Funnyhouse of a Negro*," *Theatre Southwest*, 8–16, Apr. 1989

The Owl Answers, 1965

  Fletcher, W. L., "Who Put the 'Tragic' in the Tragic Mulatto?" pp. 262–268 in H. K. Chinoy and L. W. Jenkins, eds., *Women in American Theatre*, rev. and enl. ed. (pp. 260–266 in 1981 ed.)

  Keyssar, H., "Rites and Responsibilities: The Drama of Black American Women," pp. 226–240 in E. Brater, ed., *Feminine Focus*

SKIP KENNON
SEE WILLY HOLTZMAN, SKIP KENNON, and MICHAEL KORIE

JEROME KERN
SEE OSCAR HAMMERSTEIN II and JEROME KERN

JEAN KERR

Mary, Mary, 1961
    TheaterWeek, 1:38, 7 Mar. 1988

ROBERT KERR

And the Air Didn't Answer, 1988
    New Yorker, 64:91, 3 Oct. 1988
    TheaterWeek, 2:7, 12 Sept. 1988
    Village Voice, 33:110+, 4 Oct. 1988

Finnegan's Funeral Parlor and Ice Cream Shoppe, 1989
    Chansky, D., "Younger than Springtime . . . Sharp as Tacks," *TheaterWeek,*
        3:29–33, 25 Sept. 1989
    TheaterWeek, 3:42, 9 Oct. 1989

WENDY ANN KESSELMAN

My Sister in This House, 1980
    Hart, L., " 'They Don't Even Look like Maids Anymore': Wendy Kessel-
        man's *My Sister in This House,*" pp. 131–146 in Hart, ed., *Making a
        Spectacle*
    Keyssar, H., "Nooks, Crannies and New Directions: Collective Scripts, Gay
        Drama, Feminist Dramas by Men and the Example of Wendy Kessel-
        man," pp. 167–184 in Keyssar's *Feminist Theatre*
    Mandl, B., "Disturbing Women: Wendy Kesselman's *My Sister in This
        House,*" pp. 246–253 in J. Schlueter, ed., *Modern American Drama*
    Schroeder, P. R., "Locked behind the Proscenium: Feminist Strategies in
        Getting Out and *My Sister in This House,*" *Modern Drama,* 32(1):104–
        114, Mar. 1989

JOSEPH KESSELRING

Arsenic and Old Lace, 1941
    Nelson, T. G. A., *Comedy,* pp. 85–86

LYLE KESSLER

Robbers, staged reading in 1988
    TheaterWeek, 1:5, 16 May 1988

The Watering Place, 1969
    Counts, M. L., *Coming Home,* pp. 88, 89–90, 94–95, 115, 137, 148–149,
        170–171, 181
    Leonard, W. T., *Once Was Enough,* pp. 204–205

PAUL KESTER and GEORGE MIDDLETON

The Cavalier (dramatization of novel by G. W. Cable), 1902
    Ware, E., "George W. Cable's *The Cavalier,* an American Best Seller and
    Theatrical Attraction," *Southern Literary Journal,* 19(2):70–80, 1987

LARRY KETRON

No Time Flat, 1988
    TheaterWeek, 1:6, 18 Apr. 1988
    Village Voice, 33:108, 17 May 1988

Rib Cage, 1978
    Counts, M. L., *Coming Home,* p. 69

KID CREOLE
SEE AUGUST DARNELL

JEROME KILTY

Margaret Sanger: Unfinished Business, 1989
    TheaterWeek, 3:11, 18 Sept. 1989

SUSAN KIM

Death and the Maiden, 1990
    American Theatre, 7:13, May 1990

WILLIAM A. KIMBALL

The Leading Man, 1936
    Kazacoff, G., *Dangerous Theatre,* pp. 286–287

Spring Afternoon, 1936
    Kazacoff, G., *Dangerous Theatre,* pp. 281–282

GEORGE KING and RUBY LERNER

Bananaland: A Central American Theme Park, 1988
    Evans, P., "*Bananaland*: PR, Propaganda, and Infotainment," *The Drama
    Review,* 33(3[T123]):95–102, Fall 1989

LARRY L. KING

Durham, B., "The Play's the Thing," *Texas Techsan,* 42(5):10–13, Sept.-Oct.
    1989
Phillips, M., "Lone Star Playwright: Larry L. King" (interview), *TheaterWeek,*
    2:18–23, 6 Feb. 1989
Playbill, 7:37, 31 May 1989

The Golden Shadows Old West Museum (based on a short story by M. Blackmon), 1989
  American Theatre, 5:11, Jan. 1989
  TheaterWeek, 2:5, 17 Apr. 1989

The Night Hank Williams Died, 1988
  Buckley, M., "Darren McGavin: The Natural," *TheaterWeek,* 2:12–17, 17 Apr. 1989
  Davis, K. W., "King's Drama Offers Genial Comedy, Biting Satire," *Texas Books in Review,* 10:29, Fall 1990
  Commonweal, 116:210–212, 7 Apr. 1989
  Playbill, 7:42, 31 Mar. 1989
  Nation, 248:355–356, 13 Mar. 1989
  New York, 22:92–93, 6 Feb. 1989
  New Yorker, 65:89, 20 Feb. 1989
  TheaterWeek, 1:6, 29 Feb. 1988
  TheaterWeek, 2:10, 9 Jan. 1989
  TheaterWeek, 2:6, 5 June 1989
  Village Voice, 34:79 + , 28 Feb. 1989

LARRY L. KING and CAROL HALL

Diamondbacks, in progress
  TheaterWeek, 3:12, 19 Mar. 1990

LARRY L. KING, PETER MASTERSON, and CAROL HALL

Best Little Whorehouse in Texas (based on King's article in *Playboy* in 1974), 1978
  Green, S., *Broadway Musicals,* p. 250
  New York, 11:83 + , 8 May 1978
  New Yorker, 54:67, 1 May 1978
  Newsweek, 91:74, 1 May 1978
  Plays and Players, 25:36–38, Aug. 1978
  Time, 111:95–96, 1 May 1978

STEPHEN KING

An Evening at God's (a "one-minute play"), 1990
  Carpenter, B., "Just Add Water . . . ," *TheaterWeek,* 3:32–33, 28 May 1990

SIDNEY KINGSLEY

Harap, L., *Dramatic Encounters,* pp. 99–100

Dead End, 1935
  Marcuson, L. R., *The Stage Immigrant,* pp. 85–89

Detective Story, 1949
  Marcuson, L. R., *The Stage Immigrant,* pp. 164–168

Men in White, 1934
    Stephens, J. L., "Women in Pulitzer Prize Plays, 1918–1949," pp. 245–253
    in H. K. Chinoy and L. W. Jenkins, eds., *Women in American Theatre,*
    rev. and enl. ed. (pp. 243–251 in 1981 ed.)

MICHAEL KIRBY

Kirby, M., *A Formalist Theatre*
Shank, T., "Michael Kirby: The Structuralist Workshop," pp. 149–154 in
Shank's *American Alternative Theater*

JACK KIRKLAND

Tobacco Road (dramatization of novel by E. Caldwell), 1933
    Howard, W. L., "Caldwell on Stage and Screen," pp. 59–72 in E. T. Arnold,
    ed., *Erskine Caldwell Reconsidered*

JAMES KIRKWOOD

Kirkwood, J., *Diary of a Mad Playwright* (excerpt printed in *Playbill,* 8:S1–S15,
31 Mar. 1990)

JAMES KIRKWOOD, NICOLAS DANTE, MARVIN HAMLISCH, and EDWARD KLEBAN

A Chorus Line, 1975
    Bordman, G., "How to Remember Broadway's Baby," *TheaterWeek,* 3:18–
    23, 12 Mar. 1990
    Filichia, P., "*A Chorus Line* at 14," *TheaterWeek,* 3:42, 11 Sept. 1989
    Flinn, D. M., *What They Did for Love*
    Gottfried, M., "The End of *A Chorus Line,*" *TheaterWeek,* 3:22–25, 7 May
    1990
    Green, S., *Broadway Musicals,* p. 243
    Haun, H., "A Tony Memory: *A Chorus Line,*" *Playbill,* 6:12, 14, 16, June
    1988
    Kelly, K., *One Singular Sensation*
    Mandelbaum, K., A Chorus Line *and the Musicals of Michael Bennett* (ex-
    cerpt printed in *Playbill,* 7:S1–S16, 30 Sept. 1989)
    ———, "On Writing *A Chorus Line* and the Musicals of Michael Bennett,"
    TheaterWeek, 2:31–37, 15 May 1989
    Philip, R., "Michael Bennett and the Making of *A Chorus Line,*" *Dance*
    Magazine, 49:62–65, June 1975
    Schmitt, N. C., "A Popular Contemporary Work: *A Chorus Line,*" pp. 77–
    91 in Schmitt's *Actors and Onlookers*
    Viagas, R., T. Walsh, and B. Lee, *On the Line*
    America, 134:40, 17 Jan. 1976
    Dance Magazine, 49:62–65, June 1975
    Dance Magazine, 57:102, Nov. 1983
    Intellect, 104:531, Apr. 1976
    Mademoiselle, 81:98–99, July 1975
    Nation, 220:734, 14 June 1975

New Republic, 172:20+, 21 June 1975
New York, 16:92–93, 17 Oct. 1983
New York Times Magazine, pp. 18–20+, 2 May 1976
New Yorker, 51:84, 2 June 1975
New Yorker, 51:78+, 25 Aug. 1975
Newsweek, 85:49, 2 June 1975
Newsweek, 85:85–86, 9 June 1975
Newsweek, 86:86, 3 Nov. 1975
Newsweek, 86:66–70, 1 Dec. 1975
People Weekly, 20:34–41, 17 Oct. 1983
People Weekly, 33:121–123, 23 Apr. 1990
Playbill, 6:73, June 1988
Plays and Players, 23:40, July 1976
Plays and Players, 23:20–21, Sept. 1976
Saturday Review, 2:50, 9 Aug. 1975
Saturday Review, 2:16–19, 26 July 1975
Saturday Review, 4:50, 16 Oct. 1976
TheaterWeek, 1:32, 11 Apr. 1988
TheaterWeek, 1:4, 8 Aug. 1988
TheaterWeek, 3:9, 8 Jan. 1990
TheaterWeek, 3:8, 5 Mar. 1990
TheaterWeek, 4:12–13, 17 Dec. 1990
Theatre Crafts, 19:10, Nov. 1985
Time, 105:60, 2 June 1975
Time, 106:47–48, 28 July 1975
Time, 135:53, 5 Mar. 1990
Vogue, 165:120–123+, Aug. 1975

JAMES KIRKWOOD and JIM PIAZZA

Stage Struck, 1989
TheaterWeek, 2:4, 17 Apr. 1989

JOHN KISHLINE
SEE JOHN SCHNEIDER, JOHN KISHLINE, and OTHERS

LAURENCE KLAVAN

The Magic Act, 1987
TheaterWeek, 2:7, 6 Mar. 1989

EDWARD KLEBAN
SEE JAMES KIRKWOOD, NICOLAS DANTE, MARVIN HAMLISCH, and EDWARD KLEBAN

CHARLES KLEIN

Harap, L., *Dramatic Encounters,* p. 80

JON KLEIN

Southern Cross, 1989
    American Theatre, 6:9–10, Nov. 1989

BARRY KLEINBORT

Angelina (musical version of F. Gilroy's play *That Summer—That Fall*), 1989
    Filichia, P., "Only 175 Minutes from Broadway," *TheaterWeek,* 2:16–23, 23
    Jan. 1989
    TheaterWeek, 2:6, 7 Aug. 1989

KEVIN KLING

Mpls/St Paul, 16:84 + , Dec. 1988
Writer's Digest, 68:6–9, Aug. 1988

Home and Away, 1990
    American Theatre, 7:11, Nov. 1990

Lloyd's Prayer, 1988
    American Theatre, 5:n. pag. (text of play, special pull-out section), Nov.
    1988

PERCIVAL KNIGHT

Thin Ice, 1922
    Counts, M. L., *Coming Home,* pp. 137–138, 199

CHRISTOPHER KNOWLES

Drateln, D. von, "Christopher Knowles, Galerie Dorrie & Priess" (tr. Joachim
    Neugroschel), *Artforum,* 26:159–160, May 1988
Shyer, L., "Secret Sharers," *American Theatre,* 6:12–19, Sept. 1989

ARTHUR KOBER

Harap, L., *Dramatic Encounters,* pp. 34, 40, 119–120

Having Wonderful Time, 1937
    Marcuson, L. R., *The Stage Immigrant,* pp. 111–117

HOWARD KOCH

Lonely Man, 1937
    Kazacoff, G., *Dangerous Theatre,* pp. 230–232

KENNETH KOCH

Auslander, P., *The New York School of Poets as Playwrights*
Tranter, J., "An Interview with Kenneth Koch," *Scripsi,* 4(2):177–185, Nov. 1986

HARRY KONDOLEON

Elle, 3:46, Mar. 1988

The Fairy Garden, 1984
> Gross, R. F., "Between the Devil and the Deep Blue Sea: Reification and Gay Identity in Kondoleon's *The Fairy Garden* and *Zero Positive,*" *Essays in Theatre,* 8(1):23–33, Nov. 1989
> Hall, R., "Eleven Different Directions," *American Theatre,* 5:32–33, Dec. 1988
> Shewey, D., "Gay Theatre Grows Up," *American Theatre,* 5:10–17, 52–53, May 1988
> *American Theatre,* 4:10, Feb. 1988

Love Diatribe, 1990
> *New Yorker,* 66:82–83, 31 Dec. 1990
> *TheaterWeek,* 4:7, 3 Dec. 1990

Play Yourself, 1988
> *American Theatre,* 5:9, May 1988

The Poet's Corner, 1988
> *TheaterWeek,* 1:9, 23 May 1988

Self-Torture and Strenuous Exercise, 1987
> *American Theatre,* 4:10, Feb. 1988

Zero Positive, 1988
> Gross, R. F., "Between the Devil and the Deep Blue Sea: Reification and Gay Identity in Kondoleon's *The Fairy Garden* and *Zero Positive,*" *Essays in Theatre,* 8(1):23–33, Nov. 1989
> *American Theatre,* 5:n pag. (text of play; special pull-out section), Sept. 1988
> *New Yorker,* 64:85, 20 June 1988
> *TheaterWeek,* 1:4, 25 Apr. 1988
> *Village Voice,* 33:105, 14 June 1988

ARTHUR KOPIT

Auerbach, D., "Arthur L. Kopit 1937– ," pp. 125–139 in M. C. Roudané, ed., *Contemporary Authors Bibliographical Series*
King, K., "Arthur Kopit," pp. 167–178 in King's *Ten Modern American Playwrights*
Przemecka, I., "European Influence on the Theatre of Edward Albee, Arthur Kopit and Sam Shepard," pp. 491–495 in M. Jurak, ed., *Cross-Cultural Studies*
Weaver, L. H., "Arthur Kopit (10 May 1937–)," pp. 226–238 in P. C. Kolin, ed., *American Playwrights since 1945*
American Theatre, 6:52, Sept. 1989
American Theatre, 6:57, Sept. 1989

Bone-the-Fish (original title of *Road to Nirvana,* which see), 1989
    Time, 133:71, 17 Apr. 1989

The Day the Whores Came out to Play Tennis, 1965
    Shrager, S., *Scatology in Modern Drama,* p. 51

End of the World (also known as *End of the World with Symposium to Follow*),
    1984 (revised 1987)
        Adler, T. P., "Public Faces, Private Graces: Apocalypse Postponed in Ar-
        thur Kopit's *End of the World,*" *Studies in the Literary Imagination,*
        21(2):107–118, Fall 1988

Indians, 1968
    Zinman, T. S., "Search and Destroy: The Drama of the Vietnam War,"
        Theatre Journal, 42:5–26, Mar. 1990
    TheaterWeek, 1:57, 23 May 1988

Road to Nirvana (formerly titled *Bone-the-Fish,* which see), 1990
    Playbill, 8:29, 30 June 1990
    TheaterWeek, 3:9, 23 Apr. 1990
    TheaterWeek, 4:7, 24 Sept. 1990

ARTHUR KOPIT and MAURY YESTON

Nine (musical based on F. Fellini's film *8½*), 1982
    Green, S., *Broadway Musicals,* p. 262
    TheaterWeek, 3:19, 25 Dec. 1989

BRAD KORBESMEYER

Incident at San Bajo, 1990
    Filichia, P., "New Directions," *TheaterWeek,* 3:42–43, 22 Jan. 1990

HOWARD KORDER

Boy's Life, 1988
    Paller, M., "Center Stage: The Atlantic Theater Company: A New *Life* in
        the Theater," *TheaterWeek,* 1:6–9, 15 Feb. 1988
    Shirakawa, S. H., "Strange Romances," *TheaterWeek,* 1:20–27, 25 Apr.
        1988
    New Republic, 198:26, 4 Apr. 1988
    New Yorker, 64:82–83, 28 Mar. 1988
    TheaterWeek, 1:28, 4 Jan. 1988
    TheaterWeek, 1:4, 25 Jan. 1988
    TheaterWeek, 1:6, 8 Feb. 1988
    TheaterWeek, 1:7, 30 May 1988
    Village Voice, 33:101, 8 Mar. 1988

The Pope's Nose (short plays, sketches, and monologues: *The Facts, Man in a
    Restaurant, Girls' Talk, The Middle Kingdom,* and *The Laws*), 1990
    TheaterWeek, 3:7, 4 June 1990

Search and Destroy, 1990
  Stayton, R., "The Fear Years," *American Theatre,* 6:8–9, Feb. 1990
  American Theatre, 7:1–15, June 1990 (text of play; special pull-out section)
  TheaterWeek, 3:6, 8 Jan. 1990

MICHAEL KORIE
SEE WILLY HOLTZMAN, SKIP KENNON, and MICHAEL KORIE

CAPPY KOTZ and PHRIN

In Search of the Hammer, 1983
  Case, S.-E., *Feminism and Theatre,* pp. 73–74

HY KRAFT

Café Crown, 1942
  Harap, L., *Dramatic Encounters,* pp. 133–134
  Kazan, E., *Elia Kazan,* pp. 191–192, 193, 201
  Marcuson, L. R., *The Stage Immigrant,* pp. 117–122
  Shirakawa, S. H., "Crown Matrimonial: Anne Jackson and Eli Wallach"
    (interview), *TheaterWeek,* 2:10–17, 31 October 1988
  Catholic World, 154:729–730, Mar. 1942
  Commonweal, 35:394, 6 Feb. 1942
  New Republic, 199:27–28, 12 Dec. 1988
  New York, 21:109, 7 Nov. 1988
  New Yorker, 17:28, 31 Jan. 1942
  New Yorker, 64:121, 14 Nov. 1988
  Theatre Arts, 26:220–221, Apr. 1942
  Village Voice, 33:99–100, 8 Nov. 1988

HY KRAFT, ALBERT HAGUE, and MARTY BRILL

Café Crown (musical version of Kraft's play), 1964
  Filichia, P., "*Café Crown*: The Musical?" *TheaterWeek,* 2:33–38, 5 Dec.
    1988
  Dance Magazine, 38:26–27, May 1964
  New Yorker, 40:130, 25 Apr. 1964

LARRY KRAMER

Kramer, L., *Reports from the Holocaust*
———, "Whose Bad Taste?" *American Theatre,* 6:9, Dec. 1989 (excerpted from
  his Introduction to *Just Say No*)
Paller, M., " 'Dangerous, Unpopular, and Controversial': An Encounter with
  Larry Kramer," *TheaterWeek,* 2:8–17, 17 Oct. 1988
Simpson, J. C., "Using the Rage to Fight the Plague" (interview), *Time,* 135:7–
  8, 5 Feb. 1990
New York Woman, 4:149, Sept. 1989
Manhattan, inc., 5:88, Sept. 1988
Pittsburgh Magazine, 19:31–32, Apr. 1988

Just Say No, 1988
>*New York,* 21:109–110, 7 Nov. 1988
>*New Yorker,* 64:134, 137–138, 7 Nov. 1988
>*TheaterWeek,* 2:6, 26 Sept. 1988

The Normal Heart, 1985
>Clum, J. M., " 'A Culture That Isn't Just Sexual': Dramatizing Gay Male History," *Theatre Journal,* 41:169–189, May 1989
>Gutwillig, S., "A Look Back in Anguish," *TheaterWeek,* 3:33–38, 25 Dec. 1989
>Shewey, D., "Gay Theatre Grows Up," *American Theatre,* 5:10–17, 52–53, May 1988
>*Chicago,* 36:101–103, July 1987
>*Maclean's,* 101:65, 14 Mar. 1988
>*TheaterWeek,* 3:18–19, 14 May 1990

Reports from the Holocaust (an excerpt from Kramer's book *Reports from the Holocaust* presented with *Jesse Helms Speaks,* which see, under the title *Indecent Materials*), 1990
Playbill, 9:34, 31 Oct. 1990
TheaterWeek, 4:15, 3 Sept. 1990
TheaterWeek, 4:44, 10 Sept. 1990

SHERRY KRAMER

New York Woman, 4:58, Oct. 1989

What a Man Weighs, 1990
>Spillane, M., "Librarians in Love," *TheaterWeek,* 3:40, 18 June 1990
>*American Theatre,* 6:62, Dec. 1989
>*New York,* 23:73–74, 4 June 1990
>*Village Voice,* 35:91 + , 5 June 1990

NORMAN KRASNA

Dear Ruth, 1944
>Counts, M. L., *Coming Home,* pp. 167–168

John Loves Mary, 1947
>Counts, M. L., *Coming Home,* pp. 98–99, 164, 168, 195

JOANNA KRAUS

The Devil's Orphan, winner of a 1988–1989 Indiana playwriting contest
>*American Theatre,* 6:108, Oct. 1989

HENRY KREISEL

Brenner, R. F., "Henry Kreisel—European Experience and Canadian Reality: A State of Mind," *World Literature Written in English*, 28(2):269–287, Autumn 1988

He Who Sells His Shadow, 1956 (a radio play)
>Riedel, W., "The Lost Shadow: Henry Kreisel's and Carl Weiselberger's Use of Adelbert von Chamisso's Literary Motif," *Canadian Review of Comparative Literature*, 14(2):211–222, June 1987

HENRY KRIEGER
SEE TOM EYEN and HENRY KRIEGER

JOHN KRIZANC

The Half of It, 1989
>*Maclean's*, 102:76, 4 Dec. 1989

Tamara, 1981
>Costache, I., "Il Vittoriale e D'Annunzio verso le coste del Pacifico," *Sipario*, 487:18–20, Mar.-Apr. 1989
>Filichia, P., "Center Stage: From *The Night of January 16th* to *Tamara*: It Couldn't Happen in a Movie," *TheaterWeek*, 1:8–11, 4 Jan. 1988
>Frassica, P., "Con D'Annunzio in camera da letto," *Sipario*, 487:20–22, Mar.-Apr. 1989
>MacLean, D., "Center Stage: *Tamara* Producer Moses Znaimer Establishes a New Medium," *TheaterWeek*, 1:12–15, 4 Jan. 1988
>Shirakawa, S. H., "Theater Trends: Isn't It Romantic?" *TheaterWeek*, 1:23–25, 18 Jan. 1988
>———, "Theater Trends: Political Action Plays," *TheaterWeek*, 1:13–15, 21 Mar. 1988
>*Connoisseur*, 218:138–143, May 1988
>*Film Comment*, 24:52–55, Mar./Apr. 1988
>*Harper's*, 277:12 + , Dec. 1988
>*Manhattan, inc.*, 5:142–145, Feb. 1988
>*New York*, 21:46, 4 Jan. 1988
>*Playbill*, 8:24, 31 Aug. 1990
>*TheaterWeek*, 3:13, 25 June 1990
>*Theatre Crafts*, 22:12, Feb. 1988
>*Town & Country*, 142:258–267, Nov. 1988
>*Village Voice*, 32:155 + , 15 Dec. 1987
>*Westways*, 80:6, Sept. 1988

LISA KRON

Paradykes Lost, 1988
>*Village Voice*, 33:97 + , 22 Mar. 1988

D. D. KUGLER
SEE RICHARD ROSE and D. D. KUGLER

MAGGIE KULIK

With All Coherence Gone, 1988
  TheaterWeek, 1:7, 23 May 1988

CASEY KURTTI

Three Ways Home, 1988
  New Yorker, 64:112, 6 June 1988
  TheaterWeek, 1:5, 18 Apr. 1988
  Village Voice, 33:116+, 24 May 1988

TONY KUSHNER

The Illusion (adaptation of P. Corneille's *L'Illusion Comique*), 1990
  Popkin, H., "Another Hit in Hartford," *TheaterWeek*, 3:42, 5 Feb. 1990
  American Theatre, 6:12, Mar. 1990
  Village Voice, 33:100, 8 Nov. 1988

WILLIAM POPE. L

Candide (based on story by Voltaire), 1989
  American Theatre, 6:9, July/Aug. 1989

LESLIE LABOWITZ

Sproutime, 1980
  Case, S.-E., *Feminism and Theatre*, pp. 58–59

ALSO SEE SUZANNE LACY and LESLIE LABOWITZ

MICHAEL JOHN LaCHIUSA

Eulogy for Mister Hamm, 1990
  American Theatre, 7:13, May 1990

SUZANNE LACY

Case, S.-E., *Feminism and Theatre*, p. 57

SUZANNE LACY and LESLIE LABOWITZ

Three Weeks in May, 1977
    Forte, J., "Women's Performance Art: Feminism and Postmodernism,"
    pp. 251–269 in S.-E. Case, ed., *Performing Feminisms* (rpt. of *Theatre
    Journal*, 40(2):217–235, May 1988)

MYRNA LAMB

Keyssar, H., "A Network of Playwrights," pp. 102–125 in Keyssar's *Feminist Theatre*

Apple Pie, 1974
Moore, H., "Woman Alone, Women Together," pp. 186–191 in H. K. Chinoy and L. W. Jenkins, eds., *Women in American Theatre,* rev. and enl. ed. (pp. 184–190 in 1981 ed.)

But What Have You Done For Me Lately?, 1969
Case, S.-E., *Feminism and Theatre,* p. 67
Natalle, E. J., *Feminist Theatre,* pp. 34–36 and elsewhere

ALONZO D. LAMONT, JR.

That Serious He-Man Ball, 1987
American Theatre, 5:50, Mar. 1989
Village Voice, 32:126 + , 1 Dec. 1987

MILLARD LAMPELL

The Wall (dramatization of novel by J. Hersey), 1960 (revised 1964)
Skloot, R., *The Darkness We Carry,* pp. 48–50

JAMES LAPINE

Table Settings, 1980
Cohen, E. M., *Working on a New Play,* pp. 20, 194–195

JAMES LAPINE and WILLIAM FINN

Falsettoland (third play of *Marvin's Trilogy*; the first is *In Trousers* by Finn, which see; the second is *March of the Falsettos* by Finn, which see), 1990
Botto, L., "*Falsettoland,*" *Playbill,* 9:56, 59–60, 31 Dec. 1990
Mandelbaum, K., "Urban Landscape," *TheaterWeek,* 3:42–43, 16 July 1990
Commonweal, 117:756–757, 21 Dec. 1990
Nation, 251:574–575, 12 Nov. 1990
New York, 23:47–48, 16 July 1990
Newsweek, 116:68, 8 Oct. 1990
TheaterWeek, 1:4, 11 July 1988
TheaterWeek, 3:9, 25 June 1990
TheaterWeek, 3:11, 23 July 1990
TheaterWeek, 4:37, 1 Oct. 1990
Time, 136:83, 1 Oct. 1990
Time, 136:54, 31 Dec. 1990

JAMES LAPINE and STEPHEN SONDHEIM

Into the Woods, 1986

Chase, A., "Onto the Road with *Into the Woods," TheaterWeek,* 2:8–15, 23 Jan. 1989

Flatow, S., "Sing a Song of Sondheim," *Playbill,* 6:14, 18, 20, 22–23, Jan. 1988

Mankin, N., "Contemporary Performance: The Emergence of the Fairy Tale," *Performing Arts Journal,* 11(1[31]):48–53, 1988

———, comp., "The PAJ Casebook #2: *Into the Woods," Performing Arts Journal,* 11(1[31]):47–66, 1988 (spec. sect.)

America, 157:458, 12 Dec. 1987

Commonweal, 115:18–19, 15 Jan. 1988

Connoisseur, 219:42, Apr. 1989

Dance Magazine, 62:64, Jan. 1988

Detroit Monthly, 12:38, May 1989

Drama, no. 167:40, 1988

Georgia Review, 42:602–603, Fall 1988

Horizon, 31:27–28, Jan./Feb. 1988

Hudson Review, 41:182–184, Spring 1988

Jet, 64:56–57, 13 June 1988

Los Angeles, 33:164–165, Jan. 1988

Los Angeles, 34:218+, Mar. 1989

Nation, 245:726–727, 12 Dec. 1987

New Leader, 70:18–19, 28 Dec. 1987

New Republic, 197:29–30, 21 Dec. 1987

New York, 20:50–51, 21 Sept. 1987

New York, 20:74–76+, 28 Sept. 1987

New York, 20:109–110, 16 Nov. 1987

New Yorker, 63:147–148, 16 Nov. 1987

Newsweek, 110:106–107, 16 Nov. 1987

Playbill, 9:96–97, 30 Nov. 1990

San Diego Magazine, 41:42+, Mar. 1989

TheaterWeek, 3:19, 25 Dec. 1989

Theatre Crafts, 22:28–32+, Jan. 1988

Time, 130:96–97, 16 Nov. 1987

Time, 135:100, 1 Jan. 1990

Village Voice, 32:109, 18 Nov. 1987

Vogue, 178:118, Feb. 1988

W, 16:25, 14 Dec. 1987

Sunday in the Park with George, 1984

Brustein, R., "Singing the Set," pp. 171–174 in Brustein's *Who Needs Theatre* (rpt. of *New Republic,* 190:25–26, 18 June 1984)

Cohen, E. M., *Working on a New Play,* pp. 20, 91, 129

Green, S., *Broadway Musicals,* p. 269

Kakutani, M., "Stephen Sondheim and James Lapine," pp. 186–193 in Kakutani's *The Poet at the Piano*

Playbill, 8:105, 31 May 1990

  TheaterWeek, 3:19, 25 Dec. 1989
  TheaterWeek, 3:22, 30 Apr. 1990

LARRY LARSON

Hulbert, D., "Actors Are the Spark for Atlanta's Writers," *American Theatre*, 7:44–45, June 1990

LARRY LARSON and LEVI LEE

Some Things You Need to Know before the World Ends (A Final Evening with the Illuminati), 1981
  American Theatre, 5:n. pag., May 1988 (text of play; special pull-out section)

ALSO SEE LEVI LEE, LARRY LARSON, and REBECCA WACKLER

ORRIE LASHIN and MILO HASTINGS

Class of '29, 1936
  Kazacoff, G., *Dangerous Theatre*, pp. 58–61

JOHN LATOUCHE
SEE HUGH WHEELER, LEONARD BERNSTEIN, RICHARD WILBUR, JOHN LATOUCHE, and STEPHEN SONDHEIM

ARTHUR LAURENTS

Home of the Brave, 1945
  Harap, L., *Dramatic Encounters*, p. 132
  Marcuson, L. R., *The Stage Immigrant*, pp. 154–159

ARTHUR LAURENTS, LEONARD BERNSTEIN, and STEPHEN SONDHEIM

West Side Story (based on J. Robbins's conception of Shakespeare's *Romeo and Juliet*), 1957
  Green, S., *Broadway Musicals*, pp. 174–175
  Ilson, C., "Broadway Innovation: *West Side Story*," pp. 33–43 in Ilson's *Harold Prince*

ARTHUR LAURENTS, RICHARD RODGERS, and STEPHEN SONDHEIM

Do I Hear a Waltz? (musical version of Laurents's play *The Time of the Cuckoo*), 1965
  Green, S., *Broadway Musicals*, p. 210
  TheaterWeek, 1:36–37, 14 Mar. 1988

ARTHUR LAURENTS, CHARLES STROUSE, and RICHARD MALTBY, JR.

Nick and Nora (musical based on characters created by D. Hammett), scheduled for 1991
　　TheaterWeek, 4:29–30, 13 Aug. 1990

ARTHUR LAURENTS, JULE STYNE, and STEPHEN SONDHEIM

Gypsy (musical based on the memoirs of G. R. Lee), 1959
　　Green, S., *Broadway Musicals,* pp. 182–183
　　Israel, L., "Move Over Ethel, Here Comes Tyne," *TheaterWeek,* 3:16–20, 27 Nov. 1989
　　Mandelbaum, K., "Hold Your Hats and Hallelujah: *Gypsy*'s Back," *TheaterWeek,* 3:22–25, 27 Nov. 1989
　　————, "Musical Comedy Heaven," *TheaterWeek,* 3:40, 11 Dec. 1989
　　Samelson, J., "Tyne's Turn," *Playbill,* 8:20, 22, 24, 26–28, 30 Nov. 1989
　　Walker, S., "Tyne's Turn," *TheaterWeek,* 3:33–35, 28 Aug. 1989
　　America, 162:14, 6–13 Jan. 1990
　　Connoisseur, 219:44 + , Nov. 1989
　　Dance Magazine, 64:62, Apr. 1990 (Joan Acocella)
　　Dance Magazine, 64:62, Apr. 1990 (Robert Sandla)
　　Hudson Review, 43:127–129, Spring 1990
　　Nation, 250:68, 8–15 Jan. 1990
　　New Republic, 202:27–28, Jan. 1990
　　New Yorker, 65:142–143, 4 Dec. 1989
　　People Weekly, 32:88–89, 3 July 1989
　　TheaterWeek, 1:60, 16 May 1988
　　TheaterWeek, 3:40, 15 Jan. 1990
　　TheaterWeek, 3:25, 2 July 1990
　　TheaterWeek, 4:36–37, 1 Oct. 1990
　　Time, 134:87, 27 Nov. 1989

SHIRLEY LAURO

Open Admissions, 1981 (revised 1984)
　　Cohen, E. M., *Working on a New Play,* pp. 195–196

A Piece of My Heart (based on oral histories in K. Walker's book), 1989
　　American Theatre, 6:9, May 1989

S. K. LAUSER

Women of Destiny (dramatization of his novel *The Heart Is Compelled*), 1936
　　Kazacoff, G., *Dangerous Theatre,* pp. 75–78

EMMET LAVERY

Bentley, J., *Hallie Flanagan,* pp. 277–278, 308–310, 352, 373–376

Monsignor's Hour, 1936
　　Kazacoff, G., *Dangerous Theatre,* pp. 209–211

EDDIE LAWRENCE

Animals (three plays: *The Beautiful Mariposa*, 1952; *Louie and the Elephant*; and *Sort of an Adventure*; the three first previewed in 1971 as *Louis and the Elephant*, with the third play being titled *The Adventure of Eddie Greshaw*), 1981
 Leonard, W. T., *Once Was Enough*, pp. 4–6

JACK LAWRENCE
SEE JEROME CHODOROV, JACK LAWRENCE, and STAN FREEMAN

JEROME LAWRENCE

"Writers of the World Answer Our Questionnaire" (interview), *Soviet Literature*, 5[470]:119–121, 1987
Playbill, 8:28, 30 Apr. 1990

JEROME LAWRENCE and ROBERT E. LEE

A Call on Kuprin (dramatization of novel by M. Edelman), 1961
 Ilson, C., *Harold Prince*, pp. 59–61

Inherit the Wind, 1955
 Playbill, 8:55–56, 31 Jan. 1990

Only in America (dramatization of book by H. Golden), 1959
 Marcuson, L. R., *The Stage Immigrant*, pp. 183–189

JEROME LAWRENCE, ROBERT E. LEE, and JERRY HERMAN

Mame (musical version of the novel by P. Dennis and the play based upon it by Lawrence and Lee, *Auntie Mame*), 1966
 Green, S., *Broadway Musicals*, p. 217
 TheaterWeek, 1:56, 23 May 1988

ALSO SEE NORMAN COUSINS, JEROME LAWRENCE, and ROBERT E. LEE

JOHN HOWARD LAWSON

Harap, L., *Dramatic Encounters*, pp. 94–96

Processional, 1925
 Demastes, W. W., *Beyond Naturalism*, p. 20
 Marcuson, L. R., *The Stage Immigrant*, pp. 57–62

Success Story, 1932
 Kazan, E., *Elia Kazan*, pp. 59, 64, 74–79, 82, 85, 86, 89, 95, 111
 Marcuson, L. R., *The Stage Immigrant*, pp. 43–48

JOHN LAZARUS

David for Queen, 1989
   van der Veen, J., "Theatre Transcends Issues: *David for Queen* by John
   Lazarus," *Canadian Theatre Review,* 59:42–46, Summer 1989

WILFORD LEACH

TheaterWeek, 1:2, 4 July 1988

WILLIAM S. LEAVENGOOD

Leavengood, W. S., "Actor Disaster," *TheaterWeek,* 3:38–41, 16 July 1990
———, "California Here I Come," *TheaterWeek,* 3:23–25, 29 Jan. 1990

Florida Crackers, 1989
   Ledford, L. A., "Drugs in the Sun," *TheaterWeek,* 2:42–43, 19 June 1989
   TheaterWeek, 2:6, 8 May 1989
   Village Voice, 34:119 + , 20 June 1989

BARBARA LEBOW

Hersh, A., "Author, Author: Finding the Connections: Barbara Lebow,"
   TheaterWeek, 1:24–25, 22 Feb. 1988
Hulbert, D., "Actors Are the Spark for Atlanta's Writers," *American Theatre,*
   7:44–45, June 1990

The Keepers, 1988
   American Theatre, 5:10–11, Nov. 1988

A Shayna Maidel, 1985
   Botto, L., "Blood Relations," *Playbill,* 6:41–44, Mar. 1988
   Village Voice, 32:112, 17 Nov. 1987

STANLEY LEBOWSKY
SEE PETER BELLWOOD, STANLEY LEBOWSKY, and FRED TOBIAS

ELIZABETH LeCOMPTE

Shank, T., "Spalding Gray and Elizabeth LeCompte: The Wooster Group," pp.
   170–179 in Shank's *American Alternative Theater*
Solomon, A., "Doubly Marginalized: Women in the Avant-Garde," pp. 363–
   371 in H. K. Chinoy and L. W. Jenkins, eds., *Women in American Theatre,*
   rev. and enl. ed. (new to this ed.)

ELIZABETH LeCOMPTE and OTHERS

Frank Dell's The Temptation of Saint Anthony (based on G. Flaubert's novel and
   other sources; Part Three of *The Road to Immortality*; Part One is *Route 1 &
   9 (The Last Act),* which see; Part Two is *L.S.D. (. . . Just the High Points
   . . .),* which see, 1988
   American Theatre, 6:12, Nov. 1989

TheaterWeek, 3:43, 9 Oct. 1989
Village Voice, 33:104, 25 Oct. 1988

Hula, 1981
  Savran, D., "From the Rhode Island Trilogy to *Hula*: Simple Demonstrations of the Law of Physics," pp. 47–167 in Savran's *The Wooster Group*

L.S.D. (. . . Just the High Points . . .) (Part Two of *The Road to Immortality*;
  Part One is *Route 1 & 9 (The Last Act),* which see; Part Three is *Frank Dell's
  The Temptation of Saint Anthony,* which see), 1984 (updated regularly)
  Aronson, A., "The Wooster Group's *L.S.D. (. . . Just the High Points
    . . .),*" *The Drama Review,* 23(1):13–30, 1985
  Demastes, W. W., "Spalding Gray's *Swimming to Cambodia* and the Evolution of an Ironic Presence," *Theatre Journal,* 41:75–94, Mar. 1989
  Erickson, J., "Appropriation and Transgression in Contemporary American
    Performance: The Wooster Group, Holly Hughes, and Karen Finley,"
    Theatre Journal, 42:225–236, May 1990
  Savran, D., "*L.S.D. (. . . Just the High Points . . .)*: History as Hallucination," pp. 169–200 in Savran's *The Wooster Group*
  Village Voice, 32:83+, 10 Feb. 1987
  Village Voice, 32:97, 17 Feb. 1987

Point Judith (the epilogue to *Three Places in Rhode Island,* which see), 1979
  Savran, D., "From the Rhode Island Trilogy to *Hula*: Simple Demonstrations of the Law of Physics," pp. 47–167 in Savran's *The Wooster Group*

Route 1 & 9 (The Last Act), 1981
  "Gray Areas: More Angry Words on *Route 1 & 9,*" *Village Voice,* 32:87,
    27 Jan. 1987
  Savran, D., "*Route 1 & 9 (The Last Act)*: The Disintegration of *Our Town,*"
    pp. 9–45 in Savran's *The Wooster Group*
  Village Voice, 32:85+, 13 Jan. 1987 (Michael Feingold)
  Village Voice, 32:85+, 13 Jan. 1987 (Erika Munk)
  Village Voice, 32:85–87, 13 Jan. 1987 (Thulani Davis)

Rumstick Road (Part Two of *Three Places in Rhode Island,* which see), 1977
  Schmitt, N. C., "Family Plays: *Long Day's Journey into Night* and *Rumstick
    Road,*" pp. 39–76 in Schmitt's *Actors and Onlookers*

Three Places in Rhode Island (trilogy: *Sahonnet Point,* 1975; *Rumstick Road,*
  1977, which see; *Nyatt School,* 1978), 1979
  Demastes, W. W., "Spalding Gray's *Swimming to Cambodia* and the Evolution of an Ironic Presence," *Theatre Journal,* 41:75–94, Mar. 1989
  Savran, D., "From the Rhode Island Trilogy to *Hula*: Simple Demonstrations of the Law of Physics," pp. 47–167 in Savran's *The Wooster
    Group*

CHARLES LEDERER, LUTHER DAVIS, ROBERT WRIGHT, GEORGE FORREST, and ALEXANDER BORODIN

Kismet (musical based on a play by E. Knoblock), 1953
    Green, S., *Broadway Musicals,* p. 158
    Stevens, R., "*Kismet* Tempts Fate Again," *TheaterWeek,* 1:28–33, 8 Aug. 1988

PAUL LEDOUX and DAVID YOUNG

Fire, 1984
    Kentridge, C., "Great Balls of *Fire*" (interview), *TheaterWeek,* 2:36–41, 13
    Feb. 1989

LESLIE LEE

Black Eagles, 1990
    American Theatre, 7:12, Apr. 1990
    TheaterWeek, 4:9, 13 Aug. 1990

Ground People (formerly known as *The Rabbit Foot,* which see), 1990
    American Theatre, 7:11, June 1990
    Playbill, 8:32, 30 Apr. 1990
    TheaterWeek, 3:11, 23 Apr. 1990
    TheaterWeek, 3:40, 21 May 1990
    Village Voice, 35:119+, 15 May 1990

The Rabbit Foot (see *Ground People*), 1989
    American Theatre, 5:14, Feb. 1989

LESLIE LEE, CHARLES STROUSE, and LEE ADAMS

Golden Boy (revised musical version of play by C. Odets), 1989
    Playbill, 7:33+, 30 Apr. 1989
    TheaterWeek, 2:7, 20 Mar. 1989
    TheaterWeek, 2:4, 24 Apr. 1989

LEVI LEE

Hulbert, D., "Actors Are the Spark for Atlanta's Writers," *American Theatre,*
    7:44–45, June 1990

LEVI LEE, LARRY LARSON, and REBECCA WACKLER

Tent Meeting, 1985
    Village Voice, 32:96, 14 Apr. 1987
    Village Voice, 32:89–90, 21 Apr. 1987

ALSO SEE PHILIP DePOY, LEVI LEE, and REBECCA WACKLER
AND LARRY LARSON and LEVI LEE

MARK LEE

Rebel Armies Deep into Chad, 1990
    Playbill, 8:34, 30 Apr. 1990

ROBERT E. LEE

"Writers of the World Answer Our Questionnaire" (interview), *Soviet Literature,* 5[470]:119–121, 1987
Playbill, 8:28, 30 Apr. 1990

ALSO SEE NORMAN COUSINS, JEROME LAWRENCE,
and ROBERT E. LEE
AND JEROME LAWRENCE and ROBERT E. LEE
AND JEROME LAWRENCE, ROBERT E. LEE, and JERRY HERMAN

JOHN LEGUIZAMO

Mambo Mouth, 1990
    Hurley, J., "The Man behind *Mambo Mouth,*" *TheaterWeek,* 4:27–29, 31
    Dec. 1990

JIM LEHRER

TV Guide, 35:17–19, 3 Oct. 1987

Chili Queen, 1987
    American Theatre, 4:5–6, Feb. 1988

Church Key Charlie Blue, 1988
    American Theatre, 4:5–6, Feb. 1988

JOHN LEICHT

Milwaukee Magazine, 12:19, Mar. 1987

ALSO SEE KERMIT FRAZIER and JOHN LEICHT

MITCH LEIGH

Schaeffer, M., "Searching for the Old Razzle-Dazzle" (interview), *TheaterWeek,*
    1:44–49, 16 May 1988
TheaterWeek, 1:39, 25 Jan. 1988

ALSO SEE DALE WASSERMAN, MITCH LEIGH, and JOE DARION

DAVID LEMOS

More than Names, 1988
    American Theatre, 5:13, Oct. 1988
    American Theatre, 5:11, Jan. 1989

GARY LENNON

Blackout, 1990
    TheaterWeek, 4:10, 15 Oct. 1990

JIM LEONARD, JR.

V & V Only, 1988
   American Theatre, 5:9, May 1988
   TheaterWeek, 1:4–5, 30 May 1988

ROBERT LEPAGE

Echo (dramatization of novel by A. Diamond, *A Nun's Diary*), 1989
   Maclean's, 102:95 + , 20 Nov. 1989

ROBERT LEPAGE and MICHAEL LEVINE

Tectonic Plates, 1988 (revised 1989)
   American Theatre, 6:31–32, May 1989

ALAN JAY LERNER

Lees, G., *Inventing Champagne*
Lerner, A. J., *The Musical Theatre*
——, *A Hymn to Him,* ed. B. Green
Playbill, 8:47, 30 Nov. 1989

ALAN JAY LERNER and FREDERICK LOEWE

My Fair Lady (musical version of G. B. Shaw's play *Pygmalion*), 1956
   Green, S., *Broadway Musicals,* pp. 168–169
   Journal of Canadian Studies, 23:115–116, Winter 1988–1989
   TheaterWeek, 1:36, 14 Mar. 1988

ALAN JAY LERNER and CHARLES STROUSE

Dance a Little Closer (musical version of R. E. Sherwood's play *Idiot's Delight*),
   1983
   Leonard, W. T., *Once Was Enough,* pp. 35–42
   TheaterWeek, 4:38–39, 3 Dec. 1990

ALAN JAY LERNER and KURT WEILL

Love Life (musical whose book was revised in 1990 by Thomas Babe), 1948
   Green, S., *Broadway Musicals,* p. 138
   Mandelbaum, K., "The First Concept Musical," *TheaterWeek,* 3:38–40, 2
      July 1990
   Stearns, D. P., "Kurt Weill in America," *American Theatre,* 7:6–7, June
      1990

RUBY LERNER
SEE GEORGE KING and RUBY LERNER

IRA LEVIN

Fletcher, R., "Rosemary's Bubbala," *TheaterWeek,* 2:56–60, 7 Nov. 1988

Break a Leg, 1974
Leonard, W. T., *Once Was Enough,* pp. 19–21

Cantorial, 1988
Botto, L., "Ira Levin's Singing Ghost," *Playbill,* 7:40, 43–45, 30 June 1989
Nation, 248:462–463, 3 Apr. 1989
TheaterWeek, 2:4, 17 Oct. 1988
Village Voice, 33:100, 8 Nov. 1988

Victoria's Room, 1973
Steele, T., "New York Deaf Theater," *TheaterWeek,* 4:40–41, 31 Dec. 1990

JACK LEVIN

Good Neighbor (originally titled *The Good Neighbor*), 1941
Leonard, W. T., *Once Was Enough,* pp. 66–67

MEYER LEVIN

Model Tenement, banned from production in 1937
Kazacoff, G., *Dangerous Theatre,* pp. 227–228

MICHAEL LEVINE
SEE ROBERT LEPAGE and MICHAEL LEVINE

BENN LEVY

Topaze (adaptation of play by M. Pagnol), 1930
Leonard, W. T., *Once Was Enough,* pp. 194–195

MAYA LEVY

Lutenbacher, C., "'So Much More Than Just Myself': Women Theatre Artists in the South," pp. 253–263 in J. Redmond, ed., *Women in Theatre*

JIM LEWIS
SEE GRACIELA DANIELE, JIM LEWIS, WILLIAM FINN,
and ASTOR PIAZZOLLA

SINCLAIR LEWIS and JOHN C. MOFFIT

It Can't Happen Here (dramatization of Lewis's novel), 1936
Bentley, J., *Hallie Flanagan,* pp. 241–245
Kazacoff, G., *Dangerous Theatre,* pp. 46, 116–126

LUDWIG LEWISOHN

Adam, 1929
    Harap, L., *Dramatic Encounters,* pp. 117–118

MARK LIEB

Terry by Terry (two one-acts: *Terry Won't Talk* and *Terry Rex*), 1988
    Raymond, R., "Serious Comedy: The Manhattan Punch Line,"
        TheaterWeek, 1:22–27, 9 May 1988
    TheaterWeek, 1:5–6, 2 May 1988

K. C. LIGON

Isle of Dogs, winner of the 1989 Deep South Writers' Conference playwriting
    award
    American Theatre, 6:62, Dec. 1989

RAFAEL LIMA

Miami, 39:16, Mar. 1987

Parting Gestures, 1989
    TheaterWeek, 3:8+ , 27 Nov. 1989
    Village Voice, 34:121, 26 Dec. 1989

El Salvador, 1987
    American Theatre, 6:10, July/Aug. 1989
    TheaterWeek, 3:15, 18 Sept. 1989
    Georgia Review, 42:596–597, Fall 1988

A. B. LINDLEY

Love and Friendship, 1809
    Harap, L., *The Image of the Jew in American Literature,* p. 202

HOWARD LINDSAY

TheaterWeek, 1:41, 28 Mar. 1988

She Loves Me Not, 1933
    Harap, L., *Dramatic Encounters,* p. 118

HOWARD LINDSAY and RUSSEL CROUSE

The Great Sebastians, 1956
    American Theatre, 5:9, Sept. 1988

State of the Union, 1945
    Stephens, J. L., "Women in Pulitzer Prize Plays, 1918–1949," pp. 245–253

in H. K. Chinoy and L. W. Jenkins, eds., *Women in American Theatre,*
rev. and enl. ed. (pp. 243–251 in 1981 ed.)

HOWARD LINDSAY, RUSSEL CROUSE, OSCAR HAMMERSTEIN II, and RICHARD RODGERS

The Sound of Music (musical based on *The Trapp Family Singers* by M. A.
Trapp), 1959
Flatow, S., "Debby Boone . . . Plays Maria von Trapp," *Playbill,* 8:50–51,
31 Mar. 1990
———, *"The Sound of Music," Playbill,* 8:52–53, 28 Feb. 1990
Green, S., *Broadway Musicals,* pp. 184–185
Mandelbaum, K., "Some Enchanted Evening," *TheaterWeek,* 3:40–41, 26
Mar. 1990
New Yorker, 66:74–75, 26 Mar. 1990
TheaterWeek, 2:57–58, 26 Sept. 1988

ROMULUS LINNEY

Wilmeth, D. B., "An Interview with Romulus Linney," *Studies in American
Drama, 1945–Present,* 2:71–84, 1987
———, "Romulus Linney (21 September 1930–)," pp. 239–249 in P. C. Kolin,
ed., *American Playwrights since 1945*

Heathen Valley (dramatization of his novel), 1988
Hurley, D. F., "Down in the Valley, the Valley So Low," *Appalachian
Journal,* 16(1):52–55, Fall 1988
American Theatre, 7:10, June 1990
San Diego Magazine, 41:58 + , Nov. 1988
TheaterWeek, 1:5, 20 June 1988
TheaterWeek, 2:9, 19 Dec. 1988
Village Voice, 33:104, 27 Dec. 1988

Holy Ghosts, 1974
TheaterWeek, 3:10, 22 Jan. 1990
TheaterWeek, 3:42–43, 12 Feb. 1990

Juliet, 1988
New Yorker, 64:73, 25 July 1988

Three Poets, 1989
Village Voice, 34:133, 28 Nov. 1989

Tonight We Love, 1990
American Theatre, 7:13, May 1990
TheaterWeek, 3:41, 25 June 1990

2, 1990
London, T., "6 Humana Plays Take the Woman's-Eye View," *American
Theatre,* 7:37–38, June 1990
TheaterWeek, 3:34, 30 Apr. 1990

KEN LIPMAN

Rosetta Street, 1990
  TheaterWeek, 4:10–11, 10 Dec. 1990
  TheaterWeek, 4:9, 17 Dec. 1990

JAMES LIPTON and LAURENCE ROSENTHAL

Sherry! (musical version of *The Man Who Came to Dinner,* play by G. S. Kaufman and M. Hart), 1967
  Driscoll, T., "Forgotten Musicals: *Sherry!" TheaterWeek,* 1:36–38, 4 Jan. 1988

HOMER LITTLE
SEE MYLA JO CLOSSER and HOMER LITTLE

ROBERT LITZ

Domino, 1988
  Nation, 246:726–727, 21 May 1988
  TheaterWeek, 1:4, 25 Apr. 1988

MYRTLE SMITH LIVINGSTON

Brown-Guillory, E., *Their Place on the Stage,* pp. 4–5, 10, 146

For Unborn Children, 1926
  Fletcher, W. L., "Who Put the 'Tragic' in the Tragic Mulatto?" pp. 262–268 in H. K. Chinoy and L. W. Jenkins, eds., *Women in American Theatre,* rev. and enl. ed. (pp. 260–266 in 1981 ed.)

FRANK LOESSER

The Most Happy Fella (musical version of *They Knew What They Wanted,* play by S. Howard), 1956
  Block, G., "Frank Loesser's Sketchbooks for *The Most Happy Fella," Musical Quarterly,* 73(1):60–78, 1989
  Green, S., *Broadway Musicals,* p. 170
  TheaterWeek, 1:55, 2 May 1988

ALSO SEE ABE BURROWS, JO SWERLING, and FRANK LOESSER
AND ABE BURROWS, JACK WEINSTOCK, WILLIE GILBERT, and FRANK LOESSER
AND SAMUEL SPEWACK and FRANK LOESSER

FREDERICK LOEWE

Lees, G., *Inventing Champagne*
Time, 131:94, 29 Feb. 1988

ALSO SEE ALAN JAY LERNER and FREDERICK LOEWE

JOHN LOGAN

Chicago, 36:41, Oct. 1987

Never the Sinner (based on the Leopold/Loeb murder case), 1989
    Playbill, 8:104, 31 May 1990
    TheaterWeek, 3:12, 14 Aug. 1989

Speaking in Tongues (about the death of Pier Paolo Pasolini), 1988
    American Theatre, 5:8, June 1988

JOSHUA LOGAN

American Theatre, 5:52, Sept. 1988
TheaterWeek, 1:7, 25 July 1988
Time, 132:73, 25 July 1988

ALSO SEE S. N. BEHRMAN, JOSHUA LOGAN, and HAROLD ROME
AND OSCAR HAMMERSTEIN II, JOSHUA LOGAN,
and RICHARD RODGERS

QUINCY LONG

Something about Baseball, 1988
    New Yorker, 64:74, 75, 25 July 1988

The Virgin Molly, 1990
    Istel, J., "Immaculate Conscription," *American Theatre,* 6:10–11, Mar. 1990

ANITA LOOS

Carey, G., *Anita Loos*
Raymond, G., "A Girl Like Her" (interview with Gary Carey), *TheaterWeek,*
2:20–29, 16 Jan. 1989

Chéri (dramatization of novels by Colette), 1959
    TheaterWeek, 2:8, 22 May 1989

ALSO SEE JOHN EMERSON and ANITA LOOS

EDUARDO IVAN LOPEZ

A Silent Thunder, 1990
    TheaterWeek, 3:11, 2 July 1990
    TheaterWeek, 3:43, 23 July 1990

Spanish Eyes, 1990
  American Theatre, 7:13, May 1990
  TheaterWeek, 3:10, 14 May 1990

JOSEFINA LOPEZ

Real Women Have Curves, 1990
  Bensussen, M., "Whose Language Is It?" *American Theatre,* 7:82–83, Oct. 1990

W. W. LORD

André, 1856
  Harap, L., *The Image of the Jew in American Literature,* pp. 210–211

STEVEN LOTT

MacBeth in Hell, 1989
  TheaterWeek, 3:43, 9 Oct. 1989

PATRICIA LOUGHREY

The Inner Circle, 1988
  American Theatre, 5:10, Jan. 1989

NIKKI LOUIS and OTHERS

Changing Faces, 1988
  American Theatre, 4:6, Feb. 1988

SAMUEL LOW

The Politician Out-Witted, written 1788, first performed 1987
  Theatre Journal, 40:275–276, May 1988

FLORENCE LOWE and CAROLINE FRANCKE

The 49th Cousin, 1960
  Marcuson, L. R., *The Stage Immigrant,* pp. 269–275

ROBERT LOWELL

Axelrod, S. G., and L. Strahan, *Robert Lowell*
Bloom, H., ed., *Robert Lowell*
Meyers, J., ed., *Robert Lowell*
Stuprich, M., "Robert Lowell (1 March 1917–12 September 1977)," pp. 250–258 in P. C. Kolin, ed., *American Playwrights since 1945*

The Old Glory (three plays: *Endecott and the Red Cross,* a dramatization of N.
Hawthorne's story of that title and of his story "The Maypole of Merry
Mount"; *My Kinsman, Major Molineaux,* a dramatization of N. Hawthorne's
story; and *Benito Cereno,* a dramatization of H. Melville's novella), 1964
    Bouchard, L. D., "'Waiting on Providence': *The Old Glory,*" pp. 141–168
    in Bouchard's *Tragic Method and Tragic Theology*
    Shirakawa, S. H., "American Place: The Original Underground Theater,"
    TheaterWeek, 2:22–29, 7 Nov. 1988
    Strout, C., "Refractions of History: Lowell's Revision of Hawthorne and
    Melville in *The Old Glory,*" pp. 100–116 in Strout's *Making American
    Tradition* (rpt. of *Southern Review,* 25(3):549–562, Summer 1989)

Prometheus Bound (adaptation of play by Aeschylus), 1967
    Bouchard, L. D., "An Interpretive Addendum: *Prometheus Bound,*"
    pp. 168–175 in Bouchard's *Tragic Method and Tragic Theology*

JACKIE LUBECK and FRANÇOIS ABU SALEM

The Story of Kufur Shamma, date of première unknown
    "Notes and Comments," *New Yorker,* 65:23–24, 28 Aug. 1989
    New York, 22:45, 7 Aug. 1989

CRAIG LUCAS

Flatow, S., "Getting *Reckless,*" *TheaterWeek,* 2:8–15, 3 Oct. 1988
Hopkins, B., "Craig Lucas" (interview), *BOMB,* 28:56–59, Summer 1989
London, T., "Opening a Door Up Left," *American Theatre,* 5:38–41, Mar. 1989
Lucas, C., "A Gay Life in the Theatre," *American Theatre,* 7:24–27, 29, 68,
    Nov. 1990
TheaterWeek, 3:12, 6 Aug. 1990
Village Voice, 35:74, 29 May 1990
W, 19:21, 30 Apr. 1990

Prelude to a Kiss, 1988
    Flatow, S., "Atypical Love Story," *Playbill,* 8:8, 10, 12, 31 July 1990
    Raymond, G., "Prelude to a . . . Star," *TheaterWeek,* 3:21–23, 19 Mar. 1990
    Riedel, M., "Kiss and Tell," *TheaterWeek,* 3:39, 26 Mar. 1990
    American Theatre, 4:11, Mar. 1988
    American Theatre, 7:7, June 1990
    Commonweal, 117:456, 10 Aug. 1990
    New Republic, 202:27–28, 16 Apr. 1990
    New York, 23:87–88, 26 Mar. 1990
    New York, 23:125–126, 14 May 1990
    New Yorker, 66:74, 26 Mar. 1990
    TheaterWeek, 3:25, 4 Sept. 1989
    TheaterWeek, 3:13, 19 Feb. 1990
    TheaterWeek, 3:16, 28 May 1990
    Time, 136:54, 31 Dec. 1990
    Village Voice, 35:99 + , 27 Mar. 1990
    Village Voice, 35:63, 15 May 1990

Village Voice, 35:74, 29 May 1990

Reckless, 1983 (revised several times)
   American Theatre, 5:10, Nov. 1988
   American Theatre, 5:n. pag., Jan. 1989 (text of play; special pull-out section)
   American Theatre, 6:66, Dec. 1989
   Commonweal, 115:687–688, 16 Dec. 1989
   Georgia Review, 43:576–577, Fall 1989
   New Republic, 199:28, 31 Oct. 1988
   New York, 21:75, 10 Oct. 1988
   New Yorker, 64:85, 10 Oct. 1988
   New Yorker, 65:90, 20 Feb. 1989
   Playbill, 7:101–102, 31 Dec. 1988
   TheaterWeek, 2:5, 19 Sept. 1988
   Time, 132:85, 31 Oct. 1988
   Village Voice, 33:109, 4 Oct. 1988

CRAIG LUCAS and CRAIG CARNELIA

Three Postcards, 1987
   Chicago, 37:115–116, Jan. 1988
   Village Voice, 32:105, 26 May 1987

CLARE BOOTHE LUCE

Morris, S., "In Search of Clare Boothe Luce," *New York Times Magazine,* pp. 22–27 + , 31 Jan. 1988
American Spectator, 21:30–31, Jan. 1988
Playbill, 6:4, Feb. 1988

ALSO SEE CLARE BOOTHE

WILLIAM LUCE

The Belle of Amherst (based on the life and writings of E. Dickinson), 1976
   Gentile, J. S., *Cast of One,* p. 138
   Helle, A. P., "Re-Presenting Women Writers Onstage: A Retrospective to the Present," pp. 195–208 in L. Hart, ed., *Making a Spectacle*

Bravo, Caruso, 1991
   TheaterWeek, 3:16, 30 July 1990

CHARLES LUDLAM

Bentley, E., "Ludlam's Magic Ring," *TheaterWeek,* 3:26, 23 Apr. 1990
"Charles Ludlam: 1943–1987," *Village Voice,* 32:88, 9 June 1987
Essman, J., "Big Wigs in the Mainstream," *TheaterWeek,* 3:19–22, 23 Apr. 1990
Ludlam, C., "Observations on Acting," *American Theatre,* 7:36–39, 123–124, Oct. 1990

—————, *The Complete Plays of Charles Ludlam,* ed. S. Samuels and E. Quinton
Shirakawa, S. H., "Everett Quinton: After Charles," *TheaterWeek,* 1:34–39, 11
    July 1988
Andy Warhol's Interview, 19:78+, Dec. 1989
Playbill, 8:58, 30 Nov. 1989
The Drama Review, 31:8–9, Winter 1987
Village Voice, 32:88+, 9 June 1987 (Michael Feingold)
Village Voice, 32:98, 9 June 1987 (Michael T. Smith)
Village Voice, 32:98, 9 June 1987 (Guy Trebay)
Village Voice, 32:97–98, 4 Aug. 1987

Big Hotel, 1967
    Helbing, T., "There's a Small Hotel," *TheaterWeek,* 3:43, 16 Oct. 1989
    Playbill, 8:48, 31 Oct. 1989
    TheaterWeek, 3:4, 2 Oct. 1989
    Village Voice, 34:107+, 10 Oct. 1989 (Gordon Rogoff)
    Village Voice, 34:100, 10 Oct. 1989 (Otis Stuart)

Camille: A Tear-Jerker (based on A. Dumas *fils'* novel and play, *La dame aux
    Camélias*), 1973
    Botto, L., "Ridiculous *Camille,*" *Playbill,* 8:48, 51–53, 30 Sept. 1990
    Nation, 251:575, 12 Nov. 1990
    Playbill, 9:33, 31 Oct. 1990
    TheaterWeek, 4:31, 10 Sept. 1990

The Isle of the Hermaphrodites, or the Murdered Minion, 1988
    American Theatre, 5:13, Oct. 1988
    TheaterWeek, 2:7, 10 Oct. 1988

Medea: A Tragedy (based on many translations of Euripides's play and on other
    sources), 1985
    Village Voice, 32:110, 17 Nov. 1987

The Mystery of Irma Vep, 1984
    Playbill, 9:64, 31 Dec. 1990
    San Diego Magazine, 40:48+, July 1988
    Theatre Journal, 42:247–248, May 1990

Der Ring Gott Farblonjet, 1977
    Nation, 250:717, 21 May 1990
    Playbill, 8:32, 30 Apr. 1990
    TheaterWeek, 3:41, 30 Apr. 1990
    Village Voice, 35:103, 24 Apr. 1990

Stage Blood, 1974
    TheaterWeek, 1:6, 11 July 1988

CHARLES LUDLAM and BILL VEHR

Turds in Hell, 1969
    Shirakawa, S. H., "Audience Notes: Alternating Currents," *TheaterWeek,*
    1:36–38, 29 Feb. 1988
    TheaterWeek, 1:29, 25 Jan. 1988

KEN LUDWIG

Sandla, R., "The Playwright in the Grey Flannel Suit" (includes an interview),
    TheaterWeek, 2:52–60, 20 Mar. 1989
Washingtonian, 22:24–25, Jan. 1987

Lend Me a Tenor (originally titled *Opera Buffa*), 1988
    Barbour, D., "Philip Bosco: A Night at the Opera," *TheaterWeek,* 2:10–
    17, 6 Mar. 1989
    American Theatre, 5:44, Mar. 1989
    Nation, 248:534–535, 17 Apr. 1989
    New York, 22:74–75, 13 Mar. 1989
    New Yorker, 65:74, 13 Mar. 1989
    Village Voice, 34:95–96, 14 Mar. 1989

Sullivan and Gilbert, 1984
    Maclean's, 101:55, 18 July 1988
    TheaterWeek, 1:6, 20 June 1988

BRENDA SHOSHANNA LUKEMAN

Double Blessing, 1989
    Helbing, T., "Bells are Ringing," *TheaterWeek,* 2:41, 17 July 1989
    TheaterWeek, 2:6, 3 July 1989

CHARLES MacARTHUR
SEE BEN HECHT and CHARLES MacARTHUR

GALT MacDERMOT
SEE WILLIAM DUMARESQ and GALT MacDERMOT
AND GEROME RAGNI, JAMES RADO, and GALT MacDERMOT

ANN-MARIE MacDONALD

Goodnight Desdemona, 1989
    Fortier, M., "Shakespeare with Difference: Genderbending and Genre-
    bending in *Goodnight Desdemona,*" *Canadian Theatre Review,* 59:47–51,
    Summer 1989
    Maclean's, 103:66, 29 Jan. 1990

LEUEEN MacGRATH
SEE GEORGE S. KAUFMAN and LEUEEN MacGRATH

EDUARDO MACHADO

Gray, A., "The Big If," *American Theatre,* 6:18–21, 56, June 1989
Henry, W. A., III, "Visions from the Past," *Time,* 132:82–83, 11 July 1988

Machado, E., tr., *The Day You'll Love Me* (play by José Ignacio Cabrujas), *American Theatre*, 6:1–11, Sept. 1989 (text of play; special pull-out section)

Broken Eggs (the third play of the Floating Islands trilogy; the first is *The Modern Ladies of Guanabacoa*, the second *Fabiola*), 1984
  Osborn, M. E., ed., *On New Ground*, pp. vi–viii (Preface), 143–148, 149–189 (text of play)

A Burning Beach, 1988
  Shirakawa, S. H., "American Place: The Original Underground Theater," *TheaterWeek*, 2:22–29, 7 Nov. 1988
  TheaterWeek, 2:8, 31 Oct. 1988
  Village Voice, 33:104, 15 Nov. 1988

Cabaret Bambu, 1989
  TheaterWeek, 2:6, 7 Aug. 1989

Once Removed, 1987
  American Theatre, 4:10, Feb. 1988

Related Retreats, 1990
  Village Voice, 35:114, 24 Apr. 1990

Stevie Wants to Play the Blues (A Jazz Play), 1990
  Glore, J., "Gender-Bender Blues," *American Theatre*, 7:8–9, Apr. 1990
  TheaterWeek, 3:15, 19 Mar. 1990

EDUARDO MACHADO and SERGIO GARCIA-MARRUIZ

Don Juan in N.Y.C., 1988
  TheaterWeek, 2:8, 31 Oct. 1988

PERCY MacKAYE

The Scarecrow (dramatization of N. Hawthorne's story "Feathertop"), 1908
  Marks, P., "*The Scarecrow*: Percy MacKaye's Adaptation of 'Feathertop,'" *Nathaniel Hawthorne Review*, 14(1):13–15, Spring 1988

STEELE MacKAYE

Money-Mad, 1890
  Harap, L., *The Image of the Jew in American Literature*, p. 216

JAMES BOVELL MACKENZIE

Thayandenegea, published 1898
  Jones, E. H., *Native Americans as Shown on the Stage*, p. 136

BARTON MacLANE

Rendezvous, 1932
Counts, M. L., *Coming Home,* pp. 61–62, 112–113, 149, 178

ARCHIBALD MacLEISH

Engler, B., "Der 'doppelte' Sündenfall ins menschliche Selbstbewusst-Sein: Alttestamentliche Typologie in Dramen Archibald MacLieschs, Howard Nemerovs, Arthur Millers und Jean-Claude von [sic] Itallies," pp. 591–609 in F. Link, ed., *Paradeigmata*

The Fall of the City, 1937
French, W., " 'That Never Realized, Never Abandoned Dream,' " *Pembroke Magazine,* 7:123–131, 1976
Novak, G. D., "A Poet's Gift to Radio: Archibald MacLeish's *The Fall of the City,*" *West Georgia College Review,* 19:1–9, May 1987
Roulston, R., "Recollections of the First Broadcast of *The Fall of the City,*" *Pembroke Magazine,* 7:93–94, 1976

J.B.: A Play in Verse, 1958
Calhoun, R. J., "Archibald MacLeish's *J.B.*—A Retrospective Look," *Pembroke Magazine,* 7:74–77, 1976
Kazan, E., *Elia Kazan,* pp. 582–584, 592, 682–683
MacLeish, A., "MacLeish Speaks to the Players" (ed. B. A. Drabeck and H. E. Ellis), *Pembroke Magazine,* 7:78–87, 1976
Siebald, M., "Archibald MacLeishs *J.B.* und das Buch Hiob," pp. 759–774 in F. Link, ed., *Paradeigmata*
Stout, J. P., "Re-Visions of Job: *J.B.* and 'A Masque of Reason,' " *Essays in Literature,* 14(2):225–239, Fall 1987
Walters, T. N., " 'A Work of a Man': A Personal Appreciation of MacLeish's *J.B.,*" *Pembroke Magazine,* 7:65–73, 1976

JOAN MacLEOD

Amigo's Blue Guitar, 1990
Maclean's, 103:66, 29 Jan. 1990

WENDY MacLEOD

Apocalyptic Butterflies, 1988
TheaterWeek, 2:6, 29 May 1989
TheaterWeek, 4:41–42, 10 Dec. 1990

The House of Yes, 1990
TheaterWeek, 4:41–42, 10 Dec. 1990

ALEXANDER MACOMB

Pontiac; or, The Siege of Detroit, 1838
Jones, E. H., *Native Americans as Shown on the Stage,* pp. 32–33

DAVID MAGIDSON

New Hampshire Profiles, 36:90 + , Aug. 1987

ANN MAGNUSON

Transmissions, 1987
  Artforum, 26:135–136, Nov. 1987

JAMES MAGRUDER

Nesteggs for Armageddon, 1989
  TheaterWeek, 3:12, 6 Nov. 1989

MATTHEW MAGUIRE

Propaganda, 1987
  Village Voice, 32:92, 19 May 1987

RICHARD MAIBAUM

A Moral Entertainment, 1938
  Kazacoff, G., *Dangerous Theatre,* pp. 180–183

CHARLES MAIR

Tecumseh, 1886
  Jones, E. H., *Native Americans as Shown on the Stage,* p. 35

RUTH MALECZECH and HERSCHEL GARFEIN

Sueños (adaptation of various works by others, especially by E. Galeano), 1989
  Berreby, D., "Spanish for Dreams," *TheaterWeek,* 2:54–59, 27 Feb. 1989
  American Theatre, 5:13, Feb. 1989
  Village Voice, 34:89–90, 7 Mar. 1989

GAIL KRIEGEL MALLIN

Holy Places, 1979
  Moore, H., "Woman Alone, Women Together," pp. 186–191 in H. K. Chinoy and L. W. Jenkins, eds., *Women in American Theatre,* rev. and enl.
  ed. (pp. 184–190 in 1981 ed.)

KAREN MALPEDE

Betsko, K., and R. Koenig, *Interviews with Contemporary Women Playwrights,*
  pp. 259–273
Case, S.-E., *Feminism and Theatre,* pp. 72–73
Neff, R., "Theater People: Judith Malina: Living Tradition, Living Theater,"
  TheaterWeek, 1:24–27, 25 Jan. 1988

Better People: A Surreal Comedy about Genetic Engineering, 1990
  TheaterWeek, 3:39–40, 26 Feb. 1990
  Theatre Journal, 42:369–370, Oct. 1990
  Village Voice, 35:102, 13 Feb. 1990

The End of the War, 1977
  Natalle, E. J., *Feminist Theatre,* pp. 41–44 and elsewhere

Rebeccah, 1976
  Malpede, K., "*Rebeccah*: Rehearsal Notes," pp. 308–310 in H. K. Chinoy
    and L. W. Jenkins, eds., *Women in American Theatre,* rev. and enl. ed.
    (pp. 311–315 in 1981 ed.)

Us, 1987
  Koenig, R., "Malina Steers New Path for The Living Theatre," *American
    Theatre,* 4:48–49, Mar. 1988
  Village Voice, 33:87, 5 Jan. 1988

RICHARD MALTBY, JR.
SEE ARTHUR LAURENTS, CHARLES STROUSE,
and RICHARD MALTBY, JR.

DAVID MAMET

Blumberg, M., "Eloquent Stammering in the Fog: O'Neill's Heritage in Mamet,"
  pp. 97–111 in S. Bagchee, ed., *Perspectives on O'Neill*
Bruster, D., "David Mamet and Ben Jonson: City Comedy Past and Present,"
  Modern Drama, 33:333–346, Sept. 1990
Carroll, D., *David Mamet*
Davis, J. M., and J. Coleman, "David Mamet: A Classified Bibliography," *Stud-
  ies in American Drama, 1945–Present,* 1:83–101, 1986
Dean, A., "Musings on Mamet," *Drama,* no. 169:25–26, 1988
Demastes, W. W., "David Mamet's Dis-Integrating Drama," pp. 67–94 in De-
  mastes's *Beyond Naturalism*
Harriott, E., "David Mamet: Comedies of Bad Manners," pp. 61–76, and "In-
  terview with David Mamet," pp. 77–97, in Harriott's *American Voices*
Hubert-Leibler, P., "Dominance and Anguish: The Teacher-Student Relation-
  ship in the Plays of David Mamet," *Modern Drama,* 31(4):557–570, Dec. 1988
Kim, M., "Mamet's World of Collapse," *Journal,* 21:29–44, 1988
King, K., "David Mamet," pp. 179–186 in King's *Ten Modern American Play-
  wrights*
Kolin, P. C., "David Mamet's *Writing in Restaurants*: A Primary and Secondary
  Bibliography," *Analytical & Enumerative Bibliography,* 2(4):160–167, 1988
London, T., "Chicago Impromptu," *American Theatre,* 7:14–23, 60–64, July/
  Aug. 1990
Lundin, E., "Mamet and Mystery," *Publications of the Mississippi Philological
  Association,* 106–114, 1988
Mamet, D., " 'He's the Kind of Guy Who . . .': An Essay on Dramatic Char-
  acter," *TheaterWeek,* 3:12–17, 22 Jan. 1990
————, "One April, 1988" (poem), *Paris Review,* 30:197, Summer 1988

————, *Some Freaks*

————, "Two Men" (poem), *Paris Review,* 32:43, Spring 1990

Myers, L., "Critic, Cornered: Michael Feingold Speaks Out" (interview), *TheaterWeek,* 1:28–34, 11 Jan. 1988

Nuwer, H., "A Life in the Theatre: David Mamet" (interview), *Rendezvous,* 21(1):1–7, Fall 1985

Peereboom, J. J., "Mamet from Afar," pp. 189–200 in G. Debusscher, H. I. Schvey, and M. Maufort, eds., *New Essays on American Drama*

Pinazzi, A., "David Mamet: Il teatro ritrova la parola," *Il Ponte,* 43(1):119–136, Jan.-Feb. 1987

Roudané, M. C., "An Interview with David Mamet," *Studies in American Drama, 1945–Present,* 1:73–81, 1986

Rouyer, P., "David Mamet: Une Nouvelle Ecriture Amèricaine," *Revue Française d'Etudes Américaines,* 13(32):215–226, Apr. 1987

Savran, D., "David Mamet," pp. 132–144 in Savran's *In Their Own Words*

Schlueter, J., "David Mamet 1947– ," pp. 141–169 in M. C. Roudané, ed., *Contemporary Authors Bibliographical Series*

Schvey, H. I., "The Plays of David Mamet: Games of Manipulation and Power" (includes an interview), *New Theatre Quarterly,* 4:77–86 + , Feb. 1988

Trigg, J., "David Mamet (30 November 1947–)," pp. 259–288 in P. C. Kolin, ed., *American Playwrights since 1945*

Van Wert, W. F., "Psychoanalysis and 'House of Games,'" *Film Quarterly,* 43:3–10, Summer 1990

Wiles, T. J., "Talk Drama: Recent Writers in the American Theater," *Amerikastudien,* 32(1):65–79, 1987

American Theatre, 5:44, Mar. 1989

Andy Warhol's Interview, 17:140–141, Oct. 1987

Boston, 80:29, June 1988

Chicago, 37:104 + , May 1988

Elle, 2:106 + , June 1987

Pacific Northwest, 20:18, Oct. 1986

W, 16:26, 21 Sept. 1987

American Buffalo, 1975

Cohen, E. M., *Working on a New Play,* pp. 115–116

Bobby Gould in Hell (presented with Shel Silverstein's *The Devil and Billy Markham* under the title *Oh, Hell*), 1989

Greene, A., "A Woman in Hell," *TheaterWeek,* 3:22–23, 18 Dec. 1989

New Republic, 202:28, 29 Jan. 1989

New York, 22:105, 18 Dec. 1989

New Yorker, 65:77–79, 25 Dec. 1989

TheaterWeek, 3:13, 23 Oct. 1989

Time, 134:78, 18 Dec. 1989

Village Voice, 34:116, 19 Dec. 1989

Duck Variations, 1972

Callens, J., "'Allemaal mooie woorden, de eenden leggen de eieren' of David Mamets *Duck Variations,*" *Documenta,* 5(4):229–251, 1987

Edmond, 1982
  Savran, D., *Danger,* n. pag.

The Frog Prince (presented with Israel Horovitz's *It's Called the Sugar Plum*
  under the title *Love in the Afternoon*), 1985
  TheaterWeek, 3:12, 5 Feb. 1990

Glengarry Glen Ross, 1983
  Brustein, R., "Show and Tell," pp. 67–71 in Brustein's *Who Needs Theatre*
    (rpt. of *New Republic,* 190:27–29, 7 May 1984
  Forbes, D., "Dirty Dealing," *American Theatre,* 4:12–18, Feb. 1988
  Hasenberg, P., "'Always Be Closing': Struktur und Thema von David Ma-
    mets *Glengarry Glen Ross,*" *Anglistik & Englischunterricht,* 35:177–191,
    1988
  Kolin, P. C., "Mitch and Murray in David Mamet's *Glengarry Glen Ross,*"
    Notes on Contemporary Literature, 18(2):3–5, Mar. 1988
  Roudané, M. C., "Public Issues, Private Tensions: David Mamet's *Glen-
    garry Glen Ross,*" *South Carolina Review,* 19(1):35–47, Fall 1986
  San Diego Magazine, 41:50+, Dec. 1988

A Life in the Theatre, 1977
  Playbill, 8:64, 31 Jan. 1990

The Revenge of the Space Pandas; or, Binky Rudich and the Two-Speed Clock,
  1977
  TheaterWeek, 3:8, 7 May 1990

The Shawl, 1985
  Kolin, P. C., "Revealing Illusions in David Mamet's *The Shawl,*" *Notes on
    Contemporary Literature,* 16(2):9–10, Mar. 1986

Speed-the-Plow, 1988
  Henry, W. A., III, "Madonna Comes to Broadway," *Time,* 131:98–99, 16
    May 1988
  American Theatre, 5:7, July/Aug. 1988
  American Theatre, 6:1, Apr. 1989
  Commonweal, 115:371, 17 June 1988
  Drama, no. 169:411–43, 1988
  Georgia Review, 42:601–602, Fall 1988
  Hudson Review, 41:516–518, Autumn 1988
  Los Angeles, 33:160+, July 1988
  Nation, 246:874–875, 18 June 1988
  New Leader, 71:20–21, 13 June 1988
  New Republic, 198:29–31, 6 June 1988
  New York, 21:106, 16 May 1988
  New York Review of Books, 35:3–4+, 21 July 1988
  New Yorker, 64:95, 16 May 1988
  Newsweek, 111:82–83, 16 May 1988
  People Weekly, 29:48–49, 2 May 1988
  Playbill, 7:88, 31 Mar. 1989

TheaterWeek, 1:55, 16 May 1988
Time, 131:92, 14 Mar. 1988
Vanity Fair, 51:32 + , Apr. 1988
Village Voice, 33:105–106, 17 May 1988
Village Voice, 33:57, 19 July 1988
W Supplement, 17:1–8, 27 June 1988

Squirrels, 1974
Commonweal, 117:117–118, 23 Feb. 1990

Two War Scenes, 1990
American Theatre, 7:13, May 1990

Uncle Vanya (adaptation of play by A. Chekhov), 1988
American Theatre, 7:12, May 1990
Theatre Journal, 41:101–103, Mar. 1989

DAVID MAMET and SHEL SILVERSTEIN

Life from the Empire Hotel (a radio drama performed before a live audience), 1990
TheaterWeek, 3:8, 5 Feb. 1990

TIM MANER

Icarus, 1988
Village Voice, 33:122–123, 20 Dec. 1988

EMILY MANN

Betsko, K., and R. Koenig, *Interviews with Contemporary Playwrights,* pp. 274–286
Gray, A., "The Big If," *American Theatre,* 6:18–21, 56, June 1989
Kolin, P. C., and L. Daniel, "Emily Mann: A Classified Bibliography," *Studies in American Drama, 1945–Present,* 4:223–266, 1989
Savran, D., "Emily Mann," pp. 145–160, in Savran's *In Their Own Words*
American Theatre, 6:44, Feb. 1990
TheaterWeek, 3:9, 2 July 1990

Annulla, an Autobiography, 1985 revision of *Annulla Allen: Autobiography of a Survivor* (1977)
Hersh, A., "A Survivor's Voice," *American Theatre,* 5:8–9, Nov. 1988
Village Voice, 33:100, 8 Nov. 1988

Execution of Justice, 1983
Feldshuh, D., "In Praise of Docudrama" (letter), *American Theatre,* 6:62, Mar. 1990
Hall, R., "Eleven Different Directions," *American Theatre,* 5:32–33, Dec. 1988

Shewey, D., "Gay Theatre Grows Up," *American Theatre,* 5:10–17, May 1988

Still Life, 1980
  Counts, M. L., *Coming Home,* pp. 55–56, 75, 148, 162–163, 178
  Savran, D., *Danger,* n. pag.
  Zinman, T. S., "Search and Destroy: The Drama of the Vietnam War,"
    Theatre Journal, 42:5–26, Mar. 1990

ALSO SEE NTOZAKE SHANGE, EMILY MANN,
and BAIKIDA CARROLL

J. HARTLEY MANNERS

The House Next Door, 1909
  Harap, L., *Dramatic Encounters,* pp. 76–77

KEITH MANO

Resistance, 1988
  Village Voice, 33:105–106, 14 June 1988

JOE MANTEGNA

Bleacher Bums, 1989
  Chicago, 38:22, July 1989
  Los Angeles, 34:230+, Oct. 1989
  Sports Illustrated, 70:16, 26 June 1989

WARREN MANZI

Perfect Crime, 1987 (revised frequently)
  Godfrey, T., "Foul Play on Broadway," *Armchair Detective,* 21(1):5–14,
    Winter 1988
  Henderson, K., "Murder, He Writes," *TheaterWeek,* 2:34–36, 12 Dec. 1988
  TheaterWeek, 2:5, 12 Sept. 1988
  Village Voice, 32:86, 7 July 1987

MAX MARCIN

Cheating Cheaters, 1916
  Harap, L., *Dramatic Encounters,* p. 80

TOM MARDIROSIAN

Saved from Obscurity, 1988
  Horwitz, S., "Will *Obscurity* Put Tom Mardirosian in the Limelight,"
    TheaterWeek, 2:54–60, 21 Nov. 1988
  New York, 21:145, 24 Oct. 1988
  Village Voice, 33:103, 25 Oct. 1988

Subfertile, 1990
  New York, 23:115–116, 19 Nov. 1990
  Playbill, 9:36, 31 Oct. 1990
  Playbill, 9:46, 31 Dec. 1990
  TheaterWeek, 3:17, 26 Mar. 1990
  TheaterWeek, 4:11, 10 Sept. 1990

DEBORAH MARGOLIN

Little Women: The Tragedy, 1989
  Village Voice, 34:100, 27 June 1989

970-Debb, 1990
  TheaterWeek, 4:43, 1 Oct. 1990

DAVID MARGULIES

The Loman Family Picnic, 1989
  Coen, S., "No Picnic," *TheaterWeek,* 2:40, 10 July 1989
  American Theatre, 6:7–8, July/Aug. 1989
  TheaterWeek, 2:5–6, 12 June 1989
  Village Voice, 34:97 + , 27 June 1989

What's Wrong with This Picture?, 1990
  TheaterWeek, 3:7, 18 June 1990
  TheaterWeek, 3:38, 9 July 1990

MRS. MARIOTT

The Chimera; or, Effusions of Fancy: A Farce in Two Acts, 1795
  Schofield, M. A., "The Happy Revolution: Colonial Women and the
  Eighteenth-Century Theater," pp. 29–37 in J. Schlueter, ed., *Modern
  American Drama*

RON MARK

Jugger's Rain, 1989
  American Theatre, 6:48, Feb. 1990

CHARLES MAROWITZ

Marowitz, C., "A Rebuttal [to Martin Gottfried's response to the following
  entry]," *TheaterWeek,* 3:28–29, 26 Feb. 1990
———, "1980–1990: [Frank] Rich Years or Lean Years," *TheaterWeek,* 3:16–
23, 19 Feb. 1990
TheaterWeek, 4:11, 24 Sept. 1990

Sherlock's Last Case, 1984
  Marowitz, C., "The *Sherlock* File," *TheaterWeek,* 1:49–55, 23 May 1988
  (excerpt from Marowitz's forthcoming book *The Sherlock Log*)

American Theatre, 6:14, Dec. 1989

Wilde West, 1989
 American Theatre, 6:10, Apr. 1989

DAVID MARTIN
SEE LANGSTON HUGHES and DAVID MARTIN

HUGH MARTIN
SEE HUGH WHEELER, HUGH MARTIN, and RALPH BLANE

JANE MARTIN (pseudonym)

Vital Signs, 1990
 London, T., "6 Humana Plays Take the Woman's-Eye View," *American Theatre,* 7:37–38, June 1990
 TheaterWeek, 3:33, 30 Apr. 1990

JUDITH MARTIN

Any Friend, 1988
 TheaterWeek, 1:29, 25 Jan. 1988

MARTY MARTIN

Gertrude Stein Gertrude Stein Gertrude Stein, 1979
 Helle, A. P., "Re-Presenting Women Writers Onstage: A Retrospective to the Present," pp. 195–208 in L. Hart, ed., *Making a Spectacle*

MEL MARVIN
SEE JOHN BISHOP, MEL MARVIN, and ROBERT SATULOFF

ARTHUR MARX and ROBERT FISHER

Groucho: A Life in Review, 1986
 Los Angeles, 34:238 + , Nov. 1989
 Village Voice, 31:92, 21 Oct. 1986

LAURENCE MASLON
SEE SILAS JONES and LAURENCE MASLON

JACKIE MASON and MIKE MORTMAN

A Teaspoon Every Four Hours, 1969
 Leonard, W. T., *Once Was Enough,* pp. 189–191

TIMOTHY MASON

Bearclaw, 1984
 Wilcox, M., ed., *Gay Plays,* 2:7–8 (Introduction), 73, 75–101 (text of play)

Only You, 1987
　　TheaterWeek, 1:23–25, 18 Jan. 1988
　　Village Voice, 32:102, 29 Dec. 1987

JANE MAST
SEE MAE WEST

JOE MASTEROFF

Hirsch, F., *Harold Prince and the American Musical Theater,* pp. 57–58, 59–61, 66–68

JOE MASTEROFF, JOHN KANDER, and FRED EBB

Cabaret (musical version of J. Van Druten's play *I Am a Camera,* a dramatization of *Berlin Stories* by C. Isherwood), 1966 (revised 1987)
　　Green, S., *Broadway Musicals,* p. 219
　　Harap, L., *Dramatic Encounters,* p. 132
　　Hirsch, F., "The Prince of Difference," *American Theatre,* 6:18–23, 43–44, Apr. 1989 (excerpted from Hirsch's *Harold Prince and the American Musical*)
　　Ilson, C., "A Re-Vision: *Cabaret,*" pp. 339–341 in Ilson's *Harold Prince*
　　———, *Harold Prince,* pp. 136–152
　　America, 158:42, 16 Jan. 1988
　　Dance Magazine, 62:73–74, Jan. 1988
　　Journal of Canadian Studies, 22:120–121, Winter 1987/1988
　　Playbill, 6:6, Feb. 1988

PETER MASTERSON
SEE LARRY L. KING, PETER MASTERSON, and CAROL HALL

WILLIAM MASTROSIMONE

Cat's-Paw, 1986
　　TheaterWeek, 2:8, 6 Feb. 1989

Extremities, 1981
　　Davis, T. C., "*Extremities* and *Masterpieces*: A Feminist Paradigm of Art and Politics," *Modern Drama,* 32(1):89–103, Mar. 1989

Shivaree, 1983
　　Los Angeles, 33:244+, Oct. 1988

Sunshine, 1989
　　TheaterWeek, 3:10–11, 4 Dec. 1989
　　Village Voice, 34:121, 26 Dec. 1989

CORNELIUS MATHEWS

False Pretenses, 1856
　　Miller, T. L., "The Image of Fashionable Society in American Comedy, 1840–1870," pp. 243–252 in J. L. Fisher and S. Watt, eds., *When They Weren't Doing Shakespeare*

The Politicians, 1840
    Grimsted, D., *Melodrama Unveiled,* pp. 163–164

JOHN MAXWELL and TOM DUPREE

Oh, Mr. Faulkner, Do You Write?, 1981
    Barry, M. N., *"Oh, Mr. Faulkner, Do You Write?" Mississippi,* 5:65–66,
    July/Aug. 1987

NATHAN MAYER

Beyond a Reasonable Doubt, 1989
    Ledford, L. S., "Legal Eagles," *TheaterWeek,* 2:34–38, 20 Mar. 1989
    TheaterWeek, 2:5, 6 Feb. 1989

MAXIM MAZUNDAR

TheaterWeek, 1:8, 30 May 1988

DES McANUFF

Stevens, L., "Last Exit to La Jolla," *TheaterWeek,* 3:37–39, 4 June 1990

ALSO SEE RICHARD NELSON, TIM RICE, BENNY ANDERSSON,
and BJÖRN ULVAEUS

HELEN McAVITY
SEE ELEANOR HARRIS HOWARD and HELEN McAVITY

JAMES DABNEY McCABE

Watson, C. S., "Confederate Drama: The Plays of John Hill Hewitt and James
Dabney McCabe," *Southern Literary Journal,* 22[21]:100–112, Spring 1989

ROBBIE McCAULEY

Indian Blood, 1987
    Artforum, 26:120–121, Jan. 1988

ALSO SEE
LAURIE CARLOS, JESSICA HAGEDORN, and ROBBIE McCAULEY

MARION ISAAC McCLINTON

Walkers, 1989
    American Theatre, 6:10, June 1989

JAMES J. McCLOSKEY

Across the Continent; or, Scenes from New York Life and the Pacific Railroad,
1870
   Jones, E. H., *Native Americans as Shown on the Stage,* pp. 109–110

MICHAEL McCLURE

McClure, M., *Scratching the Beat Surface*

VKTMS: Orestes in Scenes, 1988
   TheaterWeek, 2:9, 19 Dec. 1988
   TheaterWeek, 2:60, 2 Jan. 1989
   Village Voice, 33:103 + , 23 Dec. 1988

CARSON McCULLERS

Carr, V. S., "Carson McCullers: Novelist Turned Playwright," *Southern Quarterly,* 25(3):37–51, Spring 1987
———, *Understanding Carson McCullers*
Cook, R. M., *Carson McCullers*
Kimball, S. L., "Reflections on Reflections," *Pembroke Magazine,* 20:4–8, 1988
Madden D., "Tennessee and Carson: Notes on a Concept for a Play," *Pembroke Magazine,* 20:96–103, 1988
McBride, M., "Loneliness and Longing in Selected Plays of Carson McCullers and Tennessee Williams," pp. 143–150 in J. Schlueter, ed., *Modern American Drama*
McDowell, M. B., "Carson McCullers 1917–1967," pp. 171–188 in M. C. Roudané, ed., *Contemporary Authors Bibliographical Series*
Shapiro, A. M., J. R. Bryer, and K. Field, *Carson McCullers*
Wilson, M. A., "Carson McCullers (19 February 1917–29 September 1967)," pp. 289–296 in P. C. Kolin, ed., *American Playwrights since 1945*

The Member of the Wedding (dramatization of her novel), 1950
   Helbing, T., "Esther Rolle: Invitation to the *Wedding,*" *TheaterWeek,* 2:12–19, 3 Apr. 1989
   Nation, 248:825, 12 June 1989
   New York, 22:100, 10 Apr. 1989
   New Yorker, 65:114, 10 Apr. 1989
   Village Voice, 34:97, 11 Apr. 1989

HEATHER McCUTCHEON

3 A.M., 1990
   Village Voice, 35:110, 3 Apr. 1990

JOHN McGEE

Jefferson Davis, 1936
   Bentley, J., *Hallie Flanagan,* pp. 216–217
   Kazacoff, G., *Dangerous Theatre,* pp. 115–116

HOWARD McGRATH

Men at Work, 1936
   Kazacoff, G., *Dangerous Theatre,* pp. 281–282

KEN McGUIRE

Grin and Bare It! (adaptation of play by T. Cushing, which see), 1970
   New Yorker, 46:81, 28 Mar. 1970

DENNIS McINTYRE

Spillane, M., "Playwright Dennis McIntyre: 1942–1990," *TheaterWeek,* 3:24–26,
   12 Mar. 1990
American Theatre, 7:63–64, Apr. 1990
Playbill, 8:32, 30 June 1990

Established Price, 1987
   Forbes, D., "Dirty Dealing," *American Theatre,* 4:12–18, Feb. 1988
   TheaterWeek, 3:4, 25 Dec. 1989

Modigliani, 1978
   American Theatre, 6:12–13, Oct. 1989

National Anthems, 1987 (revised 1988)
   American Theatre, 5:58, Jan. 1989
   Massachusetts Review, 30:130–131, Spring 1989
   Playbill, 6:28, May 1988
   TheaterWeek, 3:24, 4 Sept. 1989

LULIE HARD McKINLEY

One More Spring (dramatization of novel by R. Nathan), 1937
   Kazacoff, G., *Dangerous Theatre,* pp. 206–207

ELLEN McLAUGHLIN

Infinity's House, 1990
   London, T., "6 Humana Plays Take the Woman's-Eye View," *American
      Theatre,* 7:37–38, June 1990
   American Theatre, 7:66, Nov. 1990
   TheaterWeek, 3:33–34, 30 Apr. 1990

JOHN McLAUGHLIN

Lycanthrope, 1989
   TheaterWeek, 3:13, 25 Sept. 1989

SHEILA McLAUGHLIN

She Must Be Seeing Things, 1987
    de Lauretis, T., "Sexual Indifference and Lesbian Representation," pp. 17–
        39 in S.-E. Case, ed., *Performing Feminisms* (rpt. of *Theatre Journal,*
        40(2):155–177, May 1988)

JOHN McLIAM

The Sin of Pat Muldoon, 1957
    Marcuson, L. R., *The Stage Immigrant,* pp. 205–212

JAMES McLURE

Lone Star, 1979
    Counts, M. L., *Coming Home,* pp. 80–81, 134, 159, 194, 200

Max and Maxie, 1989
    TheaterWeek, 2:9, 16 Jan. 1989
    Village Voice, 34:90+, 31 Jan. 1989

Pvt. Wars, 1979
    Counts, M. L., *Coming Home,* pp. 80, 81–82, 105, 194, 197

TERRENCE McNALLY

Bennetts, L., "Lanford Wilson & Terrence McNally: On Love, Responsibility,
    and Sexual Obsession," *Vogue,* 178:216+, Feb. 1988
de Sousa, G. U., "Terrence McNally (3 November 1939–)," pp. 297–308 in
    P. C. Kolin, ed., *American Playwrights since 1945*
Paller, M., "Terrence McNally: Grand Passion in a Naturalistic Landscape,"
    TheaterWeek, 2:14–19, 19 June 1989
Smith, L., "Provocative Playwright," *Playbill,* 6:67–70, July 1988
Elle, 4:44, June 1989
Playbill, 7:53, 28 Feb. 1989 (interview)
TheaterWeek, 1:7, 9 May 1988
TheaterWeek, 3:18, 26 Mar. 1990

Bad Habits (two one-acts: *Dunelawn* and *Ravenswood*), 1971
    TheaterWeek, 3:13, 19 Feb. 1990
    TheaterWeek, 3:12, 26 Mar. 1990
    TheaterWeek, 3:42, 2 Apr. 1990
    Village Voice, 35:99+, 27 Mar. 1990

Botticelli, televised 1968, produced on stage 1971
    Zinman, T. S., "Search and Destroy: The Drama of the Vietnam War,"
        Theatre Journal, 42:5–26, Mar. 1990

Bringing It All Back Home, 1969
    Counts, M. L., *Coming Home,* pp. 174–175, 201, 203, 207

Frankie and Johnny in the Clair de Lune, 1987
    Sheward, D., "Johnny's Back and Frankie's Got Him," *TheaterWeek,* 2:40–45, 15 Aug. 1988
    Shirakawa, S. H., "Theater Trends: Isn't It Romantic?" *TheaterWeek,* 1:23–25, 18 Jan. 1988
    ————, "Theater Trends: Two for the Road," *TheaterWeek,* 1:20–23, 4 Jan. 1988
    American Theatre, 4:8, Jan. 1988
    TheaterWeek, 2:10–11, 14 Nov. 1988
    Village Voice, 32:103+, 10 Nov. 1987

Hope (presented with I. Horovitz's *Faith* and L. Melfi's *Charity*), 1988
    American Theatre, 5:48, Feb. 1989
    TheaterWeek, 1:4–5, 8 Aug. 1988
    TheaterWeek, 2:6, 5 Dec. 1988
    Village Voice, 34:89–90, 3 Jan. 1989

The Lisbon Traviata, 1985 (later revised)
    Botto, L., "A Night at the Opera," *Playbill,* 8:66, 68, 71–73, 30 Nov. 1989
    Hall, R., "Eleven Different Directions," *American Theatre,* 5:32–33, Dec. 1988
    Helbing, T., "Divas Need Love Too," *TheaterWeek,* 2:43, 26 June 1989
    Marowitz, C., "Los Angeles in Review," *TheaterWeek,* 4:38–39, 31 Dec. 1990
    Shewey, D., "Gay Theatre Grows Up," *American Theatre,* 5:10–17, 52–53, May 1988
    American Theatre, 7:58, June 1990
    Nation, 249:766, 18 Dec. 1989
    New York, 22:71, 19 June 1989
    New York, 22:130–131, 13 Nov. 1989
    New Yorker, 65:74–76, 19 June 1989
    Playbill, 7:56, 30 Sept. 1989
    TheaterWeek, 2:4, 22 May 1989
    TheaterWeek, 2:8, 17 July 1989
    TheaterWeek, 3:12, 14 Aug. 1989
    TheaterWeek, 3:42, 13 Nov. 1989
    Time, 134:120, 13 Nov. 1989
    Village Voice, 34:97, 13 June 1989

The Ritz (originally titled *The Tubs*), 1973 (revised 1975)
    Leonard, W. T., *Once Was Enough,* pp. 163–167

Up in Saratoga (adaptation of B. Howard's play *Saratoga*), 1989
    American Theatre, 5:14, Mar. 1989
    TheaterWeek, 2:40, 26 Sept. 1988
    San Diego Magazine, 41:60+, May 1989

TERRENCE McNALLY, JOHN KANDER, and FRED EBB

The Kiss of the Spider Woman (musical version of novel by M. Puig), 1990
    Backalenick, I., "Kevin Gray: From *Spider Woman* to *Phantom,*"
        TheaterWeek, 3:18–21, 2 July 1990
    Harris, J., "Will the Critics Kill *Kiss of the Spider Woman?*" *TheaterWeek,*
        3:5–6, 11 June 1990
    Mandelbaum, K., "*Kiss* and Tell," *TheaterWeek,* 3:38–39, 11 June 1990
    Seff, R., "This *Kiss* Could Be the Start of Something Big," *TheaterWeek,*
        3:17–20, 21 May 1990
    American Theatre, 7:12, July/Aug. 1990
    TheaterWeek, 3:10, 19 Feb. 1990
    TheaterWeek, 3:10, 21 May 1990
    Time, 135:59, 12 Feb. 1990

The Rink, 1984 (revised 1988)
Mandelbaum, K., "Another Time Around *The Rink,*" *TheaterWeek,* 1:56–57,
    18 July 1988
TheaterWeek, 1:4, 25 Jan. 1988
TheaterWeek, 3:21–22, 25 Dec. 1989

WILLIAM J. McNALLY

A Good Bad Woman, 1925
    Brown, J., "The Good Old Days of Censorship," *American Theatre,* 7:60–
        63, Dec. 1990

SCOTT McPHERSON

Marvin's Room, 1990
    Abarbanel, J., "Desperate Living," *American Theatre,* 7:8–9, Dec. 1990
    American Theatre, 6:12, Mar. 1990
    American Theatre, 7:66, Nov. 1990
    TheaterWeek, 4:10, 12 Nov. 1990

FRED G. MEADER

Buffalo Bill, the King of Border Men (dramatization of magazine serial by N.
    Buntline, pseudonym of E. Z. C. Judson), 1871
    Jones, E. H., *Native Americans as Shown on the Stage,* p. 111

ALSO SEE NED BUNTLINE and FRED G. MEADER

LOUISA MEDINA

Nick of the Woods; or, The Jibbenainosay (dramatization of novel by R. M.
    Bird), 1838)
    Jones, E. H., *Native Americans as Shown on the Stage,* pp. 74–77 and else-
        where

CASSANDRA MEDLEY

Ma Rose, 1986 (revised (1988)
    American Theatre, 5:12, Dec. 1988
    TheaterWeek, 2:4, 3 Oct. 1988
    Village Voice, 33:106, 1 Nov. 1988

MURRAY MEDNICK

Sand, published 1967
    Shrager, S., *Scatology in Modern Drama*, pp. 54–57

MARK MEDOFF

Henderson, K., "Home on the Range: Mark Medoff" (interview), *TheaterWeek*,
  2:42–47, 2 Jan. 1988
New Mexico Magazine, 66:75 + , Nov. 1988

Children of a Lesser God, 1979
    Bartow, A., "Controversy and Gordon Davidson" (interview), *American*
      Theatre, 5:24–30, 54–55, May 1988
    Brustein, R., "The Play You're Not Allowed to Hate," pp. 61–63 in Bru-
      stein's *Who Needs Theatre* (rpt. of *New Republic*, 182:23–24, 7 June 1980)
    Horn, B., "Speech vs. Language: An Overview of Communication," *Essays*
      in Arts & Sciences, 17:29–39, May 1988
    Willmott, G., "Mark Medoff" (interview), *Kaleidoscope*, 11:28–33, Sum-
      mer 1985

The Heart Outright (sequel to *When You Comin' Back, Red Ryder?*), 1989
    Playbill, 7:30 + , 31 Aug. 1989
    TheaterWeek, 2:6, 22 May 1989

The Majestic Kid, 1988
    New York, 21:110–111, 12 Dec. 1988
    Playbill, 7:30, 31 Jan. 1989
    TheaterWeek, 2:5, 3 Oct. 1988
    TheaterWeek, 2:7, 28 Nov. 1988
    Village Voice, 33:120, 13 Dec. 1988

Stumps, 1990
    Playbill, 8:50, 31 May 1990

When You Comin' Back, Red Ryder?, 1973
    Erben, R., "The Western Holdup Play: The Pilgrimage Continues," *Western*
      American Literature, 23(4):311–322, Feb. 1989

CHARLES L. MEE, JR.

Gray, A., "The Big If," *American Theatre*, 6:18–21, 56, June 1989
Mee, C. L., Jr., "Looking for Trouble," *American Theatre*, 7:36–40, 69, Sept.
  1990

Solomon, A., "Charles L. Mee, Jr.: The Theatre of History" (interview), *Performing Arts Journal*, 11(1[31]):67–76, 1988
Wetzsteon, R., "Can Theatre Do the Right Thing?" (interview), *American Theatre*, 6:23–25, 112–114, Oct. 1989
Village Voice, 34:97, 23 May 1989

The Constitutional Convention, The Sequel, published 1988
    Mee, C. L., Jr., "*The Constitutional Convention, The Sequel*" (text of play), *Performing Arts Journal*, 11(1[31]):77–88, 1988

The Imperialists at the Club Cave Canem, 1988
    Giessen, N., "La Cave aux Folles," *TheaterWeek*, 1:52–55, 8 Aug. 1988
    TheaterWeek, 1:6, 27 June 1988

The Investigation of the Murder in El Salvador, written 1984, revised 1988 for a workshop production
    American Theatre, 6:8, June 1989
    TheaterWeek, 2:8, 1 May 1989

ALSO SEE MARTHA CLARKE, CHARLES L. MEE, JR.,
and RICHARD PEASLEE

GREG MEHRTEN

It's a Man's World, 1985
    Village Voice, 32:90, 9 June 1987

LEONARD MELFI

Birdbath, 1965
    TheaterWeek, 1:28, 4 Jan. 1988

Charity (presented with I. Horovitz's *Faith* and T. McNally's *Hope*), 1988
    American Theatre, 5:48, Feb. 1989
    TheaterWeek, 1:4–5, 8 Aug. 1988
    TheaterWeek, 2:6, 5 Dec. 1988
    Village Voice, 34:89–90, 3 Jan. 1989

ALSO SEE JULES FEIFFER, DAN GREENBURG, LEONARD MELFI,
SAM SHEPARD, and OTHERS

THOMAS MELONCON

Whatever Happened to Black Love?, 1990
    TheaterWeek, 4:8, 12 Nov. 1990

ALEJANDRO MEMBRENO

Peter Breaks Through, 1989
    Chansky, D., "Younger than Springtime . . . Sharp as Tacks," *TheaterWeek*, 3:29–33, 25 Sept. 1989
    TheaterWeek, 3:42, 9 Oct. 1989

IVAN MENCHELL

Elle, 4:170 + , Oct. 1988

The Cemetery Club, 1989
    Chase, T., "The Graveyard Shift," *TheaterWeek,* 3:27–29, 21 May 1990
    Sneerwell, R., "Club Dead," *TheaterWeek,* 3:37, 28 May 1990
    Nation, 251:29–30, 2 July 1990
    New York, 23:74, 28 May 1990
    New Yorker, 66:101, 28 May 1990
    TheaterWeek, 2:7, 1 May 1989
    TheaterWeek, 2:7, 8 May 1989
    TheaterWeek, 3:24, 30 July 1990

GIAN CARLO MENOTTI

Andy Warhol's Interview, 17:56–57, Mar. 1987 (interview)

The Consul, 1950
    TheaterWeek, 1:36, 14 Mar. 1988

Goya, 1986
    New Yorker, 62:90–91, 22 Dec. 1986
    Opera News, 51:14–18, Nov. 1986
    Ovation, 7:12 + , Nov. 1986
    Time, 128:70, 1 Dec. 1986
    TV Guide, 34:18–19, 15 Nov. 1986
    Vanity Fair, 49:27, Oct. 1986
    Village Voice, 31:115, 2 Dec. 1986

The Medium, 1946
    San Diego Magazine, 39:62 + , July 1987

The Telephone, 1947
    San Diego Magazine, 39:62 + , July 1987

MARY MERCIER

Johnny No-Trump, 1967
    Goldman, W., *The Season,* pp. 67–69, 72, 256, 393
    Jacobs, S., *On Stage* (a book about this play)
    Leonard, W. T., *Once Was Enough,* pp. 94–96
    Stasio, M., "On *Johnny No-Trump,*" pp. 408–425 in Stasio's *Broadway's Beautiful Losers* (text of play on pp. 343–407)

EVE MERRIAM

Betsko, K., and R. Koenig, *Interviews with Contemporary Women Playwrights,* pp. 288–311

And I Ain't Finished Yet, 1981
    New Yorker, 57:98–99, 21 Dec. 1981

The Club, 1976
    America, 135:373, 27 Nov. 1976
    Mademoiselle, 83:142–143, Feb. 1977
    Ms., 5:34+, Mar. 1977
    New York, 9:75, 1 Nov. 1976
    New Yorker, 52:64, 25 Oct. 1976

EVE MERRIAM, PAULA WAGNER, and JACK HOFSISS

Out of Our Father's House, 1975
    Mael, P., "A Rainbow of Voices," pp. 317–321 in H. K. Chinoy and L. W.
    Jenkins, eds., *Women in American Literature,* rev. and enl. ed. (pp. 320–
    324 in 1981 ed.)

ROBERT MERRILL
SEE GEORGE ABBOTT and ROBERT MERRILL
AND JOSEPH STEIN, ROBERT RUSSELL, and ROBERT MERRILL

KRES MERSKY

Algerian Romance, 1989
    TheaterWeek, 2:7, 6 Feb. 1989

STEPHEN METCALFE

Emily, 1988
    New York, 21:88–89, 9 May 1988
    New Yorker, 64:100, 9 May 1988
    Village Voice, 33:98+, 3 May 1988

White Linen, 1988
    TheaterWeek, 1:4, 2 May 1988

White Man Dancing, 1990
    American Theatre, 7:13, July/Aug. 1990

ALLEN MEYER and MICHAEL NOWAK

The Signal Season of Dummy Hoy, 1987
    Shirakawa, S. H., "Theater Trends: Dramatic Disabilities," *TheaterWeek,*
    1:24–27, 11 Jan. 1988

BOB MEYER and JACK CLARK

M: The Murderer (based on F. Lang's 1931 film *M*), 1990
    American Theatre, 7:14, Oct. 1990

MARLANE MEYER

Etta Jenks, 1988
 Hersh, A., "The Women's Project Goes It Alone," *TheaterWeek,* 1:34–39,
  25 Apr. 1988
 Drama, no. 168:42–44, 1988
 TheaterWeek, 1:9, 28 Mar. 1988

The Geography of Luck, 1989
 Los Angeles, 34:230+, Oct. 1989
 Time, 133:73, 12 June 1989

Kingfish, 1988
 Henry, W. A., III, "Two Tales of One City," *Time,* 132:92, 3 Oct. 1988
 Sagal, P., "A Native Californian Playwright Goes Public," *TheaterWeek,*
  3:30–31, 1 Jan. 1990
 American Theatre, 6:10, Feb. 1990
 Village Voice, 35:96+, 9 Jan. 1990

MICHAEL MEYER

Lunatic and Lover, 1988
 Village Voice, 33:88, 30 Aug. 1988

JAN MEYEROWITZ
SEE LANGSTON HUGHES and JAN MEYEROWITZ

CAROLYN MEYERS and TERRY BAUM

Dos Lesbos: Play by, for and about Perverts, 1981
 Case, S.-E., *Feminism and Theatre,* p. 77
 Dolan, J., "'Lesbian' Subjectivism in Realism: Dragging at the Margins of
  Structure and Ideology," pp. 40–53 in S.-E. Case, ed., *Performing Fem-
  inisms*
 Hart, L., "Canonizing Lesbians?" pp. 275–292 in J. Schlueter, ed., *Modern
  American Drama*

PATRICK MEYERS

K2, 1982
 TheaterWeek, 3:13, 19 Feb. 1990

SIDNEY MICHAELS

Tricks of the Trade, 1980
 Leonard, W. T., *Once Was Enough,* pp. 198–199

ROBERT MIDDLEMASS
SEE HOLWORTHY HALL and ROBERT MIDDLEMASS

GEORGE MIDDLETON

Middleton, G., *These Things Are Mine!*

The Road Together, 1923
  Leonard, W. T., *Once Was Enough,* pp. 167–169

ALSO SEE GUY BOLTON and GEORGE MIDDLETON
AND PAUL KESTER and GEORGE MIDDLETON

GEORGE H. MILES

De Soto; or, The Hero of the Mississippi, 1852
  Jones, E. H., *Native Americans as Shown on the Stage,* pp. 37, 47

HENRY MILES
SEE CHARLES HORNER and HENRY MILES

EDNA ST. VINCENT MILLAY

Patton, J. J., "The Variety of Language in Millay's Verse Plays," *Tamarack,*
  3(1):8–16, Fall 1985–Winter 1986

ALAN MILLER

The Fox (dramatization of D. H. Lawrence's novella), 1982
  TheaterWeek, 2:9, 14 Nov. 1988
  Village Voice, 31:125–126, 23 Dec. 1986

ARTHUR MILLER

Abbott, A. S., "Arthur Miller and Tennessee Williams," pp. 129–147 in Abbott's *The Vital Lie*
Balakian, J., "A Conversation with Arthur Miller," *Michigan Quarterly Review,* 29(2):158–170, Spring 1990
Ben-Zvi, L., "'Home Sweet Home': Deconstructing the Masculine Myth of the Frontier in Modern American Drama," pp. 217–225 in D. Mogen, M. Busby, and P. Bryant, eds., *The Frontier Experience and the American Dream*
Bigsby, C., "'Dwustronne lustro' Arthura Millera," *Dialog,* 32(11–12[374–375]):142–144, Nov.–Dec. 1987 (tr. Ewa Krasińska)
Bigsby, C. W. E., *File on Miller*
Bloom, H., ed., *Arthur Miller*
Carson, N., *Arthur Miller*
Cox, B., "Twelve Days at Mow-Hat," *Drama,* no. 169:5–6, 1988
Demastes, W. W., *Beyond Naturalism,* pp. 25, 26, 29, 35, 70–71, 88, 92, 93
Denby, D., "All My Sins," *New Republic,* 198:30–34, 8 Feb. 1988
Engler, B., "Der 'doppelte' Sündenfall ins menschliche Selbstbewusst-Sein: Alt-

testamentliche Typologie in Dramen Archibald MacLeischs, Howard Neme-rovs, Arthur Millers und Jean-Claude von [sic] Itallies," pp. 591–609 in F. Link, ed., *Paradeigmata*

Feldman, R. L., "Arthur Miller's Neglected Article on the Nazi War Criminals' Trials: A Vision of Evil," *Resources for American Literary Study,* 15(2):187–196, Autumn 1985

Goldfarb, A., "Arthur Miller (17 October 1915–)," pp. 309–338 in P. C. Kolin, ed., *American Playwrights since 1945*

Goodman, C., "The Fox's Cubs: Lillian Hellman, Arthur Miller, and Tennessee Williams," pp. 130–142 in J. Schlueter, ed., *Modern American Drama*

Guo, J., "My Interview with Arthur Miller," *Foreign Literatures,* 5:31–38, 1987

Harap, L., *Dramatic Encounters,* pp. 121–131, 139

Kazan, E., *Elia Kazan,* pp. 178, 299, 318–321, 348, 356, 358–359, 361, 365–368, 371, 401–402, 408–409, 410–416, 420, 421, 426, 427, 438–450, 460–461, 471–472, 486, 487, 508, 529, 530, 539–540, 565, 586, 605, 629–630, 650, 656, 659–660, 666–668, 673–674, 687, 690, 698, 699, 718, 746, 818

Martin, R. A., "Arthur Miller: Public Issues, Private Tensions," *Studies in the Literary Imagination,* 21(2):97–106, Fall 1988

Mason, J. D., "Paper Dolls: Melodrama and Sexual Politics in Arthur Miller's Early Plays," pp. 103–115 in J. Schlueter, ed., *Feminist Rereadings in Modern American Drama*

Mathur, S. C., "The Plays of Arthur Miller," *Triveni,* 56(2):64–67, 1987

McKinney, P. S., "Jung's 'Anima' in Arthur Miller's Plays," *Studies in American Drama, 1945–Present,* 3:41–63, 1988

Miller, A., "Bees" (story), *Michigan Quarterly Review,* 29:153–157, Spring 1990

Moss, L., "'Lack of Tension': An Interview with Arthur Miller," *Foreign Literatures,* 5:23–30, 1987

Myers, L., "Critic, Cornered: Michael Feingold Speaks Out" (interview), *TheaterWeek,* 1:28–34, 11 Jan. 1988

Paller, M., "TheaterBook: Arthur Miller's New Autobiography, *Timebends,*" *TheaterWeek,* 1:41–43, 4 Jan. 1988

Raymond, G., "Author, Author: Bending Time with Arthur Miller" (interview), *TheaterWeek,* 1:20–23, 25 Jan. 1988

———, "Miller-time in London: An American Playwright in Exile," *TheaterWeek,* 3:30–31, 16 Apr. 1990

Roudané, M. C., ed., *Conversations with Arthur Miller*

Sanoff, P., "'The Theater Must Be Bread, Not Cake'" (interview), *U.S. News & World Report,* 104:54–55, 11 Jan. 1988

Savran, D., *Danger,* n. pag.

Schlueter, J., "Arthur Miller 1915– ," pp. 189–270 in M. C. Roudané, ed., *Contemporary Authors Bibliographical Series*

Schlueter, J., and J. K. Flanagan, *Arthur Miller*

Schroeder, P. R., "Arthur Miller: Illuminating Process," pp. 76–104 in Schroeder's *The Present of the Past in Modern American Drama*

Schvey, H. I., "Arthur Miller: Songs of Innocence and Experience," pp. 75–98 in G. Debusscher, H. I. Schvey, and M. Maufort, eds., *New Essays on American Drama*

"Uneasy about the Germans," *New York Times Magazine,* pp. 46–47 + , 6 May 1990

American Theatre, 7:53, June 1990

American Theatre, 7:47, Dec. 1990
Detroit, 10:14, Nov. 1987
TheaterWeek, 4:16, 29 Oct. 1990
Wigwag, 1:14+, Oct. 1989

After the Fall, 1964

Alter, I., "Betrayal and Blessedness: Explorations of Feminine Power in *The Crucible, A View from the Bridge,* and *After the Fall,"* pp. 116–145 in J. Schlueter, ed., *Feminist Rereadings in Modern American Drama*

Centola, S. R., "The Monomyth and Arthur Miller's *After the Fall,"* *Studies in American Drama, 1945–Present,* 1:49–60, 1986

Kazan, E., *Elia Kazan,* pp. 610, 629–630, 635, 685–686, 698–690, 692, 693, 764, 803

Playbill, 8:48, 31 Aug. 1990

All My Sons, 1947

Bloom, H., ed., *Arthur Miller's* All My Sons

Centola, S. R., "Bad Faith and *All My Sons,"* pp. 123–133 in H. Bloom, ed., *Arthur Miller's* All My Sons

Counts, M. L., *Coming Home,* pp. 85–86, 88, 133–134, 199

Kazan, E., *Elia Kazan,* pp. 319–323, 329, 366, 426

Village Voice, 32:90, 5 May 1987

The American Clock (adaptation of S. Terkel's book *Hard Times*), 1979

TheaterWeek, 1:5, 4 July 1988

The Archbishop's Ceiling, 1974 (revised 1984)

Schlueter, J., "Power Play: Arthur Miller's *The Archbishop's Ceiling,"* *CEA Critic,* 49(2–4):134–138, Winter-Summer 1986–1987

Clara (one of the two one-acts comprising Miller's *Danger: Memory!*), 1987

American Theatre, 6:15, Dec. 1989

The Crucible, 1953

Alter, I., "Betrayal and Blessedness: Explorations of Feminine Power in *The Crucible, A View from the Bridge,* and *After the Fall,"* pp. 116–145 in J. Schlueter, ed., *Feminist Rereadings in Modern American Drama*

Arnold, M., "Just Plain Justine," *Playbill,* 8:45–47, 30 Apr. 1990

Dukore, B. F., Death of a Salesman *and* The Crucible

Erickson, J., "Appropriation and Transgression in Contemporary American Performance: The Wooster Group, Holly Hughes, and Karen Finley," *Theatre Journal,* 42:225–236, May 1990

Kazan, E., *Elia Kazan,* pp. 367, 449–450, 472

Savran, D., *"L.S.D. (. . . Just the High Points . . .)*: History as Hallucination," pp. 169–220 in Savran's *The Wooster Group*

———, "The Wooster Group, Arthur Miller and *The Crucible,"* *The Drama Review,* 29(2):99–109, Summer 1985 (parts of this article are included in the article immediately above)

Weales, G., ed., The Crucible: *Text and Criticism*

Nation, 250:716, 21 May 1990

New York, 23:103–104, 9 Apr. 1990
Playbill, 8:64–65, 31 July 1990
San Diego Magazine, 41:50+, Dec. 1988
TheaterWeek, 3:10, 8 Jan. 1990
TheaterWeek, 3:43, 16 Apr. 1990
TheaterWeek, 3:22, 30 Apr. 1990
Village Voice, 35:102, 10 Apr. 1990

Death of a Salesman, 1949
  Austin, G., *Feminist Theories for Dramatic Criticism,* pp. 1, 47–51, 52, 55
  ———, "The Exchange of Women and Male Homosocial Desire in Arthur
    Miller's *Death of a Salesman* and Lillian Hellman's *Another Part of the
    Forest,*" pp. 59–66 in J. Schlueter, ed., *Feminist Rereadings of Modern
    American Drama*
  Becker, B. J., "*Death of a Salesman*: Arthur Miller's Play in the Light of
    Psychoanalysis," *American Journal of Psychoanalysis,* 47(3):195, 1987
  Bloom, H., ed. *Arthur Miller's* Death of a Salesman
  Bloomgarden, K., "The Unfinished Memoirs of Kermit Bloomgarden" (ed.
    and introd. Christine Conrad), *American Theatre,* 5:24–29, 53–56, Nov.
    1988
  Bodmer, G. R., "A Sartrean Reading of Arthur Miller's *Death of a Sales-
    man,*" *Journal of Evolutionary Psychology,* 9(3–4):297–302, Aug. 1988
  Brustein, R., "Show and Tell," pp. 67–71 in Brustein's *Who Needs Theatre*
    (rpt. of *New Republic,* 190:27–29, 7 May 1984)
  Burgard, P. J., "Two Parts Ibsen, One Part American Dream: On Deri-
    vation and Originality in Arthur Miller's *Death of a Salesman,*" *Orbis
    Litterarum,* 43(4):336–353, 1988
  Di Giuseppe, R., "The Shadows of the Gods: Tragedy and Commitment
    in *Death of a Salesman,*" *Quaderni di Lingue e Letterature,* 14:109–128,
    1989
  Dolan, J., "Bending Gender to Fit the Canon: The Politics of Production,"
    pp. 318–344 in L. Hart, ed., *Making a Spectacle*
  ———, *The Feminist Spectator as Critic,* pp. 5, 31–33
  Dukore, B. F., Death of a Salesman *and* The Crucible
  Fichandler, Z., "Casting for a Different Truth," *American Theatre,* 5:18–
    23, May 1988
  Graybill, R. V., "Why Does Biff Boff Bimbos? Innocence as Evil in *Death
    of a Salesman,*" *Publications of the Arkansas Philological Association,*
    13(2):46–53, Fall 1987
  Hadomi, L., "Fantasy and Reality: Dramatic Rhythm in *Death of a Sales-
    man,*" *Modern Drama,* 31(2):157–174, June 1988
  Kakutani, M., "Arthur Miller," pp. 161–164 in Kakutani's *The Poet at the
    Piano* (rpt. of *The New York Times,* May 1984)
  Kazan, E., *Elia Kazan,* pp. 74, 115, 146, 162, 301, 338, 355–368, 373, 402,
    426, 502, 530, 667
  Mathur, S. C., "Willy Loman the Apotheosis of the Modern Man," *Triveni,*
    57(1):37ff, 1988
  Miller, A., "The Birth of *Death of a Salesman,*" *Playbill,* 6:n. pag., Feb.
    1988 (excerpt from Miller's autobiography *Timebends*)

———, "The Inspiration for Willy Loman," *Playbill*, 6:n. pag., Feb. 1988
(excerpt from Miller's autobiography *Timebends*)
Morse, D. E., "The 'Life Lie' in Three Plays by O'Neill, Williams, and
Miller," pp. 273–277 in M. Jurak, ed., *Cross-Cultural Studies*
Sewall, R. B., "*Death of a Salesman*," pp. 175–194 in Sewall's *The Vision
of Tragedy*
Stanton, K., "Women and the American Dream of *Death of a Salesman*,"
pp. 67–102 in J. Schlueter, ed., *Feminist Rereadings of Modern American
Drama*
Stephens, J. L., "Women in Pulitzer Prize Plays, 1918–1949," pp. 245–253
in H. K. Chinoy and L. W. Jenkins, eds., *Women in American Theatre*,
rev. and enl. ed. (pp. 243–251 in 1981 ed.)

An Enemy of the People (adaptation of play by H. Ibsen), 1950
Miller, A., "Ibsen's Warning," *Index on Censorship*, 18(6–7):74–76, July–
Aug. 1989
Playbill, 7:64, 31 Dec. 1988

Incident at Vichy, 1964
Issacharoff, M., "Comic Space," pp. 185–198 in J. Redmond, ed., *The
Theatrical Space*

The Price, 1968
Ohtsuka, K., "*The Price*: Two Different Attitudes toward Life," *Chu-Shi-
koku Studies in American Literature*, 24:66–80, June 1988
Encounter, 74:75, Apr. 1990
Journal of Dramatic Theory and Criticism, 4(2):210–211, Spring 1990

They Too Arise, 1937 (revision of *No Villain*, 1936)
Kazacoff, G., *Dangerous Theatre*, pp. 238–242

Two-Way Mirror (London title for the 1982 U.S. *2 by A.M.*; two one-acts: *Elegy
for a Lady* and *Some Kind of Love Story*), 1984
Kurdi, M., "The Deceptive Nature of Reality in Arthur Miller's *Two-Way
Mirror*," pp. 267–271 in M. Jurak, ed., *Cross-Cultural Studies*
Playbill, 7:89, 31 Mar. 1989

A View from the Bridge, 1955 (revised 1956)
Alter, I., "Betrayal and Blessedness: Explorations of Feminine Power in
The Crucible, A View from the Bridge, and *After the Fall*," pp. 116–145
in J. Schlueter, ed., *Feminist Rereadings of Modern American Drama*
Marcuson, L. R., *The Stage Immigrant*, pp. 220–226
Rothenberg, A., and E. D. Shapiro, "The Defense of Psychoanalysis in
Literature: *Long Day's Journey into Night* and *A View from the Bridge*,"
pp. 169–185 in J. H. Stroupe, ed., *Critical Approaches to O'Neill*
Hudson Review, 50:637–638, Winter 1988
Playbill, 6:40, Feb. 1988
Playbill, 6:12 + , Apr. 1988

ARTHUR MILLER and STANLEY SILVERMAN

Up from Paradise (a dramatic oratorio, adapted from Miller's play *The Creation of the World and Other Business*), 1974
  Cohen, E. M., *Working on a New Play,* pp. 187–188

CINCINNATUS HINER MILLER
SEE JOAQUIN MILLER

JASON MILLER

That Championship Season, 1972
  Cohen, E. M., *Working on a New Play,* p. 4
Playbill, 6:72, June 1988

JOAQUIN MILLER (Cincinnatus Hiner Miller)

An Oregon Idyl, published 1910
  Jones, E. H., *Native Americans as Shown on the Stage,* p. 159

MAY MILLER

Brown-Guillory, E., *Their Place on the Stage,* pp. 4–7, 12–13, 15, 18–19, 33

ROGER MILLER
SEE WILLIAM HAUPTMAN and ROGER MILLER

SIGMUND MILLER

Masquerade, 1959
  Leonard, W. T., *Once Was Enough,* pp. 115–116

SUSAN MILLER

Keyssar, H., "Nooks, Crannies and New Directions: Collective Scripts, Gay Drama, Feminist Dramas by Men and the Example of Wendy Kesselman," pp. 167–184 in Keyssar's *Feminist Theatre*

For Dear Life, 1988
  New York, 22:56, 23 Jan. 1989
  TheaterWeek, 2:8, 2 Jan. 1989
  Village Voice, 34:91, 17 Jan. 1989

Nasty Rumors and Final Remarks, 1979
  Moore, H., "Woman Alone, Women Together," pp. 186–191 in H. K. Chinoy and L. W. Jenkins, eds., *Women in American Theatre,* rev. and enl. ed. (pp. 184–190 in 1981 ed.)

TIM MILLER

Miller, T., "In [My] Own Words," *TheaterWeek,* 3:15–18, 16 July 1990

JASON MILLIGAN

Navy Wife, 1990
   TheaterWeek, 3:10, 21 May 1990

RON MILNER

Checkmates, 1988
   Horwitz, S., "*Checkmates*: The Next Generation," *TheaterWeek,* 1:16–22,
      8 Aug. 1988
   Shirakawa, S. H., "*Checkmates*: Finding the Dream," *TheaterWeek,* 1:8–
      14, 8 Aug. 1988
   ———, "Woodie Agonistes," *TheaterWeek,* 2:48–51, 26 Sept. 1988
   Commonweal, 116:21–22, 13 Jan. 1989
   Essence, 19:25, Nov. 1988
   Georgia Review, 43:577, Fall 1989
   New York, 21:142+, 22 Aug. 1988
   TheaterWeek, 1:5, 6 June 1988
   TheaterWeek, 1:7, 11 July 1988
   TheaterWeek, 1:6, 25 July 1988
   Village Voice, 33:85, 16 Aug. 1988
   Village Voice, 33:103–104, 25 Oct. 1988

RON MILNER, RICHARD BLACKFORD, and MAYA ANGELOU

King (musical about the final years of Martin Luther King, Jr.; Milner was
   replaced by Richard Nelson, who was replaced by Lonne Elder III), 1990
   Jet, 77:59, 9 Apr. 1990
   Newsweek, 115:62, 7 May 1990
   Playbill, 8:50, 30 Apr. 1990
   Playbill, 8:64–65, 30 June 1990
   TheaterWeek, 3:8, 18 Dec. 1989

A. J. MINOR

Masks and Faces, 1933
   Leonard, W. T., *Once Was Enough,* p. 115

JIM MIRRIONE

Zwickler, P. "Author, Author: The Stage as Classroom" (interview),
   TheaterWeek, 1:26–27, 18 Jan. 1988

JOSEPH MITCHELL
SEE KERRY SHAW and JOSEPH MITCHELL

LOFTEN MITCHELL

Bigsby, C. W. E., "Three Black Playwrights: Loften Mitchell, Ossie Davis,
   Douglas Turner Ward," pp. 148–167 in E. Hill, ed., *The Theatre of Black*

Americans, Vol. 1 of two vols. rptd. as one in 1987; same pagination in both
eds. (rpt. of *The Black American Writer,* ed. Bigsby, 2:137–155)
Brown-Guillory, E., *Their Place on the Stage,* pp. 26, 32, 34, 37

MATT MITLER

Miss Lonelyhearts (a new dramatization of N. West's novella), 1989
    Playbill, 7:38, 31 May 1989

FELIX MITTERER

Jailbird, 1990
    Village Voice, 35:98, 9 Jan. 1990

JOHN C. MOFFIT
SEE SINCLAIR LEWIS and JOHN C. MOFFIT

LESLIE MOHN

White Boned Demon, 1988
    American Theatre, 6:9, Apr. 1989

URSULE MOLINARO

Breakfast Past Noon, 1968
    Moore, H., "Woman Alone, Women Together," pp. 186–191 in H. K. Chi-
    noy and L. W. Jenkins, eds., *Women in American Theatre,* rev. and enl.
    ed. (pp. 184–190 in 1981 ed.)

MEREDITH MONK

Solomon, A., "Doubly Marginalized: Women in the Avant-Garde," pp. 363–
    371 in H. K. Chinoy and L. W. Jenkins, eds., *Women in American Theatre,*
    rev. and enl. ed. (new to this ed.)
Westfall, S. R., "The Silver Lining in the Mushroom Cloud: Meredith Monk's
    Opera/Music Theater," pp. 264–274 in J. Schlueter, ed., *Modern American
    Drama*

LINDA MONTANO

Case, S.-E., *Feminism and Theatre,* p. 59

MICHAEL DORN MOODY

The Shortchanged Review, 1976
    Counts, M. L., *Coming Home,* pp. 58–60

WILLIAM VAUGHN MOODY

The Great Divide, 1906
    American Theatre, 5:7–8, Dec. 1988

CHRISTOPHER MOORE

The Last Season (about Jackie Robinson), 1988
  American Theatre, 4:48, Feb. 1988

HONOR MOORE

Moore, H., ed. and introd., *The New Women's Theatre*
————, "Woman Alone, Women Together," pp. 186–191 in H. K. Chinoy and
L. W. Jenkins, eds., *Women in American Theatre*, rev. and enl. ed. (pp. 184–
190 in 1981 ed.)

Mourning Pictures, 1974
  Keyssar, H., "A Network of Playwrights," pp. 102–125 in Keyssar's *Feminist Theatre*
  Leonard, W. T., *Once Was Enough*, pp. 131–132

WESLEY MOORE

Swim Visit, 1990
  TheaterWeek, 3:8, 11 June 1990

HENRY C. MOOREHEAD

Tan-Go-Ru-A, 1856
  Jones, E. H., *Native Americans as Shown on the Stage*, p. 88

CHERRÍE MORAGA

Giving Up the Ghost, 1984
  Case, S.-E., "From Split Subject to Split Britches," pp. 126–146 in E. Bra-
    ter, ed., *Feminine Focus*
  de Lauretis, T., "Sexual Indifference and Lesbian Representations," pp.
    17–39 in S.-E. Case, ed., *Performing Feminisms* (rpt. of *Theatre Journal*,
    40(2):155–177, May 1988)
  Herrera-Sobek, M., "The Politics of Rape: Sexual Transgression in Chicano
    Fiction," pp. 171–181 in Herrera-Sobek and H. M. Viramones, eds., *Chi-
    cano Creativity and Criticism* (rpt. of *Americas Review*, 15(3–4):171–188,
    Fall-Winter 1987)
  Yarbro-Bejarano, Y., "The Female Subject in Chicano Theatre: Sexuality,
    'Race,' and Class," pp. 131–149 in S.-E. Case, ed., *Performing Feminisms*
    (rpt. of *Theatre Journal*, 38(4):389–407, Dec. 1986)

Shadow of a Man, 1990
  American Theatre, 7:10–11, Dec. 1990

CONRADO MORALES
SEE NICOLAS DANTE

WARD MOREHOUSE III

Broadway after Dark (about Ward Morehouse), 1990
  TheaterWeek, 3:19–20, 26 Mar. 1990
  TheaterWeek, 3:10, 18 June 1990

My Four Mothers, 1987
  TheaterWeek, 1:6, 23 May 1988

RICK MORGAN

Cleveland Magazine, 17:80 + , Sept. 1988

BRIAN RICHARD MORI

Adult Fiction, 1990
  American Theatre, 7:10, 58–59, June 1990

MICHAEL MORIARTY

A Special Providence, 1990
  Playbill, 8:34, 30 Apr. 1990

BOB MORRIS

A Circle, 1988
  TheaterWeek, 1:4, 2 May 1988
  Village Voice, 33:94, 12 July 1988

TONI MORRISON

Alexander, H. S., "Toni Morrison: An Annotated Bibliography of Critical Articles and Essays, 1975–1984," *College Language Association Journal*, 33(1): 81–93, Sept. 1989
Davis, C., "Interview with Toni Morrison," *Présence Africaine*, 145:141–150, 1988
Hudson-Weems, C., *Toni Morrison*
Koenen, A., "'The One out of Sequence': An Interview with Toni Morrison, New York, April 1980," pp. 207–221 in G. H. Lenz, ed., *History and Tradition in Afro-American Culture*
Lester, R. K., "An Interview with Toni Morrison, Hessian Radio Network, Frankfurt, West Germany," pp. 47–54 in N. Y. McKay, ed., *Critical Essays on Toni Morrison*
McKay, N. Y., ed., *Critical Essays on Toni Morrison*

MIKE MORTMAN
SEE JACKIE MASON and MIKE MORTMAN

CARLOS MORTON

Henry, W. A., III, "Visions from the Past," *Time,* 132:82–83, 11 July 1988

El Jardin, 1988
  TheaterWeek, 1:7, 1 Aug. 1988
  Village Voice, 33:86, 16 Aug. 1988

Johnny Tenorio (adaptation of *Don Juan Tenorio* by J. Zorilla y Moral and *El Burlador de Seville* by Tirso de Molina), 1988
  Theatre Journal, 41:231–233, May 1989

MARTHA MORTON

A Bachelor's Romance, 1896
  Abramson, D., "'The New Path': Nineteenth-Century American Women Playwrights," pp. 38–51 in J. Schlueter, ed., *Modern American Drama*

SUSAN MOSAKOWSKI

The Cabinet of Dr. Caligari (based on R. Weine's 1919 film, based on a novel by H. Janowitz and C. Mayer), 1987
  American Theatre, 4:12, Jan. 1988
  Artforum, 26:141, Mar. 1988
  Film Comment, 24:52–55, Mar./Apr. 1988

Cities Out of Print, 1990
  TheaterWeek, 3:17, 26 Mar. 1990

LELAND MOSS

American Theatre, 7:63, Apr. 1990

SHANNY MOW

The Odyssey (dramatization of Homer's epic), 1989
  American Theatre, 6:12, Nov. 1989

ANNA CORA OGDEN MOWATT

Gentile, J. S., *Cast of One,* pp. 25–30
Grimsted, D., *Melodrama Unveiled,* pp. 85, 89, 105, 116n, 152, 156n

Fashion; or, Life in New York, 1845
  Abramson, D., "'The New Path': Nineteenth-Century American Women Playwrights," pp. 38–51 in J. Schlueter, ed., *Modern American Drama*

Ito, A., "Early American Drama, III: The Flattering of an Age," *Language and Culture*, 5:1–25, 1984

Miller, T. L., "The Image of Fashionable Society in American Comedy, 1840–1870," pp. 243–252 in J. L. Fisher and S. Watt, eds., *When They Weren't Doing Shakespeare*

JOHN C. MOYNIHAN

Little Lulu in a Tight Orange Dress, 1988
American Theatre, 4:10–11, Mar. 1988

LAVONNE MUELLER

Violent Peace, 1990
Commonweal, 117:259, 20 Apr. 1990
New York, 23:75–76, 19 Mar. 1990
TheaterWeek, 3:10, 26 Feb. 1990
Village Voice, 35:104+, 13 Mar. 1990

HEINER MÜLLER
SEE ROBERT WILSON and HEINER MÜLLER

PAUL MULLIN

Ellison and Eden, 1990
TheaterWeek, 3:10–11, 5 Feb. 1990

DONALD MURRAY, THEODORE PEZMAN, and RENA VALE

The Sun Rises in the West, 1938
Kazacoff, G., *Dangerous Theatre*, pp. 254–257

JOHN MURRAY and ALLEN BORETZ

Room Service, 1937
Playbill, 8:55, 31 Jan. 1990

JUDITH SARGENT STEVENS MURRAY

The Traveller Returned, 1796
Schofield, M. A., "The Happy Revolution: Colonial Women and the Eighteenth-Century Theater," pp. 29–37 in J. Schlueter, ed., *Modern American Drama*

Virtue Triumphant (earlier titled *The Medium, or Happy Tea Party*), 1795
Schofield, M. A., "The Happy Revolution: Colonial Women and the Eighteenth-Century Theater," pp. 29–37 in J. Schlueter, ed., *Modern American Drama*

JOHN MURRELL

October, 1988
  Maclean's, 101:61, 28 Nov. 1988

LINDA MUSSMAN

M.A.C.B.E.T.H. (based on Shakespeare's tragedy), 1990
  TheaterWeek, 4:32, 19 Nov. 1990

Mary Surratt (the fourth section of her Civil War Chronicles; the other three, in
  order, are: *If Kansas Goes, Cross Way Cross,* and *Blue Scene Grey*), 1988
  American Theatre, 5:6–7, May 1988

LARRY MYERS

Children Anonymous, 1990
  TheaterWeek, 3:9, 2 July 1990
  TheaterWeek, 4:44, 17 Sept. 1990

White Boys Can't Rap, 1990
  Village Voice, 35:111–112, 8 May 1990

VLADIMIR NABOKOV

Bloom, H., ed., *Vladimir Nabokov*
Parker, S. J., *Understanding Nabokov*

LEE NAGRIN

Dragon's Nest, 1990
  Village Voice, 35:122, 15 May 1990

N. RICHARD NASH

Breaking the Tie, 1989
  American Theatre, 6:57, Sept. 1989

Come as You Are, 1990
  TheaterWeek, 3:8–9, 29 Jan. 1990

N. RICHARD NASH, TOM JONES, and HARVEY SCHMIDT

110 in the Shade (musical version of Nash's play *The Rainmaker*), 1963
  Green, S., *Broadway Musicals,* p. 203

WILLIAM ROBERT NAVE

Starry Road to the Ice Machine (three related plays), 1989
  TheaterWeek, 3:6, 16 Oct. 1989

LARRY NEAL

Neal, L., "Into Nationalism, Out of Parochialism," pp. 95–102 in E. Hill, ed., *The Theater of Black Americans,* Vol. 2 of two vols. rptd. as one in 1987 (pp. 293–300 in 1987 ed.; rpt. of *Performance,* 1(2):32–40, Apr. 1972)
————, "The Black Arts Movement," *The Drama Review,* 12(4):29–39, Summer 1968

DEBRA NEFF

Twice Shy, 1989
    Chansky, D., "Younger than Springtime . . . Sharp as Tacks," *TheaterWeek,* 3:29–33, 25 Sept. 1989
    TheaterWeek, 3:42, 9 Oct. 1989

JANET NEIPRIS

Betsko, K., and R. Koenig, *Interviews with Contemporary Women Playwrights,* pp. 312–323

RALPH NELSON

The Wind Is Ninety, 1943
    Counts, M. L., *Coming Home,* pp. 172–174, 206

RICHARD NELSON

Greene, A., "Some Success Abroad," *TheaterWeek,* 3:24–25, 19 Feb. 1990
Nelson, R., ed., Strictly Dishonorable *and Other Lost American Plays*
————, "The Progressive Jeremiad, Critical Theory and the End of Republican Virtue," *Clio,* 16:359–379, Summer 1987
Savran, D., "Richard Nelson," pp. 161–177 in Savran's *In Their Own Words*

Between East and West, 1988
    Playbill, 6:53, Mar. 1988

Jitterbugging (updated version of A. Schnitzler's play *La Ronde*), 1989
    Frank, G., "Letter from Woodstock," *TheaterWeek,* 3:19, 25 Sept. 1989

The Return of Pinocchio, 1986
    American Theatre, 3:5, Oct. 1986

Some Americans Abroad, 1989
    Raymond, G., "Two British Directors Abroad," *TheaterWeek,* 3:29–31, 5 Mar. 1990
    America, 162:587, 9 June 1990
    Commonweal, 117:190, 23 Mar. 1990
    Hudson Review, 42:629–636, Winter 1990
    Nation, 250:394–395, 19 Mar. 1990
    New Republic, 202:28, 26 Mar. 1990

New York, 23:133–134, 26 Feb. 1990
New Yorker, 66:99–100, 26 Feb. 1990
TheaterWeek, 3:9, 15 Jan. 1990
TheaterWeek, 3:38, 26 Feb. 1990
Village Voice, 35:87–88, 27 Feb. 1990

RICHARD NELSON, TIM RICE, BENNY ANDERSSON, and BJÖRN ULVAEUS

Chess, 1986 in London (Nelson did the book for this musical for the 1988 New
    York production; Des McAnuff and Robert Coe did further revisions in 1990)
  Ganzl, K., "*Chess:* Round Three," *TheaterWeek,* 3:31–35, 19 Feb. 1990
  Mandelbaum, K., "*Chess* Variations," *TheaterWeek,* 2:54–58, 22 Aug. 1988
    (about the recording)
  Morley, S., "Opening Gambit," *Playbill,* 6:14, 18, July 1988
  Shirakawa, S. H., "Check Mate," *TheaterWeek,* 1:37–41, 23 May 1988
  America, 158:536, 21 May 1988
  Drama, no. 161:33, 1986
  Encounter, 68:31–32, May 1987
  Georgia Review, 42:595, Fall 1988
  Los Angeles, 33:160+, July 1988
  Nation, 246:726, 21 May 1988
  New Leader, 71:22–23, 27 June 1988
  New York, 21:34, 9 May 1988
  New York, 21:87–88, 9 May 1988
  New Yorker, 64:100, 9 May 1988
  Newsweek, 109:64–65, 30 Mar. 1987
  Newsweek, 111:73, 9 May 1988
  Plays and Players, 394:22–23, July 1986
  TheaterWeek, 3:6, 18 Sept. 1989
  TheaterWeek, 3:4, 25 Dec. 1989
  TheaterWeek, 3:22, 25 Dec. 1989
  TheaterWeek, 3:11, 5 Feb. 1990
  Theatre Crafts, 22:70–78, Oct. 1988
  Time, 131:80, 9 May 1988
  Time, 133:102, 2 Jan. 1989
  Vanity Fair, 51:34+, May 1988
  Village Voice, 33:105, 10 May 1988 (Michael Feingold)
  Village Voice, 33:105, 10 May 1988 (Alisa Solomon)
  Vogue, 178:94, Apr. 1988

ALSO SEE RON MILNER, RICHARD BLACKFORD, and MAYA ANGELOU

HOWARD NEMEROV

Engler, B., "Der 'doppelte" Sündenfall ins menschliche Selbstbewusst-Sein: Alttestamentliche typologie in Dramen Archibald MacLeischs, Howard Neme-
  rovs, Arthur Millers und Jean-Claude von [sic] Itallies," pp. 591–609 in F.
  Link, ed., *Paradeigmata*

SALLY NEMETH

Mill Fire, 1989
    American Theatre, 6:12–13, May 1989
    TheaterWeek, 3:12, 25 Sept. 1989

Spinning into the Blue, 1990
    TheaterWeek, 4:24, 20 Aug. 1990

ROBERT NEMIROFF, CHARLOTTE ZALTZBERG, JUDD WOLDIN, and ROBERT BRITTAN

Raisin (musical version of L. Hansberry's play *A Raisin in the Sun*), 1973
    Green, S., *Broadway Musicals,* p. 239
    Woll, A., *Black Musical Theatre,* pp. xiv, 249, 261–263, 271–272, 276

BERNARD SLADE NEWBOUND
SEE BERNARD SLADE

MOLLY NEWMAN

Shooting Stars, 1987
    Village Voice, 33:102 + , 22 Nov. 1988

HARRY L. NEWTON and A. S. HOFFMAN

Glickman, the Glazier, 1904
    Harap, L., *The Image of the Jew in American Literature,* pp. 229–230

The Troubles of Rozinski, 1904
    Harap, L, *The Image of the Jew in American Literature,* p. 230

DIANE NEY

Washingtonian, 24:33 + , May 1989

ANNE NICHOLS

Abie's Irish Rose, 1922
    Abramson, D., and L. Harris, "Anne Nichols: $1,000,000.00 Playwright,"
        pp. 153–157 in H. K. Chinoy and L. W. Jenkins, eds., *Women in Amer-
        ican Theatre,* rev. and enl. ed. (same pagination in 1981 ed.; rpt. of
        Players, 51:123–125, 1976)
    Harap, L., *Dramatic Encounters,* pp. 32, 115
    Marcuson, L. R., *The Stage Immigrant,* pp. 24–30
    TheaterWeek, 1:56, 23 May 1988

DON NIGRO

Grotesque Lovesongs, 1990
  New York, 23:152, 3 Dec. 1990
  New Yorker, 66:139, 10 Dec. 1990

GLORIA NISSENSON
SEE GEORGE ABBOTT, JOSEPH TURRIN, and GLORIA NISSENSON

MORDECAI MANUEL NOAH

She Would Be a Soldier; or, The Plains of Chippewa, 1819
  Jones, E. H., *Native Americans as Shown on the Stage,* pp. 24–25 and else-
    where

JANET NOBLE

Away Alone, 1989
  Hurley, J., *"Away Alone," TheaterWeek,* 3:37–39, 5 Mar. 1990
  TheaterWeek, 3:13, 27 Nov. 1989
  Village Voice, 34:121, 26 Dec. 1989

MILTON NOBLES

The Phoenix, 1875
  Harap, L., *The Image of the Jew in American Literature,* pp. 224–225

JOHN FORD NOONAN

A Critic and His Wife, 1989
  Spencer, S., "John Ford Noonan" (interview), *BOMB,* 28:16–17, Summer
    1989

Friends in High Places, 1989
  TheaterWeek, 2:8, 24 Apr. 1989

Stay Away a Little Closer, 1990
  American Theatre, 7:13, May 1990
  TheaterWeek, 3:41, 25 June 1990

Talking Things Over with Chekhov, staged reading in 1985
  TheaterWeek, 3:10, 23 Apr. 1990
  TheaterWeek, 3:38, 28 May 1990
  TheaterWeek, 3:11, 25 June 1990

MARSHA NORMAN

Betsko, K., and R. Koenig, *Interviews with Contemporary Women Playwrights,*
  pp. 324–342
Dolan, J., *The Feminist Spectator as Critic,* pp. 4, 19–40

Harriott, E., "Marsha Norman: Getting Out," pp. 129–147, and "Interview with Marsha Norman," pp. 148–163, in Harriott's *American Voices*

Hart, L., "Doing Time: Hunger for Power in Marsha Norman's Plays," *Southern Quarterly,* 25(3):67–69, Spring 1987

Hubert, L. L., "Marsha Norman 1947– ," pp. 271–287 in M. C. Roudané, ed., *Contemporary Authors Bibliographical Series*

Kane, L., "The Way Out, the Way In: Paths to Self in the Plays of Marsha Norman," pp. 255–274 in E. Brater, ed., *Feminine Focus*

Keyssar, H., "Success and Its Limits: Mary O'Malley, Wendy Wasserstein, Nell Dunn, Beth Henley, Catherine Hayes, Marsha Norman," pp. 148–166 in Keyssar's *Feminist Theatre* (Norman's *Getting Out* and *'night, Mother* considered)

McDonnell, L. J., "Diverse Similitude: Beth Henley and Marsha Norman," *Southern Quarterly,* 25(3):95–104, Spring 1987

Nischik, R. M., " 'Look Back in Gender': Beziehungskonstellationen in dramen von Beth Henley und Marsha Norman—Einige Grundzüge des Zeitgenössischen Feministischen Theaters in den USA," *Anglistik & Englischunterricht,* 35:61ff., 1988

Savran, D., "Marsha Norman," pp. 178–192 in Savran's *In Their Own Words*

Spencer, J. S., "Marsha Norman's *She-tragedies,*" pp. 147–165 in L. Hart, ed., *Making a Spectacle*

Wolfe, I. H., "Marsha Norman: A Classified Bibliography," *Studies in American Drama, 1945–Present,* 3:148–175, 1988

———, "Marsha Norman (21 September 1947–)," pp. 339–348 in P. C. Kolin, ed., *American Playwrights since 1945*

Writer's Digest, 68:34–38, Sept. 1988

Getting Out, 1977

    Case, S.-E., "From Split Subject to Split Britches," pp. 126–146 in E. Brater, ed., *Feminine Focus*

    Moore, H., "Woman Alone, Women Together," pp. 186–191 in H. K. Chinoy and L. W. Jenkins, eds., *Women in American Theatre,* rev. and enl. ed. (pp. 184–190 in 1981 ed.)

    Scharine, R. G., "Caste Iron Bars: Marsha Norman's *Getting Out* as Political Theatre," pp. 185–198 in J. Redmond, ed., *Women in Theatre*

    Schroeder, P. R., "Locked beyind the Proscenium: Feminist Strategies in *Getting Out* and *My Sister in This House,*" *Modern Drama,* 32(1):104–114, Mar. 1989

The Holdup, 1983

    Erben, R., "The Western Holdup Play: The Pilgrimage Continues," *Western American Literature,* 23(4):311–322, Feb. 1989

    Wattenberg, R., "Feminizing the Frontier Myth: Marsha Norman's *The Holdup,*" *Modern Drama,* 33(4):507–517, Dec. 1990

'night, Mother, 1983

    Browder, S., " 'I Thought You Were Mine': Marsha Norman's *'night, Mother,*" pp. 109–113 in M. Pearlman, ed., *Mother Puzzles*

    Brustein, R., "Don't Read This Review!" pp. 64–67 in Brustein's *Who Needs Theatre* (rpt. of *New Republic,* 188:25–27, 2 May 1983)

    Burkman, K. H., "The Demeter Myth and Doubling in Marsha Norman's '*night, Mother,*" pp. 254–263 in J. Schlueter, ed., *Modern American Drama*

Demastes, W. W., "New Voices Using New Realism: Fuller, Henley, and Norman," pp. 125–154 in Demastes's *Beyond Naturalism* (the specific part of this chapter dealing with this play has the subtitle "Marsha Norman and '*night, Mother,*" pp. 144–152

Dolan, J., "Bending Gender to Fit the Canon: The Politics of Production," pp. 318–344 in L. Hart, ed., *Making a Spectacle*

Forte, J., "Realism, Narrative, and the Feminist Playwright—a Problem of Reception," *Modern Drama*, 32(1):115–127, Mar. 1989

Greiff, L. K., "Fathers, Daughters, and Spiritual Sisters: Marsha Norman's '*night, Mother* and Tennessee Williams's *The Glass Menagerie,*" *Text and Performance Quarterly,* 9(3):224–228, July 1989

Morrow, L., "Orality and Identity in '*night, Mother* and *Crimes of the Heart,*" *Studies in American Drama, 1945–Present,* 3:23–29, 1988

Nischik, R. M., " 'Look Back in Gender': Beziehungskonstellationen in Dramen von Beth Henley and Marsha Norman—einige Grundzüge des zeitgenössischen feministischen Theaters in den USA," *Anglistik & Englischunterricht,* 35:61–89, 1988

Porter, L. R., "Women Re-Conceived: Changing Perceptions of Women in Contemporary American Drama," *Conference of College Teachers of English Studies,* 54:53–59, Sept. 1989

Spencer, J. S., "Norman's '*night, Mother*: Psycho-Drama of Female Identity," *Modern Drama,* 30(3):364–375, Sept. 1987

The Pool Hall, 1978
  Seff, R., "The Boob Tube Gets a Touch of Class," *TheaterWeek,* 3:28–32, 4 Dec. 1989

Sarah and Abraham, 1988 (workshop production)
  American Theatre, 4:11, Feb. 1988

Traveler in the Dark, 1984 (later revised)
  Commonweal, 117:117, 23 Feb. 1990
  Playbill, 8:29, 28 Feb. 1990
  TheaterWeek, 3:9, 8 Jan. 1990
  Village Voice, 35:102, 30 Jan. 1990

MARSHA NORMAN and LUCY SIMON

The Secret Garden (musical version of novel by F. H. Burnett), 1989
  American Theatre, 6:15, Dec. 1989
  American Theatre, 7:12, July/Aug. 1990
  Playbill, 9:48, 30 Nov. 1990
  TheaterWeek, 2:6, 31 July 1989

FRANKLIN P. NORTON

Financier of New York, 1915
  Harap, L., *Dramatic Encounters,* p. 74

MICHAEL NOWAK
SEE ALLEN MEYER and MICHAEL NOWAK

MAXWELL NURNBERG
SEE HAROLD CLARKE and MAXWELL NURNBERG

JOYCE CAROL OATES

Bloom, H., ed., *Joyce Carol Oates*
Johnson, G., *Understanding Joyce Carol Oates*

The Eclipse (see *In Darkest America*), 1990
    American Theatre, 7:13, May 1990
    TheaterWeek, 3:41, 25 June 1990

I Stand before You Naked, 1990
    TheaterWeek, 4:34–35, 31 Dec. 1990

In Darkest America (two one-acts: *Tone Clusters,* which see, and *The Eclipse,* which see), 1990
    London, T., "6 Humana Plays Take the Woman's-Eye View," *American Theatre,* 7:37–38, June 1990
    Springer, P. G., "Placing Bets in Louisville," *TheaterWeek,* 3:32–35, 30 Apr. 1990

Tone Clusters (see *In Darkest America*), 1990
    American Theatre, 7:68, May 1990

DANIEL O'CONNOR

The Blue Dahlia (adaptation of R. Chandler's film script), 1989
    Los Angeles, 34:229, Apr. 1989

JAMES O'CONNOR

Deep to Center, 1990
    TheaterWeek, 3:8, 8 Jan. 1990
    TheaterWeek, 3:42, 5 Mar. 1990

MICHAEL O'CONNOR
SEE BILL IRWIN, DOUG SKINNER, and MICHAEL O'CONNOR

ROBERT PATRICK O'CONNOR
SEE ROBERT PATRICK

SEAN O'CONNOR

Who Collects the Pain?, 1990
    TheaterWeek, 4:43–44, 8 Oct. 1990

CLIFFORD ODETS

Brustein, R., "The Prodigal Clifford Odets," pp. 22–29 in Brustein's *Who Needs Theatre*
Cooperman, R., *Clifford Odets*
Demastes, W. W., *Beyond Naturalism*, pp. 20, 22, 23–24, 25, 29, 71, 84
Groman, G. L., "Clifford Odets' Musical World: The Failed Utopia," *Studies in American Jewish Literature*, 5:80–88, 1986
Harap, L., *Dramatic Encounters*, pp. 100–106
"Hollywood & Its Discontents," *American Film*, 13:28–34, May 1988
Kazan, E., *Elia Kazan*, pp. 27, 78, 80, 85–91, 105, 112–113, 116, 119–120, 123–126, 153, 157–163, 172, 175, 182–183, 211, 240, 273, 352, 423, 445, 446, 462–463, 465, 471, 475, 505, 652, 659, 662–665, 750, 783, 818
Miller, G., *Clifford Odets*
Odets, C., "Odets in Hollywood" (excerpts from Odets's diary; see next entry), *Los Angeles*, 33:161–168, June 1988
———, *The Time is Ripe*, ed. W. Gibson
Weales, G., "Clifford's Children; or, It's a Wise Playwright Who Knows His Own Father," *Studies in American Drama, 1945–Present*, 2:3–18, 1987

Awake and Sing!, 1935
    Kazan, E., *Elia Kazan*, pp. 102, 110, 113, 119–120, 121–123, 133, 153, 154, 182, 663
    Marcuson, L. R., *The Stage Immigrant*, pp. 97–105
    Mishra, K., "Clifford Odets' *Awake and Sing!*: A Leftist Play," *Panjab University Research Bulletin (Arts)*, 18(1):69–81, Apr. 1987
    Skloot, R., "Clifford Odets's Dog of Betrayal: *Awake and Sing!* in Performance," *Journal of Dramatic Theory and Criticism*, 4(2):179–187, Spring 1990

The Big Knife, 1949
    Miller, G., "The Muse of Money," *American Theatre*, 5:96–97, Oct. 1988

The Flowering Peach, 1954
    Theatre Journal, 40:422–424, Oct. 1988

Golden Boy, 1937
    Chinoy, H. K., "A Salute to the Group's Legacy," *American Theatre*, 4:22, Mar. 1988
    Kazan, E., *Elia Kazan*, pp. 80, 124, 161–164, 168, 170, 172, 342, 362
    Marcuson, L. R., *The Stage Immigrant*, pp. 105–111
    Miller, G., "The Muse of Money," *American Theatre*, 5:96–97, Oct. 1988
    American Theatre, 6:46, Apr. 1989
    Theatre Journal, 40:422–424, Oct. 1088

Paradise Lost, 1935
    Kazan, E., *Elia Kazan*, pp. 133, 147–150, 156, 163, 184

The Silent Partner, unfinished play
    Kazan, E., *Elia Kazan*, pp. 87–88, 153–154

Till the Day I Die, 1935
  Pütz, M., "Male Chauvinism," *Notes and Queries,* 36(3[234]):360–361,
  Sept. 1989

Waiting for Lefty, 1935
  Kazan, E., *Elia Kazan,* pp. 106, 112–119, 123, 147, 158, 163, 449, 468–
  469, 538, 664
  Marcuson, L. R., *The Stage Immigrant,* pp. 73–77

CLIFFORD ODETS, WILLIAM GIBSON, CHARLES STROUSE, and LEE ADAMS

Golden Boy (musical version of Odets's play), 1964
  Green, S., *Broadway Musicals,* p. 210

MARK O'DONNELL

Andy Warhol's Interview, 18:22, June 1988

MIRA-LANI OGLESBY
SEE REZA ABDOH and MIRA-LANI OGLESBY

FRANK O'HARA (Francis Russell O'Hara)

Auslander, P., *The New York School of Poets as Playwrights*

Try! Try!, 1951
  Counts, M. L., *Coming Home,* pp. 157–158

JOHN O'KEEFE

Elle, 4:58, Aug. 1989

Shimmer, 1989
  Helbing, T., "Iowa Stubborn," *TheaterWeek,* 3:40, 14 Aug. 1989
  Village Voice, 34:91–92, 17 Jan. 1989

VID, 1990
  TheaterWeek, 4:33, 19 Nov. 1990

JOHN OLIVE

Killers, 1988
  American Theatre, 5:9, July/Aug. 1988

The Voice of the Prairie, 1987
  TheaterWeek, 2:8, 2 Jan. 1989
  TheaterWeek, 4:10, 17 Dec. 1990

THOMAS OLSON

Lord of the Flies (dramatization of novel by W. Golding), 1988
  American Theatre, 5:8, May 1988

MICHAEL ONDAATJE

Hickey, B., "Michael Ondaatje's Return: *Running in the Family*," pp. 37–40 in M. Jurak, ed., *Cross-Cultural Studies*

Thieme, J., "'Historical Relations': Modes of Discourse in Michael Ondaatje's *Running in the Family*," *Journal of Indian Writing in English*, 16(2):136, 1988

The Collected Works of Billy the Kid, 1975

    Harrison, K., "Montage in *The Collected Works of Billy the Kid*," *Journal of Canadian Poetry*, 3(1):32–38, Winter 1980

    Jones, M., "*The Collected Works of Billy the Kid*: Scripting the Docudrama," *Canadian Literature*, 122–123:26–38, Autumn-Winter 1989

    Kamboureli, S., "Outlawed Narrative: Michael Ondaatje's *The Collected Works of Billy the Kid*," *Sagetrieb*, 7(1):115–129, Spring 1988

    Kelly, R. A., "Outlaw and Explorer: Recent Adventurers in the English-Canadian Long Poem," *Antigonish Review*, 79:27–34, Autumn 1989

JOHN O'NEAL

Barron, E. A., "Sayings from the Life and Writings of John O'Neal," *Southern Quarterly*, 25(4):65–72, Summer 1987

Barron, E. A., and D. R. Mott, "John O'Neal: An Interview," *Southern Quarterly*, 25(4):75–84, Summer 1987

RUSSELL O'NEILL

Don't Call Back, 1974

    Leonard, W. T., *Once Was Enough*, pp. 43–45

EUGENE O'NEILL

"A Decade's Riches: Articles in the *Newsletter*, 1977–1986," *Eugene O'Neill Newsletter*, 11(1):27–32, Spring 1987

"A Special Centennial Salute to Eugene O'Neill, I, II, & III," *Eugene O'Neill Newsletter*, 12(1): Spring 1988; 12(2): Summer-Fall 1988; 12(3): Winter 1988 (spec. issues)

Abbott, A. S., "Eugene O'Neill," pp. 113–128 in Abbott's *The Vital Lie*

Alvarez, C. G., "O'Neill and Tragedy—a Longing to Die," *Estudos Anglo-Americanos*, 12–13:24–29, 1988–1989

Antush, J. V., "Eugene O'Neill: Modern and Postmodern," *Eugene O'Neill Review*, 13(1):14–26, Spring 1989

Astington, J. H., "Shakespeherian Rags," *ModernDrama*, 31:73–80, Mar. 1988

Bagchee, S., "On Blake and O'Neill," *Eugene O'Neill Review*, 14(1–2):25–38, Spring-Fall 1990

———, ed., *Perspectives on O'Neill*

———, "Reading O'Neill's Poetry," pp. 79–96 in Bagchee, ed., *Perspectives on O'Neill*

Barlow, J. E., "O'Neill's Many Mothers: Mary Tyrone, Josie Hogan and Their Antecedents," pp. 7–16 in S. Bagchee, ed., *Perspectives on O'Neill*

Behrendt, P. F., "Images of Women and the Burden of Myth: Plagues on the

Houses of Gorky and O'Neill," pp. 161–169 in J. Redmond, ed., *Drama and Philosophy*

Bentley, E., "The Life and Hates of Eugene O'Neill," pp. 27–56 in Bentley's *Thinking about the Playwrights*, (rpt. of P. Miller, ed., *Major Writers of America*, 2:557–576)

Bentley, J., *Hallie Flanagan*, pp. 280, 283–284, and elsewhere

Ben-Zvi, L., "Freedom and Fixity in the Plays of Eugene O'Neill," *Modern Drama*, 31(1):16–27, Mar. 1988

———, " 'Home Sweet Home': Deconstructing the Masculine Myth of the Frontier in Modern American Drama," pp. 217–225 in D. Mogen, M. Busby, and P. Bryant, eds., *The Frontier Experience and the American Dream*

———, "O'Neill and Absurdity," pp. 35–55 in E. Brater and R. Cohn, eds., *Around the Absurd*

Berlin, N., *Eugene O'Neill*

———, "The Beckettian O'Neill," *Modern Drama*, 31(1):28–34, Mar. 1988

Black, S. A., "O'Neill's Dramatic Process," *American Literature*, 59(1):58ff., 1987

Bloom, H., ed., *Eugene O'Neill*

Blumberg, M., "Eloquent Stammering in the Fog: O'Neill's Heritage in Mamet," pp. 97–111 in S. Bagchee, ed., *Perspectives on O'Neill*

Bogard, T., *Contour in Time*, rev. ed.

———, "First Love: Eugene O'Neill and 'Boutade,' " *Eugene O'Neill Newsletter*, 12(1):3–9, Spring 1988

Bryer, J. R., "Eugene O'Neill's Letters to Donald Pace: A Newly Discovered Correspondence," pp. 133–150 in M. Maufort, ed., *Eugene O'Neill and the Emergence of American Drama*

Buckley, M., "An Interview with Colleen Dewhurst," *TheaterWeek*, 3:34–38, 2 Oct. 1989

Burr, S., "O'Neill's Ghostly Women," pp. 37–47 in J. Schlueter, ed., *Feminist Rereadings of Modern American Drama*

Carpenter, F. I., "Eugene O'Neill and the Orient: A Forward Glance," *Eugene O'Neill Review*, 13(1):27–28, Spring 1989

"Celebrating the O'Neill Centennial," *Sunset*, 181:16, Sept. 1988

Chioles, J., "Aeschylus and O'Neill: A Phenomenological View," pp. 53–81 in J. H. Stroupe, ed., *Critical Approaches to O'Neill*

Chothia, J., "Questions of Significance: Some Recent Work in O'Neill Studies," *Journal of American Studies*, 23(2):311–314, Aug. 1989

Como, R. M., "O'Neill, Beckett and Dürrenmatt: The Shared Genre," *Eugene O'Neill Review*, 13(2):63–72, Fall 1989

Cunningham, F. R., " 'Authentic Tidings of Invisible Things,': Beyond James Robinson's *Eugene O'Neill and Oriental Thought*," *Eugene O'Neill Review*, 13(1):29–39, Spring 1989

Dardis, T., "O'Neill: 'Turn Back the Universe, and Give Me Yesterday,' " pp. 211–256 in Dardis's *The Thirsty Muse*

Demastes, W. W., *Beyond Naturalism*, pp. 6, 20–22, 23, 26, 29, 35, 70, 97–99, 105, 120–121

Donahue, F., "Eugene O'Neill: Llamada a escena," *Atenea*, 457:1119–1130, 1988

Egri, P., "Critical Approaches to the Birth of Modern American Tragedy: The Significance of Eugene O'Neill," *Acta Litteraria Academiae Scientiarum Hungaricae*, 30(3–4):243–271, 1988

————, "Epic Retardation and Diversion: Hemingway, Strindberg and O'Neill," *Neohelicon,* 35(4):316–325, 1987

————, "Synge and O'Neill: Inspiration and Influence," pp. 261–268 in W. Zach and H. Kosok, eds., *Literary Interrelations,* Vol. 2

Eisen, K., "Eugene O'Neill's Joseph: A Touch of the Dreamer," *Comparative Drama,* 23(4):344–358, Winter 1989–1990

Erens, P., "Portrait of the Playwright as a Young Man," *Connecticut Magazine,* 51:82 + , Feb. 1988

Floyd, V., "O'Neill at Work: A Pen in Trust to Art," *Eugene O'Neill Newsletter,* 12(2):33–38, Summer-Fall 1988

"Focus on 'Games People Play': Family Relationships in O'Neill's Plays," *Eugene O'Neill Newsletter,* 11(2):[spec. sect.], Summer-Fall, 1987

Gallup, D. C., "Carlotta Monterey O'Neill, 1954–1970," pp. 282–310 in Gallup's *Pigeons on the Granite*

Garvey, S. H., "Notes on a Work in Progress: An Interview with Barbara Gelb," *Eugene O'Neill Newsletter,* 11(1):21–25, Spring 1987

Gelb, B., "In Search of O'Neill," *Eugene O'Neill Newsletter,* 12(2):3–8, Summer-Fall 1988

Goodwin, D. W., "O'Neill: Alcohol and the Irish," pp. 123–137 in Goodwin's *Alcohol and the Writer*

Grabes, H., "The Legacy of Eugene O'Neill," pp. 29–40 in G. Debusscher, H. I. Schvey, and M. Maufort, eds., New Essays on American Drama

Gray, P. "New Views of a Playwright's Long Journey," *Time,* 132:120–121, 7 Nov. 1988

Griffin, E. G., "O'Neill and the Tragedy of Culture," *Modern Drama,* 31(1):1–15, Mar. 1988

Halfmann, U., ed., *Eugene O'Neill*

————, ed., *Eugene O'Neill: Comments on the Drama and the Theater*

————, " 'With Clenched Fist . . .': Observations on a Recurrent Motif in the Drama of Eugene O'Neill," pp. 107–121 in M. Maufort, ed., *Eugene O'Neill and the Emergence of American Drama*

Hamilton, J. W., "Eugene O'Neill and Addison's Disease," *Perspectives in Biology and Medicine,* 30(2):231 + , 1987

Hammerman, H. J., "On Collecting O'Neill," *Eugene O'Neill Review,* 13(1):47–54, Spring 1989

Harap, L., "American Drama Comes of Age: Eugene O'Neill," pp. 81–86 in Harap's *Dramatic Encounters*

Hayes, R., "Eugene O'Neill: The Tragic in Exile," introd. Eric Bentley, *TheaterWeek,* 3:34, 36–38, 26 Mar. 1990 (the Hayes article rpt. of *Theatre Arts,* Oct. 1963)

Hinden, M., "Paradise Lost: O'Neill and American History," *Eugene O'Neill Newsletter,* 12(1):39–40, 45–48, Spring 1988

————, "When Playwrights Talk to God: Peter Shaffer and the Legacy of O'Neill," pp. 199–213 in J. H. Stroupe, ed., *Critical Approaches to O'Neill*

Hornby, R., "O'Neill's Metadrama," *Eugene O'Neill Newsletter,* 12(2)13–18, Summer-Fall 1988

Horovitz, I., "The Legacy of O'Neill," *Eugene O'Neill Newsletter,* 11(1):3–10, Spring 1987

Jiji, V., "Reviewers' Responses to the Early Plays of Eugene O'Neill: A Study in Influence," *Theatre Survey,* 29(1):69–86, May 1988

Kalson, A. E., and L. M. Schwerdt, "Eternal Recurrence and the Shaping of O'Neill's Dramatic Structures," *Comparative Drama*, 24:133–150, Summer 1990

Kobernick, M., *Semiotics of the Drama and the Style of Eugene O'Neill*

Kusuhara, T., "Nihon ni okeru O'Neill-geki no Juyô," *Eigo Seinen*, 134:420–422, n.d.

Lui Haiping, "Eugene O'Neill in China," *Theatre Survey*, 29:87–101, May 1988

———, "Taoism in O'Neill's Tao House Plays," *Eugene O'Neill Newsletter*, 12(2):28–33, Summer-Fall 1988

Manheim, M., "Eugene O'Neill and the Founders of Modern Drama," pp. 47–57 in M. Maufort, ed., *Eugene O'Neill and the Emergence of American Drama*

———, "O'Neill's Early Debts to David Belasco," *Theatre History Studies*, 6:124–131, 1986

———, "O'Neill's Transcendence of Melodrama in the Late Plays," *Eugene O'Neill Newsletter*, 12(2):22–28, Summer-Fall 1988

Maufort, M., ed., *Eugene O'Neill and the Emergence of American Drama*

———, "Mariners and Mystics: Echoes of *Moby Dick* in O'Neill," *Theatre Annual*, 43:31–52, 1988

Maufort, M. J., "Eugene O'Neill: Dramaturge américain," *L'Artichaut*, 5(2):9–14, Oct. 1987, and 5(3):10–16, Dec. 1987

———, "Visions du nouveau monde: Eugene O'Neill et Herman Melville," *Revue de Philologie et d'Histoire*, 65(4):1003–1004, May 1986

McDonough, E. J., *Quntero Directs O'Neill*

Miller, J. Y., "From Nabokov to the Nobel: Two Decades of First Night O'Neill Criticism," *Eugene O'Neill Newsletter*, 12(2):8–13, Summer-Fall 1988

Moleski, J. J., "Eugene O'Neill and the Cruelty of Theater," pp. 37–52 in J. H. Stroupe, ed., *Critical Approaches to O'Neill*

Moleski, J. J., and J. H. Stroupe, "Jean Anouilh and Eugene O'Neill: Repetition as Negativity," pp. 187–198 in Stroupe, ed., *Critical Approaches to O'Neill* (rpt. of *Comparative Drama*, 20(4):315–326, Winter 1986–1987)

Morehouse, R., "A Theatregoer's Notebook: Homage to O'Neill," *Playbill*, 6:22–23, July 1988

Mutô, S., "O'Neill to Bokushin," *Eigo Seinen*, 134:417–419, n.d.

"O'Neill and the American Theatre," *Modern Drama*, 31(1):[spec. issue], Mar. 1988

O'Neill, E., *As Ever, Gene*, ed. N. L. Roberts and A. W. Roberts

———, *The Eugene O'Neill Songbook*, col. and annot. T. Bogard

———, *O'Neill: Complete Plays*, 3 vols., ed. T. Bogard

———, *Selected Letters of O'Neill*, ed. T. Bogard and J. R. Bryer

———, *The Unfinished Plays*, ed. V. Floyd

———, *The Unknown O'Neill*, ed. T. Bogard

O'Neill, M. C., "Confession as Artifice in the Plays of Eugene O'Neill," *Renascence*, 39(3):430–441, Spring 1987

Ouyang, J., "O'Neill, an American Playwright Who Bemoans the Fate of Mankind," *Foreign Literature Studies*, 42(4):3–11, Dec. 1988

Paller, M., "Eugene O'Neill: The Tributes Cometh," *TheaterWeek*, 2:31–35, 31 Oct. 1988

———, "Finding the Quintessential O'Neill: José Quintero," *TheaterWeek*, 1:8–13, 27 June 1988

Pasquier, M.-C., "You Are One of Us, You Are a Russian," pp. 77–83 in M. Maufort, ed., *Eugene O'Neill and the Emergence of American Drama*

Patrachkova, C., "L'illusion en tant qu'autodefense (dans quelques Pieces d'Eugene O'Neill, de Tennessee Williams et d'Edward Albee)," *Literaturna Misul,* 31(9):73–79, 1987

Pettegrove, J. P. "Karl Ragnow Gierow on O'Neill, October 6, 1970," *Eugene O'Neill Newsletter,* 11(1):32–34, Spring 1987

Pinaev, S. M., "Tragicheskaia simbolika Iudzhina O'Nila," *Filologicheskie Nauki,* 6:30–38, 1989

Porter, L., *The Banished Prince*

Prasad, H. M., *The Dramatic Art of Eugene O'Neill*

Proehl, G. S., "Foucault on Discourse: O'Neill as Discourse: *LDJN*(4:125–154) Tyrone and Edmund," *Journal of Dramatic Theory and Criticism,* 4(2):51–62, Spring 1990

Putzel, S. D., "Whiskey, Blarney and Land: Eugene O'Neill's Conceptions and Misconceptions of the Irish," pp. 125–131 in W. Zach and H. Kosok, eds., *Literary Interrelations,* Vol. 3.

Qian, J., "A Long Day's Journey That Tries but Fails to Get beyond the Horizon," *Waiguoyu,* 2(60):34–39, Apr. 1989

Quintero, J., "Carlotta and the Master," *New York Times Magazine,* pp. 56+, 1 May 1988

Quiroga, O., "Eugene O'Neill, un mensaje humanista que perdura," *Suplemento Lit. La Nación,* 20:6, Nov. 1988

Raleigh, J. H., "Eugene O'Neill," pp. 480–518 in J. R. Bryer, ed., *Sixteen Modern American Authors,* Vol. 2

———, "Strindberg and O'Neill as Historical Dramatists, pp. 59–75 in M. Maufort, ed., *Eugene O'Neill and the Emergence of American Drama*

Roy, E., "The Archetypal Unity of Eugene O'Neill's Drama," pp. 1–15 in J. H. Stroupe, ed., *Critical Approaches to O'Neill*

Ryan, P., "Eugene O'Neill a Hundred Years On," *Drama,* no. 170:27–30, 1988

Schroeder, P. R., "Eugene O'Neill: What the Past Has Made Them," pp. 29–52 in Schroeder's *The Presence of the Past in Modern American Drama*

Sen, K., "Eugene O'Neill and the Concept of 'Psychic Fate,'" *Journal of the Department of English,* 21(1–2):55–66, 1986–1987

Shaugnessy, E. L., *Eugene O'Neill in Ireland*

Sheaffer, L., "Correcting Some Errors in Annals of O'Neill," pp. 83–114 in J. H. Stroupe, ed., *Critical Approaches to O'Neill*

———, *O'Neill*

———, "Taasinge or Tharsing?" *Eugene O'Neill Newsletter,* 11(1):26, Spring 1987

Simon, J., "Brothers under the Skin: Eugene O'Neill and Tennessee Williams," pp. 62–76 in Simon's *The Sheep from the Goats* (rpt. of *Hudson Review,* 39:553–565, Winter 1987)

Smith, M., and R. Eaton, *Eugene O'Neill*

Smith, M. C., and R. B. Eaton, "Four Letters by Eugene O'Neill," *Eugene O'Neill Newsletter,* 11(3):12–18, Winter 1987

Stanciu, V., "O'Neill și renașterea tragediei," *Steaua,* 37(12[475]):44+, Dec. 1986

Stroupe, J. H., ed., *Critical Approaches to O'Neill*

———, "Eugene O'Neill and the Creative Process: A Road to Xanadu," pp. 115–133 in Stroupe, ed., *Critical Approaches to O'Neill*

Sun, B., "In Commemoration of the Centenary of Eugene O'Neill," *Waiguoyu,* 6[58]:33–36, Dec. 1988

Swortzell, L., "O'Neill and the Marionette: *Über* and Otherwise," *Eugene O'Neill Newsletter,* 11(3):3–7, Winter 1987

Törnqvist, E., "From *A Wife for a Life* to *A Moon for the Misbegotten*: O'Neill's Play Titles," pp. 97–105 in M. Maufort, ed., *Eugene O'Neill and the Emergence of American Drama*

Uchino, T., "O'Neill no Melodramatism," *Eigo Seinen,* 134:409–411, n.d.

Vena, G., "Carlotta Takes Center-Stage: A Review of *My Gene*," *Eugene O'Neill Newsletter,* 11(1):19–21, Spring 1987

Voelker, P., ed., "Eugene O'Neill 1888–1953," *Theatre Annual,* 43:[spec. issue], 1988

———, "Success and Frustration at Harvard: Eugene O'Neill's Relationship with George Pierce Baker (1914–1915)," pp. 15–29 in M. Maufort, ed., *Eugene O'Neill and the Emergence of American Drama*

Voelker, P. D., "O'Neill's First Families: *Warnings* through *The Personal Equation*," *Eugene O'Neill Newsletter,* 11(2):13–18, Summer-Fall 1987

Vysots'ka, N., "Dotork do fatumu," *Vsesvit,* 11[719]:139–142, Nov. 1988

Wainscott, R. H., *Staging O'Neill*

Watt, S., "O'Neill and Otto Rank: Doubles, 'Death Instincts,' and the Trauma of Birth," pp. 17–36 in J. H. Stroupe, ed., *Critical Approaches to O'Neill* (rpt. of *Comparative Drama,* 20(3):211–230, Fall 1986)

Weales, G., "The Postman Cometh," *Gettysburg Review,* 2(4):647–657, Autumn 1989

Wilkins, F. C., " 'Arriving with a Bang': O'Neill's Literary Reputation," pp. 5–13 in M. Maufort, ed., *Eugene O'Neill and the Emergence of American Drama*

———, "O'Neill at 100," *Americana,* 16:47–52, July/Aug. 1988

———, "O'Neill's Secular Saints," *Eugene O'Neill Review,* 14(1–2):67–78, Fall 1990

Wilson, S. M., "Sea Island Sanctuary: Eugene O'Neill's Former Workspace-Retreat," *Southern Accents,* 13(5):54–61, June 1990

Xia, Y., "Exploration of O'Neill's Philosophy of Life," *Foreign Literature Studies,* 37(3):76–81, Sept. 1987

Zapf, H., "Drama und Postmoderne: Zur Aktualität Eugene O'Neills," *Forum Modernes Theater,* 3(2):142 +, 1988

American Theatre, 5:88–89, Oct. 1988

Chicago, 37:117 +, Dec. 1988

Connecticut Magazine, 51:83 +, Feb. 1988

New England Monthly, 5:31–32, Mar. 1988

Playbill, 6:66, June 1988

TheaterWeek, 2:5, 17 Oct. 1988

Vanity Fair, 51:130, Oct. 1988

Ah, Wilderness!, 1933

    Bermel, A., "O'Neill's Funny Valentine," *Eugene O'Neill Newsletter,* 12(2):18–22, Summer-Fall 1988

    Henry, W. A., III, "A Coney Island of the Mind," *Time,* 131:56–57, 27 June 1988

Hersh, A., "Colleen Dewhurst: At Home with the O'Neills," *TheaterWeek*, 1:8–10, 20 June 1988

Littlejohn, D., "O'Neill, Light and Dark," *American Theatre*, 5:16, Dec. 1988

Paton, A., "Long Day's Journal," ed. David Littlejohn, *American Theatre*, 5:14–21, 48–51, Dec. 1988

America, 159:64–65, 23–30 July 1988

Eugene O'Neill Newsletter, 12(1):68–70, Spring 1988

Eugene O'Neill Review, 13(1):72–74, Spring 1989

Eugene O'Neill Review, 14(1–2):89–94, Spring-Fall 1990

Nation, 247:178–179, 27 Aug.–3 Sept. 1988

New York, 21:48–49, 11 July 1988

New Yorker, 64:60, 4 July 1988

Theatre Journal, 40:545–548, Dec. 1988

Village Voice, 33:85, 5 July 1988

All God's Chillun Got Wings, 1924

Fletcher, W. L., "Who Put the 'Tragic' in the Tragic Mulatto?" pp. 262–268 in H. K. Chinoy and L. W. Jenkins, eds., *Women in American Theatre*, rev. and enl. ed. (pp. 260–266 in 1981 ed.)

Kolin, P. C., "*All God's Chillun Got Wings* and *Macbeth*," *Eugene O'Neill Newsletter*, 12(1):55–61, Spring 1988

Mandl, B., "Theatricality and Otherness in *All God's Chillun Got Wings*," pp. 48–56 in J. Schlueter, ed., *Feminist Rereadings of Modern American Drama*

Press, M., "Black Man-White Woman: The 'Lynch Pattern' as Morality Play," pp. 157–168 in K. Hartigan, ed., *Text and Presentation*

Tuck, S., "White Dreams, Black Nightmares: *All God's Chillun Got Wings* and *Light in August*," 12(1):48–55, Spring 1988

Anna Christie, 1921

Adler, T. P., "Beyond Synge: O'Neill's *Anna Christie*," *Eugene O'Neill Newsletter*, 12(1):34–39, Spring 1988

Antush, J. V., "Eugene O'Neill: Modern and Postmodern," *Eugene O'Neill Review*, 13(1):14–26, Spring 1989

Garvey, S. H., "*Anna Christie* in New Haven: A Theatrical Odyssey," *Eugene O'Neill Review*, 14(1–2):53–70, Spring-Fall 1990

Reed, T., "O'Neill's Nausikaa Episode," *Eugene O'Neill Newsletter*, 11(3):8–9, Winter 1987

Stephens, J. L., "Women in Pulitzer Prize Plays, 1918–1949," pp. 245–253 in H. K. Chinoy and L. W. Jenkins, eds., *Women in American Theatre*, rev. and enl. ed. (pp. 243–251 in 1981 ed.)

Beyond the Horizon, 1920

Black, S. A., "America's First Tragedy," *English Studies in Canada*, 13(2):195–203, June 1987

Murphy, B., "*Beyond the Horizon*'s Narrative Sentence: An American Intertext for O'Neill," *Theatre Annual*, 41:49–62, 1986

Stephens, J. L., "Women in Pulitzer Prize Plays, 1918–1949," pp. 245–253

in H. K. Chinoy and L. W. Jenkins, eds., *Women in American Theatre,*
rev. and enl. ed. (pp. 243–251 in 1981 ed.)
Eugene O'Neill Newsletter, 12(3):48–50, Winter 1988

Bound East for Cardiff (also see *The Sea Plays* and *S.S. Glencairn*), 1916
Maufort, M., "O'Neill's Variations on an Obituary Motif in *Bound East for
Cardiff* and *Hughie,*" *Revue Belge de Philologie et d'Histoire,* 66(3):602–
612, 1988
Williams, G. J., "Turned Down in Provincetown: O'Neill's Debut Re-Examined," *Eugene O'Neill Newsletter,* 12(1):17–27, Spring 1988 (revision
of article in *Theatre Journal,* 37(2):155–166, May 1985)

The Calms of Capricorn (a play in O'Neill's unfinished cycle of eleven plays
which was to have been called *A Tale of Possessors Self-Dispossessed*)
Jackson, E. M., "Dramatic Form in Eugene O'Neill's *The Calms of Capricorn,*" *Eugene O'Neill Newsletter,* 12(3):35–42, Winter 1988

Children of the Sea (early version of *Bound East for Cardiff,* which see), written
1914
Williams, G. J., "Turned Down in Provincetown: O'Neill's Debut Re-Examined," *Eugene O'Neill Newsletter,* 12(1):17–27, Spring 1988 (revision
of article in *Theatre Journal,* 37(2):155–166, May 1985)

Desire under the Elms, 1924
Gordenstein, A., "A Few Thousand Battered Books: Eugene O'Neill's Use
of Myth in *Desire under the Elms* and *Mourning Becomes Electra,*" *Ilha
do Desterro,* 15–16(1–2):136–146, 1986
Kalson, A. E., "Up-Staged and Off-Staged by the Director and Designer:
The Hairy Ape and *Desire under the Elms* in London," *Eugene O'Neill
Newsletter,* 11(2):36–40, Summer-Fall 1987
Kolin, P. C., "Parallels between *Desire under the Elms* and *Sweet Bird of
Youth,*" *Eugene O'Neill Review,* 13(2)23–25, Summer-Fall 1989
Mandl, B., "Family Ties: Landscape and Gender in *Desire under the Elms,*"
Eugene O'Neill Newsletter, 11(2):19–23, Summer-Fall 1987
Robinson, H., "A Glasnost Menagerie," *American Theatre,* 5:24–29, Sept.
1988
Robinson, J. A., "Buried Children: Fathers and Sons in O'Neill and She-
pard," pp. 151–157 in M. Maufort, ed., *Eugene O'Neill and the Emer-
gence of American Drama*
———, "O'Neill's Indian *Elms,*" *Eugene O'Neill Review,* 13(1):40–46,
Spring 1989
Robinson, L. S., "On the Sources and Motives behind Ts'ao Yü's *Thun-
derstorm*: A Qualitative Analysis," *Tamkang Review,* 16(2):177–192, Win-
ter 1985
Eugene O'Neill Review, 13(2):80–89, Fall 1989
TheaterWeek, 1:6, 11 July 1988
TheaterWeek, 2:2, 17 Oct. 1988

The Dreamy Kid, 1919

Williams, G. J., *"The Dreamy Kid:* O'Neill's Darker Brother," *Theatre Annual,* 43:3–14, 1988

The Emperor Jones, 1920

Abiteboul, M., "Civilisation et régression dans *L'Empéreur Jones* d'Eugene O'Neill et *Vacances d'été* de Francis Ebejer: Le Progrès est-il un mythe?" *Commonwealth Essays and Studies,* 10(1):49–56, Autumn 1987

Cooley, J., "In Search of the Primitive: Black Portraits in Eugene O'Neill and Other Village Bohemians," pp. 51–64 in V. A. Kramer, ed., *The Harlem Renaissance Re-Examined*

——, "White Writers and the Harlem Renaissance," pp. 13–22 in A. Singh, W. S. Shiver, and S. Brodwin, eds., *The Harlem Renaissance*

Larabee, A. E., "'Meeting the Outside Face to Face': Susan Glaspell, Djuna Barnes, and O'Neill's *The Emperor Jones,"* pp. 77–85 in J. Schlueter, ed., *Modern American Drama*

Singh, V., "O'Neill's Yank and Jones: The Dislocated Characters," *Panjab University Research Bulletin (Arts),* 18(1):45–54, Apr. 1987

Viswanathan, R., *"The Jungle Book* and O'Neill," *Eugene O'Neill Newsletter,* 11(2):3–7, Summer-Fall 1987

Woll, A., *Black Musical Theatre,* pp. 74, 165–66, 174

Four Plays of the Sea (see *The Sea Plays* and *S.S. Glencairn*)

Gold, 1921

Maufort, M., "Eugene O'Neill and the Shadow of Edmond Dantes: The Pursuit of Dramatic Unity in *Where the Cross Is Made* (1918) and *Gold* (1920)," pp. 89–97 in G. Debusscher and M. Maufort, eds., *American Literature in Belgium*

The Great God Brown, 1926

Manheim, M., *"The Great God Brown* in the light of O'Neill's Last Plays," *Eugene O'Neill Review,* 14(1–2):5–15, Spring-Fall 1990

Richardson, B., *"The Great God Brown* and the Theory of Character," *Eugene O'Neill Review,* 14(1–2):16–24, Spring-Fall 1990

Stephens, J. L., "Subverting the Demon-Angel Dichotomy: Innovation and Feminist Intervention in Twentieth-Century Drama," *Text and Performance Quarterly,* 9(1):53–64, Jan. 1989

The Hairy Ape, 1922

Chothia, J., "Theatre Language: Word and Image in *The Hairy Ape,"* pp. 31–46 in M. Maufort, ed., *Eugene O'Neill and the Emergence of American Drama*

Jurich, M., "Men of Iron, Beasts of Clay: The Confluence of Folk-Tale and Drama in 'Joe Magarac' and *The Hairy Ape,"* *Eugene O'Neill Newsletter,* 12(2):38–45, Summer-Fall 1988

Kalson, A. E., "Up-Staged and Off-Staged by the Director and Designer: *The Hairy Ape* and *Desire under the Elms* in London," *Eugene O'Neill Newsletter,* 11(2):36–40, Summer-Fall 1987

Massa, A., "Intention and Effect in *The Hairy Ape,"* *Modern Drama,* 31(1):41–51, Mar. 1988

Singh, V., "O'Neill's Yank and Jones: The Dislocated Characters," *Panjab University Research Bulletin (Arts)*, 18(1):45–54, Apr. 1987

Viswanathan, R., "*The Jungle Book* and O'Neill," *Eugene O'Neill Newsletter*, 11(2):3–7, Summer-Fall 1987

Whitlatch, M., "Eugene O'Neill and Class Consciousness in *The Hairy Ape*," *Zeitschrift für Anglistik und Amerikanistik*, 35(3):223–227, 1987

Zapf, H., "O'Neill's *Hairy Ape* and the Reversal of Hegelian Dialectics," *Modern Drama*, 35(1):35–40, Mar. 1988

Eugene O'Neill Review, 13(1):70–72, Spring 1989

Theatre Journal, 40:114–116, Mar. 1988

Theatre Journal, 40:545–548, Dec. 1988

Hughie, 1958

Bigsby, C. W. E., "O'Neill's Endgame," pp. 159–168 in M. Maufort, ed., *Eugene O'Neill and the Emergence of American Drama*

Bloom, S. F., "Waiting for the Dough: O'Neill's *Hughie*," *Eugene O'Neill Newsletter*, 12(3):28–35, Winter 1988

Ichinose, K., "Performance Text to shite no *Hughie*: Togaki wo tôshite," *Eigo Seinen*, 134:412–413, n.d.

Maufort, M., "O'Neill's Variations on an Obituary Motif in *Bound East for Cardiff* and *Hughie*," *Revue Belge de Philologie et d'Histoire*, 66(3):602–612, 1988

McKelly, J. C., "Ain't It the Truth: *Hughie* and the Power of Fiction," *Eugene O'Neill Newsletter*, 11(1):15–19, Spring 1987

Smith, S. H., "Actors Constructing an Audience: *Hughie*'s Post-Modern Aura," pp. 169–180 in M. Maufort, ed., *Eugene O'Neill and the Emergence of American Drama*

Chicago, 37:117+, Dec. 1988

Eugene O'Neill Newsletter, 12(2):82–83, Summer-Fall 1988

Eugene O'Neill Review, 13(1):74–76, Spring 1989

The Iceman Cometh, 1946

Austin, G., *Feminist Theories for Dramatic Criticism*, pp. 29–37

Behrendt, P. F., "Images of Women and the Burden of Myth: Plagues on the Houses of Gorky and O'Neill," pp. 161–169 in J. Redmond, ed., *Drama and Philosophy*

Berlin, N., ed., *Eugene O'Neill: Three Plays*

———, "O'Neill and Comedy: *The Iceman Cometh*," *Eugene O'Neill Newsletter*, 12(3):3–8, Winter 1988

Berry, D. W. "Albee and the Iceman: O'Neill's Influence on *Who's Afraid of Virginia Woolf?*" *Eugene O'Neill Newsletter*, 11(3):18–21, Winter 1987

Black, S. A., "Tragic Anagnorisis in *The Iceman Cometh*," pp. 17–32 in S. Bagchee, ed., *Perspectives on O'Neill*

Bloom, H., ed., *Eugene O'Neill's* The Iceman Cometh

Brustein, R., "Souls on Ice," pp. 98–101 in Brustein's *Who Needs Theatre* (rpt. of *New Republic*, 193:41–43, 28 Oct. 1985)

Garvey, S. H., "The Origins of the O'Neill Renaissance: A History of the 1956 Productions of *The Iceman Cometh* and *Long Day's Journey into Night*," *Theatre Survey*, 29:51–68, May 1988

Hornby, R., "O'Neill's 'Death of a Salesman,'" *Journal of Dramatic Theory and Criticism*, 2(2):53–59, Spring 1988

Morse, D. E., "The 'Life Lie' in Three Plays by O'Neill, Williams, and Miller," pp. 273–277 in M. Jurak, ed., *Cross-Cultural Studies*

Neu, J., "Life-Lies and Pipe Dreams: Self-Deception in Ibsen's *The Wild Duck* and O'Neill's *The Iceman Cometh*," *Philosophical Forum*, 19(4): 241+, 1988

Porter, L. R., "*The Iceman Cometh* as Crossroad in O'Neill's Long Journey," *Modern Drama*, 31(1):52–62, Mar. 1988

Robinson, J. A., "Ghost Stories: *Iceman*'s Absent Women and Mary Tyrone," *Eugene O'Neill Newsletter*, 12(3):14–19, Winter 1988

Shafer, Y., "In Ibsen's Back Room: Related Patterns in *The Iceman Cometh* and *The Wild Duck*," *Eugene O'Neill Newsletter*, 12(3):8–14, Winter 1988

Stanich, L., "*The Iceman Cometh* as Ethnographic Text," *Eugene O'Neill Review*, 12(2):55–62, Fall 1989

American Theatre, 7:11, Nov. 1990

Eugene O'Neill Newsletter, 12(3):51–52, Winter 1988

TheaterWeek, 1:56–57, 2 May 1988

Time, 136:54, 31 Dec. 1990

Ile (see *The Sea Plays*), 1917

In the Zone (see *The Sea Plays* and *S.S. Glencairn*), 1917

Lazarus Laughed, 1928

King, W. D., "'It Brought the World to This Coast': The World Premiere of Eugene O'Neill's *Lazarus Laughed* at the Pasadena Community Playhouse," *Theatre Survey*, 29:1–36, May 1988

Sarlós, R. K., "'Write a Dance': *Lazarus Laughed* as O'Neill's Dithyramb of the Western Hemisphere," *Theatre Survey*, 29(1):37–49, May 1988

Long Day's Journey into Night, 1956

Adler, T. P., "'Daddy Spoke to Me!': Gods Lost and Found in *Long Day's Journey into Night* and *Through a Glass Darkly*," pp. 161–168 in J. H. Stroupe, ed., *Critical Approaches to O'Neill* (rpt. of *Comparative Drama*, 20(4):341–348, Winter 1986–1987)

Astington, J. H., "Shakespeherian Rags," *Modern Drama*, 31(1):73–80, Mar. 1988

Barbour, D., "The Actor as Daredevil: Kevin Spacey," *TheaterWeek*, 1:32–38, 27 June 1988

Barlow, J. E., "Mother, Wife, Mistress, Friend, and Collaborator: Carlotta Monterey and *Long Day's Journey into Night*," pp. 123–131 in M. Maufort, ed., *Eugene O'Neill and the Emergence of American Drama*

Berlin, N., ed., *Eugene O'Neill: Three Plays*

———, "O'Neill's Shakespeare," *Eugene O'Neill Review*, 13(1):5–13, Spring 1989

Black, S. A., "O'Neill's Dramatic Process," *American Literature*, 59(1):58–70, Mar. 1987

———, "The War among the Tyrones," *Eugene O'Neill Newsletter*, 11(2):29–31, Summer-Fall 1987

Bloom, H., ed., *Eugene O'Neill's* Long Day's Journey into Night

Chothia, J., " 'Native Eloquence': Multiple Voices in *Long Day's Journey into Night,*" *Eugene O'Neill Newsletter,* 12(3):24–28, Winter 1988

Flèche, A., " 'A Monster of Perfection': O'Neill's 'Stella,' " pp. 25–36 in J. Schlueter, ed., *Feminist Rereadings of Modern American Drama*

Garner, S. B., Jr., *The Absent Voice,* pp. 18, 19, 34, 170

Garvey, S. H., "The Origins of the O'Neill Renaissance: A History of the 1956 Productions of *The Iceman Cometh* and *Long Day's Journey into Night,*" *Theatre Survey,* 29:51–68, May 1988

Gierow, K. R., "*Long Day's Journey* Was the 'Wrong' Play" (tr. Pat M. Ryan), *Theatre Survey,* 29:103–112, May 1988

Henry, W. A., III, "A Coney Island of the Mind," *Time,* 131:56–57, 27 June 1988

Hersh, A., "Colleen Dewhurst: At Home with the O'Neills," *TheaterWeek,* 1:8–10, 20 June 1988

Hinden, M., Long Day's Journey into Night: *Native Eloquence*

———, "Missing Lines in *Long Day's Journey into Night,*" *Modern Drama,* 32(2):177–182, June 1989

———, "The Pharmacology of *Long Day's Journey into Night,*" *Eugene O'Neill Review,* 14(1–2):47–51, Spring-Fall 1990

Ishizuka, K., "Sakusha 'Fazai' no Jiden Geki: *Yoru eno Nagai Tabiji* Saikô," *Eigo Seinen,* 134:414–416, n.d.

Lindman-Strafford, K., "Modern som martyr," *Finsk Tidskrift,* 225–226(7): 414–423, 1989

Littlejohn, D., "O'Neill, Light and Dark," *American Theatre,* 5:16, Dec. 1988

Lloyd, D. W., "Mystical Experience in *Long Day's Journey into Night,*" *Unisa English Studies,* 24(2):17–21, Sept. 1986

Mandl, B., "Wrestling with the Angel in the House: Mary Tyrone's Long Journey," *Eugene O'Neill Newsletter,* 12(3):19–24, Winter 1988

Manheim, M., "The Transcendence of Melodrama in *Long Day's Journey into Night,*" pp. 33–42 in S. Bagchee, ed., *Perspectives on O'Neill*

Mann, B. J., "O'Neill's 'Presence' in *Long Day's Journey into Night,*" *Theatre Annual,* 43:15–30, 1988

Marcuson, L. R., *The Stage Immigrant,* pp. 197–205

Maufort, M., "American Flowers of Evil: *Long Day's Journey into Night* and Baudelaire," pp. 13–28 in G. Debusscher, H. I. Schvey, and Maufort, eds., *New Essays on American Drama*

———, "Eugene O'Neill and Poetic Realism: Tragic Form in the Belgian Premiere of *Long Day's Journey into Night,*" *Theatre Survey,* 29:117–125, May 1988

———, "The Tyrone Family in Bruges: A Belgian *Long Day's Journey into Night,*" *Eugene O'Neill Newsletter,* 11(2):32–35, Summer-Fall, 1987

Moorton, R. F., Jr., "The Author as Oedipus in *Mourning Becomes Electra* and *Long Day's Journey into Night,*" *Papers on Language and Literature,* 25(3):304–325, Summer 1989

Paton, A., "Long Day's Journal" (ed. by David Littlejohn), *American Theatre,* 5:14–21, 48–51, Dec. 1988

Raleigh, J. H., "Communal, Familial, and Personal Memories in O'Neill's *Long Day's Journey into Night,*" *Modern Drama,* 31(1):63–72, Mar. 1988

Robinson, J. A., "Ghost Stories: *Iceman*'s Absent Women and Mary Tyrone," *Eugene O'Neill Newsletter,* 12(3):14–19, Winter 1988

Rothenberg, A., and E. D. Shapiro, "The Defense of Psychoanalysis in Literature: *Long Day's Journey into Night* and *A View from the Bridge,*" pp. 169–185 in J. H. Stroupe, ed., *Critical Approaches to O'Neill*

Savran, D., *The Wooster Group,* pp. 133–157

Schmitt, N. C., "Family Plays: *Long Day's Journy into Night* and *Rumstick Road,*" pp. 39–76 in Schmitt's *Actors and Onlookers*

Simon, B., "A Mistake My Being Born a Man: O'Neill's *Long Day's Journey into Night,*" pp. 177–211 in Simon's *Tragic Drama and the Family*

Stuart, O., "Backstage with the Tyrone Brothers" (interview), *Theater-Week,* 1:30–35, 25 July 1988

Törnqvist, E., "Ingmar Bergman Directs *Long Day's Journey into Night,*" *New Theatre Quarterly,* 5(2):374–383, Nov. 1989

Vena, G., "Congruency and Coincidence in O'Casey's *Juno* and O'Neill's *Journey,*" *English Studies,* 68(3):249–263, June 1987

America, 159:64, 23–30 July 1988

American Theatre, 5:6, June 1988

Eugene O'Neill Newsletter, 12(1):64–66, Spring 1988

Eugene O'Neill Newsletter, 12(1):68, Spring 1988

Eugene O'Neill Newsletter, 12(2):83–85, Summer-Fall 1988

Eugene O'Neill Newsletter, 12(3):50–51, Winter 1988

Eugene O'Neill Review, 14(1–2):101–103, Spring-Fall 1990

Nation, 247:178, 27 Aug.–3 Sept. 1988

New York, 21:48–49, 11 July 1988

New Yorker, 64:59–60, 4 July 1988

Theatre Journal, 40:545–548, Dec. 1988

Village Voice, 33:85, 5 July 1988

The Long Voyage Home (also see *The Sea Plays* and *S.S. Glencairn*), 1917

Bernstein, M., "Hollywood's 'Arty Cinema': John Ford's *The Long Voyage Home,*" *Wide Angle,* 10(1):30–45, 1988

Marco Millions, 1928

Cooperman, R., "*Marco Millions*: O'Neill's Other Comedy," *Eugene O'Neill Review,* 13(2):36–44, Fall 1989

Liao, K., "On O'Neill's *Marco Millions,*" *Foreign Literature Studies,* 38(4):40–45, 102, Dec. 1987

Robinson, J. A., "Taoism and O'Neill's *Marco Millions,*" pp. 135–146 in J. H. Stroupe, ed., *Critical Approaches to O'Neill* (rpt. of *Comparative Drama,* 14(3):251–262, Fall 1980)

American Theatre, 5:11–12, Dec. 1988

Eugene O'Neill Newsletter, 12(2):76–79, Summer-Fall 1988

A Moon for the Misbegotten, 1947

Manheim, M., "O'Neill's Transcendence of Melodrama in *A Touch of the Poet* and *A Moon for the Misbegotten,*" pp. 147–159 in J. H. Stroupe, ed., *Critical Approaches to O'Neill* (rpt. of *Comparative Drama,* 16(3): 238–250, Fall 1982)

Marcuson, L. R., *The Stage Immigrant,* pp. 197–205

Ready, R., "The Play of the Misbegotten," *Modern Drama,* 31(1):81–90, Mar. 1988

Robinson, J. A., "The Metatheatrics of *A Moon for the Misbegotten,*" pp. 61–75 in S. Bagchee, ed., *Perspectives on O'Neill*

Spånberg, S.-J., "*A Moon for the Misbegotten* as Elegy: An Intertextual Reading," *Studia Neophilologica,* 61(1):23–36, 1989

American Theatre, 7:12, Apr. 1990

Eugene O'Neill Review, 13(2):77–80, Fall 1989

Eugene O'Neill Review, 14(1–2):95–100, Spring-Fall 1990

Eugene O'Neill Review, 14(1–2):103–107, Spring-Fall 1990

The Moon of the Caribbees (see *The Sea Plays* and *S.S. Glencairn*), 1918

More Stately Mansions, 1962

Bower, M. G., ed., More Stately Mansions: *The Unexpurgated Edition*

Jackson, E. M., "Dramatic Form in Eugene O'Neill's *The Calms of Capricorn,*" *Eugene O'Neill Newsletter,* 12(3):35–42, Winter 1988

Eugene O'Neill Review, 14(1–2):85–89, Spring-Fall 1990

Mourning Becomes Electra, 1939

Ahmed, S., "Euripides's *Electra* and Eugene O'Neill's *Mourning Becomes Electra*: A Study in Sexual Jealousy," *Meerut Journal of Comparative Literature and Language,* 1(2):19–32, Oct. 1988

Berlin, N., ed., *Eugene O'Neill: Three Plays*

Counts, M. L., *Coming Home,* pp. 83–84, 126, 135–136, 150, 180, 210

Deng, S., "On O'Neill's *Mourning Becomes Electra* (Tragic Trilogy)," *Foreign Literature Studies,* 36(2):85–90, June 1987

Egri, P., "The Electra Complex of Puritan Morality and the Epic Ambition of O'Neillian Tragedy," pp. 43–60 in S. Bagchee, ed., *Perspectives on O'Neill*

Gordenstein, A., "A Few Thousand Battered Books: Eugene O'Neill's Use of Myth in *Desire under the Elms* and *Mourning Becomes Electra,*" *Ilha do Desterro,* 15–16(1–2):136–146, 1986

Maufort, M., "The Legacy of Melville's *Pierre*: Family Relationships in *Mourning Becomes Electra,*" *Eugene O'Neill Newsletter,* 11(2):23–28, Summer-Fall 1987

———, "*Typee* Revisited: O'Neill's *Mourning Becomes Electra* and Melville," pp. 85–96 in Maufort, ed., *Eugene O'Neill and the Emergence of American Drama*

Moorton, R. F., "What's in a Name? The Significance of 'Mannon' in *Mourning Becomes Electra,*" *Eugene O'Neill Newsletter,* 12(3):42–44, Winter 1988

Moorton, R. F., Jr., "The Author as Oedipus in *Mourning Becomes Electra* and *Long Day's Journey into Night,*" *Papers on Language and Literature,* 25(3):304–325, Summer 1989

Nugent, S. G., "Masking Becomes Electra: O'Neill, Freud, and the Feminine," *Comparative Drama,* 22:37–55, Spring 1988

Sands, J., "*Electra*'s First Hazel: An Interview with Mary Arbenz," *Eugene O'Neill Newsletter,* 11(1):34–37, Spring 1987

Wainscott, R. H., "Exploring the Religion of the Dead: Philip Moeller

Directs O'Neill's *Mourning Becomes Electra,*" *Theatre History Studies,* 7:28–39, 1987

Weckermann, H.-J., "Das Haus Pyncheon und das Haus Mannon: Der Amerikanische einfluss in O'Neills *Mourning Becomes Electra,*" *Literatur in Wissenschaft und Unterricht,* 21(3):202+, 1988

Werner, B. C., "Eugene O'Neill's *Paradise Lost*: The Theme of the Islands in *Mourning Becomes Electra,*" *Ball State University Forum,* 27(1):46–52, Winter 1986

Eugene O'Neill Newsletter, 12(1):66–68, Spring 1988

Eugene O'Neill Newsletter, 12(2):76–79, Summer-Fall 1988

Eugene O'Neill Review, 13(2):73–77, Fall 1989

The Rope, 1918

Seff, R., "The Boob Tube Gets a Touch of Class," *TheaterWeek,* 3:28–32, 4 Dec. 1989

Eugene O'Neill Review, 13(2):94–96, Fall 1989

S.S. Glencairn (four plays: *The Moon of the Caribbees*; *In the Zone*; *Bound East for Cardiff,* which see; and *The Long Voyage Home,* which see), 1924

Larson, K. A., "O'Neill's Tragic Quest for Belonging: Psychological Determinism in the *S.S. Glencairn* Quartet," *Eugene O'Neill Review,* 13(2):12–22, Fall 1989

Maufort, M., "Eugene O'Neill's Innovative Craftsmanship in the *Glencairn* Cycle (1914–1917)," *Eugene O'Neill Newsletter,*" 12(1):27–33, Spring 1988

American Theatre, 5:7–8, Apr. 1988

Eugene O'Neill Newsletter, 12(2)79–80, Summer-Fall 1988

Nation, 247:663–664, 12 Dec. 1988

The Sea Plays (*In the Zone, The Long Voyage Home,* and *Ile*; also see *S.S. Glencairn*)

Eugene O'Neill Newsletter, 12(3):47–48, Winter 1988

The Sea Plays (*The Moon of the Caribees*; *In the Zone*; *Bound East for Cardiff,* which see; and *The Long Voyage Home,* which see; also see *S.S. Glencairn*)

Eugene O'Neill Review, 13(1):65–68, Spring 1989

Servitude, 1914

Miller, R. R., "O'Neill's *Servitude,* Shaw's *Candida,* and the Comic Vision," pp. 147–156 in K. Hartigan, ed., *Text and Presentation*

Strange Interlude, 1928

Curtin, K., "*We Can Always Call Them Bulgarians,*" pp. 115–118

Egri, P., "Epic Retardation and Diversion: Hemingway, Stringberg and O'Neill," *Zeitschrift für Anglistik und Amerikanistik,* 33(4):324–330, 1985

———, "High Culture and Popular Culture in Eugene O'Neill: *Strange Interlude,*" pp. 55–76 in C. Kretzoi, ed., *High and Low in American Culture*

———, "The Aftermath of World War I and the Fictionalization of Drama (Eugene O'Neill: *Strange Interlude*)," *Acta Litteraria Academiae Scientiarum Hungaricae,* 29(1–2):75–96, 1987

Eisen, K., "Novelization and the Drama of Consciousness in *Strange Interlude*," *Eugene O'Neill Review*, 14(1–2):39–46, Spring-Fall 1990

Smith, M., and R. Eaton, "Lewys v. O'Neill Again—or, Who Was That Lady?" *Eugene O'Neill Review*, 13(2):45–54, Fall 1989

Stephens, J. L., "Women in Pulitzer Prize Plays, 1918–1949," pp. 245–253 in H. K. Chinoy and L. W. Jenkins, eds., *Women in American Theatre*, rev. and enl. ed. (pp. 243–251 in 1981 ed.)

Eugene O'Neill Newsletter, 12(2):80–82, Summer-Fall 1988

Theatre Journal, 41:245–247, May 1989

The Straw, 1921

Marcuson, L. R., *The Stage Immigrant*, pp. 34–37

Eugene O'Neill Review, 13(2):89–94, Fall 1989

Eugene O'Neill Review, 14(1–2):79–85, Spring-Fall 1990

TheaterWeek, 3:11, 6 Nov. 1989

A Touch of the Poet, 1957

Bermel, A., "A Crutch of the Poet," *Eugene O'Neill Newsletter*, 11(1):10–14, Spring 1987

Blank, M., "Eugene O'Neill in South Africa: Margaret Webster's Production of *A Touch of the Poet*," *Theatre Survey*, 29:113–116, May 1988

Jackson, E. M., "Dramatic Form in Eugene O'Neill's *The Calms of Capricorn*," *Eugene O'Neill Newsletter*, 12(3):35–42, Winter 1988

Manheim, M., "O'Neill's Transcendence of Melodrama in *A Touch of the Poet* and *A Moon for the Misbegotten*," pp. 147–159 in J. H. Stroupe, ed., *Critical Approaches to O'Neill* (rpt. of *Comparative Drama*, 16(3): 238–250, Fall 1982)

Marcuson, L. R., *The Stage Immigrant*, pp. 244–252

Mason, J. D., "The Metatheatre of O'Neill: Actor as Metaphor in *A Touch of the Poet*," *Theatre Annual*, 43:53–66, 1988

Raymond, G., "A National Standard: The Young Vic," *TheaterWeek*, 2:42–47, 28 Nov. 1988

———, "An Interview with Vanessa Redgrave," *TheaterWeek*, 2:14–20, 31 July 1989

Encounter, 71:76–77, June 1988

Eugene O'Neill Newsletter, 12(1):62–64, Spring 1988

Eugene O'Neill Newsletter, 12(2):71–76, Summer-Fall 1988

Playbill, 6:42, May 1988

Theatre Journal, 41:110–112, Mar. 1989

Where the Cross Is Made, 1918

Maufort, M., "Eugene O'Neill and the Shadow of Edmond Dantes: The Pursuit of Dramatic Unity in *Where the Cross Is Made* (1918) and *Gold* (1920)," pp. 89–97 in G. Debusscher and M. Maufort, eds., *American Literature in Belgium*

A Wife for a Life, 1913

Törnqvist, E., "O'Neill's Firstborn," *Eugene O'Neill Review*, 13(2):5–11, Fall 1989

Voelker, P. D., "Biography, Autobiography and Artistry in *A Wife for a Life*," *Eugene O'Neill Newsletter,* 12(1):10–17, Spring 1988

JASON R. ORTON

Arnold, 1854
Harap, L., *The Image of the Jew in American Literature,* p. 210

PAUL OSBORN

American Theatre, 5:49, July/Aug. 1988

The Vinegar Tree, 1930
Catholic World, 132:461, 31 Jan. 1931
Drama, 21:14, Feb. 1931
Life, 96:18–19, 12 Dec. 1930
Nation, 131:658+, 10 Dec. 1930
New Statesman, 3:798, 18 June 1931
TheaterWeek, 1:4, 18 Jan. 1988
Theatre Magazine, 53:25, 31 Jan. 1931

PAUL OSBORNE, KENNETH JACOBSON, and RHODA ROBERTS

Hot September (musical version of W. Inge's play *Picnic*), 1965
Mandelbaum, K., "Theater Music: The Daring Blue Pear Label," *Theater-Week,* 1:40–42, 25 Jan. 1988

GORDON OSMOND

A Matter of Tone, 1989
TheaterWeek, 2:6–7, 1 May 1989

GEORGE OSTERMAN

Dr. Jekyll and Mr. Hyde (dramatization of novel by R. L. Stevenson), 1989
Riedel, M., "The Hyde Chronicles," *TheaterWeek,* 3:42, 8 Jan. 1990
Village Voice, 34:115–116, 19 Dec. 1989

STUART OSTROW

Stages (consists of five "stages" or segments: *Denial, Anger, Bargaining, Depression,* and *Acceptance*), 1978
Leonard, W. T., *Once Was Enough,* pp. 174–175

ERIC OVERMYER

Booth, S. V., "Dramaturg in Search of an Axis," *American Theatre,* 7:62–63, Sept. 1990
Fletcher, R., "On the Verge with Eric Overmyer," *TheaterWeek,* 1:44–49, 11 July 1988

Overmyer, E., "An Open Letter to David Hare," *American Theatre*, 6:4, Jan. 1990
Robinson, M., "Don't Fence Them In," *American Theatre*, 6:28–34, Sept. 1989
Elle, 4:132 + , Feb. 1989
Village Voice, 34:41, 21 Feb. 1989

In Perpetuity throughout the Universe, 1988
    American Theatre, 5:5–6, June 1988
    TheaterWeek, 1:4, 13 June 1988
    Village Voice, 33:122 + , 28 June 1988

Mi Vida Loca, 1990 (work-in-progress)
    TheaterWeek, 3:13, 30 Apr. 1990

On the Verge, or The Geography of Yearning, 1985
    Savran, D., *Danger*, n. pag.
    Cleveland Magazine, 18:12, Jan. 1989
    Village Voice, 32:92, 17 Mar. 1987

ERIC OVERMYER and AUGUST DARNELL

In a Pig's Valise, 1989
    American Theatre, 5:11, Jan. 1989
    Elle, 3:142 + , Feb. 1989
    New York, 22:138, 27 Feb. 189
    New Yorker, 65:66–67, 27 Feb. 1989
    TheaterWeek, 2:9, 16 Jan. 1989
    Village Voice, 34:41, 21 Feb. 1989
    Village Voice, 34:103, 21 Feb. 1989

ROBERT DALE OWEN

Pocahontas, a Historical Drama, 1837
    Jones, E. H., *Native Americans as Shown on the Stage*, pp. 55–57

ROCHELLE OWENS

Betsko, K., and R. Koenig, *Interviews with Contemporary Women Playwrights*, pp. 343–352
Coleman, C. B., "The Androgynous Muse: An Interview with Rochelle Owens," *Theater*, 20(2):19–23, Spring 1989
Keyssar, H., "A Network of Playwrights," pp. 102–125 in Keyssar's *Feminist Theatre*

Chucky's Hunch, 1981
    Murray, T., "The Play of Letters: Possession and Writing in *Chucky's Hunch*," pp. 186–209 in E. Brater, ed., *Feminine Focus*

OyamO (Charles Gordon)

Gray, A., "The Big If," *American Theatre,* 6:18–21, 56, June 1989
Nixon, W., "House of Playwrights," *TheaterWeek,* 2:48–52, 19 Sept. 1988

The Return of the Been-To, 1989
    Hurley, J., "Opening at the Door," *TheaterWeek,* 2:26–30, 6 Mar. 1989

Singing Joy, 1988
    New Yorker, 64:75, 25 July 1988

The Stalwarts, 1990
    American Theatre, 7:13, May 1990
    Village Voice, 35:106, 12 June 1990

ELIZABETH PAGE

Spare Parts, 1990
    TheaterWeek, 3:14, 19 Mar. 1990
    TheaterWeek, 3:42, 26 Mar. 1990
    Village Voice, 35:100, 27 Mar. 1990

SILVIO MARTINEZ PALAU

The English Only Restaurant, 1990
    TheaterWeek, 4:37, 20 Aug. 1990

CHAZZ PALMINTERI

A Bronx Tale, 1989
    TheaterWeek, 3:43, 6 Nov. 1989
    Village Voice, 34:103, 31 Oct. 1989

RALPH PAPE

Girls We Have Known, 1988
    TheaterWeek, 1:37, 21 Mar. 1988

Say Goodnight, Gracie, 1979
    Cohen, E. M., *Working on a New Play,* pp. 10, 156–157, 161

CHARLES PARDEY

Nature's Nobleman, 1851
    Miller, T. L., "The Image of Fashionable Society in American Comedy,
    1840–1870," pp. 243–252 in J. L. Fisher and S. Watt, eds., *When They
    Weren't Doing Shakespeare*

DOROTHY PARKER and ARNAUD d'USSEAU

Ladies of the Corridor, 1953
    Curtin, K., "*We Can Always Call Them Bulgarians,*", pp. 301–302
    America, 90:157, 7 Nov. 1953

Catholic World, 178:230–231, Dec. 1953
Commonweal, 59:197–198, 27 Nov. 1953
Nation, 177:378, 7 Nov. 1953
New Republic, 129:21, 9 Nov. 1953
New Yorker, 29:58–60, 31 Oct. 1953
Newsweek, 42:65, 2 Nov. 1953
Saturday Review, 36:32, 7 Nov. 1953
Saturday Review, 36:47, 12 Dec. 1953
Theatre Arts, 38:20, Jan. 1954
Time, 62:82, 2 Nov. 1953

LOUIS N. PARKER

Disraeli, 1911
  Harap, L., *Dramatic Encounters,* p. 77

SUZAN-LORI PARKS

Village Voice, 34:99 + , 19 Sept. 1989
Village Voice, 35:76, 29 May 1990

The Death of the Last Black Man in the Whole Entire World, 1990
  American Theatre, 7:14, Oct. 1990
  TheaterWeek, 4:42, 8 Oct. 1990

Imperceptible Mutabilities in the Third Kingdom (A Tetraptych), 1989
  Village Voice, 34:99 + , 26 Sept. 1989

PETER PARNELL

TheaterWeek, 4:8, 31 Dec. 1990

Hyde in Hollywood, 1989
  Levy, L. M., "A Partnership for the Theater," *TheaterWeek,* 3:32–34, 18
  Dec. 1989
  New York, 22:105–106, 18 Dec. 1989
  TheaterWeek, 3:12, 14 Aug. 1989
  TheaterWeek, 3:24, 4 Sept. 1989
  TheaterWeek, 3:10, 23 Oct. 1989
  Village Voice, 34:119, 12 Dec. 1989

LINDA PARVIS-BAILEY

Lutenbacher, C., "'So Much More Than Just Myself': Women Theatre Artists
  in the South," pp. 380–382 in H. K. Chinoy and L. W. Jenkins, eds., *Women
  in American Theatre,* rev. and enl. ed. (new to this ed.; excerpted from a
  paper Lutenbacher presented at the 1987 Themes in Drama Conference in
  Riverside, CA, later printed in J. Redmond, ed., *Women in Theatre,* pp. 253–
  263)

JOHN PATRICK (John Patrick Goggan)

TheaterWeek, 1:61, 16 May 1988

ROBERT PATRICK (Robert Patrick O'Connor)

Myers, L., "Robert Patrick: Song of Myself" (interview), *TheaterWeek,* 2:53–57, 19 Sept. 1988

Patrick, R., "Let's Not Talk about Me" (letter to editor), *TheaterWeek,* 4:6, 12 Nov. 1990

Explanation of a Xmas Wedding, 1987
   Village Voice, 33:90, 12 Jan. 1988

The Haunted Host, 1964
   TheaterWeek, 3:6, 4 Dec. 1989

Hello, Bob, 1990
   TheaterWeek, 4:8, 8 Oct. 1990

Judas, 1973
   Playbill, 7:24+, 31 July 1989

Kennedy's Children, 1973
   Counts, M. L., *Coming Home,* pp. 63, 116–117, 136–137

Men in Art (two one-acts: *Let Me Not Mar That Perfect Dream* and *The Last Stroke*), 1988
   TheaterWeek, 1:4, 15 Feb. 1988

Untold Decades (a seven-part series), 1988
   TheaterWeek, 1:4, 4 Apr. 1988

KEVIN PATTERSON

A Most Secret War (dramatization of *Alan Turing: The Enigma* by A. Hodges), 1987
   Shirakawa, S. H., "Audience Notes: Turing Versions," *TheaterWeek,* 1:17–19, 25 Jan. 1988
   Village Voice, 32:102–103, 29 Dec. 1987

JAMES KIRK PAULDING

Grimsted, D., *Melodrama Unveiled,* pp. 152, 157, 190, 231–232

JOHN HOWARD PAYNE

Grimsted, D., *Melodrama Unveiled,* pp. 34, 39, 56–57, 91, 99, 108, 110, 141, 146, 154, 156n, 159, 165–168, 229, 254, 258

Trial without Jury (also known as *The Maid and the Magpie*), 1815
    Harap, L., *The Image of the Jew in American Literature*, pp. 207–208

SYBILLE PEARSON

Phantasie, 1988
    American Theatre, 6:7–8, Apr. 1989
    New York, 22:56–57, 23 Jan. 1989

RICHARD PEASLEE

Hurley, J., "Composer Richard Peaslee," *TheaterWeek*, 4:22, 15 Oct. 1990

ALSO SEE MARTHA CLARKE, RICHARD COE, RICHARD PEASLEE,
            and STANLEY WALDEN
    AND MARTHA CLARKE, RICHARD GREENBERG,
            and RICHARD PEASLEE
    AND MARTHA CLARKE, CHARLES L. MEE, JR.,
            and RICHARD PEASLEE
    AND MARTHA CLARKE and RICHARD PEASLEE

ERIC PELTONIEMI
SEE STEVEN DIETZ and ERIC PELTONIEMI

ROB PENNY

Good Black . . . , 1988
    TheaterWeek, 2:8, 31 Oct. 1988

S. J. PERELMAN

Gale, S. H., "Around the World in Eighty Ways: S. J. Perelman as Screenwriter," *Studies in American Humor,* 4(3):142–160, Fall 1985

The Beauty Part, 1961
    Stasio, M., "On *The Beauty Part*," pp. 158–176 in Stasio's *Broadway's
    Beautiful Losers* (text of play on pp. 81–157)

COLERIDGE-TAYLOR PERKINSON
SEE PAUL CARTER HARRISON and COLERIDGE-TAYLOR PERKINSON

ARNOLD PERL

The World of Sholom Aleichem (adaptation of short stories by Aleichem and
    others), 1953
    Harap, L., *Dramatic Encounters*, pp. 135–136

MARTIN PERLMAN
SEE ROBERT WILSON, HEINER MÜLLER,
CHRISTOPHER ESCHENBACH, and MARTIN PERLMAN

ROBERT PERRING

Beds (three one-acts: *Julia Calls, The Late Lonely Performance,* and *My Brother's Keeper*), 1988
    TheaterWeek, 1:5, 8 Aug. 1988

Best Man, 1987
    TheaterWeek, 1:4, 1 Feb. 1988

A Cup of Change, 1987 (a staged reading)
    American Theatre, 4:8–9, Mar. 1988
    TheaterWeek, 1:4, 1 Feb. 1988

CHARLIE PETERS

Hollywood Scheherazade, 1989
    TheaterWeek, 3:6, 11 Sept. 1989
    TheaterWeek, 3:43, 9 Oct. 1989

DON PETERSEN

Does a Tiger Wear a Necktie?, 1967
    TheaterWeek, 3:6, 21 Aug. 1989

ERIC PETERSON
SEE JOHN GRAY and ERIC PETERSON

LISA PETERSON and DAVID BUCKNAM

The Waves (dramatization of passages from V. Woolf's works), 1990
    Village Voice, 35:104, 22 May 1990

PEGGY PETTIT

Women Preachers, 1990
    Village Voice, 35:122, 15 May 1990

A. WASHINGTON PEZET
SEE ARTHUR GOODMAN and A. WASHINGTON PEZET

THEODORE PEZMAN
SEE DONALD MURRAY, THEODORE PEZMAN, and RENA VALE

PHRIN
SEE CAPPY KOTZ and PHRIN

DONN PIATT

Blennerhassett's Island, published 1893
    Jones, E. H., *Native Americans as Shown on the Stage,* pp. 134–135

JIM PIAZZA
SEE JAMES KIRKWOOD and JIM PIAZZA

ASTOR PIAZZOLLA
SEE GRACIELA DANIELE, JIM LEWIS, WILLIAM FINN,
and ASTOR PIAZZOLLA

JOHN PIELMEIER

Nixon, W., "House of Playwrights," *TheaterWeek,* 2:48–52, 19 Sept. 1988

Agnes of God, 1980
    Hutchings, W., "*Equus* of Convent: *Agnes of God,*" pp. 139–146 in K. V.
    Hartigan, ed., *From the Bard to Broadway*
    Porter, L. R., "Women Re-Conceived: Changing Perceptions of Women in
    Contemporary American Drama," *Conference of College Teachers of En-
    glish Studies,* 54:53–59, Sept. 1989

Sleight of Hand, 1987
    Godfrey, T., "Foul Play on Broadway," *Armchair Detective,* 21(1):5–14,
    Winter 1988

PEDRO JUAN PIETRI

Maffi, M., "The Nuyorican Experience in the Plays of Pedro Pietri and Miguel
Piñero," pp. 483–489 in M. Jurak, ed., *Cross-Cultural Studies*

JAMES PILGRIM

Yankee Jack; or, The Buccaneers of the Gulf, 1852
    Harap, L., *The Image of the Jew in American Literature,* p. 211

DARRYL PINCKNEY
SEE ROBERT WILSON and DARRYL PINCKNEY

MIGUEL PIÑERO

Maffi, M., "The Nuyorican Experience in the Plays of Pedro Pietri and Miguel
Piñero," pp. 483–489 in M. Jurak, ed., *Cross-Cultural Studies*
American Theatre, 5:52, Sept. 1988
TheaterWeek, 1:2, 4 July 1988
Village Voice, 33:121, 28 June 1988

Short Eyes, 1974
    Ruiz, A., "Raza, sexo y política en *Short Eyes* de Miguel Piñero," *Americas
    Review,* 15(2):93–102, Summer 1987

GORDON PINSENT

Brass Rubbings, 1989
    Maclean's, 102:62, 3 Apr. 1989

JOSEPH PINTAURO

Gray, A., "The Big If," *American Theatre,* 6:18–21, 56, June 1989

Beside Herself (developed from his short story), 1989
 Coen, S., "Joe Pintauro's 'Magical Realism,'" *TheaterWeek,* 3:24–26, 23
  Oct. 1989
 Konik, M., "The UPS Man Always Rings Twice," *TheaterWeek,* 3:43, 30
  Oct. 1989
 Commonweal, 116:643, 17 Nov. 1989
 New York, 22:101, 30 Oct. 1989
 New Yorker, 65:130–132, 6 Nov. 1989
 TheaterWeek, 3:25, 4 Sept. 1989
 Village Voice, 34:103–104, 31 Oct. 1989

Moving Targets ("a group of nine scenes," the first five of which were presented
 earlier as *Wild Blue,* which see), 1990
 TheaterWeek, 3:8, 22 Jan. 1990
 TheaterWeek, 3:42, 12 Feb. 1990

Wild Blue (also see *Moving Targets*), 1987
 Village Voice, 32:96, 1 Sept. 1987

SAL PIRO
SEE RICHARD IORIO, TONY BONDI, and SAL PIRO

JOHN FARO PiROMAN

The Palace of Amateurs, 1983
 TheaterWeek, 1:4–5, 1 Feb. 1988

DEAN PITCHFORD
SEE LAWRENCE D. COHEN, MICHAEL GORE, and DEAN PITCHFORD

ALPHONSUS PITTMAN

Glaap, A.-R., "Back to the Future: Al Pittman, *A Rope against the Sun*—A
 Slice of Canadiana," *Anglistik und Englischunterricht,* 33:55–65, 1987

SYLVIA PLATH

Three Women, a Poem for Three Voices, 1962
 Wood, D., "Sylvia Plath's *Three Women,*" *Kyushu American Literature,*
  28:45–53, Oct. 1987

CHANNING POLLOCK

Grange, W., "Channing Pollock: The American Theatre's Forgotten Polemicist,"
 Zeitschrift für Anglistik und Amerikanistik, 35(2):158–163, 1987

The Fool, 1922
  Harap, L., *Dramatic Encounters,* pp. 114–115

SHARON POLLOCK

Bessai, D., "Sharon Pollock's Women: A Study in Dramatic Process," pp. 126–136 in S. Neuman and S. Kamboureli, eds., *A Mazing Space*
Saddlemyer, A., "Two Canadian Women Playwrights," pp. 251–256 in M. Jurak, ed., *Cross-Cultural Studies*

Blood Relations, 1980 (produced in 1979 as *My Name Is Lisbeth*)
  Case, S.-E., "From Split Subject to Split Britches," pp. 126–146 in E. Brater, ed., *Feminine Focus*

BERNARD POMERANCE

The Elephant Man, 1977
  Holladay, W. E., and S. Watt, "Viewing the Elephant Man," *PMLA,* 104(5):868–881, Oct. 1989
  Jiji, V., "Multiple and Virtual: Theatrical Space in *The Elephant Man,*" pp. 247–257 in J. Redmond, ed., *The Theatrical Space*
  Kelley, M. A., "Life near Death: Art of Dying in Recent American Drama," pp. 117–127 in K. Hartigan, ed., *Text and Performance*
  Ricks, V., "Pomerance's *The Elephant Man,*" *Explicator,* 46(4):48–49, Summer 1988
  Playbill, 6:74, June 1988

Melons, 1986
  Honegger, G., "How American It Is: Lessons from the Melon Patch," *Theater,* 19(2):58–64, Spring 1988
  Playbill, 6:50, Jan. 1988

TOM POOLE

Wild Raspberries (suggested by I. Bergman's film *Wild Strawberries*), 1988
  American Theatre, 5:9, July/Aug. 1988

COLE PORTER
SEE BELLA SPEWACK, SAMUEL SPEWACK, and COLE PORTER

ESTELA PORTILLO (Estela Portillo Trambley)

Miguelez, A., "Aproximaciones al nuevo teatro chicano de autor único," *Explicación de Textos Literarios,* 15(2):8–18, 1986–1987 (Portillo's *Sun Images* considered)

CHAIM POTOK

Istel, J., "Chaim Potok's World Moves onto the Stage," *American Theatre,* 7:54–55, June 1990 (Potok's *Out of the Depths, The Chosen: The Musical,* and *Sins*

of the Father considered, the latter consisting of two one-acts adapted from his novels *The Promise* and *My Name Is Asher Lev*)
Kauvar, E. M., "An Interview with Chaim Potok," *Contemporary Literature,* 27(3):291 + , 1986

CHAIM POTOK, PHILIP SPRINGER, and MITCHELL BERNARD

The Chosen: The Musical (musical version of Potok's novel), 1987
    Nation, 246:176, 6 Feb. 1988
    New York, 21:84, 18 Jan. 1988
    New Yorker, 63:74, 18 Jan. 1988

STEPHEN POULIOT

Grandma Moses—An American Primitive, 1986
    Mabery, D. L., "Cloris Leachman Becomes Grandma Moses," *Theater-Week,* 2:10–13, 29 May 1989
    American Theatre, 6:35–36, Apr. 1989
    Detroit Monthly, 12:36, June 1989
    People Weekly, 31:112–113, 22 May 1989
    TheaterWeek, 2:6, 27 Feb. 1989

EZRA POUND

Bloom, H., ed., *Ezra Pound*
"Ezra Pound Centenary Issue," *San Jose Studies,* 12(3):[spec. issue], Fall 1986

The Women of Trachis (adaptation of Sophocles's play), published 1954
    Olcott, M., "Metre and Translation in Pound's *Women of Trachis,*" *San Jose Studies,* 12(3):111–118, Fall 1986

EZRA POUND and RUDD FLEMING

Elektra (adaptation of Sophocles's play), 1987
    Coleman, C. B., "Pound's *Elektra* at CSC," *Theater,* 19(3): 83–86, Summer-Fall 1988
    Gainor, J. E., "*Elektra* by Ezra Pound: The Classic Stage Company, November 1–29, 1987," *Paideuma,* 16(3):127–131, Winter 1987
    Reid, R., ed., Electra: *A Play by Ezra Pound and Rudd Fleming*
    Nation, 246:99–100, 23 Jan. 1988
    Village Voice, 32:109–110, 17 Nov. 1987

REINALDO POVOD

Henry, W. A., III, "Visions from the Past," *Time,* 132:82–83, 11 July 1988

Cuba and His Teddy Bear, 1986
    Cohen, E. M., *Working on a New Play,* pp. 32, 132

La Puta Vida Trilogy, 1987
　　Nation, 246:99, 23 Jan. 1988
　　Village Voice, 32:125–126, 1 Dec. 1987

FRANCIS POWERS

The First Born, 1897
　　Harap, L., *The Image of the Jew in American Literature,* p. 237

TONI PRESS

Patsy's Legacy, 1989 playwriting-award winner
　　American Theatre, 6:62, Dec. 1989

DANIEL S. PRESTON

Columbus; or, A Hero of the New World, 1887
　　Jones, E. H., *Native Americans as Shown on the Stage,* p. 136

HENRY CLAY PREUSS

Fashions and Follies of Washington Life, published 1857
　　Jones, E. H., *Native Americans as Shown on the Stage,* pp. 102–105, 127

REYNOLDS PRICE

Price, R., *Clear Pictures* (autobiography)

August Snow (part of a trilogy, *New Music,* which see; the other two plays are
　　Night Dance and *Better Days*), 1985
　　　American Theatre, 6:1–12, Jan. 1990 (text of play; special pull-out section)

New Music (a trilogy of full-length plays: *August Snow,* which see; *Night Dance*;
　　and *Better Days*), 1989
　　　Chase, A., "Letter from Ohio," *TheaterWeek,* 3:12–13, 20 Nov. 1989
　　　Levine, M., "Price Is a Connoisseur of Recreational Talk," *American
　　　　Theatre,* 6:44–45, Nov. 1989
　　　American Theatre, 6:57, Sept. 1989
　　　TheaterWeek, 3:13, 23 Oct. 1989

DOLORES PRIDA

Prida, D., "The Show Does Go On: Testimonio," pp. 181–188 in A. Horno-
　　Delgado, E. Ortega, N. M. Scott, and N. S. Sternbach, eds., *Breaking Bound-
　　aries*
Umpierre, L. M., "Interview with Dolores Prida," *Latin American Theatre Re-
　　view,* 22(1):81–85, Fall 1988

Coser y Cantar (A Piece of Cake), 1981
    Sandoval, A., "Dolores Prida's *Coser y cantar*: Mapping the Dialectics of
    Ethnic Identity and Assimilation," pp. 201–220 in A. Horno-Delgado, E.
    Ortega, N. M. Scott, and N. S. Sternbach, eds., *Breaking Boundaries*

JAMES PRIDEAUX

Tusitala (Teller of Tales) (about Robert Louis Stevenson), 1988
    TheaterWeek, 1:6, 4 July 1988

TOM PRIDEAUX

Prideaux, T., *Love or Nothing*

POLLY ANN PRITCHARD
SEE DELIA A. HEYWOOD

MICHAEL PROCASSION
SEE MICHAEL CRISTOFER

DEBORAH PRYOR

Briar Patch, 1989
    Ungaro, J., *"Briar Patch," TheaterWeek,* 3:42, 8 Jan. 1990
    TheaterWeek, 3:8, 27 Nov. 1989
    Village Voice, 34:118, 19 Dec. 1989

The Love Talker, 1987 (revised 1988)
    TheaterWeek, 1:6–7, 18 Apr. 1988
    Village Voice, 33:116, 24 May 1988

JAMES PURDY

Sun of the Sleepless (two one-acts: *Heatstroke* and *Souvenirs*), 1989
    American Theatre, 6:8, Apr. 1989
    TheaterWeek, 2:4, 20 Mar. 1989
    Village Voice, 34:81–82, 4 Apr. 1989

'Til the Eagle Hollers (two one-acts), 1990
    TheaterWeek, 3:40, 26 Feb. 1990
    Village Voice, 35:87–88, 27 Feb. 1990

JAN QUACKENBUSH

Perfect Partners, 1988
    TheaterWeek, 1:5, 11 Apr. 1988

EVERETT QUINTON

A Tale of Two Cities (dramatization of novel by C. Dickens), 1989
    American Theatre, 6:11, Apr. 1989

DAVID RABE

Demastes, W. W., "David Rabe's Assault on Rationalism and Naturalism" pp. 35–65 in Demastes's *Beyond Naturalism*

Herget, W., "David Rabes Vietnam-Trilogie zwischen Expressionismus und Naturalismus," *Anglistik & Englischunterricht*, 35:137–151, 1988 (Rabe's *The Basic Training of Pavlo Hummel, Sticks and Bones,* and *Streamers* considered)

King, K., "David Rabe," pp. 187–196 in King's *Ten Modern American Playwrights*

Kolin, P. C., *David Rabe*

————, "An Interview with David Rabe," *Journal of Dramatic Theory and Criticism*, 3(2):135–156, Spring 1989

————, "David Rabe (10 March 1940–)," pp. 349–68 in Kolin, ed., *American Playwrights since 1945*

Myers, L., "Critic, Cornered: Michael Feingold Speaks Out" (interview), *TheaterWeek*, 1:28–34, 11 Jan. 1988

Savran, D., "David Rabe," pp. 193–206 in Savran's *In Their Own Words*

Simard, R., "David Rabe 1940– ," pp. 289–303 in M. C. Roudané, ed., *Contemporary Authors Bibliographical Series*

————, "David Rabe: Subjective Realist," pp. 117–129 in Simard's *Postmodern Drama*

Playbill, 6:72, June 1988

The Basic Training of Pavlo Hummel, 1971
    Zinman, T. S., "Search and Destroy: The Drama of the Vietnam War," *Theatre Journal*, 42:5–26, Mar. 1990

The Chameleon, 1959
    Kolin, P. C., "Notices of David Rabe's First Play, *The Chameleon* (1959)," *Resources for American Literary Study*, 17(1):95–107, Spring 1990

Corners (a "one-minute play"), 1990
    Carpenter, B., "Just Add Water . . . ," *TheaterWeek*, 3:32–33, 28 May 1990

Hurlyburly, 1984
    Brustein, R., "Painless Destistry," pp. 72–75 in Brustein's *Who Needs Theatre* (rpt. of *New Republic*, 191:27–29, 6 Aug. 1984)

    Kolin, P. C., "*Hurlyburly* in Stockholm," *Theatre History Studies*, 10:229–237, 1990

    ————, "Staging *Hurlyburly*: David Rabe's Parable for the 1980s," *Theatre Annual*, 41:63–78, 1986

    Los Angeles, 34:190+, Jan. 1989

    People Weekly, 31:190+, Jan. 1989

    TheaterWeek, 3:25–26, 25 Dec. 1989

In the Boom Boom Room (revision of his 1973 play *Boom Boom Room*), 1974
    Kolin, P. C., "Therapists in Susan Glaspell's *Suppressed Desires* and David Rabe's *In the Boom Boom Room*," *Notes on Contemporary Literature*, 18(5):2–3, Nov. 1988

The Orphan, 1973
    Colakis, M., "The House of Atreus Myth in the Seventies and Eighties: David Rabe's *The Orphan* and Joyce Carol Oates's *Angel of Light,*" *Classical and Modern Literature,* 9(2):125–130, Winter 1989
    Counts, M. L., *Coming Home,* pp. 83–84

Sticks and Bones, 1969
    Counts, M. L., *Coming Home,* pp. 57–58, 82–83, 89, 95, 109, 124–126, 129–130, 132, 144–145, 169, 173, 196, 198, 200
    Zinman, T. S., "Search and Destroy: The Drama of the Vietnam War," *Theatre Journal,* 42:5–26, Mar. 1990
    TheaterWeek, 3:19, 14 May 1990

Streamers, 1976
    Kolin, P. C., "Rabe's *Streamers,*" Explicator, 45(1):63–64, Fall 1986
    Poli, L., "'La mancata apertura,'" *Cristallo,* 26(2):97–100, Aug. 1984
    Zinman, T. S., "Search and Destroy: The Drama of the Vietnam War," *Theatre Journal,* 42:5–26, Mar. 1990

Those the River Keeps, 1989
    TheaterWeek, 3:8, 30 Oct. 1989
    TheaterWeek, 3:9, 2 July 1990

JAMES RADO
SEE NEXT ENTRY

GEROME RAGNI, JAMES RADO, and GALT MacDERMOT

Hair, 1967
    Filichia, P., "The Naked Truth," *TheaterWeek,* 1:46–51, 25 Apr. 1988
    Green, S., *Broadway Musicals,* p. 224
    Los Angeles, 33:160 +, July 1988
    Newsweek, 112:83, 5 Dec. 1988
    TheaterWeek, 1:59, 25 Apr. 1988
    TheaterWeek, 1:52–54, 27 June 1988
    Vanity Fair, 51:100, May 1988

AISHAH RAHMAN

Unfinished Women Cry in No Man's Land While a Bird Dies in a Gilded Cage, 1977
    Moore, H., "Woman Alone, Women Together," pp. 186–191 in H. K. Chinoy and L. W. Jenkins, eds., *Women in American Theatre,* rev. and enl. ed. (pp. 184–190 in 1981 ed.)
    Wilkerson, M. B., "Music as Metaphor: New Plays of Black Women," pp. 61–75 in L. Hart, ed., *Making a Spectacle*

AYN RAND

The Night of January 16th, 1936
    Journal of Canadian Studies, 22:137–138, Winter 1987/1988

ARTHUR McKEE RANKIN

Beasley, D., "McKee Rankin: The Actor as Playwright," *Theatre History in Canada,* 10(2):115–131, Fall 1989

REBECCA RANSOM

Austin, G., "Author, Author: Coming to Terms: Rebecca Ransom" (interview), *TheaterWeek,* 1:19–21, 14 Mar. 1988

SAMSON RAPHAELSON

The Jazz Singer, 1925
   Harap, L., *Dramatic Encounters,* pp. 116–117
   Marcuson, L. R., *The Stage Immigrant,* pp. 37–43

JOE RAPOSO
SEE WILLIAM GIBSON and JOE RAPOSO

DAVID STEVEN RAPPOPORT

Cave Life, 1988
   Filichia, P., "Author, Author: He *Is* Rappaport [sic]" (interview), *TheaterWeek,* 1:19–21, 15 Feb. 1988
   Shirakawa, S. H., "Strange Romances," *TheaterWeek,* 1:20–27, 25 Apr. 1988
   Nation, 246:319, 5 Mar. 1988
   New Yorker, 64:97–98, 22 Feb. 1988
   TheaterWeek, 1:4, 25 Jan. 1988
   Village Voice, 33:90 + , 23 Feb. 1988

GEORGE RATTNER

Out to Lunch, 1989
   TheaterWeek, 3:6, 13 Nov. 1989

DAVID RAYFIEL

P.S. 193, 1962
   Counts, M. L., *Coming Home,* pp. 60, 110–111, 181

GORDON RAYFIELD

Bitter Friends, 1989
   TheaterWeek, 2:6, 6 Feb. 1989
   Village Voice, 34:79–80, 28 Feb. 1989

GEORGE LANSING RAYMOND

Columbus, 1893
   Jones, E. H., *Native Americans as Shown on the Stage,* p. 136

HARRIETTE FANNING READ

The New World, published 1848
    Jones, E. H., *Native Americans as Shown on the Stage,* pp. 87–88

JAMES REANEY

Three Desks, 1967
    McNamara, T., *"Three Desks*: A Turning Point in James Reaney's Drama,"
    Queen's Quarterly, 94(1):15–32, Spring 1987

DENNIS J. REARDON

The Happiness Cage, 1970
    Counts, M. L, *Coming Home,* p. 122

The Leaf People, 1975
    Cohen, E. M., *Working on a New Play,* pp. 121–122

KEITH REDDIN

Big Time: Scenes from a Service Economy, 1987
    Ouderkirk, C., "Facing Reality in Chelsea," *TheaterWeek,* 1:46–51, 18 July
      1988
    American Theatre, 4:12, Jan. 1988
    American Theatre, 5:8, July/Aug. 1988
    Chicago, 37:71 + , Mar. 1988
    New York, 21:48, 1 Aug. 1988
    Massachusetts Review, 30:128–129, Spring 1989
    Village Voice, 33:95, 26 July 1988

Life during Wartime, 1990
    Henry, W. A., III, "Myth, Ambition and Anger," *Time,* 136:78, 23 July
      1990
    American Theatre, 7:10, June 1990

Nebraska, 1989
    Stevens, L., "Letter from La Jolla," *TheaterWeek,* 2:13, 7 Aug. 1989
    American Theatre, 6:8–9, July/Aug. 1989
    San Diego Magazine, 41:42 + , Aug. 1989

Rum and Coke, 1986
    Brustein, R., "Highballs and Ballups," pp. 91–95 in Brustein's *Who Needs*
    Theatre (rpt. of *New Republic* 194:24–26, 3 Mar. 1986)

CHARLENE REDICK

Autumn Elegy, 1989
    Time, 133:71, 17 Apr. 1989

PETER REED

Witness, 1986
  Art in America, 75:152, Feb. 1987

SYLVIA REGAN

The Fifth Season, 1953
  Harap, L., *Dramatic Encounters,* p. 134
  Marcuson, L. R., *The Stage Immigrant,* pp. 172–177

Morning Star, 1940
  Harap, L., *Dramatic Encounters,* p. 134

HOWARD REIFSNYDER

The Guys in the Truck, 1982
  Leonard, W. T., *Once Was Enough,* pp. 71–73

BERNARD REINES

Forward the Heart, 1949
  Counts, M. L., *Coming Home,* pp. 107–109, 163, 198

ELMER LEOPOLD REIZENSTEIN
SEE ELMER RICE

JONATHAN REYNOLDS

Geniuses, 1982
  TheaterWeek, 1:8, 28 Mar. 1988

RONALD RIBMAN

Egan, P. J., "Ronald Ribman: A Classified Bibliography," *Studies in American Drama, 1945–Present,* 2:97–117, 1987
——, "Ronald Ribman (28 May 1932–)," pp. 369–378 in P. C. Kolin, ed., *American Playwrights since 1945*

Cold Storage, 1977
  Kelley, M. A., "Life near Death: Art of Dying in Recent American Drama," pp. 117–127 in K. Hartigan, ed., *Text and Presentation*

ELMER RICE (Elmer Leopold Reizenstein)

Bentley, J., *Hallie Flanagan,* pp. 187–188, 197–198, 210–216, and elsewhere
Demastes, W. W., *Beyond Naturalism,* pp. 19–20
Harap, L., *Dramatic Encounters,* pp. 79, 87–89

The Adding Machine, 1923
    TheaterWeek, 1:37, 14 Mar. 1988

Judgment Day, 1934
    Bentley, J., *Hallie Flanagan,* pp. 289, 292–293

Love among the Ruins, 1963
    Counts, M. L., *Coming Home,* p. 158

Street Scene, 1929
    Marcuson, L. R., *The Stage Immigrant,* pp. 77–85
    Stephens, J. L., "Women in Pulitzer Prize Plays, 1918–1949," pp. 245–253
    in H. K. Chinoy and L. W. Jenkins, eds., *Women in American Theatre,*
    rev. and enl. ed. (pp. 243–251 in 1981 ed.)

We, the People, 1933
    Marcuson, L. R., *The Stage Immigrant,* pp. 69–73

ELMER RICE, KURT WEILL, and LANGSTON HUGHES

Street Scene (musical version of Rice's play), 1947
    Flatow, S., "*Street Scene,*" *Playbill,* 8:56, 58–59, 30 Sept. 1990
    Green, S., *Broadway Musicals,* p. 132
    Mandelbaum, K., "Mean Streets," *TheaterWeek,* 4:38–39, 8 Oct. 1990

TIM RICE
SEE RICHARD NELSON, TIM RICE, BENNY ANDERSSON, and BJÖRN ULVAEUS

GARY RICHARDS

Dividends, 1990
    TheaterWeek, 3:14, 19 Feb. 1990
    TheaterWeek, 3:40–41, 19 Mar. 1990

CLAIBE RICHARDSON
SEE KENWARD ELMSLIE and CLAIBE RICHARDSON

JACK RICHARDSON

Xmas in Las Vegas, 1965
    Stasio, M., "On *Xmas in Las Vegas,*" pp. 323–341 in Stasio's *Broadway's
    Beautiful Losers* (text of play on pp. 263–322)

WILLIS RICHARDSON

Peterson, B. L., "Willis Richardson: Pioneer Playwright," pp. 113–125 in E.
Hill, ed., *The Theater of Black Americans,* Vol. 1 of two vols. rptd. as one in
1987; same pagination in both eds. (rpt. of *Black World,* 24(6):40–48, 86–88,
Apr. 1975)

Sanders, L. C., " 'How Shall the Negro Be Portrayed?': Willis Richardson and Randolph Edmonds, the Pioneers," pp. 19–61 in Sanders's *The Development of Black Theater in America*

The Broken Banjo, 1926
    Walker, E. P., "Krigwa, a Theatre by, for, and about Black People," *Theatre Journal,* 40:347–356, Oct. 1988

Compromise, 1926
    Walker, E. P., "Krigwa, a Theatre by, for, and about Black People," *Theatre Journal,* 40:347–356, Oct. 1988

JANE RICHLOVSKY
SEE TERRI KAPSALIS and JANE RICHLOVSKY

RANDOM RIDEOUT

Goin' Home, 1928
    Counts, M. L., *Coming Home,* pp. 71–72, 139, 199, 206

DONALD RIFKIN

A Perfect Diamond, 1990
    TheaterWeek, 3:9–10, 14 May 1990
    TheaterWeek, 3:45, 18 June 1990

LYNN RIGGS

Braunlich, P. C., *Haunted by Home*

The Cherokee Night, 1932
    Braunlich, P. C., "*The Cherokee Night* by R. Lynn Riggs," *Midwest Quarterly,* 30(1):45–59, Autumn 1988
    Kazacoff, G., *Dangerous Theatre,* pp. 152–155

BRADFORD RILEY

Foreclosure, 1988
    TheaterWeek, 1:9, 23 May 1988
    Village Voice, 33:108, 14 June 1988

BARBARA RING and RUDOLPH ELIE

Whom Dreams Possess, 1939
    Kazacoff, G., *Dangerous Theatre,* pp. 205–206

GWEN PHARIS RINGWOOD

Lynde, D., "The Dowser Character in the Plays of Gwen Pharis Ringwood," *Ariel,* 18(1):27–37, Jan. 1987

DAVID RISK

The Emperor's New Dress, 1989
  TheaterWeek, 3:10, 11 Sept. 1989

ANNA CORA MOWATT RITCHIE
SEE ANNA CORA OGDEN MOWATT

JOSÉ RIVERA

Each Day Dies with Sleep, 1990
  American Theatre, 7:13, May 1990
  New York, 23:75, 28 May 1990
  TheaterWeek, 3:11–12, 7 May 1990
  TheaterWeek, 3:41, 11 June 1990
  Village Voice, 35:79–80, 29 May 1990

The House of Ramon Iglesia, 1983
  Osborn, M. E., ed., *On New Ground,* pp. vi–viii (Preface), 191–196, 197–242 (text of play)

The Promise, 1988
  American Theatre, 5:5, May 1988
  American Theatre, 5:50, Mar. 1989

Slaughter in the Lake, 1988
  New Yorker, 64:73, 25 July 1988

KAREN RIZZO

The Hot Seat, 1990
  TheaterWeek, 4:44, 17 Sept. 1990

MAX ROACH
SEE LeROI JONES and MAX ROACH

TIM ROBBINS
SEE ADAM SIMON and TIM ROBBINS

RHODA ROBERTS
SEE PAUL OSBORN, KENNETH JACOBSON, and RHODA ROBERTS

LANIE ROBERTSON

AIDS Alive, 1988
  Shirakawa, S. H., "*AIDS Alive*: Playing in Time," *TheaterWeek,* 2:18–24, 17 Oct. 1988
  TheaterWeek, 1:4–5, 25 July 1988
  Village Voice, 33:121–122, 29 Nov. 1988

Alfred Stieglitz Loves O'Keeffe, 1988
   American Theatre, 5:11–12, Nov. 1988
   San Diego Magazine, 41:42 + , Mar. 1989
   TheaterWeek, 2:8, 14 Nov. 1988

Nasty Little Secrets, 1988
   Shirakawa, S. H., "Lanie Robertson: What the Playwright Saw,"
      TheaterWeek, 2:34–40, 28 Nov. 1988
   Playbill, 7:38, 31 May 1989
   TheaterWeek, 2:8–9, 14 Nov. 1988
   TheaterWeek, 2:7, 17 Apr. 1989
   Village Voice, 33:125 + , 6 Dec. 1988

JOHN HOVEY ROBINSON

Nick Whiffles, 1858
   Jones, E. H., *Native Americans as Shown on the Stage,* pp. 78–79

EDWARD ROBOAK
SEE MORTON THAW and EDWARD ROBOAK

BRUCE E. RODGERS

Lost Electra, to be premièred 1991
   American Theatre, 7:68, Sept. 1990

RICHARD RODGERS

Botto, L., "Something Wonderful," *Playbill,* 8:22, 30 Apr. 1990
Chapin, T. S., comp., *Rodgers and Hammerstein Rediscovered*
Hirsch, F., *Harold Prince and the American Musical Theatre,* pp. 10, 18–21, 74,
   76, 80
Mates, J., *America's Musical Stage,* pp. 121, 150, 182–184, 187, 188, 189–190,
   193, 197, 199
American Heritage, 41:20 + , Sept./Oct. 1990
Playbill, 8:47, 30 Nov. 1989

ALSO SEE GEORGE ABBOTT, RICHARD RODGERS,
and LORENZ HART
AND ARTHUR LAURENTS, RICHARD RODGERS,
and STEPHEN SONDHEIM
AND OSCAR HAMMERSTEIN II, BENJAMIN F. GLAZER,
and RICHARD RODGERS
AND OSCAR HAMMERSTEIN II and RICHARD RODGERS
AND HOWARD LINDSAY, RUSSEL CROUSE,
OSCAR HAMMERSTEIN II, and RICHARD RODGERS

ROBERT ROGERS

Ponteach; or, The Savages of America, published 1766
   Jones, E. H., *Native Americans as Shown on the Stage,* pp. 4–8 and elsewhere

Tanner, L. E., and J. N. Krasner, "Exposing the 'Sacred Juggle': Revolutionary Rhetoric in Robert Rogers' *Ponteach*," *Early American Literature*, 24(1):4–19, 1989

ROXANNE ROGERS

Andy Warhol's Interview, 18:38, May 1988

SAMUEL SHEPARD ROGERS
SEE SAM SHEPARD

RICHARD ROHMAN

Tell My Story, 1939
Leonard, W. T., *Once Was Enough*, pp. 191–192

LAWRENCE ROMAN

Alone Together, 1984
TheaterWeek, 1:7+, 23 May 1988

HAROLD ROME

TheaterWeek, 1:57, 23 May 1988

ALSO SEE
S. N. BEHRMAN, JOSHUA LOGAN, and HAROLD ROME
AND HORTON FOOTE and HAROLD ROME

LLOYD ROSE

American Splendor (based on H. Pekar's adult comic book series), 1987
American Theatre, 4:12, Jan. 1988

NORMAN ROSE
SEE GEORGE GONNEAU and NORMAN ROSE

PHILIP ROSE
SEE OSSIE DAVIS, PETER UDELL, PHILIP ROSE, and GARY GELD

REGINALD ROSE

Twelve Angry Men (based on his television play and film version of it), 1985
TheaterWeek, 4:8–9, 8 Oct. 1990

RICHARD ROSE and D. D. KUGLER

Newhouse (adaptation of *Don Juan* by Tirso de Molina and *Oedipus the King* by Sophocles), 1989
Bemrose, J., "Drama's Daredevil," *Maclean's*, 102:62–63, 1 May 1989
Theatre Journal, 42:117–118, Mar. 1990

SHELDON ROSEN

Nixon, W., "House of Playwrights," *TheaterWeek*, 2:48–52, 19 Sept. 1988

Ned and Jack, 1978
    Leonard, W. T., *Once Was Enough,* pp. 137–138

SETH ZVI ROSENFELD

Brothers, Mothers and Others (two one-acts), 1989
    Village Voice, 34:100 +, 16 May 1989

The Writing on the Wall, 1990
    TheaterWeek, 3:40–41, 26 Feb. 1990
    Village Voice, 35:106, 13 Mar. 1990

THEODORE ROSENGARTEN
SEE JENNIFER HADLEY, MICHAEL HADLEY,
and THEODORE ROSENGARTEN

LAURENCE ROSENTHAL
SEE JAMES LIPTON and LAURENCE ROSENTHAL

RACHEL ROSENTHAL

Case, S.-E., *Feminism and Theatre,* pp. 60–61 (Rosenthal's *The Arousing (Shock, Thunder)*; *Bonsoir, Dr. Schön*; and *Gaia, mon amour* considered)
Forte, J., "Women's Performance Art: Feminism and Postmodernism," pp. 251–269 in S.-E. Case, ed., *Performing Feminisms* (rpt. of *Theatre Journal,* 40(2):217–235, May 1988)
Lampe, E., "Rachel Rosenthal Creating Her Selves," *The Drama Review,* 32:170–190, Spring 1988

L.O.W. in Gaia, 1986
    Performing Arts Journal, 10(3):76–94, 1987 (text of performance piece)

My Brazil, 1979
    Champagne, L., ed., *Out from Under,* pp. ix–xiv (Introduction), 72–75, 77–87 (text of performance piece)

Rachel's Brain, 1987
    Artforum, 26:145–146, Nov. 1987

TOM ROSS

Words from the Moon, 1987
    Village Voice, 33:89 +, 12 Jan. 1988

LEO ROST

The Dietrich Process, 1989
  Playbill, 7:34+, 30 Apr. 1989
  TheaterWeek, 2:7, 27 Feb. 1989

ARI ROTH

Oh, the Innocents, 1990
  American Theatre, 7:10, 58, June 1990

BEATRICE ROTH

Broken Cups, 1989
  Village Voice, 34:94, 30 May 1989

The Father, 1985
  Champagne, L., ed., *Out from Under,* pp. ix–xiv (Introduction), 34–36, 37–
  44 (text of performance piece)

SUSANNA HASWELL ROWSON

Schofield, M. A., "The Happy Revolution: Colonial Women and the Eighteenth-
Century Theater," pp. 29–37 in J. Schlueter, ed., *Modern American Drama*

Slaves in Algiers, 1794
  Harap, L., *The Image of the Jew in American Literature,* pp. 205–206

EDWIN MILTON ROYLE

The Squaw Man, 1905
  Jones, E. H., *Native Americans as Shown on the Stage,* pp. 152–156 and
  elsewhere

HARRY RUBY
SEE GEORGE S. KAUFMAN, MORRIE RYSKIND, BERT KALMAR, and HARRY RUBY

GENE RUFFINI

Il Capo, 1989
  TheaterWeek, 3:8, 13 Nov. 1989

TOM RUSHFIELD

Chekhov in Love, 1989
  TheaterWeek, 2:11, 27 Mar. 1989

BILL RUSSELL

Elegies for Angels, Punks, and Raging Queens (An AIDS Anthology), 1989
    TheaterWeek, 2:5–6, 8 May 1989
    TheaterWeek, 3:14, 19 Feb. 1990
    TheaterWeek, 3:5, 26 Feb. 1990
    Village Voice, 35:106, 6 Mar. 1990

ROBERT RUSSELL
SEE JOSEPH STEIN, ROBERT RUSSELL, and ROBERT MERRILL

JAMES RYAN

Door to Cuba, 1988
    New Yorker, 64:74–75, 25 July 1988

FLORENCE RYERSON and COLIN CLEMENTS

Harriett, 1943
    Kazan, E., *Elia Kazan,* pp. 222–224, 225, 231, 235, 243

GEORGE RYGA

Boire, G., "George Ryga: A Tribute," *Canadian Literature,* 118:189–190, Autumn 1988
Martinez, J., "An Interview with George Ryga," *Journal of Canadian Fiction,* 35–36:106–121, 1986
Minami, Y., "George Ryga to Canada Engeki," *Eigo Seinen,* 133:176–178, 1987

The Ecstasy of Rita Joe, 1967
    Boire, G., "Wheels on Fire: The Train of Thought in George Ryga's *The Ecstasy of Rita Joe,*" *Canadian Literature,* 113–114:62–74, Summer-Fall 1987
    Grace, S., "The Expressionist Legacy in the Canadian Theatre: George Ryga and Robert Gurik," *Canadian Literature,* 118:47–58, Autumn 1988

MORRIE RYSKIND
SEE GEORGE S. KAUFMAN and MORRIE RYSKIND
AND GEORGE S. KAUFMAN, MORRIE RYSKIND,
GEORGE GERSHWIN, and IRA GERSHWIN
AND GEORGE S. KAUFMAN, MORRIE RYSKIND, BERT KALMAR,
and HARRY RUBY

LEENY SACK

The Survivor and the Translator, 1980
    Champagne, L., ed., *Out from Under,* pp. ix–xiv (Introduction), 120–122, 123–151 (text of performance piece)

HOWARD SACKLER

The Great White Hope, 1967
Fichandler, Z., "Casting for a Different Truth," *American Theatre,* 5:18–23, May 1988
Fletcher, W. L., "Who Put the 'Tragic' in the Tragic Mulatto?" pp. 262–268 in H. K. Chinoy and L. W. Jenkins, eds., *Women in American Theatre,* rev. and enl. ed. (pp. 260–266 in 1981 ed.)
Chicago, 38:141–143, Apr. 1989

EDWARD SAKAMOTO

The Life of the Land, 1987
Village Voice, 32:98, 23 June 1987

Stew Rice, 1987
American Theatre, 4:12–13, Jan. 1988

LUIS RAFAEL SÁNCHEZ

Quintuplets, 1984
Hudson Review, 42:286–287, Summer 1989
Village Voice, 34:98, 11 Apr. 1989

SONIA SANCHEZ

Melhem, D. H., "Sonia Sanchez: Will and Spirit" (interview), *MELUS,* 12(3):73–98, Fall 1985

Sister Son/ji, 1969
Keyssar, H., "Rites and Responsibilities: The Drama of Black American Women," pp. 226–240 in E. Brater, ed., *Feminine Focus*

MILCHA SANCHEZ-SCOTT

Henry, W. A., III, "Visions from the Past," *Time,* 132:82–83, 11 July 1988

The Architect Piece, in development
Bannon, B. M., "Letter from Sundance," *TheaterWeek,* 3:15–16, 18 Sept. 1989

Roosters, 1987
Osborn, M. E., ed., *On New Ground,* pp. vi-viii (Preface), 243–248, 249–280) text of play)
Village Voice, 32:98, 31 Mar. 1987

Stone Wedding, 1988
American Theatre, 5:8, Dec. 1988

DONALD T. SANDERS

Old New York: New Year's Day (dramatization of novella by E. Wharton), 1988
    TheaterWeek, 1:4, 2 May 1988

SUSAN SANDLER

Crossing Delancy, 1985
    Levy, L. M., *"Driving Miss Daisy* with Eddie Murphy and Bette Mid-
    ler . . .?" *TheaterWeek,* 3:26–30, 4 Sept. 1989

TOM SANKEY

The Golden Screw; or, That's Your Thing, Baby, 1966
    Shrager, S., *Scatology in Modern Drama,* p. 51

LUIS SANTEIRO

South Florida, 42:26, May 1989

The Lady from Havana, 1990
    TheaterWeek, 4:14–15, 10 Sept. 1990

Mixed Blessings (loosly based on Molière's play *Tartuffe*), 1989
    Chase, A., *"Tartuffe*: Cuban Style," *TheaterWeek,* 2:21–25, 24 July 1989
    American Theatre, 6:13, May 1989
    TheaterWeek, 2:7, 13 Mar. 1989
    Time, 133:72–73, 12 June 1989

WILLIAM SAROYAN

Ėmin, A., "Dobrota—chto eshche?: Predvoennaia dramaturgiia Uil-'iama Sa-
    roiana," *Literaturnaia Armeniia,* 9[346]: 85–93, Sept. 1987
Foard, E. C., *William Saroyan*
Lee, L., and B. Gifford, *Saroyan*
Shirinian, L., "William Saroyan and the Autobiographical Pact: A Look at His
    Last Published Book," *Armenian Review,* 39(3):23–31, 1986

Hello Out There, 1941
    Hinz, K., "Das kurzdrama im englishchunterricht: Beispiel: *Hello Out
    There,"* *Praxis des Neusprachlichen Unterrichts,* 34(2):127 + , 1987

The Time of Your Life, 1939
    Everding, R. G., *"The Time of Your Life*: 'A Fragment in a Nightmare of
    an Idiot," *McNeese Review,* 32:11–22, 1986–1989
    Stephens, J. L., "Women in Pulitzer Prize Plays, 1918–1949," pp. 245–253
    in H. K. Chinoy and L. W. Jenkins, eds., *Women in American Theatre,*
    rev. and enl. ed. (pp. 243–251 in 1981 ed.)

STEVEN SATER

Arnold (see *Carbondale Dreams*), 1989
  Village Voice, 35:88, 27 Feb. 1990

Beth (see *Carbondale Dreams*), 1989
  TheaterWeek, 3:11, 16 Oct. 1989

Bradley (see *Carbondale Dreams*), 1989
  TheaterWeek, 3:11, 16 Oct. 1989

Carbondale Dreams: Bradley, Beth, and Arnold (the first three parts of a planned
  five-part work; the two other plays are to be *Barone* and *David*; see *Arnold,
  Beth,* and *Bradley*), 1989
    TheaterWeek, 3:15, 12 Feb. 1990
    TheaterWeek, 3:41–42, 26 Feb. 1990
    TheaterWeek, 3:12, 16 Apr. 1990

ROBERT SATULOFF
SEE JOHN BISHOP, MEL MARVIN, and ROBERT SATULOFF

OSCAR SAUL
SEE OSCAR SAUL HALPERN

GEORGE SAVAGE

All My Life, 1936
  Kazacoff, G., *Dangerous Theatre,* pp. 281–282

See How They Run, 1938
  Kazacoff, *Dangerous Theatre,* pp. 272–275

GEORGE SCARBOROUGH and DAVID BELASCO

The Heart of Wetona, 1916
  Jones, E. H., *Native Americans as Shown on the Stage,* pp. 160–162

DORE SCHARY

Brightower, 1970
  Leonard, W. T., *Once Was Enough,* pp. 22–23

RICHARD SCHECHNER

Kaye, N., "Theory and Practice of the Indeterminate Theatre" (interview), *New
  Theatre Quarterly,* 5(20):348–360, Nov. 1989
Schechner, R., *Performance Theory,* rev. and enl. ed.
Shank, T., "Richard Schechner: The Performance Group," pp. 93–103 in
  Shank's *American Alternative Theater*

Dionysus in 69, 1968
  Hornby, R., *Drama, Metadrama, and Perception,* pp. 62, 98–99
  Schechner, R., ed., *The Performance Group:* Dionysus in 69

JOAN SCHENKAR

Patraka, V. M., "An Interview with Joan Schenkar," *Studies in American Drama, 1945–Present,* 4:187–202, 1989
———, "Feminism and the Jewish Subject in the Plays of Sachs, Atlan, and Schenkar," pp. 160–174 in S.-E. Case, ed., *Performing Feminisms*
———, "Mass Culture and Metaphors in Joan Schenkar's Plays," pp. 25–40 in L. Hart, ed., *Making a Spectacle*

Between the Acts, 1989
  TheaterWeek, 2:6, 6 Mar. 1989
  Village Voice, 34:96+ , 14 Mar. 1989

Signs of Life, 1979
  Wilson, A., "History and Hysteria: Writing the Body in *Portrait of Dora* and *Signs of Life,*" *Modern Drama,* 32(1): 73–88, Mar. 1989

ROBERT SCHENKKAN

Heaven on Earth, 1989
  New Yorker, 65:110, 20 Nov. 1989
  TheaterWeek, 3:13, 6 Nov. 1989
  TheaterWeek, 3:42, 13 Nov. 1989

SILVIA GONZALEZ SCHERER

The Empty Boxcar, 1989 (workshop production)
  American Theatre, 6:58, Sept. 1989

MURRAY SCHISGAL

Road Show, 1987
  Village Voice, 32:93+ , 2 June 1987

EDWIN SCHLOSS

Money Talks, 1990
  New York, 23:62, 17 Sept. 1990
  New Yorker, 66:91, 17 Sept. 1990
  TheaterWeek, 3:14, 30 July 1990

HARVEY SCHMIDT
SEE TOM JONES and HARVEY SCHMIDT
AND N. RICHARD NASH, TOM JONES, and HARVEY SCHMIDT

CAROLEE SCHNEEMAN

Case, S.-E., *Feminism and Theatre*, pp. 57–58
Forte, J., "Women's Performance Art: Feminism and Postmodernism," pp. 251–269 in S.-E. Case, ed., *Performing Feminisms* (Schneeman's *Interior Scroll* and *Meat Joy* considered; rpt. of *Theatre Journal*, 40(2):217–235, May 1988)

JOHN SCHNEIDER, JOHN KISHLINE, and OTHERS

A History of Sexuality (suggested by M. Foucault's multi-volume work), 1987
American Theatre, 4:6–8, Jan. 1988
Chicago, 37:59–60, July 1988

JOSHUA SCHNEIDER
SEE EVE ENSLER and JOSHUA SCHNEIDER

SEYRIL SCHOCHEN

The Moon Beseiged (about John Brown), 1950
Leonard, W. T., *Once Was Enough*, pp. 123–127

HENRY ROWE SCHOOLCRAFT

Alhalla; or, The Lord of Talladega: A Tale of the Creek War, written 1826, published 1843
Jones, E. H., *Native Americans as Shown on the Stage*, p. 87

RICHARD SCHOTTER

Taking Stock, 1990
Playbill, 9:46, 31 Dec. 1990

BUDD SCHULBERG

Kazan, E., *Elia Kazan*, pp. 27, 295, 399–400, 421, 445–446, 456, 468, 471, 486–489, 492–494, 499–500, 506–511, 515, 516, 517–518, 521, 528, 529, 560, 566, 567–569, 746

BUDD SCHULBERG and STANLEY SILVERMAN

On the Waterfront (based on Schulberg's novel and screenplay), 1988
Chase, A., "They Cover the Waterfront," *TheaterWeek*, 2:50–59, 9 Jan. 1989
American Theatre, 5:9, Dec. 1988
TheaterWeek, 2:4, 10 Oct. 1988

ARNOLD SCHULMAN

A Hole in the Head, 1957
  Harap, L., *Dramatic Encounters,* p. 134

JAMES SCHUYLER

Auslander, P., *The New York School of Poets as Playwrights*

ARTHUR SCHWARTZ
SEE FAY KANIN, MICHAEL KANIN, HOWART DIETZ,
and ARTHUR SCHWARTZ

GIL SCHWARTZ

Taking Care of Business, 1988
  American Theatre, 5:8, Apr. 1988

STEPHEN SCHWARTZ

TheaterWeek, 1:41, 29 Feb. 1988

ALSO SEE JOHN-MICHAEL TEBELAK and STEPHEN SCHWARTZ

CAROLE SCHWEID

On the Bench (a one-act play presented with Jane Stanton Hitchcock's *New
  Listings* under the collective title *The Bench*), 1990
  TheaterWeek, 3:8, 28 May 1990
  TheaterWeek, 3:42, 18 June 1990

DOUGLAS SCOTT

Mountain (about William O. Douglas), 1990
  American Theatre, 6:14, Jan. 1990
  American Theatre, 7:11, May 1990
  New York, 23:107–108, 16 Apr. 1990
  New Yorker, 66:88, 23 Apr. 1990
  Playbill, 7:32, 31 Aug. 1989
  Playbill, 9:34, 31 Oct. 1990
  TheaterWeek, 3:8, 22 Jan. 1990
  TheaterWeek, 3:42–43, 16 Apr. 1990
  Travel Holiday, 173:82, July 1990
  Village Voice, 35:119, 17 Apr. 1990

RAYMOND SCOTT
SEE SIDNEY HOWARD, WILL IRWIN, RAYMOND SCOTT,
and BERNARD HANIGHEN

ELLEN SEBASTIAN

Sanctified (based on Z. N. Hurston's essay "The Sanctified Church"), 1990
    Jacobson, L., "The Mark of Zora," *American Theatre,* 7:24–30, July/Aug.
    1990

Your Place Is No Longer with Us, 1982
    Arnold, S. K., "Multiple Spaces, Simultaneous Action and Illusion,"
    pp. 259–269 in J. Redmond, ed., *The Theatrical Space*

BUFFY SEDLACHEK

Mpls/St Paul, 16:110 + , Sept. 1988

SONDRA SEGAL
SEE CLARE COSS, SONDRA SEGAL, and ROBERTA SKLAR

CONRAD SEILER

Censored, 1936
    Kazacoff, G., *Dangerous Theatre,* pp. 258–259

JULE SELBO

Isolate, 1988
    TheaterWeek, 1:8, 28 Mar. 1988

PAUL SELIG

Terminal Bar, 1986
    Village Voice, 31:128, 16 Dec. 1986

EDGAR SELWYN

The Country Boy, 1917
    Harap, L., *Dramatic Encounters,* p. 80

ROD SERLING

The Strike (stage production of his television play), 1990
    TheaterWeek, 3:8, 8 Jan. 1990

ANNE SEXTON

Mercy Street, written 1969
    Middlebrook, D. W., "Seduction in Anne Sexton's Unpublished Play *Mercy
    Street,*" pp. 19–26 in D. H. George, ed., *Sexton*

DAVID SHABER

Bunker Reveries, 1987
  Village Voice, 32:95+ , 1 Sept. 1987

LAURA SHAMAS

Shamas, L., "Watching the House," *American Theatre,* 7:7, Sept. 1990

JOHN HERMAN SHANER

After Crystal Night, 1988
  TheaterWeek, 1:6, 29 Feb. 1988

NTOZAKE SHANGE (Paulette Williams)

Betsko, K., and R. Koenig, *Interviews with Contemporary Women Playwrights,* pp. 365–376
Brown-Guillory, E., "Alice Childress, Lorraine Hansberry, Ntozake Shange: Carving a Place for Themselves on the American Stage," pp. 25–49 in Brown-Guillory's *Their Place on the Stage*
———, "The African Continuum: The Progeny in the New World," pp. 135–150 in Brown-Guillory's *Their Place on the Stage*
DeShazer, M. K., "Rejecting Necrophilia: Ntozake Shange and the Warrior Re-Visioned," pp. 86–100 in L. Hart, ed., *Making a Spectacle*
Keyssar, H., "Communities of Women in Drama: Pam Gems, Michelene Wandor, Ntozake Shange," pp. 126–147 in Keyssar's *Feminist Theatre*
Lee, C. C., "Ntozake Shange 1948– ," pp. 305–324 in M. C. Roudané, ed., *Contemporary Authors Bibliographical Series*
Lewis, J., "An Eye on Tomorrow," *American Theatre,* 7:16–23, Nov. 1990
Timpane, J., " 'The Poetry of a Moment': Politics and the Open Form in the Drama of Ntozake Shange," pp. 198–206 in J. Schlueter, ed., *Modern American Drama* (rpt. of *Studies in American Drama, 1945–Present,* 4:91–101, 1989)
Watson, K., "Ntozake Shange (18 October 1948–)," pp. 379–386 in P. C. Kolin, ed., *American Playwrights since 1945*
Wilkerson, M. B., "Music as Metaphor: New Plays of Black Women," pp. 61–75 in L. Hart, ed., *Making a Spectacle*
Elle, 3:52, Apr. 1988

Boogie Woogie Landscapes, 1980
  Keyssar, H., "Rites and Responsibilities: The Drama of Black American Women," pp. 226–240 in E. Brater, ed., *Feminine Focus*

For Colored Girls Who Have Considered Suicide/When the Rainbow is Enuf, 1976 (revised 1977)
  Brown-Guillory, E., "Black Women Playwrights: Exorcising Myths," *Phylon,* 48(3):229–239, Fall 1987
  Geis, D. R., "Distraught Laughter: Monologue in Notozake Shange's Theater Pieces," pp. 210–225 in E. Brater, ed., *Feminine Focus*

Keyssar, H., "Rites and Responsibilities: The Drama of Black American Women," pp. 226–240 in E. Brater, ed., *Feminine Focus*

Levin, T., and G. Flowers, "Black Feminism in *For Colored Girls Who Have Considered Suicide/When the Rainbow Is Enuf,*" pp. 181–193 in G. H. Lenz, ed., *History and Tradition in Afro-American Culture*

Mael, P., "A Rainbow of Voices," pp. 317–321 in H. K. Chinoy and L. W. Jenkins, eds., *Women in American Theatre*, rev. and enl. ed. (pp. 320–324 in 1981 ed.)

Moore, H., "Woman Alone, Women Together," pp. 186–191 in H. K. Chinoy and L. W. Jenkins, eds., *Women in American Theatre*, rev. and enl. ed. (pp. 184–190 in 1981 ed.)

NTOZAKE SHANGE, EMILY MANN, and BAIKIDA CARROLL

Betsey Brown (adaptation of Shange's novel), 1989

Shange, N., and E. Mann, "Excerpt from *Betsey Brown: A Rhythm and Blues Musical,*" *Studies in American Drama, 1945–Present,* 4:3–20, 1989

American Theatre, 6:10, Apr. 1989

Georgia Review, 43:585, Fall 1989

Playbill, 8:37 +, 30 Sept. 1990

TheaterWeek, 2:6, 1 May 1989

TheaterWeek, 3:10–11, 6 Aug. 1990

BOB SHANKS

S. J. Perelman in Person, 1989

Szekrenyi, L., "S. J. Perelman: The Play, the Person," *TheaterWeek,* 2:31–32, 5 June 1989

Village Voice, 34:93–94, 30 May 1989

JOHN PATRICK SHANLEY

"Bard of the Bronx," *Harper's Bazaar,* 121:110 +, Feb. 1988

Johnson, B. D., "Writing His Own Ticket," *Maclean's,* 101:40, 4 Apr. 1988

Nixon, W., "House of Playwrights," *TheaterWeek,* 2:48–52, 19 Sept. 1988

Ouderkirk, C., "Working It Through: John Patrick Shanley," *TheaterWeek,* 2:28–33, 14 Nov. 1988

American Theatre, 5:51, Feb. 1989

Los Angeles, 33:53 +, Mar. 1988

The Big Funk, 1990

New Yorker, 66:75, 24 Dec. 1990

TheaterWeek, 4:35, 31 Dec. 1990

Danny and the Deep Blue Sea, 1983

Los Angeles, 33:164–165, Jan. 1988

Italian American Reconciliation, 1987

American Theatre, 5:12, Nov. 1988

New York, 21:103–104, 14 Nov. 1988

New Yorker, 64:121–123, 14 Nov. 1988
TheaterWeek, 3:17, 25 June 1990
Time, 132:105, 7 Nov 1988
Village Voice, 33:99, 22 Nov. 1988

Women of Manhattan, 1989
TheaterWeek, 3:8–9, 16 Oct. 1989

LEONARD SHAPIRO

Punch!, 1987
Village Voice, 32:87 + , 9 June 1987

MEL SHAPIRO

The Lay of the Land, 1990
American Theatre, 7:59, Dec. 1990
Playbill, 9:46, 30 Nov. 1990

BINA SHARIF

Watchman, 1989
TheaterWeek, 3:40, 23 Oct. 1989

IRWIN SHAW

Harap, L., *Dramatic Encounters,* pp. 112–113
Shnayerson, M., *Irwin Shaw*

Bury the Dead, 1936
TheaterWeek, 1:49, 18 Apr. 1988

The Gentle People: A Brooklyn Fable, 1939
Marcuson, L. R., *The Stage Immigrant,* pp. 131–135

ALSO SEE PETER VIERTEL and IRWIN SHAW

KERRY SHAW and JOSEPH MITCHELL

Satellite, 1935
Leonard, W. T., *Once Was Enough,* pp. 169–170

PEGGY SHAW and LOIS WEAVER

Anniversary Waltz, 1990
Commonweal, 117:259, 20 Apr. 1990
Village Voice, 35:106, 6 Mar. 1990

WALLACE SHAWN

Savran, D., "Wallace Shawn," pp. 207–222 in Savran's *In Their Own Words*

Andy Warhol's Interview, 19:73+, Mar. 1989

Aunt Dan and Lemon, 1985
  Brustein, R., "Addressing a Hostile Audience," pp. 87–91 in Brustein's
    Who Needs Theatre (rpt. of *New Republic,* 193:26–28, 9 Dec. 1985)
  TheaterWeek, 3:26, 25 Dec. 1989
  Theatre Journal, 40:114–116, Mar. 1988
  Theatre Journal, 40:121–123, Mar. 1988

Fever, 1990
  TheaterWeek, 4:38, 17 Dec. 1990

Marie and Bruce, 1979
  Brustein, R., "Two Couples," pp. 57–61 in Brustein's *Who Needs Theatre*
    (rpt. of *New Republic,* 182:28–29, 5 Apr. 1980)

EDWARD SHELDON

"The Nigger", 1909
  Fletcher, W. L., "Who Put the 'Tragic' in the Tragic Mulatto?" pp. 262–
    268 in H. K. Chinoy and L. W. Jenkins, eds., *Women in American
    Theatres,* rev. and enl. ed. (pp. 260–266 in 1981 ed.)

HARRY E. SHELLAND

The Great Libel Case, 1900
  Harap, L., *The Image of the Jew in American Literature,* p. 228

JUNE SHELLENE and RICHARD FIRE

Dealing, 1987
  Forbes, D., "Dirty Dealing," *American Theatre,* 4:12–18, Feb. 1988
  Chicago, 36:67–69, Aug. 1987

ELSA SHELLEY

Foxhole in the Parlor, 1945
  Counts, M. L., *Coming Home,* pp. 118, 119–120, 198

SAM SHEPARD (Samuel Shepard Rogers)

Ahrends, G., "Bilder inauthentischen Lebens: Sam Shepards spätere Dramen,"
  Anglistik & Englishchunterricht, 35:153–175, 1988
Allen, J., "The Man on the High Horse," *Esquire,* 110:141–144+, Nov. 1988
Antonucci, G., "Da Rosvita a Shepard: La pubblicistica teatrale," *Studium,*
  83(3):431–441, Mar.-June 1987

Auerbach, D., "Who Was Icarus's Mother? The Powerless Mother Figures in the Plays of Sam Shepard," pp. 53–64 in K. King, ed., *Sam Shepard*

Bigsby, C. W. E., "Theatre Checklist No. 3: Sam Shepard," *Theatrefacts*, 3:3–11, Aug./Oct. 1974

Blau, H., "The American Dream in American Gothic: The Plays of Sam Shepard and Adrienne Kennedy," pp. 42–64 in Blau's *The Eye of Prey*

Brookhouse, C., "Story Itself," pp. 65–72 in K. King, ed., *Sam Shepard*

Cott, J., "Strong Words," *Vogue*, 178:680–681+, Sept. 1988

Daniels, B., ed., *Joseph Chaikin and Sam Shepard*

Demastes, W. W., "Sam Shepard's Realistic Drama," pp. 97–122 in Demastes's *Beyond Naturalism* (rpt. of *Comparative Drama*, 21(3):229–248, Fall 1987, with the title "Understanding Sam Shepard's Realism")

———, "The Future of Avant-Garde Theatre and Criticism: The Case of Sam Shepard," *Journal of Dramatic Theory and Criticism*, 4(2):5–18, Spring 1990

Erben, R., "Women and Other Men in Sam Shepard's Plays," *Studies in American Drama, 1945–Present*, 2:29–41, 1987

Fennell, P. J., "Sam Shepard's Lost Sheep," pp. 3–20 in K. King, ed., *Sam Shepard*

Harriott, E., "Sam Shepard: Inventing Identities," pp. 3–16 in Harriott's *American Voices*

Hart, L., "Sam Shepard 1943– ," pp. 325–360 in M. C. Roudané, ed., *Contemporary Authors Bibliographical Series*

———, "Sam Shepard's Pornographic Visions," *Studies in the Literary Imagination,* 21(2):69–82, Fall 1988

Kakutani, M., "Sam Shepard," pp. 178–185 in Kakutani's *The Poet at the Piano* (rpt. of *The New York Times*, Jan. 1984)

King, K., "Sam Shepard," pp. 197–213 in King's *Ten Modern American Playwrights*

———, ed., *Sam Shepard*

Kleb, W., "Sam Shepard (5 November 1943–)," pp. 387–419 in P. C. Kolin, ed., *American Playwrights since 1945*

Leigh, J., "Shepard, Pound, and Bertran de Born," *Paideuma,* 14(2–3):367–375, 1985

Londré, F. H., "Sam Shepard Works Out: The Masculinization of America," *Studies in American Drama, 1945–Present*, 2:19–27, 1987

Luedtke, L. S., "From Fission to Fusion: Sam Shepard's Nuclear Families," pp. 143–166 in G. Debusscher, H. I. Schvey, and M. Maufort, eds., *New Essays on American Drama*

———, "Shepard: A Bibliographical Guide," pp. 167–188 in G. Debusscher, H. I. Schvey, and M. Maufort, eds., *New Essays in American Drama*

Myers, L., "Critic, Cornered: Michael Feingold Speaks Out" (interview), *TheaterWeek,* 1:28–34, 11 Jan. 1988

Proctor, E., "Offbeat Humor and Comic Mystery in Shepard's Plays: *La Turista, The Unseen Hand, The Mad Dog Blues,* and *Forensic and the Navigators,*" pp. 31–52 in K. King, ed., *Sam Shepard*

Przemecka, I., "European Influence on the Theatre of Edward Albee, Arthur Kopit and Sam Shepard," pp. 491–495 in M. Jurak, ed., *Cross-Cultural Studies*

Putzel, S., "Expectation, Confutation, Revelation: Audience Complicity in the Plays of Sam Shepard," *Modern Drama,* 30(2):147–160, June 1987

Rabillard, S., "Sam Shepard: Theatrical Power and American Dreams," *Modern Drama*, 30(1):58–71, Mar. 1987

Rubenstein, G. M., "The Onomastic Sam Shepard," *Names*, 37(3):231–243, Sept. 1989

Schuler, C. A., "Gender Perspective and Violence in the Plays of Maria Irene Fornes and Sam Shepard," pp. 218–228 in J. Schlueter, ed., *Modern American Drama*

Simard, R., "American Gothic: Sam Shepard's Family Trilogy," *Theatre Annual*, 41:21–36, 1986 (Shepard's *Curse of the Starving Class, Buried Child,* and *True West* considered)

————, "Sam Shepard: Emotional Renegade," pp. 75–97 in Simard's *Postmodern Drama*

Skloot, R., "Warpaths and Boulevards: Sam Shepard on the Road of American Non-Realism," *Assaph*, 100(3):207–214, 1986

Smith, S. H., "Estrangement and Engagement: Sam Shepard's Dramaturgical Strategies," *Journal of Dramatic Theory and Criticism*, 3(1):71–84, Fall 1988

Taga, M., "Sam Shepard's Pastoral Dilemmas," *Studies in the Humanities*, 14(2):116–126, Dec. 1987

Thompson, T., "Working for Sam," pp. 155–158 in K. King, ed., *Sam Shepard*

Watt, S., "Simulation, Gender, and Postmodernism: Sam Shepard and *Paris, Texas,*" *Perspectives on Contemporary Literature*, 13:73–82, 1987

Whiting, C. G., "Food and Drink in Shepard's Theater," *Modern Drama*, 31(2):175–183, June 1988

————, "Images of Women in Shepard's Theatre," *Modern Drama*, 33(4): 494–506, Dec. 1990

Wiles, T. J., "Talk Drama: Recent Writers in the American Theater," *Amerikastudien*, 32(1):65–79, 1987

Wilson, A., "Fools of Desire: The Spectator to the Plays of Sam Shepard," *Modern Drama*, 30(1):46–57, Mar. 1987

————, "Great Expectations: Language and the Problem of Presence in Sam Shepard's Writing," pp. 135–153 in K. King, ed., *Sam Shepard*

Zinman, T. S., "Visual Histrionics: Shepard's Theatre of the First Wall," *Theatre Journal*, 40:509–518, Dec. 1988

Andy Warhol's Interview, 18:71+, Sept. 1988

TheaterWeek, 3:25–26, 25 Dec. 1989

Buried Child, 1978

Adler, T. P., "Ghosts of Ibsen in Shepard's *Buried Child,*" *Notes on Modern American Literature,* 10(1):Item 3, Spring-Summer 1986

Crum, J. A., "Notes on *Buried Child,*" pp. 73–80 in K. King, ed., *Sam Shepard*

Goist, P. D., "Sam Shepard's Child Is Buried Somewhere in Illinois," *Midamerica,* 14:113–125, 1987

Griffin, P. F., "Saying 'No' in Three Modern Dramas," *Comparatist,* 12:67–78, May 1988

Inverso, M., *The Gothic Impulse in Contemporary Drama,* pp. 150–153, 156

Mann, B. J., "Character Behavior and the Fantastic in Sam Shepard's *Buried Child,*" pp. 81–94 in K. King, ed., *Sam Shepard*

Putzel, S. D., and S. R. Westfall, "The Back Side of Myth: Sam Shepard's

Subversion of Mythic Codes in *Buried Child,*" *Journal of Dramatic Theory and Criticism,* 4(1):109–124, Fall 1989

Radel, N. F., "'What's the Meaning of This Corn Tilden!' Mimeses in Sam Shepard's *Buried Child,*" pp. 177–189 in K. V. Hartigan, ed., *From the Bard to Broadway*

Robinson, J. A., "Buried Children: Fathers and Sons in O'Neill and Shepard," pp. 151–157 in M. Maufort, ed., *Eugene O'Neill and the Emergence of American Drama*

Whiting, C. G., "Digging up *Buried Child,*" *Modern Drama,* 31(4):548–556, Dec. 1988

Curse of the Starving Class, 1977

Lyons, C. R., "Text as Agent in Sam Shepard's *Curse of the Starving Class,*" *Comparative Drama,* 24:24–33, Spring 1990

Randall, P. R., "Adapting to Reality: Language in Shepard's *Curse of the Starving Class,*" pp. 121–134 in K. King, ed., *Sam Shepard*

Fool for Love, 1983

Bank, R., "Self as Other: Sam Shepard's *Fool for Love* and *A Lie of the Mind,*" pp. 227–240 in J. Schlueter, ed., *Feminist Rereadings of Modern American Drama*

Foster, D. W., "Los desperdicios del sueño americano," *La Palabra y el Hombre,* 71:53–66, July-Sept. 1989

Hart, L., "Sam Shepard's Spectacle of Impossible Heterosexuality: *Fool for Love,*" pp. 213–226 in J. Schlueter, ed., *Feminist Rereadings of Modern American Drama*

Podol, P. L., "Dimensions of Violence in the Theater of Sam Shepard: *True West* and *Fool for Love,*" *Essays in Theatre,* 7(2):149–158, May 1989

Ramsey, A., "The Boundaries of Illusion in *Fool for Love,*" *Notes on Contemporary Literature,* 19(4):9–11, Sept. 1989

Icarus's Mother, 1965

Wilhelm, A. E., "*Icarus's Mother*: Creative Transformations of a Myth," pp. 21–30 in K. King, ed., *Sam Shepard*

A Lie of the Mind, 1985

Bank, R., "Self as Other: Sam Shepard's *Fool for Love* and *A Lie of the Mind,*" pp. 227–240 in J. Schlueter, ed., *Feminist Rereadings of Modern American Drama*

Brustein, R., "The Shepard Enigma," pp. 83–87 in Brustein's *Who Needs Theatre* (rpt. of *New Republic,* 194:25–26+, 27 Jan. 1985)

Mottram, R., "Exhaustion of the American Soul: Sam Shepard's *A Lie of the Mind,*" pp. 95–106 in K. King, ed., *Sam Shepard*

Los Angeles, 33:188+, Mar. 1988

Maclean's, 101:53, 18 Jan. 1988

Theatre Journal, 40:543–545, Dec. 1988

Red Cross, 1966

Leverett, J., "Avant and After," *American Theatre,* 7:24–29+, Apr. 1990

Wilcox, L., "Language and Desire: The Abject in Shepard's *Red Cross*," pp. 107–120 in K. King, ed., *Sam Shepard*
TheaterWeek, 3:16, 23 Apr. 1990

The Tooth of Crime, 1972
    Austin, G., *Feminist Theories for Dramatic Criticism*, pp. 85–88
    Blau, H., "Comedy since the Absurd," pp. 14–41 in Blau's *The Eye of Prey* (rpt. of *Modern Drama*, 25(4):545–568, Dec. 1982)
    Mustazza, L., " 'In the Old Style': The Tragic Vision in Sam Shepard's *The Tooth of Crime*," *Text and Performance*, 9(4):277–285, Oct. 1989
    Wilcox, L., "Modernism vs. Postmodernism: Shepard's *The Tooth of Crime* and the Discourses of Popular Culture," *Modern Drama*, 30(4):560–573, Dec. 1987

True West, 1980 (revised 1982)
Glaap, A.-R., "*Der Goldene Westen* und *Die Sonne des Nordens*: Zeitgenössische Dramen aus den USA und Kanada für die gymnasiale Oberstufe," *Dei Neueren Sprachen*, 86(5):370–383, Oct. 1987
Podol, P. L., "Dimensions of Violence in the Theater of Sam Shepard: *True West* and *Fool for Love*," *Essays in Theatre*, 7(2):149–158, May 1989
Riemer, J. D., "Integrating the Psyche of the American Male: Conflicting Ideals of Manhood in Sam Shepard's *True West*," *University of Dayton Review*, 18(2):41–47, Winter-Spring 1986–1987
Smith, M., "Beckettian Symbolic Structure in Sam Shepard's *True West*: A Jungian Reading," *Journal of Evolutionary Psychology*, 10(3–4):328–334, Aug. 1989
Wattenberg, R., " 'The Frontier Myth' on Stage: From the Nineteenth Century to Sam Shepard's *True West*," *Western American Literature*, 24(3):225–241, Fall 1989
Village Voice, 35:88, 27 Feb. 1990

La Turista, 1966
    Arbiteboul, M., "La Dimension onirique dans *La Turista* de Sam Shepard: Une Version baroque du 'Voyage,' " *Etudes Anglaises*, 40(4):420–433, Oct.-Dec. 1987
    Stengel, W., "The Inside Outside World of Sam Shepard's *La Turista*," *Publications of the Arkansas Philological Association*, 13(1):45–57, Spring 1987

SAM SHEPARD and JOSEPH CHAIKIN

The War in Heaven, 1987
    American Theatre, 5:47–48, July/Aug. 1988

ALSO SEE JULES FEIFFER, DAN GREENBURG, LEONARD MELFI, SAM SHEPARD, and OTHERS

J. H. SHERBOURNE

Osceola, 1841
    Jones, E. H., *Native Americans as Shown on the Stage*, p. 36

JONATHAN MARC SHERMAN

Women and Wallace, 1988
   New Yorker, 64:91, 3 Oct. 1988
   TheaterWeek, 2:7, 12 Sept. 1988
   TheaterWeek, 3:9, 29 Jan. 1990
   Village Voice, 33:110 + , 4 Oct. 1988

MARTIN SHERMAN

Sherman, M., "Baldini Holds the Future in His Hands" (story), *Antioch Review,* 48:237–239, Spring 1990

Bent, 1979
   Clum, J. M., "'A Culture That Isn't Just Sexual': Dramatizing Gay Male History," *Theatre Journal,* 41:169–189, May 1989
   Hall, R., "Eleven Different Directions," *American Theatre,* 5:32–33, Dec. 1988
   Raymond, G., "Director Sean Mathias Talks about *Bent,*" *TheaterWeek,* 3:21, 30 Apr. 1990
   Shewey, D., "Gay Theatre Grows Up," *American Theatre,* 5:10–17, 52–53, May 1988
   Skloot, R., *The Darkness We Carry,* pp. 118–122
   Playbill, 8:48, 31 Mar. 1990
   Playbill, 8:64, 31 Mar. 1990

Cracks, 1975
   Wilcox, M., ed., *Gay Plays,* Vol. 2, pp. 7–8 (Introduction), 105–106, 107–126 (text of play)

A Madhouse in Goa (two related one-act plays: *A Table for a King* and *Keeps Rainin' All the Time*), 1989
   Henry, W. A., III, "A Time of Triumphs in London," *Time,* 134:73, 3 July 1989
   Raymond, G., "An Interview with Vanessa Redgrave," *TheaterWeek,* 2:14–20, 31 July 1989
   Hudson Review, 42:629–636, Winter 1990
   Playbill, 7:S-24, 31 July 1989
   Playbill, 8:96 + , 3 Oct. 1989
   TheaterWeek, 2:36, 3 July 1989

Passing By, 1975
   Wilcox, M., ed., *Gay Plays,* Vol. 1, pp. 6–8 (Introduction), 101, 103–120 (text of play)

When She Danced (about Isadora Duncan), 1988
   Dace, T., "Dancing in the Dark," *TheaterWeek,* 3:32–36, 5 Mar. 1990
   Raymond, G., "Two British Directors Abroad," *TheaterWeek,* 3:29–31, 5 Mar. 1990
   New York, 23:57, 5 Mar. 1990

New Yorker, 66:98, 26 Feb. 1990
Playbill, 7:69, 30 Nov. 1988
TheaterWeek, 3:24–25, 4 Sept. 1989
TheaterWeek, 3:10, 5 Feb. 1990
TheaterWeek, 3:41, 12 Mar. 1990
TheaterWeek, 3:10+, 26 Mar. 1990
Village Voice, 35:105+, 6 Mar. 1990

JOHN SHERRY

Abraham Cochrane (originally titled *Abraham's House*), 1964
    Leonard, W. T., *Once Was Enough,* pp. 1–2

CLARA HARRIOTT SHERWOOD

The Cable Car, a Howellsian Burlesque, c. 1891
    Harap, L., *The Image of the Jew in American Literature,* p. 235

ROBERT E. SHERWOOD

Harap, L., *Dramatic Encounters,* pp. 108–109

Abe Lincoln in Illinois, 1938
    Stephens, J. L., "Women in Pulitzer Prize Plays, 1918–1949," pp. 245–253
    in H. K. Chinoy and L. W. Jenkins, eds., *Women in American Theatre,*
    rev. and enl. ed. (pp. 243–251 in 1981 ed.)

Idiot's Delight, 1936
    Stephens, J. L., "Women in Pulitzer Prize Plays, 1918–1949," pp. 245–253
    in H. K. Chinoy and L. W. Jenkins, eds., *Women in American Theatre,*
    rev. and enl. ed. (pp. 243–251 in 1981 ed.)
    TheaterWeek, 1:38, 21 Mar. 1988

The Petrified Forest, 1935
    Erben, R., "The Western Holdup Play: The Pilgrimage Continues," *Western
    American Literature,* 23(4):311–322, Feb. 1989

The Road to Rome, 1927
    Mishra, K., "Sherwood's *The Road to Rome*: A Marxist Play by a Non-
    Marxian Playwright in the Twenties," *Panjab University Research Bulletin
    (Arts),* 19(1):69–75, Apr. 1988

There Shall Be No Night, 1940
    Stephens, J. L., "Women in Pulitzer Prize Plays, 1918–1949," pp. 245–253
    in H. K. Chinoy and L. W. Jenkins, eds., *Women in American Theatre,*
    rev. and enl. ed. (pp. 243–251 in 1981 ed.)

BURT SHEVELOVE and STEPHEN SONDHEIM

The Frogs (musical version of Aristophanes's play), 1974
    American Theatre, 5:8, July/Aug. 1988

R. A. SHIOMI

Shimoi, R. A., "On Playing Ball," *TheaterWeek*, 2:38–43, 27 Feb. 1989

Playing Ball, 1989
    American Theatre, 5:15–16, Mar. 1989
    Playbill, 7:42, 31 Mar. 1989
    TheaterWeek, 2:9–10, 13 Feb. 1989

REUBEN SHIP

The Investigator, 1954
    Gross, G., "A Palpable Hit: A Study of the Impact of Reuben Ship's *The Investigator,*" *Theatre History in Canada,* 10(2):152–166, Fall 1989

SAMUEL SHIPMAN and VICTOR VICTOR

The Unwritten Chapter, 1920
    Harap, L., *Dramatic Encounters,* p. 113

JOHN SHIROTA

Lucky Come Hawaii, 1990
    American Theatre, 7:10, Dec. 1990
    TheaterWeek, 4:9, 15 Oct. 1990
    TheaterWeek, 4:37, 10 Dec. 1990

LARRY SHUE

The Foreigner, 1984
    Playbill, 6:52–53, Mar. 1988

The Nerd, 1987
    Village Voice, 32:95, 31 Mar. 1987

Wenceslas Square, 1988
    Barbour, D., "Director's Chair: Jerry Zaks Explains It All for You," *TheaterWeek,* 1:26–29, 28 Mar. 1988
    Detroit Monthly, 12:38, Oct. 1989
    Nation, 246:510–511, 9 Apr. 1988
    New York, 21:72–73, 14 Mar. 1988
    New Yorker, 64:80–81, 14 Mar. 1988
    Village Voice, 33:93 + , 15 Mar. 1988

PAUL SHYRE

Hizzoner—The Mayor! (also known as *Hizzoner!*; about Fiorello LaGuardia), 1983
    Buckley, M., "On the Campaign Trail: Tony Lo Bianco," *TheaterWeek,* 2:11–15, 13 Feb. 1989

Haun, H., "Broadway's New Mayor," *Playbill,* 7:24, 28, 31 Mar. 1989
America, 160:272, 25 Mar. 1989
American Theatre, 4:7, Feb. 1988
Nation, 248:462, 3 Apr. 1989
New Yorker, 65:91, 6 Mar. 1989
TheaterWeek, 2:6, 28 Nov. 1988

GEORGE SIBBALD

Brothers, 1983
Leonard, W. T., *Once Was Enough,* pp. 29–31

LYNN SIEFERT

Coyate Ugly, 1984
TheaterWeek, 3:39–40, 7 May 1990

BEN SIEGLER

The Good Coach, 1989
New York, 22:56–57, 26 June 1989
TheaterWeek, 2:5, 5 June 1989

PAUL SIFTON

The Belt, 1927
Harap, L., *Dramatic Encounters,* p. 111

PAUL SILLS

London, T., "Chicago Impromptu," *American Theatre,* 7:14–23, 60–64, July/
Aug. 1990

Talking to Myself (dramatization of autobiography of S. Terkel), 1988
American Theatre, 5:7–8, Sept. 1988

STANLEY SILVERMAN
SEE RICHARD FOREMAN and STANLEY SILVERMAN
AND ARTHUR MILLER and STANLEY SILVERMAN
AND BUDD SCHULBERG and STANLEY SILVERMAN

SHEL SILVERSTEIN

The Devil and Billy Markham (presented with David Mamet's *Bobby Gould in
Hell* under the title *Oh, Hell*), 1989
New Republic, 202:28, 29 Jan. 1990
New York, 22:105, 18 Dec. 1989
New Yorker, 65:77–79, 25 Dec. 1989
TheaterWeek, 3:13, 23 Oct. 1989

Time, 134:78, 18 Dec. 1989
Village Voice, 34:116, 19 Dec. 1989

Hamlet (a one-act play), 1990
American Theatre, 7:13, May 1990

ALSO SEE DAVID MAMET and SHEL SILVERSTEIN

ANA MARIA SIMO

Going to New England, 1990
TheaterWeek, 3:12, 5 Mar. 1990
Village Voice, 35:104, 13 Mar. 1990

ADAM SIMON and TIM ROBBINS

Carnage, a Comedy, 1989
Russo, F., "A Religious Charade," *TheaterWeek,* 3:39, 2 Oct. 1989
American Theatre, 6:9, Nov. 1989
Playbill, 7:30, 31 Aug. 1989
Village Voice, 34:100, 26 Sept. 1989

LUCY SIMON
SEE MARSHA NORMAN and LUCY SIMON

MAYO SIMON

Elaine's Daughter, 1988
TheaterWeek, 2:6, 24 Oct. 1988

NEIL SIMON

Harap, L., *Dramatic Encounters,* pp. 139–141
"Hollywood Pays Tribute to Playwright Neil Simon—and How California Sweet It Is!" *People Weekly,* 30:99–100, 26 Sept. 1988
King, K., "Neil Simon," pp. 215–233 in King's *Ten Modern American Playwrights*
Morrow, L., "Neil Simon (4 July 1927–)," pp. 420–436 in P. C. Kolin, ed., *American Playwrights since 1945*
Roeder-Zerndt, M., "Unterhaltungskunst und Lachkultur: Überlegungen zur Situation der Amerikanischen Komödie am Beispiel Woody Allens und Neil Simons," *Anglistik & Englishchunterricht,* 35:39–59, 1988
Sato, A., "Neil Simon's Comic Vision and Its Significance," *Sophia English Studies,* 7:94–106, 1982
Playbill, 9:40, 30 Nov. 1990
Playbill, 9:46, 31 Dec. 1990
Present Tense, 15:50–51, Mar./Apr. 1988
Vanity Fair, 50:24 + , May 1987
Vanity Fair, 51:142 + , May 1988

Biloxi Blues (the second play of his semiautobiographical trilogy), 1985
  Brustein, R., "The Best of Broadway," pp. 76–79 in Brustein's *Who Needs Theatre* (rpt. of *New Republic,* 192:26–28, 20 May 1985)
  Simon, N., "An Excerpt from *Biloxi Blues,*" *Playbill,* 6:n. pag., Apr. 1988 (rpt. from Act I of the play as published by Random House)
  Vanity Fair, 50:24+, May 1987

Brighton Beach Memoirs (the first play of his semiautobiographical trilogy), 1983
  Vanity Fair, 50:24+, May 1987

Broadway Bound (the third play of his semiautobiographical trilogy), 1986
  Simon, N., "An Excerpt from *Broadway Bound,*" *Playbill,* 6:n. pag., May 1988 (rpt. from Act II of the play as published by Random House)
  Los Angeles, 33:206+, June 1988
  San Diego Magazine, 42:64+, Dec. 1989
  Time, 135:100, 1 Jan. 1990
  Vanity Fair, 50:24+, May 1987

The Gingerbread Lady, 1970
  TheaterWeek, 2:42, 17 Apr. 1989

I Ought to Be in Pictures, 1980
  TheaterWeek, 4:8, 3 Dec. 1990

Jake's Women, 1988
  American Theatre, 6:12, Mar. 1990
  Playbill, 8:43, 31 May 1990
  TheaterWeek, 1:4, 2 May 1988
  TheaterWeek, 1:6, 30 May 1988
  TheaterWeek, 3:6, 15 Jan. 1990

Last of the Red Hot Lovers, 1969
  TheaterWeek, 1:6–7, 23 May 1988
  TheaterWeek, 2:62, 13 Mar. 1989

The Odd Couple, 1965 (revised 1985)
  Filichia, P., "A Not-So-Drole *Drôle de Couple,*" *TheaterWeek,* 1:40–43, 27 June 1988

The Prisoner of Second Avenue, 1971
  TheaterWeek, 3:42, 13 Nov. 1989

Rumors, 1988
  Flatow, S., "Truth in *Rumors,*" *Playbill,* 7:8, 10, 12, 31 Jan. 1989
  Marowitz, C., "Los Angeles in Review," *TheaterWeek,* 4:12–13, 20 Aug. 1990
  Connoisseur, 219:74+, Mar. 1989
  Nation, 248:102, 23 Jan. 1989
  New York, 21:106, 28 Nov. 1988
  New Yorker, 64:110, 28 Nov. 1988

Newsweek, 112:88, 28 Nov. 1988
San Diego Magazine, 41:58+, Nov. 1988
TheaterWeek, 1:6, 30 May 1988
TheaterWeek, 2:4, 3 Oct. 1988
Time, 132:94, 28 Nov. 1988
Village Voice, 33:121, 29 Nov. 1988

GEORGE SINGER

Syringe, 1990
TheaterWeek, 3:39, 7 May 1990

JEROME SIRLIN
SEE DAVID HENRY HWANG, PHILIP GLASS, and JEROME SIRLIN

DOUG SKINNER
SEE BILL IRWIN, DOUG SKINNER, and MICHAEL O'CONNOR

GEORGE SKLAR

Life and Death of an American (originally titled *John Doe*), 1939
Kazacoff, G., *Dangerous Theatre,* pp. 138–143

ROBERTA SKLAR

Horwitz, S., "Roberta Sklar and Clare Coss," *TheaterWeek,* 2:17–21, 29 May
1989
Sklar, R., "Reflections," pp. 325–327 in H. K. Chinoy and L. W. Jenkins, eds.,
Women in American Theatre, rev. and enl. ed. (new to this ed.)

ALSO SEE CLARE COSS, SONDRA SEGAL, and ROBERTA SKLAR

BERNARD SLADE (Bernard Slade Newbound)

Special Occasions, 1982
Leonard, W. T., *Once Was Enough,* pp. 172–174

LARRY SLOAN and DOUG WRIGHT

Ubu (adaptation of A. Jarry's play *Ubu Roi*), 1989
Paller, M., "*Ubu Roi,* Not Raw," *TheaterWeek,* 2:41, 10 July 1989
New York, 22:47–48, 17 July 1989
New Yorker, 65:91, 10 July 1989

ANNA DEAVERE SMITH

Mason, S., "Smith's Specialty Is Enacting Real People," *American Theatre,*
6:50–51, Sept. 1989

Piano, 1989
American Theatre, 5:50, Mar. 1989

BARBARA BATES SMITH and MARK HUNTER

I Remane, Forever, Ivy Rowe (dramatization of novel by L. Smith), 1990
    TheaterWeek, 4:36–37, 10 Dec. 1990

BRAD L. SMITH

The Man from Aldersgate (about John Wesley), 1979
    Thiessen, C. R., "Refiner's Fire: John Wesley," *Christianity Today,*
    25(17):84, 2 Oct. 1981
    Christianity Today, 34:58, 16 July 1990

CHARLES SMITH

Chicago, 36:113–114, Sept. 1987

Jelly Belly, 1990
    American Theatre, 7:11, Nov. 1990
    TheaterWeek, 4:9, 29 Oct. 1990

EVAN SMITH

Remedial English, 1986
    Hall, R., "Eleven Different Directions," *American Theatre,* 5:32–33, Dec.
    1988
    Shewey, D., "Gay Theatre Grows Up," *American Theatre,* 5:10–17, 52–53,
    May 1988

JONATHAN B. SMITH

Siege of Algiers, 1823
    Harap, L., *The Image of the Jew in American Literature,* pp. 209–210

MARGARET SMITH

Captain Herne, U.S.A., 1893
    Fletcher, W. L., "Who Put the 'Tragic' in the Tragic Mulatto?" pp. 262–
    268 in H. K. Chinoy and L. W. Jenkins, eds., *Women in American
    Theatre,* rev. and enl. ed. (pp. 260–266 in 1981 ed.)

NOBLE MASON SMITH

Sparks in the Park, 1987
    Village Voice, 32:101 + , 6 Oct. 1987

ROGER GUENVEUR SMITH and BEN R. CALDWELL

Frederick Douglass Now, 1990
    American Theatre, 6:10–11, Feb. 1990

W[ILLIAM] H[ENRY] [SEDLEY] SMITH

The Drunkard; or, The Fallen Saved, 1843
   Ito, A., "Early American Drama, III: The Flattering of an Age," *Language and Culture,* 5:1–25, 1984

WINCHELL SMITH and JOHN E. HAZARD

Turn to the Right, 1916
   Harap, L., *Dramatic Encounters,* p. 74

LOUIS SOLOMON and HAROLD BUCHMAN

Snafu, 1944
   Counts, M. L., *Coming Home,* pp. 78–79, 94, 166–167, 195
   Catholic World, 160:261, Dec. 1944
   Commonweal, 41:102–103, 10 Nov. 1944
   Newsweek, 24:103, 6 Nov. 1944
   Theatre Arts, 29:9, Jan. 1945
   Theatre World, 41:27, 31, Jan. 1945
   Time, 44:55, 6 Nov. 1944

STEPHEN SONDHEIM

Forsburg, S. L., "Letter from Oxford," *TheaterWeek,* 3:42–43, 9 July 1990
Gordon, J., *Art Isn't Easy*
Gottfried, M., "Stephen Sondheim: State of the Art?" *TheaterWeek,* 3:11–15, 25 Dec. 1989
Hirsch, F., "A Little Sondheim Music (I)," pp. 71–84; "A Little Sondheim Music (II)," pp. 85–105; and "A Little Sondheim Music (III)," pp. 106–130 in Hirsch's *Harold Prince and the American Musical Theater*
Mandelbaum, K., "Sing a Song of Sondheim," *TheaterWeek,* 1:52–54, 2 May 1988
Martin, G., "On the Verge of Opera: Stephen Sondheim," *Opera Quarterly,* 6:76–85, Spring 1989
Mates, J., *America's Musical Stage,* pp. 51, 75, 131, 194, 198–199
Savran, D., "Stephen Sondheim," pp. 223–239 in Savran's *In Their Own Words*
Steyn, M., "A Funny Thing Happened to Sondheim," *Drama,* no. 165:11–13, 1987
Sullivan, K., "Stephen Sondheim (22 March 1930–)," pp. 437–446 in P. C. Kolin, ed., *American Playwrights since 1945*
Zadan, C., *Sondheim & Co.,* 2nd rev. and updated ed.
Playbill, 8:16, 28 Feb. 1990

ALSO SEE GEORGE FURTH and STEPHEN SONDHEIM
AND JAMES LAPINE and STEPHEN SONDHEIM
AND ARTHUR LAURENTS, LEONARD BERNSTEIN,
and STEPHEN SONDHEIM
AND ARTHUR LAURENTS, RICHARD RODGERS,
and STEPHEN SONDHEIM

AND ARTHUR LAURENTS, JULE STYNE, and STEPHEN SONDHEIM
AND BURT SHEVELOVE and STEPHEN SONDHEIM
AND HUGH WHEELER, LEONARD BERNSTEIN, RICHARD WILBUR,
JOHN LATOUCHE, and STEPHEN SONDHEIM

AARON SORKIN

Hurley, J., "Two Good Men," *TheaterWeek,* 3:26–29, 26 Mar. 1990
Fame, 2:72, Dec. 1989/Jan. 1990

A Few Good Men, 1989
    Black, K., "Dramatic Maneuvers," *Harper's Bazaar,* 123:50, Feb. 1990
    Flatow, S., *"A Few Good Men," Playbill,* 8:16, 18–19, 31 Mar. 1990
    Horwitz, S., "Beating the *Times," TheaterWeek,* 3:17–21, 28 May 1990
    Raymond, G., "An Officer and a Gentleman," *TheaterWeek,* 3:37–40, 20
        Nov. 1989
    Riedel, M., "Be All That You Can Be," *TheaterWeek,* 3:42, 4 Dec. 1989
    Wetzsteon, R., "Young Man with a Play," *New York,* 22:58–60 +, 6 Nov.
        1989
    America, 161:453, 16 Dec. 1989
    Commonweal, 117:150–151, 9 Mar. 1990
    Nation, 250:66–67, 8–15 Jan. 1990
    New York, 22:99–100, 27 Nov. 1989
    New Yorker, 65:101–103, 27 Nov. 1989
    TheaterWeek, 3:24, 4 Sept. 1989
    TheaterWeek, 3:8, 11 Sept. 1989
    TheaterWeek, 3:26, 25 Dec. 1989
    TheaterWeek, 3:38, 15 Jan. 1990
    TheaterWeek, 4:13, 3 Sept. 1990
    Village Voice, 34:121 +, 28 Nov. 1989
    Vogue, 180:98, Jan. 1990

Making Movies (originally a one-act play, *Hidden in This Picture,* 1988), 1990
    New York, 23:103, 9 Apr. 1990
    New Yorker, 66:80, 9 Apr. 1990
    Playbill, 7:32, 30 June 1989
    Playbill, 7:24, 31 July 1989
    Playbill, 8:67, 30 Apr. 1990
    TheaterWeek, 3:8, 11 Sept. 1989
    TheaterWeek, 3:10–11, 5 Mar. 1990
    Village Voice, 35:102, 10 Apr. 1990

PATTI SPEARS

A Strange Play, 1944
    Leonard, W. T., *Once Was Enough,* pp. 2–3

EULALIE SPENCE

Brown-Guillory, E., *Their Place on the Stage*, pp. 4, 16, 18–19

Fool's Errand, 1927
　　Walker, E. P., "Krigwa, a Theatre by, for, and about Black People," *Theatre Journal*, 40:347–356, Oct. 1988

Foreign Mail, 1927
　　Walker, E. P., "Krigwa, a Theatre by, for, and about Black People," *Theatre Journal*, 40:347–356, Oct. 1988

Her, 1927
　　Walker, E. P., "Krigwa, a Theatre by, for, and about Black People," *Theatre Journal*, 40:347–356, Oct. 1988

ELIZABETH SPENCER

For Lease or Sale, 1989
　　American Theatre, 5:11, Jan. 1989
　　TheaterWeek, 2:9, 9 Jan. 1989

STUART SPENCER

Human Gravity, 1988
　　New Yorker, 64:74, 25 July 1988

BELLA SPEWACK and SAMUEL SPEWACK

Spring Song, 1934
　　Marcuson, L. R., *The Stage Immigrant*, pp. 89–97

BELLA SPEWACK, SAMUEL SPEWACK, and COLE PORTER

Leave It to Me! (musical based on the Spewacks' play *Clear All Wires!*), 1938
　　Green, S., *Broadway Musicals*, p. 105

ALSO SEE BELLA COHEN

SAMUEL SPEWACK

Once There Was a Russian, 1961
　　Leonard, W. T., *Once Was Enough*, pp. 144–145

SAMUEL SPEWACK and FRANK LOESSER

Pleasures and Palaces (musical version of Spewack's play *Once There Was a Russian*), 1965
　　Leonard, W. T., *Once Was Enough*, pp. 145–146

ALSO SEE BELLA COHEN and SAMUEL SPEWACK
AND BELLA SPEWACK and SAMUEL SPEWACK
AND BELLA SPEWACK, SAMUEL SPEWACK, and COLE PORTER

LEONARD SPIGELGASS

A Majority of One, 1959
    Harap, L., *Dramatic Encounters,* pp. 134–135
    Marcuson, L. R., *The Stage Immigrant,* pp. 177–183

PHILIP SPRINGER
SEE CHAIM POTOK, PHILIP SPRINGER, and MITCHELL BERNARD

J. C. SQUIRE
SEE JOHN BALDERSTON and J. C. SQUIRE

STEPHEN STAHL

Lady Day (about Billie Holliday), 1989
    Los Angeles, 34:228, Apr. 1989

LAURENCE STALLINGS
SEE MAXWELL ANDERSON and LAURENCE STALLINGS

BARRIE STAVIS

Goldstein, E., "Barrie Stavis," *Zeitschrift für Anglistik und Amerikanistik,* 35(1):68–73, 1987

The Sun and I, 1933 (revised 1937)
    Kazacoff, G., *Dangerous Theatre,* pp. 63–65

DANIEL A. STEIN

In Windowspeak, 1988
    Georgia Review, 43:583, Fall 1989

GERTRUDE STEIN

Kellner, B., *A Gertrude Stein Companion*
Pladott, D., "Gertrude Stein: Exile, Feminism, Avant-Garde in the American Theater," pp. 111–129 in J. Schlueter, ed., *Modern American Drama*
Ryan, B. A., "Gertrude Stein: Form and Content," pp. 171–174 in H. K. Chinoy and L. W. Jenkins, eds., *Women in American Theatre,* rev. and enl. ed. (new to this ed.)

Doctor Faustus Lights the Lights, 1938
    Neuman, S., " 'Would a Viper Have Stung Her If She Had Only Had One Name?' *Doctor Faustus Lights the Lights,*" pp. 168–193 in S. Neuman and I. B. Nadel, eds., *Gertrude Stein and the Making of Literature*

The Mother of Us All, 1947
  Helle, A. P., "Re-Presenting Women Writers Onstage: A Retrospective to
    the Present," pp. 195–208 in L. Hart, ed., *Making a Spectacle*
  Martin, R. K., "*The Mother of Us All* and American History," pp. 210–222
    in S. Neuman and I. B. Nadel, eds., *Gertrude Stein and the Making of
    Literature*
  Winston, E., "Making History in *The Mother of Us All,*" *Mosaic,* 20(4):117–
    129, Fall 1987

A Play Called Not and Now, written 1936, first performed 1980
  TheaterWeek, 2:6, 13 Mar. 1989 (this version "constructed by Hanne Tier-
    ney")

GERTRUDE STEIN and AL CARMINES

A Circular Play (also called *A Play in Circles*) written 1920, first performed
  1967 with music by Carmines
  Hubert, R. R., "Gertrude Stein, Cubism, and the Postmodern Book,"
    pp. 96–125 in M. Perloff, ed., *Postmodern Genres*

GERTRUDE STEIN and VIRGIL THOMSON

Four Saints in Three Acts, 1934
  France, R., "Virgil Thomson/Gertrude Stein: A Correspondence," *Theatre
    History Studies,* 6:72–86, 1986
  Woll, A., *Black Musical Theatre,* pp. 158–159, 168, 174, 177
  Village Voice, 35:108, 6 Mar. 1990

JOSEPH STEIN

Enter Laughing (dramatization of novel by C. Reiner), 1963
  Cohen, E. M., *Working on a New Play,* pp. 183–184

JOSEPH STEIN, JERRY BOCK, and SHELDON HARNICK

Fiddler on the Roof (musical version of stories by S. Aleichem), 1964
  Cohen, E. M., *Working on a New Play,* pp. 107, 149
  Green, S., *Broadway Musicals,* p. 209
  Harap, L., *Dramatic Encounters,* p. 135
  Kissel, H., "Topol's Tevye," *Playbill,* 9:12, 15–16, 30 Nov. 1990
  Wolitz, S. L., "The Americanization of Tevye or Boarding the Jewish *May-
    flower,*" *American Quarterly,* 40(4):514–536, Dec. 1988
  America, 163:515, 22–29 Dec. 1990
  New York, 23:148, 3 Dec. 1990
  New Yorker, 66:162, 3 Dec. 1990
  Phoenix Magazine, 22:55 +, Jan. 1987
  TheaterWeek, 1:58–59, 27 June 1988
  TheaterWeek, 4:28–29, 13 Aug. 1988
  TheaterWeek, 4:40–41, 3 Dec. 1990

JOSEPH STEIN, ROBERT RUSSELL, and ROBERT MERRILL

Take Me Along! (musical version of E. O'Neill's play *Ah, Wilderness!*), 1959
   Green, S., *Broadway Musicals,* p. 183

MARK STEIN

At Long Last Leo, 1988
   American Theatre, 5:12, Dec. 1988

JOHN STEINBECK

Benson, J. J., *Looking for Steinbeck's Ghost*
Ditsky, J., "A Kind of Play: Dramatic Elements in John Steinbeck's 'The Chrysanthemums,'" *Wascana Review,* 21(1):62+, 1986
Fensch, T., ed., *Conversations with John Steinbeck*
French, W., *John Steinbeck,* 2nd ed.
Goodwin, D. W., "Steinbeck: The Dog That Didn't Bark," pp. 73–92 in Goodwin's *Alcohol and the Writer*
Steinbeck, E., and R. Wallsten, eds., *Steinbeck*
Wilson, L., "Grape Performances," *Mirabella,* 1:48–50, Apr. 1990

Of Mice and Men (dramatization of his novel), 1937
   Fichandler, Z., "Casting for a Different Truth," *American Theatre,* 5:18–23, May 1988
   Village Voice, 32:114, 3 Nov. 1987

JOHN STEPPLING

Marowitz, C., "Los Angeles in Review," *TheaterWeek,* 3:16–17, 5 Mar. 1990
California, 14:72+, Aug. 1989
Village Voice, 35:100, 10 Apr. 1990

JERRY STERNER

Horwitz, S., "Greenmail and Golden Parachutes," *TheaterWeek,* 4:22–23, 1 Oct. 1990

Crossing the Double White Line, 1990
   Playbill, 8:49, 31 May 1990

Other People's Money, 1989
   Botto, L., "Off-B'Way Takeover," *Playbill,* 7:34, 37–39, 31 July 1989
   Chambers, A., "Burned by the Market Crash, Jerry Sterner Finds Another Way to Make a Wall Street Hit," *People Weekly,* 32:123+, 4 Dec. 1989
   Eisenberg, R., "The Word from the Playwright of Wall Street" (interview), *Money,* 18:12, Oct. 1989
   Horwitz, S., "Playwright Jerry Sterner Uses *Other People's Money,*" *TheaterWeek,* 2:34–37, 31 July 1989

"Jerry Sterner: Rolling in *Other People's Money,*" *Business Week,* p. 69, 4 Dec. 1989
Nassour, E., "The Joy of Junk Bonds," *TheaterWeek,* 3:22–25, 28 May 1990
America, 160:536, 3 June 1989
Connoisseur, 219:56+, Oct. 1989
New Republic, 202:28–29, 1 Jan. 1990
New York, 22:99–100, 6 Mar. 1989
Playbill, 9:96, 31 Dec. 1990
TheaterWeek, 2:6, 13 Feb. 1989
TheaterWeek, 3:9, 1 Jan. 1990

JEFF STETSON

And the Men Shall Gather Together, written 1988 (in development)
TheaterWeek, 1:6, 30 May 1988

Fathers and Other Strangers, 1989
American Theatre, 5:49–50, Mar. 1989

Fraternity, 1989
American Theatre, 6:12, Nov. 1989

The Meeting, 1988
American Theatre, 5:10–11, Feb. 1989
American Theatre, 6:12, Nov. 1989
Theatre Journal, 41:540–541, Dec. 1989

MICHAEL STEWART, MARK BRAMBLE, and JERRY HERMAN

The Grand Tour (musical version of S. N. Behrman's play *Jacobowsky and the Colonel,* based on a play by F. Werfel), 1979
Mandelbaum, K., "Taking *The Grand Tour* Again," *TheaterWeek,* 1:34–39, 1 Aug. 1988

MICHAEL STEWART and JERRY HERMAN

Hello, Dolly! (musical version of T. Wilder's play *The Matchmaker*), 1964
Green, S., *Broadway Musicals,* pp. 204–205

Mack and Mabel, 1974 (revised 1988)
Ledford, L. S., "Bringing Back *Mack and Mabel,*" *TheaterWeek,* 1:10–17, 30 May 1988
TheaterWeek, 1:52, 27 June 1988

MARK ST. GERMAIN

Forgiving Typhoid Mary, 1990
American Theatre, 7:10, 58–59, June 1990

MARK ST. GERMAIN and RANDY COURTS

Johnny Pye and the Foolkiller (dramatization of short story by S. V. Benét), 1990
   TheaterWeek, 3:15, 12 Feb. 1990

MARY ST. JOHN

American Plan, 1933
   Bentley, J., *Hallie Flanagan*, pp. 141–142

MILAN STITT

Playbill, 7:52, 28 Feb. 1989 (interview)
TheaterWeek, 2:60, 15 Aug. 1988

DENISE STOKLOS

Casa, 1990
   Village Voice, 35:102, 16 Jan. 1990

PHILIP DEAN STOLLER

Frontier, 1988
   Village Voice, 33:108, 10 May 1988

HELEN STOLTZFUS
SEE MARTHA BOESING, ALBERT GREENBERG, and HELEN STOLTZFUS

FRANCINE STONE

Dead Sure, 1977
   Moore, H., "Woman Alone, Women Together," pp. 186–191 in H. K. Chinoy and L. W. Jenkins, eds., *Women in American Theatre*, rev. and enl. ed. (pp. 184–190 in 1981 ed.)

IRVING STONE (Irving Tennenbaum)

Truly Valiant, 1936
   Leonard, W. T., *Once Was Enough*, pp. 199–200

JOHN AUGUSTUS STONE

Metamora; or, The Last of the Wampanoags, 1829
   Jones, E. H., *Native Americans as Shown on the Stage*, pp. 65–68 and elsewhere
   McConachie, B. A., "The Theatre of Edwin Forrest and Jacksonian Hero Worship," pp. 3–18 in J. L. Fisher and S. Watt, eds., *When They Weren't Doing Shakespeare*

Walsh, D. P., "Many Metamoras: An Indian Drama in the Old Northwest," *Old Northwest,* 13(4):457–468, Winter 1986

PETER STONE

Stone, P., "How to Write the Book for a Musical Comedy," *TheaterWeek,* 4:24–31, 17 Dec. 1990 (rpt. of *Dramatist Guild Quarterly,* 25(4):8–23, Winter 1989, with the title "The Musical Comedy Book")
Playbill, 7:48 + , 28 Feb. 1989 (interview)

Full Circle (adaptation of play by E. M. Remarque), 1974
Los Angeles, 32:62, 64–65, Jan. 1987

CHARLES STOW

An Iron Creed, 1889
Harap, L., *The Image of the Jew in American Literature,* pp. 234–235

JIM STOWELL

The Green Fuse: Journeys on the Amazon, 1990
American Theatre, 7:13–14, Apr. 1990

JOHN STRADLEY

Stop Press, 1939
Leonard, W. T., *Once Was Enough,* p. 183

MICHAEL STRAIGHT

Caravaggio, 1971
Village Voice, 34:118, 19 Dec. 1989

JOHN STRAND

Burying Molière, 1990
TheaterWeek, 3:14, 21 May 1990
Village Voice, 35:106, 22 May 1990

MARK STRAND
SEE CONSTANCE CONGDON and MARK STRAND

TOM STRELICH

Dog Logic, 1988
American Theatre, 5:9, May 1988

Neon Psalms, 1985
Village Voice, 31:100 + , 4 Nov. 1986

CHARLES STROUSE
SEE ARTHUR LAURENTS, CHARLES STROUSE,
and RICHARD MALTBY, JR.
AND LESLIE LEE, CHARLES STROUSE, and LEE ADAMS
AND ALAN JAY LERNER and CHARLES STROUSE
AND CLIFFORD ODETS, WILLIAM GIBSON,
CHARLES STROUSE, and LEE ADAMS

SEBASTIAN STUART

Beverly's Yard Sale, 1988
  TheaterWeek, 1:5, 4 Apr. 1988

PRESTON STURGES

Garrand, T., "Preston Sturges and American Comedy Theater," *Studies in American Humor,* 4(3):209–214, Fall 1985

A Cup of Coffee, written 1931, first produced 1988
  Playbill, 6:58, June 1988
  TheaterWeek, 1:7, 14 Mar. 1988
  Village Voice, 33:103, 19 Apr. 1988

Strictly Dishonorable, 1929
  Marcuson, L. R., *The Stage Immigrant,* pp. 30–34
  TheaterWeek, 1:5, 2 May 1988

JULE STYNE

Buckley, M., "Jule Styne: Let Him Entertain You," *TheaterWeek,* 3:26–30, 27 Nov. 1989
Flatow, S., "Jule Styne: Some People Ain't He," *TheaterWeek,* 2:42–48, 21 Nov. 1988
TheaterWeek, 2:32, 27 Feb. 1989

ALSO SEE ARTHUR LAURENTS, JULE STYNE,
and STEPHEN SONDHEIM

KARENT SUNDE

Anton, Himself (based on Chekhov's biography and correspondence), 1989
  Theatre Journal, 42:262–266, May 1990

Kabuki Othello (adaptation of Shakespeare's play), 1986
  Village Voice, 31:99–100, 14 Oct. 1986

ARNOLD SUNDGAARD

Spirochete: A History, 1938
  Duffy, S., and B. K. Duffy, "Theatrical Responses to Technology during the Depression: Three Federal Theatre Project Plays," *Theatre History Studies,* 6:142–164, 1986

ARNOLD SUNDGAARD and MARC CONNELLY

Everywhere I Roam, 1938
    Kazacoff, G., *Dangerous Theatre,* pp. 233–235

CHARLES SUPPON
SEE HARVEY FIERSTEIN, CHARLES SUPPON, and PETER ALLEN

MARY HALL SURFACE

Most Valuable Player (about Jackie Robinson; a collaborative effort), 1988
    American Theatre, 4:10, Mar. 1988

RICHARD SUTHERLIN

Meet for Lunch, 1990
    TheaterWeek, 3:9, 30 Apr. 1990

JOSEPH SUTTON

Black Market, 1989
    TheaterWeek, 3:6, 20 Nov. 1989
    TheaterWeek, 3:39, 11 Dec. 1989

Special Interests, 1990
    Village Voice, 35:106, 6 Mar. 1990

ELIZABETH SWADOS

Russo, F., "Elizabeth Swados: Growing Up," *TheaterWeek,* 2:26–30, 3 July 1989
Shirakawa, S. H., "Theater People: A Chat with Liz" (interview), *TheaterWeek,*
    1:22–25, 28 Mar. 1988
Swados, E., *Listening out Loud*

The Red Sneaks (based on the 1947 film *The Red Shoes,* written, produced, and
    directed by E. Pressburger; based on an H. C. Andersen fairy tale), 1989
        Stearns, D. P., "Too Much Too Soon," *American Theatre,* 6:6–7, Sept. 1989
        TheaterWeek, 3:10, 14 May 1990
        TheaterWeek, 2:4–5, 19 June 1989
        Village Voice, 35:102, 5 June 1990

ROBIN SWADOS

A Quiet End, 1989
    New York, 23:96, 11 June 1990
    TheaterWeek, 3:8, 7 May 1990
    TheaterWeek, 3:28, 11 June 1990

JEFFREY SWEET

American Enterprise, 1990
    American Theatre, 6:57, Sept. 1989

The Value of Names, a one-act 1983 play later expanded into a full-length one
   Bradford, P. A., "Naming Names," *TheaterWeek,* 2:41, 19 June 1989
   TheaterWeek, 2:4, 15 May 1989
   Village Voice, 34:98+, 13 June 1989

JO SWERLING
SEE ABE BURROWS, JO SWERLING, and FRANK LOESSER

GEORGE TABORI

Schurian, A., "Der Lieb-Haber: George Tabori und sein 'Kreis,'" *Parnass,*
   6:77+, 1988
Zmij-Zielińska, D., "George Tabori: Przewyciężyć Hitlera w sobie," *Dialog,*
   33(9[384]):133–144, Sept. 1988

The Cannibals, 1968
   Skloot, R., *The Darkness We Carry,* pp. xiii, 16–17, 33, 120
   ———, *The Theatre of the Holocaust,* pp. 197–265 (text of play)

TAJ MAHAL
SEE ZORA NEALE HURSTON, LANGSTON HUGHES, and TAJ MAHAL

CLARENCE TALBOT

M.D., 1937
   Kazacoff, G., *Dangerous Theatre,* pp. 283–284

TED TALLY

Little Footsteps, 1986
   San Diego Magazine, 41:42+, Mar. 1989

Terra Nova, 1977
   Andreach, R. J., "Tally's *Terra Nova*: From Historical Journals to Existen-
   tial Journey," *Twentieth Century Literature,* 35(1):65–73, Spring 1989

BOOTH TARKINGTON

Clarence, 1919
   Counts, M. L., *Coming Home,* pp. 91–92, 150

RONALD TAVEL

Thick Dick, 1988
   Village Voice, 33:109, 31 May 1988

TERRY HODGE TAYLOR

Kennedy at Colonus (about Bobby Kennedy), 1984
   TheaterWeek, 1:4, 11 Apr. 1988

JOHN-MICHAEL TEBELAK and STEPHEN SCHWARTZ

Godspell (based on the Gospel of Matthew), 1971
    Botto, L., "The Miracle Musical," *Playbill,* 6:42, 45–47, 31 Aug. 1988
    Green, S., *Broadway Musicals,* p. 233
    Macauley, M. W., "*Godspell* Then and Now," *TheaterWeek,* 1:26–31, 20
        June 1988
    America, 159:40, 9–16 July 1988
    TheaterWeek, 1:58, 16 May 1988

LEVIN C. TEES

Tatters, the Pet of Squatters' Gulch, published 1912
    Jones, E. H., *Native Americans as Shown on the Stage,* p. 146

HOWARD TEICHMANN

Julia, Jake and Uncle Joe (dramatization of O. Atkinson's book *Over at Uncle
Joe's*), 1960
    Leonard, W. T., *Once Was Enough,* pp. 97–100

ALSO SEE GEORGE S. KAUFMAN and HOWARD TEICHMANN

BOB TELSON
SEE LEE BREUER and BOB TELSON

STEPHEN TEMPERLEY

Dance with Me, 1990 (workshop production)
    TheaterWeek, 3:20–21, 26 Mar. 1990

FIONA TEMPLETON

Strange to Relate, 1988
    Champagne, L., ed., *Out from Under,* pp. ix–xiv (Introduction), 166–169,
        171–184 (text of performance piece)

IRVING TANNENBAUM
SEE IRVING STONE

MEGAN TERRY

Betsko, K., and R. Koenig, *Interviews with Contemporary Women Playwrights,*
    pp. 377–401
Breslauer, J., and H. Keyssar, "Making Magic Public: Megan Terry's Traveling
    Family Circus," pp. 169–180 in L. Hurt, ed., *Making a Spectacle*
Gray, A., "The Big If," *American Theatre,* 6:18–21, 56, June 1989
Hart, L., "Megan Terry (22 July 1932–)," pp. 447–456 in P. C. Kolin, ed.,
    American Playwrights since 1945

Keyssar, H., "Megan Terry: Mother of American Feminist Drama," pp. 53–76 in Keyssar's *Feminist Theatre*

Laughlin, K. L., "Megan Terry 1932– ," pp. 361–378 in M. C. Roudané, ed., *Contemporary Authors Bibliographical Series*

Londré, F. H., "An Interview with Megan Terry," *Studies in American Drama, 1945–Present,* 4:177–185, 1989

"Making a Life in Art: Megan Terry Interviews," pp. 328–330 in H. K. Chinoy and L. W. Jenkins, eds., *Women in American Theatre,* rev. and enl. ed. (new to this ed.; comp. by L. W. Jenkins from two interviews with Terry, one by Dinah L. Leavitt published in the 1981 ed., pp. 285–292, the other published in K. Betsko and R. Koenig's *Interviews with Contemporary Women Playwrights,* pp. 377–401, noted above)

Savran, D., "Megan Terry," pp. 240–256 in Savran's *In Their Own Words*

Terry, M., "Anybody Is as Their Land and Air Is," *Studies in American Drama, 1945–Present,* 4:83–90, 1989

American King's English for Queens, 1978
  Natalle, E. J., *Feminist Theatre,* pp. 87–99 and elsewhere

Amtrak, 1988
  Kolin, P. C., "Megan Terry's *Amtrak*: An Iran-Contra Comedy," *Notes on Contemporary Literature,* 20(2):3–5, Mar. 1990
  Terry, M., *Amtrak* (text of play), *Studies in American Drama,* 4:21–82, 1989

Babes in the Bighouse, 1974
  Natalle, E. J., *Feminist Theatre,* pp. 48–50 and elsewhere

Family Talk, 1986
  Babnich, J., "Megan Terry and *Family Talk,*" *Centennial Review,* 32(3):296–311, Summer 1988

Headlights, 1988
  American Theatre, 5:9–10, Feb. 1989
  Theatre Journal, 42:370–372, Oct. 1990

Keep Tightly Closed in a Cool Dry Place, 1965
  Schlueter, J., "*Keep Tightly Closed in a Cool Dry Place*: Megan Terry's Transformational Drama and the Possibilities of Self," *Studies in American Drama, 1945–Present,* 2:59–69, 1987 (rptd. in Schlueter, ed., *Modern American Drama,* pp. 160–171, with the title "Megan Terry's Transformational Drama: *Keep Tightly Closed in a Cool Dry Place* and the Possibilities of Self")

100,001 Horror Stories of the Plains, 1976
  Babnich, J., "Megan Terry's *100,001 Horror Stories of the Plains*: Tall Tales and Stories from the People of the Midwest," *Mississippi Folklore Register,* 21(1–2):47–59, Spring-Fall 1988

Viet Rock: A Folk War Movie, 1966
    Shank, T., *American Alternative Theater,* pp. 38–40
    Zinman, T. S., "Search and Destroy: The Drama of the Vietnam War,"
    Theatre Journal, 42:5–26, Mar. 1990

STEVE TESICH

Baba Goya, 1973 (later in 1973 produced as *Nourish the Beast*)
    Jacobson, L., "Two by Tesich," *American Theatre,* 6:9, Mar. 1990
    Riedel, M., "Mother Knows Best," *TheaterWeek,* 3:38–40, 8 Jan. 1990

Division Street, 1980
    American Theatre, 4:11, Jan. 1988
    Village Voice, 32:100+ , 17 Feb. 1987

The Speed of Darkness, 1989
    Collins, R., "Tesich at the Frontier," *American Theatre,* 6:30–31, July/Aug.
    1989
    American Theatre, 6:1–16, July/Aug. 1989 (text of play, special pull-out
    section)
    Playbill, 7:36, 30 Apr. 1989

Square One, 1990
    Harris, J., "Art Intimidates Life," *TheaterWeek,* 3:40, 5 Mar. 1990
    Jacobson, L., "Two by Tesich," *American Theatre,* 6:9, Mar. 1990
    New York, 23:56, 5 Mar. 1990
    New Yorker, 66:89–90, 5 Mar. 1990
    TheaterWeek, 3:12, 19 Feb. 1990
    Time, 136:54, 31 Dec. 1990
    Village Voice, 35:105+ , 6 Mar. 1990

RUSS THACKER

Between the Lines, 1990
    TheaterWeek, 3:11, 14 May 1990

KRISTINE THATCHER

Niedecker, 1989
    TheaterWeek, 2:8, 20 Feb. 1989
    Village Voice, 34:96+ , 28 Mar. 1989

ROBERT THOM

Bicycle Ride to Nevada (dramatization of B. Conrad's novel *Dangerfield*), 1963
    Leonard, W. T., *Once Was Enough,* pp. 10–11

AUDREY CALLAHAN THOMAS

Mrs. Blood, 1975
    Shaw, J., "Letter to Edinburgh," *Room of One's Own,* 10(3–4):81–85, Mar.
    1986

AUGUSTUS THOMAS

Alabama, 1891
    Rainey, K. T., "Race and Reunion in Nineteenth-Century Reconciliation
    Drama," *American Transcendental Quarterly,* 2(2):155–169, June 1988

As a Man Thinks, 1911
    Harap, L., *Dramatic Encounters,* pp. 77–78

In Mizzoura, 1893
    TheaterWeek, 4:27–28, 3 Sept. 1990

LEWIS F. THOMAS

Cortez the Conqueror (based on W. H. Prescott's book *The Conquest of Mexico*),
    written 1857
    Jones, E. H., *Native Americans as Shown on the Stage,* p. 37

Osceola, 1837
    Jones, E. H., *Native Americans as Shown on the Stage,* p. 36

THOM THOMAS

Without Apologies (an "update" of O. Wilde's play *The Importance of Being
    Earnest*), 1989
    Horwitz, S., "Without Apologies to Oscar Wilde," *TheaterWeek,* 2:44–53,
    27 Feb. 1989
    Village Voice, 34:80 + , 28 Feb. 1989

DENMAN THOMPSON

The Old Homestead, 1886
    Clark, E., "The Play That Must Go On," *Yankee,* 51:62–67, 124, July 1987

JUDITH THOMPSON

Carley, D., "A Canada Nobody Knows," *American Theatre,* 4:46–47, Feb. 1988
Nunn, R., "Spatial Metaphor in the Plays of Judith Thompson," *Theatre History
    in Canada,* 10(1):3–29, Spring 1989
Toles, G., " "Cause You're the Only one I Want': The Anatomy of Love in the
    Plays of Judith Thompson," *Canadian Literature,* 118:116–135, Autumn 1988
Tomc, S., "Revisions of Probability: An Interview with Judith Thompson," *Ca-
    nadian Theatre Review,* 59:18–23, Summer 1989

Lion in the Streets, 1990
    Maclean's, 103:69, 19 Nov. 1990

RON STACKER THOMPSON
SEE RUTH BECKFORD and RON STACKER THOMPSON

VIRGIL THOMSON

Sandow, G., "The Composer and Performer and Other Matters: A Panel Discussion with Virgil Thomson and Philip Glass," ed. J. B. Clark, *American Music*, 7:181–204, Summer 1989
Time, 134:120, Oct. 1989

ALSO SEE GERTRUDE STEIN and VIRGIL THOMSON

DAVID THORNE

Beyond Evil, 1926
    Leonard, W. T., *Once Was Enough, pp. 6–9*

LEE THUNA

The Natural Look, 1967
    Leonard, W. T., *Once Was Enough*, pp. 135–136

LEONORA THUNA and HARRY CAULEY

Let Me Hear You Smile, 1973
    Leonard, W. T., *Once Was Enough*, p. 105

ZELMA TIDEN

Captain What-the-Devil, 1937
    Kazacoff, G., *Dangerous Theatre*, pp. 207–209

THOMAS TIERNEY
SEE JONATHAN BOLT, THOMAS TIERNEY, and JOHN FORSTER

LEN ELLSWORTH TILDEN

The Emigrant's Daughter, 1884
    Jones, E. H., *Native Americans as Shown on the Stage*, pp. 118–119

CANDIDO TIRADO

First Class, 1988
    TheaterWeek, 1:7, 30 May 1988
    Village Voice, 33:98 + , 21 June 1988

FRED TOBIAS
SEE PETER BELLWOOD, STANLEY LEBOWSKY, and FRED TOBIAS

KATHLEEN TOLAN

Kate's Diary, 1989
    American Theatre, 6:13, Jan. 1990
    American Theatre, 6:56, Mar. 1990

New York, 22:132, 11 Dec. 1989
TheaterWeek, 2:6, 12 June 1989
Village Voice, 34:119, 12 Dec. 1989

A Weekend near Madison, 1982
Hall, R., "Eleven Different Directions," *American Theatre,* 5:32–33, Dec. 1988
Shewey, D., "Gay Theatre Grows Up," *American Theatre,* 5:10–17, 52–53, May 1988

JEAN TOOMER

Byrd, R. P., "Jean Toomer and the Writers of the Harlem Renaissance: Was He There with Them?" pp. 209–218 in A. Singh, W. S. Shiver, and S. Brodwin, eds., *The Harlem Renaissance*
Kerman, C. E., and R. Eldridge, *The Lives of Jean Toomer*
McKay, N. Y., *Jean Toomer*
O'Daniel, T. B., ed., *Jean Toomer*

Balo, 1927
Rusch, F. L., "Jean Toomer's Early Identification: The Two Black Plays," *MELUS,* 13(1–2):115–124, Spring-Summer 1986

Kabnis, written before Apr. 1922, published in revised form in his 1923 book *Cane*
Kulii, E. A., "Literature, Biology and Folk Legal Belief: Jean Toomer's *Kabnis,*" *USF Language Quarterly,* 25(3–4):5–7, 49, 54, Spring-Summer 1987

Natalie Mann, written 1922, published 1980
Rusch, F. L., "Jean Toomer's Early Identification: The Two Black Plays," *MELUS,* 13(1–2):115–24, Spring-Summer 1986

CHARLES TOWNSEND

Border Land, 1888
Jones, E. H., *Native Americans as Shown on the Stage,* pp. 119–120

The Golden Gulch, 1893
Jones, E. H., *Native Americans as Shown on the Stage,* p. 145

Jail Bird, 1893
Harap, L., *The Image of the Jew in American Literature,* pp. 227–228

BEVERLY TRADER

Zion!, 1990
Hulbert, D., "Actors Are the Spark for Atlanta's Writers," *American Theatre,* 7:44–45, June 1990

JANE TRAHEY

Ring Round the Bathtub, 1970
    Leonard, W. T., *Once Was Enough,* pp. 162–163

ESTELA PORTILLO TRAMBLEY
SEE ESTELA PORTILLO

SOPHIE TREADWELL

Hope for a Harvest, 1941
    Marcuson, L. R., *The Stage Immigrant,* pp. 122–127

Machinal, 1928
    Bywaters, B. L., "Marriage, Madness, and Murder in Sophie Treadwell's *Machinal,*" pp. 97–110 in J. Schlueter, ed., *Modern American Drama*
    Heck-Rabi, L., "Sophie Treadwell: Agent for Change," pp. 157–162 in H. K. Chinoy and L. W. Jenkins, eds., *Women in American Theatre,* rev. and enl. ed. (same pagination in both eds.)
    Commonweal, 117:698–699, 23 Nov. 1990
    New Republic, 203:27–28, 17 Dec. 1990
    New York, 23:96, 29 Oct. 1990
    New Yorker, 66:114, 29 Oct. 1990
    Playbill, 9:45, 31 Dec. 1990
    TheaterWeek, 4:40, 5 Nov. 1990

JOSÉ TRIANA

La Noche de los Asesinos, 1965
    Alvarez-Borland, I., and others, "*La Noche de los asesinos*: Text, Staging and Audience," *Latin American Theatre Review,* 20(1):37–48, 1986

JOHN T. TROWBRIDGE

Neighbor Jackwood, 1857
    Fletcher, W. L., "Who Put the 'Tragic' in the Tragic Mulatto?" pp. 262–268 in H. K. Chinoy and L. W. Jenkins, eds., *Women in American Theatre,* rev. and enl. ed. (pp. 260–266 in 1981 ed.)

EDWARD W. TULLIDGE

Ben Israel, 1875
    Harap, L., *The Image of the Jew in American Literature,* pp. 233–234

JOSEPH DOLAN TUOTTI

Big Time Buck White (also known as *Buck White*), 1968
    Lahr, J., "Black Theatre: The American Tragic Voice," *Evergreen Review,* 13:55–63, Aug. 1969

JOSEPH TURRIN
SEE GEORGE ABBOTT, JOSEPH TURRIN, and GLORIA NISSENSON

CONVERSE TYLER

This Pretty World, 1938
    Kazacoff, G., *Dangerous Theatre,* pp. 250–253

ROYALL TYLER

The Contrast, 1787
    Pressman, R. S., "Letter to the Editor: [On 'Class Positioning and Shays'
    Rebellion']," *Early American Literature,* 22(2):230 + , Fall 1987 (correc-
    tion of entry in Supplement II to the 2nd ed.)

PETER UDELL
SEE OSSIE DAVIS, PETER UDELL, PHILIP ROSE,
and GARY GELD

ALFRED UHRY

Stark, J., "After Winning a Pulitzer for *Driving Miss Daisy,* Alfred Uhry
    Emerges as Theater's New Top Dog," *People Weekly,* 29:85 + , 23 May 1988
Uhry, A., "From Russia with Faxes," *TheaterWeek,* 3:32–33, 5 Feb. 1990
American Theatre, 5:48, June 1988
Connecticut Magazine, 51:48 + , Aug. 1988
Elle, 3:34, Jan. 1988
Playbill, 7:S-2, 30 June 1989
Southpoint, 1:40 + , Dec. 1989

Driving Miss Daisy, 1987
    Clarke, G., "Two Lives, One Ambition," *Time,* 135:62–64, 2 Apr. 1990
    Goldstein, W., "Theatre Communications Group Publishing Pulitzer Prize
        Play *Driving Miss Daisy,*" *Publishers Weekly,* 234:64–65, 26 Aug. 1988
    Haun, H., "Miss Daisy's Driving Force," *Playbill,* 7:54, 59–61, 31 Mar.
        1989
    Hulbert, D., "'Miss Daisy' Characters Are Home in Atlanta," *American
        Theatre,* 5:42–43, Dec. 1988
    Levy, L. M., "*Driving Miss Daisy* with Eddie Murphy and Bette Mid-
        ler . . . ?" *TheaterWeek,* 3:26–30, 4 Sept. 1989
    Uhry, A., *Driving Miss Daisy* (excerpt from the play), *Playbill,* 7:S-1, S-3
        through S-12, 30 June 1989
    America, 159:40 + , 9–16 July 1988
    Chicago, 38:79–80, Feb. 1989
    D Magazine, 16:15, Feb. 1989
    Jet, 78:58, 16 Apr. 1990
    Playbill, 6:69, 31 Aug. 1988
    San Diego Magazine, 41:52 + , Sept. 1989
    TheaterWeek, 2:6, 17 Oct. 1988
    TheaterWeek, 2:8–9, 10 Apr. 1989

TheaterWeek, 3:10, 9 Apr. 1990
TheaterWeek, 3:6, 14 May 1990
Village Voice, 32:93, 28 Apr. 1987

Little Johnny Jones (adaptation of musical by G. M. Cohan), 1982
     Leonard, W. T., *Once Was Enough*, pp. 105–114

ALSO SEE ALEX GORDON, ROBERT WALDMAN,
and ALFRED UHRY

BJÖRN ULVAEUS
SEE RICHARD NELSON, TIM RICE, BENNY ANDERSSON,
and BJÖRN ULVAEUS

GLADYS UNGER and WALTER ARMITAGE

African Vineyard, 1937
     Kazacoff, G., *Dangerous Theatre*, pp. 211–213

LUIS VALDEZ

Burciaga, J. A., "A Conversation with Luis Valdez" (interview), *Imagine*,
     2(2):127–141, Winter 1985
Flores, A. C., "1965–1986: El Teatro Campesino: Algunas orientaciones teó-
     ricas," *Confluencia*, 2(2):116–121, Spring 1987
González, Y. B., "Toward a Re-Vision of Chicano Theatre History: The Women
     of El Teatro Campesino," pp. 209–238 in L. Hart, ed., *Making a Spectacle*
Herrera-Sobek, M., "El teatro chicano: Teatro en transición," *Gestos*, 2(3):135–
     136, Apr. 1987
Miguelez, A., "Aproximaciones al nuevo teatro chicano de autor único," *Ex-
     plicación de Textos Literarios*, 15(2):8–18, 1986–1987
Savran, D., "Border Tactics: Luis Valdez Distills the Chicano Experience on
     Stage and Film" (interview), *American Theatre*, 4:14–21, 56–57, Jan. 1988
     (adapted from Savran's *In Their Own Words*; see next entry)
———, "Luis Valdez," pp. 257–271 in Savran's *In their Own Words*
Shank, T., "El Teatro Campesino (The Farmworkers Theatre)," pp. 74–90 in
     Shank's *American Alternative Theater*
Van Erven, E., "El Teatro Campesino," pp. 43–53 in Van Erven's *Radical
     People's Theatre*
———, "Revolutionary Voices in the American Political Theatre," pp. 24–63 in
     Van Erven's *Radical People's Theatre*
Yarbro-Bejarano, Y., "The Female Subject in Chicano Theatre: Sexuality,
     'Race,' and Class," pp. 131–149 in S.-E. Case, ed., *Performing Feminisms* (rpt.
     of *Theatre Journal*, 38(4):389–407, Dec. 1986)
American Film, 12:15, July/Aug. 1987
Time, 132:74, 11 July 1988
Village Voice, 33:29, 5 Jan. 1988

I Don't Have to Show You No Stinking Badges, 1986
     Ramirez, A., "Play in Performance: *I Don't Have to Show You No Stinking
     Badges* in San Diego," *Latin American Theatre Review*, 21(2):113, 1988

San Diego Magazine, 39:44+, June 1987

Las dos caras del patroncito, 1965 (one of the *Actos* of El Teatro Campesino)
Labinger, A. G., "The Cruciform Farce in Latin America: Two Plays,"
pp. 219–226 in J. Redmond, ed., *Farce*

Los vendidos, 1967 (revised 1988; one of the *Actos* of El Teatro Campesino)
Theatre Journal, 41:231–233, May 1989

Zoot Suit, 1978
Barrios, G., "*Zoot Suit*: The Man, the Myth, Still Lives: A Conversation
with Luis Valdez," pp. 159–164 in G. D. Keller, ed., *Chicano Cinema*

RENA VALE
SEE DONALD MURRAY, THEODORE PEZMAN, and RENA VALE

FRED VALLE

I Am a Winner, 1990
TheaterWeek, 3:16, 19 Mar. 1990
Village Voice, 35:114, 24 Apr. 1990

JOHN VAN DRUTEN

The Voice of the Turtle, 1943
New York, 21:92–93, 19–26 Dec. 1988

JEAN-CLAUDE van ITALLIE

Engler, B., "Der 'doppelte' Sündenfall ins menschliche Selbstbewusst-Sein: Alt-
testamentliche Typologie in Dramen Archibald MacLeischs, Howard Neme-
rovs, Arthur Millers und Jean-Claude von [sic] Itallies," pp. 591–609 in F.
Link, ed., *Paradeigmata*
Gray, A., "The Big If," *American Theatre,* 6:18–21, 56, June 1989
Greene, A., "An Interview with Jean-Claude van Itallie," *Studies in American
Drama, 1945–Present,* 3:134–146, 1988
————, "Jean-Claude van Itallie (25 May 1936–)," pp. 457–468 in P. C. Kolin,
ed., *American Playwrights since 1945*

America, Hurrah!, 1966
Grabes, H., "Myth and Myth Destruction in American Plays of the 60s and
70s," *Amerikastudien,* 32(1):39–48, 1987

Ancient Boys: A Requiem, 1989 (later revised)
Temerson, C., and F. Kourilsky, *Gay Plays,* Preface (n. pag.) and text of
play (pp. 329–393)

I'm Really Here, 1964
Shrager, S., *Scatology in Modern Drama,* p. 50

Three Sisters (adaptation of Chekhov's play), 1979
  Theatre Journal, 41:247–249, May 1989

JEAN-CLAUDE van ITALLIE and JOSEPH CHAIKIN

The Serpent: A Ceremony (based on Genesis), 1968
  Shank, T., *American Alternative Theater,* p. 40
  TheaterWeek, 1:58–59, 30 May 1988
  Village Voice, 33:125 + , 6 Dec. 1988

Struck Dumb, 1988
  American Theatre, 5:47–48, July/Aug. 1988

MELVIN VAN PEEBLES

Woll, A., *Black Musical Theatre,* pp. 257–261, 263, 267, 271, 277

GILDA VARESI and DOLLY BYRNE

Enter Madame, 1920
  Marcuson, L. R., *The Stage Immigrant,* pp. 17–21

RON VAWTER

Premiere, 3:40, Feb. 1990

BILL VEHR

TheaterWeek, 2:7, 22 Aug. 1988

ALSO SEE CHARLES LUDLAM and BILL VEHR

VICTOR VICTOR
SEE SAMUEL SHIPMAN and VICTOR VICTOR

GORE VIDAL

Kiernan, R. F., *Gore Vidal*

PETER VIERTEL and IRWIN SHAW

The Survivors, 1948
  Counts, M. L., *Coming Home,* pp. 86–87, 97, 107, 126–127, 158–159, 180

JAN VILLARUBIA

Lutenbacher, C., "'So Much More Than Just Myself': Women Theatre Artists
  in the South," pp. 253–263 in J. Redmond, ed., *Women in Theatre*

CRAIG VOLK

We Live in a Trailer House and Try Not to Go Crazy, 1988
    TheaterWeek, 1:5, 16 May 1988

LULA VOLLMER

Sun-Up, 1923
    France, R., "Apropos of Women and the Folk Play," pp. 145–152 in H. K.
    Chinoy and L. W. Jenkins, eds., *Women in American Theatre,* rev. and
    enl. ed. (same pagination in 1981 ed.)

KURT VONNEGUT

Make up Your Mind, 1989 (staged reading)
    TheaterWeek, 3:10, 28 Aug. 1989

JOHN VOULGARIS

Best Friends, 1989
    TheaterWeek, 3:11–12, 14 Aug. 1989
    Village Voice, 34:98, 22 Aug. 1989

REBECCA WACKLER
SEE PHILIP DePOY, LEVI LEE, and REBECCA WACKLER
AND LEVI LEE, LARRY LARSON, and REBECCA WACKLER

KEVIN WADE

Key Exchange, 1981
    Cohen, E. M., *Working on a New Play,* pp. 3, 161–162

JANE WAGNER

The Search for Signs of Intelligent Life in the Universe, 1985
    Davy, K., "Constructing the Spectator: Reception, Context, and Address
    in Lesbian Performance," *Performing Arts Journal,* 10(2[29]):43–52, 1986
    Gentile, J. S., *Cast of One,* pp. 169–172
    Maclean's, 102:37, 16 Jan. 1989

PAULA WAGNER
SEE EVE MERRIAM, PAULA WAGNER, and JACK HOFSISS

D. W. WAINWRIGHT

Wheat and Chaff, 1858
    Miller, T. L., "The Image of Fashionable Society in American Comedy,
    1840–1870," pp. 243–252 in J. L. Fisher and S. Watt, eds., *When They
    Weren't Doing Shakespeare*

CHARLES M. WALCOT

A Good Fellow, 1854
> Miller, T. L., "The Image of Fashionable Society in American Comedy, 1840–1870," pp. 243–252 in J. L. Fisher and S. Watt, eds., *When They Weren't Doing Shakespeare*

Hiawatha; or, Ardent Spirits and Laughing Water, 1856
> Jones, E. H., *Native Americans as Shown on the Stage,* pp. 94–95

DEREK WALCOTT

Hamner, R., "Exorcising the Planter-Devil in the Plays of Derek Walcott," *Commonwealth Essays and Studies,* 7(2):95–102, Spring 1985

Jeyifo, B., "On Eurocentric Critical Theory: Some Paradigms from the Texts and Sub-Texts of Post-Colonial Writing," *Kunapipi,* 11(1):107–118, 1989

Moyers, B., *Bill Moyers' World of Ideas,* ed. B. S. Flowers, pp. 426–434 (interview on PBS, 1988)

Peters, E., "The Theme of Madness in the Plays of Derek Walcott," *College Language Association Journal,* 32(2):148–169, Dec. 1988

A Branch of the Blue Nile, 1986
> Breslow, S. P., "Trinidadian Heteroglossia: A Bakhtinian View of Derek Walcott's Play *A Branch of the Blue Nile,*" *World Literature Today,* 63(1):36–39, Winter 1989

Dream on Monkey Mountain, 1967
> Euba, F., *Archetypes, Imprecators, and Victims of Fate,* pp. 153–154

Malcochon; or Six in the Rain, 1959 (produced in London in 1960 as *Six in the Rain*)
> Adekoya, O., "Between Beasthood and Godhead: An Inquiry into the Definition of Man," *Literary Half-Yearly,* 28(1):53–60, Jan. 1987

O Babylon!, 1976
> *Encounter,* 70:76, May 1988

Viva Detroit, 1990
> *American Theatre,* 7:13, July/Aug. 1990
> *American Theatre,* 7:11, Sept. 1990

STANLEY WALDEN
SEE MARTHA CLARKE, RICHARD COE, RICHARD PEASLEE, and STANLEY WALDEN

ROBERT WALDMAN
SEE ALEX GORDON, ROBERT WALDMAN, and ALFRED UHRY

GEORGE F. WALKER

The Art of War (third play of the trilogy *Power Plays*; the first is *Gossip,* 1977; the second is *Filthy Rich,* 1979), 1983
> *Village Voice,* 32:89–90, 5 May 1987

Love and Anger, 1989
    Bemrose, J., "Urban Survival," *Maclean's,* 102:76–77, 23 Oct. 1989
    TheaterWeek, 4:8 + , 19 Nov. 1990

Nothing Sacred (dramatization of I. Turgenev's novel *Fathers and Sons*), 1987
    Henry, W. A., III, "Two Tales of One City," *Time,* 132:92, 3 Oct. 1988
    Teich, J., "Taking Russia Apart," *American Theatre,* 5:6–7, Dec. 1988
    American Theatre, 5:12, Sept. 1988
    Maclean's, 101:53, 25 Jan. 1988
    TheaterWeek, 2:38, 26 Oct. 1988
    Time, 133:102, 2 Jan. 1989

JOSEPH A. WALKER

The River Niger, 1972
    Barthelemy, A., "Mother, Sister, Wife: A Dramatic Perspective," *Southern
    Review,* 21(3):770–789, 1985
    Cook, W., "Mom, Dad and God: Values in Black Theater," pp. 168–184 in
    E. Hill, ed., *The Theater of Black Americans,* Vol. 1 of two vols. rptd.
    as one in 1987; same pagination in both eds.
    Playbill, 6:72–73, June 1988

MARY WALSH

Hockey Wives, 1988
    Maclean's, 101:61, 18 Apr. 1988

SHELA WALSH

Tea with Mommy and Jack (about Jack Kerouac and his mother), 1988
    TheaterWeek, 2:6, 26 Sept. 1988
    Village Voice, 33:100, 22 Nov. 1988

DOUGLAS TURNER WARD

Bigsby, C. W. E., "Three Black Playwrights: Loften Mitchell, Ossie Davis,
    Douglas Turner Ward," pp. 148–167 in E. Hill, ed., *The Theater of Black
    Americans,* Vol. 1 of two vols. rptd. as one in 1987; same pagination in both
    eds. (rpt. of *The Black American Writer,* ed. Bigsby, 2:137–155)
Harrison, P. C., "The (R)evolution of Black Theatre," *American Theatre,* 6:30–
    32, 116–118, Oct. 1989

THEODORE WARD

Big White Fog, 1940
    Barthelemy, A., "Mother, Sister, Wife: A Dramatic Perspective," *Southern
    Review,* 21(3):770–789, 1985

MARK WAREN

. . . *Mexico,* 1989
   Theatre Journal, 42:148–149, May 1990

ANDY WARHOL

Andy Warhol's Last Love, 1978
   Shank, T., "Squat Theatre," pp. 179–189 in Shank's *American Alternative Theater*

MERCY OTIS WARREN

Case, S.-E., *Feminism and Theatre,* pp. 43–44
Robinson, A. M., "Mercy Warren, Satirist of the Revolution," pp. 131–137 in H. K. Chinoy and L. W. Jenkins, eds., *Women in American Theatre,* rev. and enl. ed. (same pagination in 1981 ed.)
Schofield, M. A., "The Happy Revolution: Colonial Women and the Eighteenth-Century Theater," pp. 29–37 in J. Schlueter, ed., *Modern American Drama*

DALE WASSERMAN, MITCH LEIGH, and JOE DARION

Man of La Mancha (musical version of Cervantes's *Don Quixote*), 1965
   Green, S., *Broadway Musicals,* pp. 214–215
   TheaterWeek, 1:56, 30 May 1988

WENDY WASSERSTEIN

Betsko, K., and R. Koenig, *Interviews with Contemporary Women Playwrights,* pp. 418–431
Cohen, E., "Uncommon Woman: An Interview with Wendy Wasserstein," *Women's Studies,* 15(1–3):257–270, 1988
Gillespie, P. P., "Wendy Wasserstein (18 October 1950–)," pp. 469–477 in P. C. Kolin, ed., *American Playwrights since 1945*
Schroeder, P. R., "Wendy Wasserstein 1950– ," pp. 379–384 in M. C. Roudané, ed., *Contemporary Authors Bibliographical Series*
Vellela, T., "The Wasserstein Chronicles" (interview), *TheaterWeek,* 2:12–19, 26 Dec. 1988
Wasserstein, W., *Bachelor Girls*
———, "Joseph Papp," *New York,* 21:106–108, 25 Apr. 1988
———, "Shopping with Him," *Gentlemen's Quarterly,* 58:196, 198, 200, Mar. 1988
New York Woman, 4:84 +, Sept. 1989
TheaterWeek, 4:8, 31 Dec. 1990
W, 18:22, 3 Apr. 1989

The Heidi Chronicles, 1988
   Harris, J., "Heidi Takes Charge," *TheaterWeek,* 3:42, 30 Oct. 1989
   ———, "The Editor Responds [to Marowitz; see item 4]," *TheaterWeek,* 4:36, 5 Nov. 1990

Horwitz, S., "'Women, Where Are We Going?'" *TheaterWeek*, 2:21–25, 8 May 1989

Marowitz, C., "Los Angeles in Review," *TheaterWeek*, 4:34–36, 5 Nov. 1990

McCree, C., "Giving Birth to Heidi," *Playbill*, 7:10, 12, 14, 16, 30 Apr. 1989

Rose, P. J., "Dear Heidi," *American Theatre*, 6:26–29, 114–116, Oct. 1989

Shapiro, W., "Chronicler of Frayed Feminism," *Time*, 133:90–92, 27 Mar. 1990

Snow, L., "Second Thoughts on *The Heidi Chronicles*," *TheaterWeek*, 2:36–37, 1 May 1989

Vellela, T., "Peter Friedman" (interview), *TheaterWeek*, 2:20–21, 26 Dec. 1988

American Theatre, 5:9, Feb. 1989
American Theatre, 6:41, Apr. 1989
American Theatre, 6:51, June 1989
Commonweal, 116:279–280, 5 May 1989
Connoisseur, 219:62 + , Sept. 1989
Georgia Review, 43:573–575, Fall 1989
Hudson Review, 42:464–465, Autumn 1989
Manhattan, inc., 6:138–141, May 1989
Nation, 248:605–606, 1 May 1989
New Republic, 200:32–34, 17 Apr. 1989
New York, 22:49, 2 Jan. 1989
New York, 22:66 + , 27 Mar. 1989
New Yorker, 64:81–82, 26 Dec. 1988
Newsweek, 113:76–77, 20 Mar. 1989
TheaterWeek, 2:61, 27 Mar. 1989
TheaterWeek, 3:24, 25 Dec. 1989
TheaterWeek, 3:7, 4 June 1990
Theatre Journal, 42:107–108, Mar. 1990
Time, 133:90, 20 Mar. 1989
Village Voice, 33:121–122, 20 Dec. 1988
Vogue, 179:266B, Mar. 1989

Uncommon Women and Others, 1977

Carlson, S. L., "Comic Textures and Female Communities 1937–1977: Clare Boothe and Wendy Wasserstein," pp. 207–217 in J. Schlueter, ed., *Modern American Drama* (rpt. of *Modern Drama*, 27(4):564–573, Dec. 1984)

Case, S.-E., *Feminism and Theatre*, p. 67

Keyssar, H., "Success and Its Limits: Mary O'Malley, Wendy Wasserstein, Nell Dunn, Beth Henley, Catherine Hayes, Marsha Norman," pp. 148–166 in Keyssar's *Feminist Theatre*

Moore, H., "Woman Alone, Women Together," pp. 186–191 in H. K. Chinoy and L. W. Jenkins, eds., *Women in American Theatre*, rev. and enl. ed. (pp. 184–190 in 1981 ed.)

ARA WATSON

Treasure Island (dramatization of R. L. Stevenson's novel), 1989
American Theatre, 6:11, Jan. 1990

LOIS WEAVER
SEE PEGGY SHAW and LOIS WEAVER

JEROME WEIDMAN

The Mother Lover, 1969
　　Leonard, W. T., *Once Was Enough,* pp. 130–131

GUS WEILL

The November People, 1978
　　Leonard, W. T., *Once Was Enough,* pp. 140–141

Rosenfeld's War, 1988
　　Shirakawa, S. H., "Check Mate," *TheaterWeek,* 1:37–42, 23 May 1988
　　TheaterWeek, 1:5, 4 Apr. 1988
　　Village Voice, 33:105, 10 May 1988

KURT WEILL

Mates, J., *America's Musical Stage,* pp. 37, 51, 64, 187, 188, 190, 195
TheaterWeek, 1:40, 29 Feb. 1988

ALSO SEE MAXWELL ANDERSON and KURT WEILL
AND PAUL GREEN and KURT WEILL
AND ALAN JAY LERNER and KURT WEILL
AND ELMER RICE, KURT WEILL, and LANGSTON HUGHES

ARNOLD WEINSTEIN and WILLIAM BOLCOM

Casino Paradise, 1990
　　American Theatre, 6:12, Mar. 1990

JACK WEINSTOCK
SEE ABE BURROWS, JACK WEINSTOCK, WILLIE GILBERT,
and FRANK LOESSER

JEFF WEISS

Frame, A., "Jeff Weiss" (interview), *BOMB,* 26:20, 1988–1989 (Weiss's *And
That's How the Rent Gets Paid, Part 4* considered)

PAUL WEITZ

Captive, 1990
　　American Theatre, 7:13, May 1990

Mango Tea, 1988
　　New Yorker, 64:73, 25 July 1988

LOUIS WEITZENKORN

Five Star Final, 1930
　　Harap, L., *Dramatic Encounters,* p. 119

DAVID WELCH
SEE MICHAEL ALASA and DAVID WELCH

GAY WELCH

Heterosexuals in Crime, 1990
　　TheaterWeek, 3:42, 6 Aug. 1990

MICHAEL WELLER

Greene, A., "The Times of Michael Weller," *American Theatre,* 5:18–22, Apr.
　　1988
Leeson, R., "Michael Weller (26 September 1942–)," pp. 478–487 in P. C.
　　Kolin, ed., *American Playwrights since 1945*
Savran, D., "Michael Weller," pp. 272–287 in Savran's *In Their Own Words*
New York Woman, 3:108, Oct. 1988

Lake No Bottom, 1990
　　American Theatre, 7:11–12, Nov. 1990
　　New York, 23:108–109, 10 Dec. 1990
　　New Yorker, 66:138, 10 Dec. 1990
　　TheaterWeek, 4:37, 10 Dec. 1990

Loose Ends, 1979
　　Nation, 246:318–319, 5 Mar. 1988
　　New York, 21:68, 22 Feb. 1988
　　New Yorker, 64:96–97, 22 Feb. 1988
　　Village Voice, 33:90, 23 Feb. 1988

Moonchildren, 1971 (originally produced in 1970 in London as *Cancer*)
　　Zinman, T. S., "Search and Destroy: The Drama of the Vietnam War,"
　　　　Theatre Journal, 42:5–26, Mar. 1990
　　New Yorker, 64:96–97, 22 Feb. 1988
　　Village Voice, 32:100 + , 29 Dec. 1987

Split, 1977
　　TheaterWeek, 3:41, 21 May 1990

Spoils of War, 1988 (revised later in the year)
　　Henderson, K., "*Spoils of War*: Michael Weller's Autobiographical Play
　　　　Comes to B'way," *Playbill,* 7:12, 14, 16, 31 Oct. 1988
　　Merla, P., "Kate Nelligan: Triumph over Diversity" (interview),
　　　　TheaterWeek, 2:12–21, 14 Nov. 1988
　　American Theatre, 5:n pag., Mar. 1989 (text of play; special pull-out section)
　　Maclean's, 101:57, 30 May 1988

Manhattan, inc., 6:104–107, Jan. 1989
Nation, 247:662–663, 12 Dec. 1988
New York, 21:88, 30 May 1988
New Yorker, 64:112, 6 June 1988
TheaterWeek, 2:6–7, 29 Aug. 1988
TheaterWeek, 3:26, 25 Dec. 1989
Theatre Crafts, 22:14, Dec. 1988
Time, 132:94, 28 Nov. 1988
Time, 133:102, 2 Jan. 1989
Village Voice, 33:99–100, 31 May 1988
Village Voice, 33:99, 22 Nov. 1988

MAC WELLMAN

Beber, N., "Dramatis Instructus," *American Theatre,* 6:22–23, 26, Jan. 1990
London, T., "Opening a Door Up Left," *American Theatre,* 5:38–41, Mar. 1989
Robinson, M., "Don't Fence Them In," *American Theatre,* 6:28–34, Sept. 1989
Wellman, M., "Against Political Theatre," *American Theatre,* 7:5, June 1990

Albanian Softshoe, 1988
    Village Voice, 33:100, 9 Feb. 1988

Bad Penny, 1989
    Village Voice, 34:97, 27 June 1989
    Village Voice, 35:74+, 29 May 1990

Cellophane, 1988
    Village Voice, 33:104+, 1 Nov. 1988

Crowbar, 1990
    Pesner, B., "Where the Underworld Can Meet the Elite," *TheaterWeek,*
        3:34–37, 26 Feb. 1990
    Commonweal, 117:223–224, 6 Apr. 1990
    Nation, 250:395–396, 19 Mar. 1990
    New Republic, 202:28–29, 26 Mar. 1990
    New York, 23:65, 12 Mar. 1990
    TheaterWeek, 3:12, 26 Feb. 1990
    TheaterWeek, 3:43, 5 Mar. 1990
    Village Voice, 35:105, 6 Mar. 1990
    Village Voice, 35:74+, 29 May 1990

Sincerity Forever, 1990
    Anderson, P., "The Sin in *Sincerity,*" *TheaterWeek,* 4:21–23, 17 Dec. 1990
    TheaterWeek, 3:13, 6 Aug. 1990

Terminal Hip: A Spiritual History of America through the Medium of Bad Language, 1989
    Village Voice, 35:99+, 16 Jan. 1990
    Village Voice, 35:74+, 29 May 1990

Whirligig, 1989
    American Theatre, 6:56, Mar. 1990
    TheaterWeek, 2:61–62, 20 Mar. 1989
    Village Voice, 33:95, 25 Apr. 1989

WIN WELLS

Gertrude Stein and a Companion, 1984
    Sheward, D., "Mixed Media: A Play Is a Play Is a Videoplay," *TheaterWeek,*
    1:22–24, 4 Apr. 1988

ANDREW WESKER

Yard Sale (two one-acts), 1988
    Village Voice, 33:90, 23 Feb. 1988

RICHARD WESLEY

The Past Is the Past, 1974
    TheaterWeek, 3:11, 4 Dec. 1989

The Talented Tenth, 1989
    American Theatre, 6:12, May 1989
    TheaterWeek, 3:6, 25 Sept. 1989
    TheaterWeek, 3:7, 6 Nov. 1989
    Village Voice, 34:122 + , 28 Nov. 1989

CHERYL WEST

Before It Hits Home, 1989 (workshop production)
    American Theatre, 6:58, Sept. 1989

MAE WEST (pseudonym: Jane Mast)

Diamond Lil, 1928
    American Theatre, 4:9–10, Mar. 1988

The Drag, 1926
    Curtin, K., "Introducing Gay Male Characters in a Broadway Play Secretly
    and by Night," pp. 69–88 in Curtin's *"We Can Always Call Them Bul-
    garians"*; also see pp. 96–99 and elsewhere

Pleasure Man, 1928
    Curtin, K., "Seventeen Live Fairies Onstage during a Presidential Year
    When New York Had to Be Good," pp. 127–139 and elsewhere in Cur-
    tin's *"We Can Always Call Them Bulgarians"*

Sex, 1926
    Life, 87:23, 20 May 1926
    Village Voice, 31:94, 8 July 1986

JOHN WEXLEY

They Shall Not Die, 1934
  Harap, L., *Dramatic Encounters,* p. 112

HUGH WHEELER

Hirsch, F., *Harold Prince and the American Musical Theater,* pp. 57, 72–73, 118,
  126, 144, 149–150
TheaterWeek, 1:37, 14 Mar. 1988

Look! We've Come Through!, 1961
  Stasio, M., "On *Look! We've Come Through,*" pp. 63–79 in Stasio's *Broadway's Beautiful Losers* (text of play on pp. 1–62)

HUGH WHEELER, LEONARD BERNSTEIN, RICHARD WILBUR, JOHN LATOUCHE, and STEPHEN SONDHEIM

Candide (revision of L. Hellman's book for the 1956 *Candide,* a musical version
  of Voltaire's story), 1973 (revised 1982)
  Brustein, R., "Musical into Opera," pp. 159–162 in Brustein's *Who Needs
  Theatre* (rpt. of *New Republic,* 187:28–29, 13 Dec. 1982)
  Green, S., *Broadway Musicals,* pp. 172, 239
  Hirsch, F., "Nights at the Opera," pp. 141–156 in Hirsch's *Harold Prince
  and the American Musical Theater*
  Ilson, C., *Harold Prince,* pp. 212–225
  TheaterWeek, 2:59–61, 19 Sept. 1988

HUGH WHEELER, HUGH MARTIN, and RALPH BLANE

Meet Me in St. Louis (stage version of the film musical), televised 1959; first
  staged 1960; revised, with a new book by Wheeler, 1989
  Buckley, M., "All Aboard for Broadway," *TheaterWeek,* 3:16–20, 6 Nov.
  1989
  Haun, H., "St. Louis to Broadway," *Playbill,* 8:8, 10, 12, 16, 31 Oct. 1989
  Mandelbaum, K., "Clunk, Clunk, Clunk Went the Trolley," *TheaterWeek,*
  3:41, 20 Nov. 1989
  Snow, L., "South African Money in a Broadway Show?" *TheaterWeek,*
  3:28–30, 23 Oct. 1989
  Commonweal, 117:52–54, 26 Jan. 1990
  New York, 22:130, 13 Nov. 1989
  New York Times Magazine, p. 78, 17 July 1988
  New Yorker, 65:110–111, 20 Nov. 1989
  TheaterWeek, 1:7, 30 May 1988
  TheaterWeek, 3:13, 2 Oct. 1989
  TheaterWeek, 3:20 + , 30 July 1990
  Village Voice, 34:138 + , 14 Nov. 1989

CHARLES WHITE

The Rehearsal; or, Barney's Old Man, published 1876
  Jones, E. H., *Native Americans as Shown on the Stage,* p. 140

EDGAR WHITE

The Case of Dr. Kola, 1987
  Shirakawa, S. H., "Theater Trends: Two for the Road," *TheaterWeek,* 1:20–
  23, 4 Jan. 1988

GEORGE WHITE

A Murderer among Us (adaptation of play by Y. Jamiaque), 1964
  Leonard, W. T., *Once Was Enough,* pp. 133–134

NORMAN H. WHITE, JR.
SEE AMBROSE ELWELL, JR.

ROBERT WHITEHEAD

Precious Land, 1937
  Kazacoff, G., *Dangerous Theatre,* pp. 214–218

RON WHYTE

American Theatre, 6:61, Dec. 1989

Disability: A Comedy, 1989
  American Theatre, 6:10, Sept. 1989

CHRISTOPHER WIDNEY

Big, Fat and Ugly with a Moustache, 1990
  Filichia, P., "Non-Traditional Family," *TheaterWeek,* 4:15–16, 1 Oct. 1990
  Playbill, 9:46, 30 Nov. 1990
  TheaterWeek, 4:9–10, 17 Sept. 1990

BERTHA WIERNIK

Destruction, 1932
  Leonard, W. T., *Once Was Enough,* pp. 42–43

RICHARD WILBUR
SEE HUGH WHEELER, LEONARD BERNSTEIN, RICHARD WILBUR,
JOHN LATOUCHE, and STEPHEN SONDHEIM

THORNTON WILDER

Blank, M., "Thornton Wilder: Broadway Production History," *Theatre History
  Studies,* 5:57–71, 1985
Gallup, D. C., "Thornton Wilder, 1947–1985," pp. 177–189 in Gallup's *Pigeons
  on the Granite*
Horgan, P., "Captain Wilder, T. N.," *American Scholar,* 59:569–575, Autumn
  1990

Kazan, E., *Elia Kazan*, pp. 192–193, 196, 197, 206, 209, 219, 220–221, 226, 339, 345

Prossnitz, G., "Thornton Wilder: Zum 90. Geburtstag," *Parnass*, 2:13+, 1987

Schroeder, P. R., "Thornton Wilder: Disparate Moments and Repetitive Patterns," pp. 53–75 in Schroeder's *The Presence of the Past in Modern American Drama*

The Long Christmas Dinner, 1966

    Playbill, 7:32, 30 Nov. 1988

The Matchmaker (revision of his play *The Merchant of Yonkers*, an adaptation of J. N. Nestroy's play *Einen Jux will er sich machen*), 1954

    Alter, M. P., "The Reception of Nestroy in America as Exemplified in Thornton Wilder's Play *The Matchmaker*," *Modern Austrian Literature*, 20(3–4):32–42, 1987

Our Town, 1939

    Bentley, J., *Hallie Flanagan*, pp. 361–362

    Erickson, J., "Appropriation and Transgression in Contemporary American Performance: The Wooster Group, Holly Hughes, and Karen Finley," *Theatre Journal*, 42:225–236, May 1990

    Haberman, D., *Our Town: An American Play*

    Joseph, K. A., "Grover's Corners Reinterpreted," pp. 70–74 in D. Radcliff-Umstead, ed., *Transformations*

    Lee, S.-K., "Zur Rezeption ostasiatischer Theatertradition in Thornton Wilders *Our Town*," *Arcadia*, 22(3):284–300, 1987

    Net, M., "The Way We Come Back into *Our Town*," *Cahiers Roumains d'Etudes Littéraires*, 1:103–116, 1988

    Newlin, J. T., Introduction, Our Town *on Stage*

    Raymond, G., "*Our Town* on TV," *TheaterWeek*, 3:38–39, 30 Oct. 1989

    Savran, D., "*Route 1 & 9 (The Last Act)*: The Disintegration of *Our Town*," pp. 9–45 in Savran's *The Wooster Group*

    Stephens, J. L., "Women in Pulitzer Prize Plays, 1918–1949," pp. 245–253 in H. K. Chinoy and L. W. Jenkins, eds., *Women in American Theatre*, rev. and enl. ed. (pp. 243–251 in 1981 ed.)

    America, 160:64, 28 Jan. 1989

    Hudson Review, 42:120–122, Spring 1989

    Nation, 248:102–103, 23 Jan. 1989

    New Republic, 200:29–31, 30 Jan. 1989

    New York, 22:48–49, 2 Jan. 1989

    New Yorker, 64:82, 19 Dec. 1988

    New Yorker, 65:111, 17 Apr. 1989

    Time, 131:71, 4 jan. 1988

    Time, 132:94, 19 Dec. 1988

Pullman Car Hiawatha, 1962

    Issacharoff, M., "Comic Space," pp. 185–198 in J. Redmond, ed., *The Theatrical Space*

The Skin of Our Teeth, 1942
    Counts, M. L, *Coming Home,* pp. 84–85, 114–115, 132–133, 182
    Kazan, E., *Elia Kazan,* pp. 192–193, 197, 205–213, 216, 217, 219–221, 223,
    225, 305, 345, 478, 479, 597
    Stephens, J. L., "Women in Pulitzer Prize Plays, 1918–1949," pp. 245–253
    in H. K. Chinoy and L. W. Jenkins, eds., *Women in American Theatre,*
    rev. and enl. ed. (pp. 243–251 in 1981 ed.)

MAX WILK

Mr. Williams and Miss Wood (based on Wilk and A. Wood's book *Represented
    by Audrey Wood*), 1989
    TheaterWeek, 3:6, 4 Dec. 1989

EDWARD WILKINS

My Wife's Mirror, 1856
    Miller, T. L., "The Image of Fashionable Society in American Comedy,
    1840–1870," pp. 243–252 in J. L. Fisher and S. Watt, eds., *When They
    Weren't Doing Shakespeare*

Young New York, 1856
    Miller, T. L., "The Image of Fashionable Society in American Comedy,
    1840–1870," pp. 243–252 in J. L. Fisher and S. Watt, eds., *When They
    Weren't Doing Shakespeare*

ESPY WILLIAMS

Watson, C. S., "The First Modern Dramatist of the South: Espy Williams,"
    Southern Quarterly, 27(2):77–91, Winter 1989

JESSE LYNCH WILLIAMS

Why Marry?, 1917
    Stephens, J. L., "Women in Pulitzer Prize Plays, 1918–1949," pp. 245–253
    in H. K. Chinoy and L. W. Jenkins, eds., *Women in American Theatre,*
    rev. and enl. ed. (pp. 243–251 in 1981 ed.)

KAREN WILLIAMS

Octopus, 1990
    TheaterWeek, 4:42, 10 Sept. 1990

PAULETTE WILLIAMS
SEE NTOZAKE SHANGE

TENNESSEE WILLIAMS (Thomas Lanier Williams)

Abbott, A. S., "Arthur Miller and Tennessee Williams," pp. 129–147 in Abbott's *The Vital Lie*

Balachandran, K., "Marriage and Family Life in Tennessee Williams," *Notes on Mississippi Writers,* 21(2):69–76, 1989

————, "Tennessee Williams in India: Stagings and Scholarship," *Notes on Mississippi Writers,* 20(1):17–27, 1988

Bloom, H., ed., *Tennessee Williams*

Bonner, T., Jr., "On Stage in New Orleans: A Photo Essay of Tennessee Williams's Plays," *Studies in American Drama, 1945–Present,* 3:79–98, 1988

Borny, G., "Williams and Kazan: The Creative Synthesis," *Australasian Drama Studies,* 8:33–47, Apr. 1986

Boxhill, R., *Tennessee Williams*

Bray, R., "Time as an Enemy in the Short Plays of Tennessee Williams," *Tennessee Williams Literary Journal,* 1(1):51–60, Spring 1989

Capote, T., "Remembering Tennessee," *Playboy,* 36:228+, Jan. 1989

Cassin, M., "Curtain Call for Tennessee," *Tennessee Williams Literary Journal,* 1(1):44, Spring 1989

Curtin, K., *"We Can Always Call Them Bulgarians,"* pp. 283–284, 299–300, 321–326

Davidson, R., "The Kindness of Friends," *Mirabella,* 1:36, 38, May 1990

Demastes, W. W., *Beyond Naturalism,* pp. 24–25

Falk, S. L., *Tennessee Williams,* 2nd ed.

Gelderman, C., "Homage to Tennessee," *American Theatre,* 5:44–45, June 1988

Goodman, C., "The Fox's Cubs: Lillian Hellman, Arthur Miller, and Tennessee Williams," pp. 130–142 in J. Schlueter, ed., *Modern American Drama*

Griffin, J., "Hellman, Williams, Hemingway and Cowley: Views and Interviews," *Canadian Review of American Studies,* 18(4):519–525, Winter 1987

Hale, A., "Two on a Streetcar," *Tennessee Williams Literary Journal,* 1(1):31–43, Spring 1989

Hall, P., "The Spirit of 'Orpheus,'" *Playbill,* 8:18, 20, 31 Oct. 1989

Kakutani, M., "Tennessee Williams," pp. 194–199 in Kakutani's *The Poet at the Piano* (rpt. of *The New York Times,* Mar. 1983)

Kazan, E., *Elia Kazan,* pp. 27, 162, 261, 273, 326, 327, 328, 329–330, 331, 334–337, 339, 340–342, 344, 346, 347–351, 352, 353–354, 356, 361, 365, 369, 373, 383, 384, 426, 433, 434, 436, 442, 443, 453, 454, 485, 488, 494–498, 540–546, 562, 564, 587, 595–596, 659, 663, 719, 746, 783, 822–823

Londré, F., *Tennessee Williams*

Londré, F. H., "Tennessee Williams (26 March 1911–24 February 1983)," pp. 488–517 in P. C. Kolin, ed., *American Playwrights since 1945*

Madden, D., "Tennessee and Carson: Notes on a Concept for a Play," *Pembroke Magazine,* 20:96–103, 1988

Mamet, D., "Epitaph for Tennessee Williams," pp. 101–102 in Mamet's *Writing in Restaurants*

McBride, M., "Loneliness and Longing in Selected Plays of Carson McCullers and Tennessee Williams," pp. 143–150 in J. Schlueter, ed., *Modern American Drama*

McHaney, P. A., "A Checklist of Tennessee Williams Scholarship," *Tennessee Williams Literary Journal,* 1(1):65–76, Spring 1989

————, "Tennessee Williams 1911–1983," pp. 385–429 in M. C. Roudané, ed., *Contemporary Authors Bibliographical Series*

Miller, J. Y., "The Three Halves of Tennessee Williams's World," *Studies in the Literary Imagination,* 21:83–95, Fall 1988

Monteiro, G., "Tennessee Williams Misremembers Hemingway," *Hemingway Review,* 10:71, Fall 1990

Murray, T. D., *Evolving Texts*

Myers, L., "Critic, Cornered: Michael Feingold Speaks Out" (interview), *TheaterWeek,* 1:28–34, 11 Jan. 1988

Parrott, J., "Tennessee Travels to Taos," *Tennessee Williams Literary Journal,* 1(1):9–13, Spring 1989

Patrachkova, C., "L'illusion en tant qu'autodefense (dans quelques Pièces d'Eugene O'Neill, de Tennessee Williams et d'Edward Albee)," *Literaturna Misul,* 31(9):73–78, 1987

Pawley, T. D., "Experimental Theatre Seminar: Or, The Basic Training of Tennessee Williams," *Iowa Review,* 19(1):65–76, Winter 1989

Pierson, C. B., "A Persistent Dream: The Tennessee Williams/New Orleans Literary Festival," *Tennessee Williams Literary Journal,* 1(1):61–64, Spring 1989

Rader, D., "Tennessee Fever," *Harper's Bazaar,* 122:364–365 + , Sept. 1989

Real, J., "An Interview with Tennessee Williams," *Southern Quarterly,* 26(3):40–49, Spring 1988

Roberts, M., "Tennessee Rising," *Vogue,* 179:706–709 + , Sept. 1989

Ross, M. B., "The Making of Tennessee Williams: Imaging a Life of Imagination," *Southern Humanities Review,* 21(2):117–131, Spring 1987

Savran, D., *Danger,* n. pag.

Schroeder, P. R., "Tennessee Williams: Memory and the Passing Moment," pp. 105–124 in Schroeder's *The Presence of the Past in Modern American Drama*

Simon, J., "Brothers under the Skin: Eugene O'Neill and Tennessee Williams," pp. 62–76 in Simon's *The Sheep from the Goats* (rpt. of *Hudson Review,* 39:553–565, Winter 1987)

Smith, B., *Costly Performances*

"The Tennessee Williams Calendar," *Tennessee Williams Literary Journal,* 1(1): 77–80, Spring 1989

Thompson, J. J., *Tennessee Williams' Plays*

Timpane, J., " 'Weak and Divided People': Tennessee Williams and the Written Woman," pp. 171–180 in J. Schlueter, ed., *Feminist Rereadings in Modern American Drama*

Van Decker, L., "A World of Light and Shadow: The Plays of Tennessee Williams," *Columbia Library Columns,* 38(2):13–21, Feb. 1989

Van Laan, T. F., " 'Shut Up!' 'Be Quiet!' 'Hush!': Talk and Its Suppression in Three Plays by Tennessee Williams," *Comparative Drama,* 22:244–265, Fall 1988

Williams, T., *Five O'Clock Angel*

Windham, D., *Lost Friendships*

Wood, A., and M. Wilk, *Represented by Audrey Wood*

American Theatre, 5:41–42, Apr. 1988

Playbill, 7:16, 30 June 1989

Playbill, 9:46, 31 Dec. 1990

TheaterWeek, 1:39, 21 Mar. 1988

TheaterWeek, 3:33, 2 Apr. 1990

Village Voice, 34:103 + , 3 Oct. 1989

Camino Real, 1953

>   Kazan, E., *Elia Kazan,* pp. 443, 485, 488, 489, 494–498, 502, 503, 545, 598
>   Miller, J. Y., "The Three Halves of Tennessee Williams's World," *Studies in the Literary Imagination,"* 21(2):83–95, Fall 1988
>   Renaux, S., "The Real and the Royal in Tennessee Williams' *Camino Real,"* *Ilha do Desterro,* 3(7):43–66, July 1982

Cat on a Hot Tin Roof, 1955

>   Backalenick, I., "A Fat Cat on a Hot Tin Roof," *TheaterWeek,* 3:22–25, 26 Mar. 1990
>   Filichia, P., "Steel Magnolia," *TheaterWeek,* 3:35–37, 16 July 1990
>   Haun, H., "Kathleen's *Cat,"* *Playbill,* 8:8, 12, 31 Mar. 1990
>   Hubbard, K., "The Original Maggie the Cat, Maria St. Just, Remembers Her Loving Friend Tennessee Williams," *People Weekly,* 33:93–95, 2 Apr. 1990
>   Kazan, E., *Elia Kazan,* pp. 540–544, 545
>   Lloyd, B., "Star Turner," *TheaterWeek,* 3:35–36, 16 Apr. 1990
>   Martin, J., "Du geste à la parole dans *Cat on a Hot Tin Roof,"* *Bulletin de la Soc. de Stylistique Anglaise,* 7:149–160, 1985
>   Stuart, J., "Sex, Lies and Kathleen Turner," *Mirabella,* 1:32, Apr. 1990
>   *America,* 164:410, 21 Apr. 1990
>   *Journal of Canadian Studies,* 24:157, Winter 1989/1990
>   *Nation,* 250:644, 7 May 1990
>   *New York,* 23:93–94, 2 Apr. 1990
>   *New Yorker,* 66:88–89, 2 Apr. 1990
>   *Newsweek,* 115:54, 2 Apr. 1990
>   *Playbill,* 6:42–43, May 1988
>   *TheaterWeek,* 1:38–39, 21 Mar. 1988
>   *TheaterWeek,* 3:24, 4 Sept. 1989
>   *Time,* 135:71–72, 2 Apr. 1990
>   *Village Voice,* 35:101, 3 Apr. 1990

Clothes for a Summer Hotel, 1980

>   Adler, T. P., "When Ghosts Supplant Memories: Tennessee Williams' *Clothes for a Summer Hotel,"* *Southern Literary Journal,* 19(2):5–19, Spring 1987
>   Anderson, H., "Tennessee Williams' *Clothes for a Summer Hotel*: Feminine Sensibilities and the Artist," *Publications of the Mississippi Philological Association,* 1–8, 1988

The Glass Menagerie, 1944

>   Berutti, E. B., "*The Glass Menagerie*: Escapism as a Way out of Fragmentation," *Estudos Anglo-Americanos,* 12–13:78–89, 1988–1989
>   Bloom, H., ed., *Tennessee Williams's* The Glass Menagerie
>   Click, P. C., "The Uncertain Universe of *The Glass Menagerie*: The Influence of the New Physics on Tennessee Williams," *Journal of American Culture,* 12:41–45, Spring 1989
>   Fichandler, Z., "Casting for a Different Truth," *American Theatre,* 5:18–23, May 1988
>   Greiff, L. K., "Fathers, Daughters, and Spiritual Sisters: Marsha Norman's

'night, Mother and Tennessee Williams's The Glass Menagerie," Text and Performance Quarterly, 9(3):224–228, July 1989

Gunn, D. W., "More Than Just a Little Chekhovian: The Sea Gull as a Source for the Characters in The Glass Menagerie," Modern Drama, 33:313–321, Sept. 1990

Henry, W. A., III, "Heartland Heartiness," Time, 132:83–84, 12 Sept. 1988

Jones, J. H., "The Missing Link: The Father in The Glass Menagerie," Notes on Mississippi Writers, 20(1):29–38, 1988

Presley, D. E., "The Glass Menagerie: An American Memory

Robinson, H., "A Glasnost Menagerie," American Theatre, 5:24–29, Sept. 1988

Thierfelder, W. R., III, "Williams's The Glass Menagerie," Explicator, 48:284–285, Summer 1990

Theatre Journal, 42:121–123, Mar. 1990

Theatre Journal, 42:267–269, May 1990

The Gnädiges Fräulein, 1966

Debusscher, G., "The Gnädiges Fräulein: Williams's Self-Portrait among the Ruins," pp. 63–74 in G. Debusscher, H. I. Schvey, and M. Maufort, eds., New Essays on American Drama

Heavenly Grass, or the Miracle at Granny's, unpublished libretto

Debusscher, G., "Tennessee Williams's Black Nativity: An Unpublished Libretto," pp. 127–133 in G. Debusscher and M. Maufort, eds., American Literature in Belgium

The Milk Train Doesn't Stop Here Anymore, 1962 (later revised)

Phillips, G., "Underrated Williams: A Reconsideration of The Seven Descents of Myrtle and The Milk Train Doesn't Stop Here Anymore," Tennessee Williams Literary Journal, 1(1):45–50, Spring 1989

Nation, 246:100, 23 Jan. 1988

New York, 21:58+, 11 Jan. 1988

The Night of the Iguana, 1959

New York, 21:48, 18 July 1988

New Yorker, 64:77, 11 July 1988

Playbill, 7:20, 31 July 1989

Village Voice, 33:92, 12 July 1988

Orpheus Descending (revision of his Battle of Angels), 1957

Guare, J., and B. Branson, "Radical Descent," Andy Warhol's Interview, 19:72–73, Oct. 1989

Harris, J., "Peter Hall Condescending," TheaterWeek, 3:41, 9 Oct. 1989

Henry, W. A., III, "Vanessa Ascending," Time, 134:109, 112, 9 Oct. 1989

Israel, L., "Orpheus Unencumbered," TheaterWeek, 3:20–23, 2 Oct. 1989

Raymond, G., "An Interview with Vanessa Redgrave," TheaterWeek, 2:14–20, 31 July 1989

————, "Orpheus Descending: Radical Politics of the Soul," TheaterWeek, 3:14–19, 2 Oct. 1989

Commonweal, 116:642–643, 17 Nov. 1989

Connoisseur, 219:44, Dec. 1989
Nation, 249:609–611, 20 Nov. 1989
New Republic, 201:25–27, 30 Oct. 1989
New York, 22:86–87, 9 Oct. 1989
New Yorker, 65:125, 9 Oct. 1989
Newsweek, 114:86, 9 Oct. 1989
Playbill, 8:97, 31 Oct. 1989
TheaterWeek, 3:20, 4 Sept. 1989
TheaterWeek, 3:38, 15 Jan. 1990
Time, 133:102, 2 Jan. 1989
Village Voice, 34:89 + , 31 Jan. 1989
Village Voice, 34:103, 3 Oct. 1989 (Gordon Rogoff)
Village Voice, 34:104 + , 3 Oct. 1989 (Michael Feingold)

Out Cry (revision of his *The Two-Character Play*), 1971
  Kahn, S. M., "Listening to *Out Cry*: Bird of Paradox in a Gilded Cage,"
    pp. 41–62 in G. Debusscher, H. I. Schvey, and M. Maufort, eds., *New
    Essays on American Drama*

Period of Adjustment, 1959
  Counts, M. L., *Coming Home,* pp. 79–80, 121, 149, 181–182

The Rose Tattoo, 1951
  Gómez García, A., "*The Rose Tattoo* y *The Roman Spring of Mrs. Stone*:
    Cara y Cruz de Una Misma Moneda," *Revista Canaria de Estudios In-
    gleses,* 16:183–192, Apr. 1988
  Marcuson, L. R., *The Stage Immigrant,* pp. 213–220

The Seven Descents of Myrtle (revised version of his *Kingdom of Earth*), 1968
  Phillips, G., "Underrated Williams: A Reconsideration of *The Seven De-
    scents of Myrtle* and *The Milk Train Doesn't Stop Here Anymore*," *Ten-
    nessee Williams Literary Journal,* 1(1):45–50, Spring 1989

Something Cloudy, Something Clear, 1981
  Clum, J. M., "*Something Cloudy, Something Clear*: Homophobic Discourse
    in Tennessee Williams," *South Atlantic Quarterly,* 88:161–179, Winter
    1989

A Streetcar Named Desire, 1947
  Adler, T. P., A Streetcar Named Desire: *The Moth and the Lantern*
  Barranger, M. S., "Three Women Called Blanche: Tandy, Hagen and
    Leigh," *Tennessee Williams Literary Journal,* 1(1):15–30, Spring 1989
  Bloom, H., ed., *Tennessee Williams's* A Streetcar Named Desire
  Burks, D. G., " 'Treatment Is Everything': The Creation and Casting of
    Blanche and Stanley in Tennessee Williams' *Streetcar*," *Library Chronicle
    of the University of Texas,* 41:16–39, 1987
  Carr, J., "The Kindness of Friends," *Playbill,* 6:18, 20, 24, May 1988
  Debusscher, G., "Trois images de las modernite chez Tennessee Williams:
    Un Micro-analyse d'*Un Tramway Nommé Désir*," *Journal of Dramatic
    Theory and Criticism,* 3(1):143–155, Fall 1988

Gilbert, S. M., and S. Gubar, *The War of the Words,* pp. 50–52, 105

Kazan, E., *Elia Kazan,* pp. 74, 96, 115, 183, 301, 327–331, 334–354, 359, 361, 364, 502, 544

Kolin, P. C., "*A Streetcar Named Desire*: A Playwrights' Forum," *Michigan Quarterly Review,* 29(2):173–203, Spring 1990

——, "Olivier to Williams: An Introduction" (includes a letter from Sir Laurence Olivier to Williams about the London premiere of *Streetcar*), *Missouri Review,* 13(3):143–157, 1991

——, "'Red-Hot!' in *A Streetcar Named Desire,*" *Notes on Contemporary Literature,* 19(4):6–8, Sept. 1989

Kolin, P. C., and S. Shao, "The First Production of *A Streetcar Named Desire* in Mainland China," *Tennessee Williams Literary Journal,* 2(1):19–31, Winter 1990–1991

Morse, D. E., "The 'Life Lie' in Three Plays by O'Neill, Williams, and Miller," pp. 273–277 in M. Jurak, ed., *Cross-Cultural Studies*

Schnathmeier, S., "The Unity of Place in Elia Kazan's Film Version of *A Streetcar Named Desire* by Tennessee Williams: A Traditional Dramatic Category Seen from a Semiotic Point of View," *Kodikas,* 10(1–2):83–93, Jan.–July 1987

Shirakawa, S. H., "Strange Romances," *TheaterWeek,* 1:20–27, 25 Apr. 1988

Spector, S., "Alternative Visions of Blanche DuBois: Uta Hagen and Jessica Tandy in *A Streetcar Named Desire,*" *Modern Drama,* 32(4):545–560, Dec. 1989

Stephens, J. L., "Women in Pulitzer Prize Plays, 1918–1949," pp. 245–253 in H. K. Chinoy and L. W. Jenkins, eds., *Women in American Theatre,* rev. and enl. ed. (pp. 243–251 in 1981 ed.)

Taylor, J. B., "*A Streetcar Named Desire*: Evolution of Blanche and Stanley," *Publications of the Mississippi Philological Association,* 63–66, 1986

Vlasopolos, A., "Authorizing History: Victimization in *A Streetcar Named Desire,*" pp. 149–170 in J. Schlueter, ed., *Feminist Rereadings in Modern American Drama*

Zuber-Skerritt, O., "Towards a Typology of Literary Translation: Drama Translation Science," *Meta,* 33(4):485–490, 1988

Nation, 246:547–548, 16 Apr. 1988

New York, 21:88+, 21 Mar. 1988

New Yorker, 64:81–82, 28 Mar. 1988

TheaterWeek, 2:61, 20 Mar. 1989

Village Voice, 33:97, 22 Mar. 1988

Summer and Smoke, 1947

Sheehy, H., "*Summer and Smoke,*" *Playbill,* 8:S1-S16, 31 July 1990 (excerpt from Sheey's book *Margo: The Life and Theatre of Margo Jones*)

American Theatre, 6:10, Jan. 1990

Los Angeles, 33:234+, Apr. 1988

TheaterWeek, 3:10, 8 Jan. 1990

Sweet Bird of Youth, 1956

Debusscher, G., "And the Sailor Turned into a Princess: New Light on the

Genesis of *Sweet Bird of Youth,*" *Studies in American Drama, 1945–Present,* 1:25–31, 1986

Kolin, P. C., "Parallels between *Desire under the Elms* and *Sweet Bird of Youth,*" *Eugene O'Neill Review,* 13(2):23–35, Fall 1989

Maclean's, 101:66, 2 May 1988

27 Wagons Full of Cotton, 1955

Seff, R., "The Boob Tube Gets a Touch of Class," *TheaterWeek,* 3:28–32, 4 Dec. 1989

TOM WILLIAMS

New Business, 1990

Weiner, B., "Dramaturgy in Denver," *TheaterWeek,* 3:30–32, 25 June 1990

WILLIAM CARLOS WILLIAMS

Whitaker, T. R., *William Carlos Williams,* rev. ed.

A Dream of Love, published 1948, revised 1961

Magid, B., "*A Dream of Love*: A Script from the Mannahatta Theatre Club Performance (1961)," *William Carlos Williams Review,* 14(2):77–78, Fall 1988

CALDER WILLINGHAM

End as a Man (dramatization of his novel), 1953

Curtin, K., *"We Can Always Call Them Bulgarians,"* pp. 299–300

Playbill, 6:36, Jan. 1988

NATHANIEL P. WILLIS

Tortesa the Usurer, 1839

Harap, L., *The Image of the Jew in American Literature,* pp. 201–202

AUGUST WILSON

Backalenick, I., "A Lesson from Lloyd Richards," *TheaterWeek,* 3:17–19, 16 Apr. 1990

Barbour, D., "August Wilson's Here to Stay," *TheaterWeek,* 1:8–14, 18 Apr. 1988

Ching, M.-L., "Wrestling against History," *Theater,* 19(3):70–71, Summer-Fall 1988

Demastes, W. W., *Beyond Naturalism,* p. 157

Glover, M. E., "Two Notes on August Wilson: The Songs of a Marked Man," *Theater,* 19(3):69–70, Summer-Fall 1988

Harrison, P. C., "The (R)evolution of Black Theatre," *American Theatre,* 6:30–32, 116–118, Oct. 1989

Henry, W. A., III, "Exorcising the Demons of Memory," *Time,* 131:77–78, 11 Apr. 1988

Hunter-Gault, C., "On Broadway: Everybody's America" (interview), *Vogue,*
   178:200+, Aug. 1988
Moyers, B., *Bill Moyers' World of Ideas,* ed. B. S. Flowers, pp. 167–180 (PBS
   interview Oct. 1988; an excerpt was reprinted in *American Theatre,* 6:12–17,
   54–56, June 1989)
Neff, R., "A Talk with Lloyd Richards," *TheaterWeek,* 1:15–19, 18 Apr. 1988
Nixon, W., "House of Playwrights," *TheaterWeek,* 2:48–52, 19 Sept. 1988
O'Neill, M. C., "August Wilson (27 April 1945–)," pp. 518–527 in P. C. Kolin,
   ed., *American Playwrights since 1945*
O'Quinn, J., "Stages of History," *American Theatre,* 5:19–23, 53, Sept. 1988
Savran, D., "August Wilson," pp. 288–305 in Savran's *In Their Own Words*
"2nd Pulitzer for Wilson," *American Theatre,* 7:52, June 1990
Shafer, Y., "An Interview with August Wilson," *Journal of Dramatic Theory and
   Criticism,* 4(1):161–174, Fall 1989
Connoisseur, 217:92–97, Mar. 1987
Pittsburgh Magazine, 20:12+, Sept. 1989
Pittsburgh Magazine, 21:28+, Jan. 1990
Playbill, 6:50, June 1988
Playbill, 8:48, 30 Nov. 1989
Playbill, 8:23, 31 July 1990
TheaterWeek, 3:25, 25 Dec. 1989
Vanity Fair, 52:102+, Apr. 1989

Fences, 1983
   Haun, H., "Batter Up, Billy Dee," *Playbill,* 6:20, 22, 24–25, Apr. 1988
   Simon, J., "The Playwright and the Audience," *TheaterWeek,* 3:26–29, 16
      Apr. 1990
   Detroit Monthly, 14:37, Jan. 1990
   Los Angeles, 33:260+, Nov. 1988
   Westways, 80:6, Nov. 1988

Joe Turner's Come and Gone, 1984 as *Mill Hand's Lunch Bucket,* revised 1985,
   1986
   Euba, F., *Archetypes, Imprecators, and Victims of Fate,* pp. 147, 151, 157
   Felton, T., "Delroy Lindo: 'A Shiny Man,'" *TheaterWeek,* 2:46–49, 15 Aug.
      1988
   America, 158:410+, 16 Apr. 1988
   Georgia Review, 42:599–600, Fall 1988
   Hudson Review, 41:518, Autumn 1988
   Massachusetts Review, 30:131–132, Spring 1989
   New Leader, 71:23, 18 Apr. 1988
   New York, 21:118, 11 Apr. 1988
   New Yorker, 64:107, 11 Apr. 1988
   Newsweek, 111:82, 11 Apr. 1988
   San Diego Magazine, 40:56+, Apr. 1988
   Time, 133:103, 20 Feb. 1989
   Village Voice, 33:104, 5 Apr. 1988

Ma Rainey's Black Bottom, 1984
   Playbill, 8:96, 31 Dec. 1989

TheaterWeek, 3:12, 13 Nov. 1989

The Piano Lesson, 1987
    Drake, S., "Spoken Music," *Playbill,* 8:18, 20, 30 Apr. 1990
    Greene, A., "Charles S. Dutton: Not Ready to Accept Defeat,"
        TheaterWeek, 3:36–39, 18 June 1990
    Migler, R., "An Elegant Duet," *Gentlemen's Quarterly,* 60:114+, Apr. 1990
    "Playwright August Wilson Wins Second Pulitzer Prize," *Jet,* 78:13, 30 Apr.
        1990
    Scher, H., "Turning 'Profit,'" *TheaterWeek,* 3:20–25, 16 Apr. 1990
    Spillane, M., "Pulitzerized *Piano,* Trying-Out *Trains,*" *TheaterWeek,* 3:37–
        38, 7 May 1990
    American Theatre, 4:6, Feb. 1988
    American Theatre, 5:14, Feb. 1989
    Chicago, 38:44, Feb. 1989
    Chicago, 38:141–143, Apr. 1989
    Commonweal, 117:422–423, 13 July 1990
    Hudson Review, 43:471–473, Autumn 1990
    Massachusetts Review, 29:90–92, Spring 1988
    Nation, 250:832–833, 11 June 1990
    New Republic, 202:28–30, 21 May 1990
    New York, 23:82–83, 7 May 1990
    New Yorker, 66:82–83, 30 Apr. 1990
    San Diego Magazine, 41:44+, July 1989
    TheaterWeek, 2:4–5, 24 July 1989
    TheaterWeek, 3:22, 4 Sept. 1989
    TheaterWeek, 3:14, 28 May 1990
    TheaterWeek, 3:24, 2 July 1990
    Time, 133:69, 30 Jan. 1989
    Time, 135:100, 1 Jan. 1990
    Time, 135:99, 23 Apr. 1990

Two Trains Running, 1990
    Dworkin, N., "Blood on the Tracks," *American Theatre,* 7:8–9, May 1990
    Spillane, M., "Pulitzerized *Piano,* Trying-Out *Trains,*" *TheaterWeek,* 3:37–
        38, 7 May 1990
    TheaterWeek, 3:18, 26 Mar. 1990
    Time, 136:54, 31 Dec. 1990

DORIC WILSON

Street Theatre, 1981
    Hall, R., "Eleven Different Directions," *American Theatre,* 5:32–33, Dec.
        1988
    Shewey, D., "Gay Theatre Grows Up," *American Theatre,* 5:10–17, 52–53,
        May 1988

LANFORD WILSON

Barbour, D., "A Talk with Lanford Wilson," *TheaterWeek,* 2:16–17, 5 Dec.
    1988

Barnett, G. A., "Recreating the Magic: An Interview with Lanford Wilson," *Ball State University Forum*, 25(2):57–74, Spring 1984

Bennetts, L., "Lanford Wilson & Terrence McNally: On Love, Responsibility, and Sexual Obsession," *Vogue*, 178:216+, Feb. 1988

Botto, L., "Circle Rep Turns 20," *Playbill*, 7:99–102, 31 Dec. 1988

Busby, M., *Lanford Wilson*

Demastes, W. W., *Beyond Naturalism*, p. 158

Harriott, E., "Lanford Wilson: To Vanish without a Trace," pp. 19–35, and "Interview with Lanford Wilson," pp. 36–58, in Harriott's *American Voices*

Jacobi, M. J., "Lanford Wilson 1937– ," pp. 431–454 in M. C. Roudané, ed., *Contemporary Authors Bibliographical Series*

——, "The Comic Vision of Lanford Wilson," *Studies in the Literary Imagination*, 21(2):119–134, Fall 1988

Kakutani, M., "Lanford Wilson," pp. 200–206 in Kakutani's *The Poet at the Piano* (rpt. of *The New York Times*, June 1984)

King, K., "Lanford Wilson," pp. 235–243 in King's *Ten Modern American Playwrights*

Robertson, C. W., "Lanford Wilson (13 April 1937–)," pp. 528–539 in P. C. Kolin, ed., *American Playwrights since 1945*

Savran, D., "Lanford Wilson," pp. 306–320 in Savran's *In Their Own Words*

Wiles, T. J., "Talk Drama: Recent Writers in the American Theater," *Amerikastudien*, 32(1):65–79, 1987

Playbill, 7:30, 31 Jan. 1989

Playbill, 7:48, 28 Feb. 1989 (interview)

Vanity Fair, 50:135, Mar. 1987

Village Voice, 33:22+, 28 June 1988

W, 16:34, 5 Oct. 1987

Angels Fall, 1982

    Erben, R., "The Western Holdup Play: The Pilgrimage Continues," *Western American Literature*, 23(4):311–322, Feb. 1989

Burn This, 1986

    Haun, H., "A Malkovich Cocktail," *Playbill*, 6:8, 12, 14, Mar. 1988

    Shirakawa, S. H., "Strange Romances," *TheaterWeek*, 1:20–27, 25 Apr. 1988

    America, 158:42, 16 Jan. 1988

    Chicago, 36:163+, Nov. 1987

    Georgia Review, 42:597–598, Fall 1988

    Hudson Review, 41:187–188, Spring 1988

    Playbill, 8:65, 31 July 1990

    TheaterWeek, 3:26, 25 Dec. 1989

    Vanity Fair, 50:135, Mar. 1987

    Village Voice, 32:112+, 27 Oct. 1987

    W, 16:25, 14 Dec. 1987

5th of July, 1978 (revised, *Fifth of July*, 1980)

    Counts, M. L., *Coming Home*, pp. 103–105, 147–148, 197, 207

    TheaterWeek, 3:42, 26 Mar. 1990

The Hot l Baltimore, 1973
  Cohen, E. M., *Working on a New Play,* p. 87

The Mound Builders, 1975
  Callens, J., "When 'The Center Cannot Hold' or the Problem of Mediation in Lanford Wilson's *The Mound Builders,*" pp. 201–226 in G. Debusscher, H. I. Schvey, and M. Maufort, eds., *New Essays on American Drama*

A Poster of the Cosmos, 1988
  New Yorker, 64:75, 25 July 1988

The Rimers of Eldritch, 1965
  Nation, 248:103–104, 23 Jan. 1989
  Village Voice, 33:119–120, 13 Dec. 1988

Talley's Folly, 1979
  Brustein, R., "Two Couples," pp. 57–61 in Brustein's *Who Needs Theatre* (rpt. of *New Republic,* 182:28, 5 Apr. 1980)

The Three Sisters (Wilson's translation of Chekhov's play), 1984
  TheaterWeek, 2:3, 8 May 1989

ROBERT WILSON

Armstrong, G. S., "Images in the Interstice: The Phenomenal Theater of Robert Wilson," *Modern Drama,* 31(4):571–587, Dec. 1988
di Niscemi, M., "Working with Robert Wilson," *Columbia Library Columns,* 38(1):12–22, Nov. 1988
Holmberg, A., "A Conversation with Robert Wilson and Heiner Müller" (interview), *Modern Drama,* 31(3):454–458, Sept. 1988
Marx, R., "Image Maker," *Opera News,* 55:24+, Sept. 1990
Pratt, D., "Robert Wilson—The Early Years," *Columbia Library Columns,* 38(1):3–11, Nov. 1988
Shank, T., "Robert Wilson," pp. 125–134 in Shank's *American Alternative Theater*
Shyer, L., *Robert Wilson and His Collaborators*
———, "Secret Sharers," *American Theatre,* 6:12–19, Sept. 1989 (excerpted from Shyer's *Robert Wilson and His Collaborators*)
[Stearns, R., and J. Rockwell], *Robert Wilson: The Theater of Images*
Swed, M., "Music Theater," *Opera News,* 53:66, Sept. 1988
Thomson, C. W., "Theaterguru Robert Wilson: Transnationales Theater der Grenzüberschreitungen am Bespiel seines Neuesten Stückes," *Parnass,* 2:80+, 1989
Wirth, A., "Interculturalism and Iconophilia in the New Theatre," *Performing Arts Journal,* 33(11[3])/34(12[1]):176–185, 1988/1989
Zurbrugg, N., "Post-modernism and the Multi-media Sensibility: Heiner Müller's *Hamletmachine* and the Art of Robert Wilson," *Modern Drama,* 31(3):439–453, Sept. 1988
American Theatre, 5:51, Feb. 1989

American Theatre, 7:63, Sept. 1990
TheaterWeek, 4:10, 3 Dec. 1990

The Golden Windows, 1982
   Fischer-Lichte, E., "The Quest for Meaning," *Stanford Literature Review,*
   3(1):137–155, Spring 1986

Swan Song (adaptation of short play by Chekhov), 1989
   Village Voice, 35:102, 3 Apr. 1990

What Room (a "three-minute play"), 1990
   Carpenter, B., "Just Add Water . . . ," *TheaterWeek,* 3:32–33, 28 May 1990
   (text of play included)

ROBERT WILSON and DAVID BYRNE

The Forest (a retelling of the *Gilgamesh*), 1988
   Marranca, B., "*The Forest* as Archive: Wilson and Interculturalism," *Per-
   forming Arts Journal,* 33(11[3])/34(12[1]):36–44, 1988/1989
   Shyer, L., "*The Forest*: A Preview of the Next Wilson-Byrne Collaboration,"
   Theater, 19(3):6–11, Summer-Fall 1988
   Hudson Review, 42:119–120, Spring 1989
   Theatre Crafts, 23:46–48+, Jan. 1989

ROBERT WILSON and PHILIP GLASS

the CIVIL warS: a tree is best measured when it is down, 1982–1984 (others also
   collaborated on this project)
   "Jenseits der interpretation: Anmerkungen zum Text von Robert Wilsons/
   Heiner Müllers *CIVIL warS,*" pp. 191–201 in A. Schöne, W. Vosskamp,
   and E. Lämmert, eds., *Kontroversen alte und neue, XI*
   Wilson, R., *Robert Wilson's* CIVIL warS: *Drawings, Models, and Docu-
   mentation,* ed. A. P. A. Belloli

Einstein on the Beach, 1976
   Brustein, R., "Expanding Einstein's Universe," pp. 123–127 in Brustein's
   Who Needs Theatre (rpt. of *New Republic,* 192:23–25, 28 Jan. 1985)
   Dance Magazine, 63:26+, Mar. 1989

ROBERT WILSON, HEINER MÜLLER, CHRISTOPHER ESCHENBACH, and MARTIN PERLMAN

Quartet, 1988 in New York City (*Quartett* for the 1987 German production;
   Eschenbach did the music for the German production, Perlman for the New
   York City production; a condensed adaptation of *Les Liaisons dangereuses* by
   C. de Laclos)
   Artforum, 26:151–152, May 1988
   Village Voice, 33:93–94, 1 Mar. 1988
   Village Voice, 35:100, 27 Mar. 1990

ROBERT WILSON and DARRYL PINCKNEY

Orlando (based on V. Woolf's novel), 1989
    Artforum, 28:27–28, Feb. 1990

DAVID WILTSE

A Dance Lesson, 1989
    TheaterWeek, 3:12–13, 23 Oct. 1989

DONALD WINDHAM

Windham, D., *Lost Friendships*

JUDD WOLDIN
SEE ROBERT NEMIROFF, CHARLOTTE ZALTZBERG, JUDD WOLDIN, and ROBERT BRITTAN

HENRY WOLF
SEE NEXT ENTRY

KEN WOLF and HENRY WOLF

My Father, My Son, 1990
    Playbill, 9:34, 31 Oct. 1990
    TheaterWeek, 4:6, 24 Sept. 1990
    TheaterWeek, 4:42–43, 1 Oct. 1990

GEORGE C. WOLFE

Gray, A., "The Big If," *American Theatre,* 6:18–21, 56, June 1989
Horwitz, S., "New Kids on the Block," *TheaterWeek,* 4:26–31, 22 Oct. 1990
Playbill, 9:46, 31 Dec. 1990

The Colored Museum, 1986
    Massachusetts Review, 22:90, Spring 1988

Spunk: Three Tales by Zora Neale Hurston (dramatization of stories by Hurston: "Sweat," "Story in Harlem Slang," and "The Gilded Six-Bits"), 1989
    Botto, L., "The Spunk of Zora," *Playbill,* 8:32, 35–37, 31 Aug. 1990
    Jacobson, L., "The Mark of Zora," *American Theatre,* 7:24–30, July/Aug. 1990
    Spillane, M., "The Genesis of *Spunk,*" *TheaterWeek,* 3:24–27, 11 June 1990
    American Theatre, 6:12, Jan. 1990
    American Theatre, 7:11, June 1990
    American Theatre, 7:1–14, Sept. 1990 (text of play; special pull-out section)
    Commonweal, 117:423, 13 July 1990
    Nation, 250:833–834, 11 June 1990
    New Yorker, 66:83, 7 May 1990

Newsweek, 115:62, 7 May 1990
TheaterWeek, 3:40, 30 Apr. 1990

RUTH WOLFF

The Abdication, 1969
  Case, S.-E., "From Split Subject to Split Britches," pp. 126–146 in E. Bra-
    ter, ed., *Feminine Focus*
  Moore, H., "Woman Alone, Women Together," pp. 186–191 in H. K. Chi-
    noy and L. W. Jenkins, eds., *Women in American Theatre,* rev. and enl.
    ed. (pp. 184–190 in 1981 ed.)

VICTOR WOLFSON

Excursion, 1937
  Harap, L., *Dramatic Encounters,* p. 120

DAVID WOLPE

The Unguided Missile (about Martha Mitchell), 1989
  American Theatre, 6:35–36, Apr. 1989
  TheaterWeek, 2:6, 6 Feb. 1989
  Village Voice, 34:80+, 28 Feb. 1989

TOM WOOD

B-Movie, the Play, 1986
  Lawson, R., "The Lost Boy: Homosexuality in *B-Movie,*" *Canadian
    Theatre Review,* 59:52–54, Summer 1989
  Maclean's, 101:53, 11 Jan. 1988

JOHN WOODWORTH

Man in the Tree, 1938
  Kazacoff, G., *Dangerous Theatre,* pp. 203–205

DALE WORSLEY

Cold Harbor, 1983
  Village Voice, 32:96+, 31 Mar. 1987

HERMAN WOUK

The Caine Mutiny Court-Martial (dramatization of part of his novel *The Caine
    Mutiny*), 1953
  Harap, L., *Dramatic Encounters,* pp. 132–133
  Marcuson, L. R., *The Stage Immigrant,* pp. 159–161
  People Weekly, 30:50–51, 31 Oct. 1988

GAYDEN WREN

Two for the Show, 1988
  TheaterWeek, 1:6, 20 June 1988

DOUG WRIGHT

Interrogating the Nude, 1989
  American Theatre, 5:47, Dec. 1988

ALSO SEE
LARRY SLOAN and DOUG WRIGHT

RAE C. WRIGHT

The Rabbit's Revenge, 1990
  Village Voice, 35:88, 27 Feb. 1990

RICHARD WRIGHT

Bloom, H., ed., *Richard Wright*
Felgar, R., *Richard Wright*
Trotman, C. J., ed., *Richard Wright*

ALSO SEE PAUL GREEN and RICHARD WRIGHT

ROBERT WRIGHT
SEE LUTHER DAVIS, ROBERT WRIGHT, GEORGE FORREST,
and MAURY YESTON
AND CHARLES LEDERER, LUTHER DAVIS, ROBERT WRIGHT,
GEORGE FORREST, and ALEXANDER BORODIN

ELIZA WYATT

The Housekeeper, 1990
  TheaterWeek, 3:10, 4 June 1990
  TheaterWeek, 3:41, 25 June 1990

WAKAKO YAMAUCHI

Arnold, S., "Dissolving the Half Shadows: Japanese American Women Playwrights," pp. 181–194 in L. Hart, ed., *Making a Spectacle*
Berson, M., "Between Worlds," *American Theatre,* 6:20–25, Mar. 1990 (based
  on Berson's Introduction to *Between Worlds*)

And the Soul Shall Dance (dramatization of her short story), 1977
  Berson, M., ed., *Between Worlds,* pp. ix–xiv (Introduction), 128–131, 132–
    174 (text of play)
  TheaterWeek, 3:13, 5 Mar. 1990
  Village Voice, 35:110, 3 Apr. 1990

The Chairman's Wife (about Madame Mao Tse-Tung), 1990
   American Theatre, 6:9–10, Jan. 1990

SUSAN YANKOWITZ

Betsko, K., and R. Koenig, *Interviews with Contemporary Women Playwrights,*
   pp. 432–449
Keyssar, H., "A Network of Playwrights," pp. 102–125 in Keyssar's *Feminist
Theatre*

Terminal, 1969 (often revised)
   Shank, T., *American Alternative Theater,* pp. 40–44

WILLIAM S. YELLOW ROBE

The Independence of Eddie Rose, 1990
   Bergart, C., "Another America," *American Theatre,* 7:11, July/Aug. 1990

LAURENCE YEP

Berson, M., "Between Worlds," *American Theatre,* 6:20–25, Mar. 1990 (based
   on Berson's introduction to *Between Worlds*)

Pay the Chinaman, 1987
   Berson, M., ed., *Between Worlds,* pp. ix–xiv (Introduction), 176–179, 180–
   196 (text of play)

MAURY YESTON
SEE LUTHER DAVIS, ROBERT WRIGHT, GEORGE FORREST,
and MAURY YESTON
AND LARRY GELBART and MAURY YESTON
AND ARTHUR KOPIT and MAURY YESTON

JOSÉ YGLESIAS

New York 1937, 1990
   TheaterWeek, 3:12, 30 Apr. 1990
   Village Voice, 35:122, 15 May 1990

ARTHUR YORINKS and PHILIP GLASS

The Fall of the House of Usher (operatic stage adaptation of E. A. Poe's short
   story), 1988
   American Theatre, 5:6–7, July/Aug. 1988

Y YORK

Nixon, W., "House of Playwrights," *TheaterWeek,* 2:48–52, 19 Sept. 1988

Rain. Some Fish. No Elephants., 1990
   American Theatre, 7:12, Apr. 1990
   TheaterWeek, 3:27, 30 Apr. 1990
   TheaterWeek, 3:40, 21 May 1990
   Village Voice, 35:102, 8 May 1990

DAVID YOUNG
SEE PAUL LEDOUX and DAVID YOUNG

JANE YOUNG and THOMAS KEITH

The Histories of Gladys, 1990
   TheaterWeek, 4:34, 31 Dec. 1990

RIDA JOHNSON YOUNG

Little Old New York, 1920
   Marcuson, L. R., *The Stage Immigrant*, pp. 21–24

SHAY YOUNGBLOOD

Shakin' the Mess Outta Misery, 1989
   American Theatre, 6:14, Dec. 1989

MARK ALAN ZAGOREN

New Jersey Monthly, 13:52, Jan. 1988

CHARLOTTE ZALTZBERG
SEE ROBERT NEMIROFF, CHARLOTTE ZALTZBERG, JUDD WOLDIN, and ROBERT BRITTAN

SUZAN ZEDER

Manna, A. L., "The Search for Self in Suzan Zeder's Plays," *Children's Literature Association Quarterly*, 14(3):142–147, Fall 1989
Pearson-Davis, S., "Female Protagonists in the Plays of Suzan Zeder," pp. 273–275 in H. K. Chinoy and L. W. Jenkins, eds., *Women in American Theatre*, rev. and enl. ed. (new to this ed.)
————, ed., *Wish in One Hand, Spit in the Other* (Zeder's *Wiley and the Hairy Man*, *The Play Called Noah's Flood*, *Step on a Crack*, *Ozma of Oz: A Tale of Time*, *Doors*, *Mother Hicks*, *In a Room Somewhere*, and *The Death and Life of Sherlock Holmes* considered, along with the texts of these plays)

ERIC ZIEGENHAGEN

Mpls/St Paul, 17:82 + , Apr. 1989

Seniority, 1988
   New Yorker, 64:91, 3 Oct. 1988
   TheaterWeek, 2:7, 12 Sept. 1988
   Village Voice, 33:110 + , 4 Oct. 1988

TOM ZIEGLER

Home Games, 1989
    America, 161:321, 11 Nov. 1989
    American Theatre, 6:14, Oct. 1989
    New York, 22:107, 16 Oct. 1989
    TheaterWeek, 3:8, 11 Sept. 1989

The Last Resort, 1988
    Detroit Monthly, 12:18, May 1989
    TheaterWeek, 1:5, 25 Jan. 1988

DICK ZIGUN

Nixon, W., "House of Playwrights," *TheaterWeek,* 2:48–52, 19 Sept. 1988

PAUL ZINDEL

Dieckman, S. B., "Paul Zindel (15 May 1936–)," pp. 540–550 in P. C. Kolin, ed., *American Playwrights since 1945*
Forman, J. J., *Presenting Paul Zindel*
Raymond, G., "The Effects of Staten Island on a Pulitzer Prize-winning Playwright," *TheaterWeek,* 2:16–21, 24 Apr. 1989

Amulets against the Dragon, 1989
    Nation, 249:30, 3 July 1989
    New York, 22:80, 17 Apr. 1989
    New Yorker, 65:111, 17 Apr. 1989
    TheaterWeek, 2:7–8, 20 Mar. 1989
    TheaterWeek, 2:3, 1 May 1989

And Miss Reardon Drinks a Little, 1967
    TheaterWeek, 3:8, 18 Dec. 1989

The Effects of Gamma Rays on Man-in-the-Moon Marigolds, 1965 (later revised)
    TheaterWeek, 1:33, 4 Apr. 1988

Ladies at the Alamo, 1975 (revised 1990)
    TheaterWeek, 3:8, 2 July 1990

Let Me Hear You Whisper, televised 1966
    Seff, R., "The Boob Tube Gets a Touch of Class," *TheaterWeek,* 3:28–32, 4 Dec. 1989

DAVID ZIPPEL
SEE LARRY GELBART, CY COLEMAN, and DAVID ZIPPEL

(*books which were examined but contain nothing relevant to this supplement or books which were not available for examination but may be of interest to the reader)

Abbott, Anthony S. *The Vital Lie: Reality and Illusion in Modern Drama.* Tuscaloosa: U of Alabama P, 1989.

Adler, Thomas P. A Streetcar Named Desire: *The Moth and the Lantern.* (MWS 47.) Boston: Twayne, 1990.

Alpert, Hollis. *The Life and Times of* Porgy and Bess: *The Story of an American Classic.* New York: Knopf, 1990.

Anderson, Jack. *Choreography Observed.* Iowa City: U of Iowa P, 1987.

Anderson, Laurie. *United States.* New York: Harper, 1984

Arnold, Edwin T., ed. *Erskine Caldwell Reconsidered.* Jackson: UP of Mississippi, 1990.

Auslander, Philip. *The New York School of Poets as Playwrights: O'Hara, Ashbery, Koch, Schuyler—and the Visual Arts.* (Lit. & the Visual Arts 3/New Foundation Ser.) New York: Peter Lang, 1989.

Austin, Gayle. *Feminist Theories for Dramatic Criticism.* Ann Arbor: U of Michigan P, 1990.

Axelrod, Steven Gould, and Linda Strahan. *Robert Lowell: A Descriptive Bibliography.* Westport, CT: Meckler, 1990.

Aycock, Wendell, and Michael Schoenecke, eds. *Film and Literature: A Comparative Approach to Adaptation.* (SC Lit 19.) Lubbock: Texas Tech UP, 1988.

Bagchee, Shyamal, ed. *Perspectives on O'Neill: New Essays.* (ELS 43.) Victoria, BC: U of Victoria, 1988.

Bartow, Arthur. *The Director's Voice.* New York: TCG, 1988.

Benson, Jackson J. *Looking for Steinbeck's Ghost.* Norman: U of Oklahoma P, 1988.

*Bentley, Eric. *The Theory of the Modern Stage: An Introduction to Modern Theatre and Drama.* 1968. New York: Penguin, 1989.

———. *Thinking about the Playwrights: Comments from Four Decades.* Evanston, IL: Northwestern UP, 1987.

Bentley, Joanne. *Hallie Flanagan: A Life in the American Theatre.* New York: Knopf, 1988.

Beranger, Jean, and Pierre Guillaume, eds. *Le Facteur religieux en Amérique du Nord, No. 7: Religion et memorie ethnique au Canada et aux Etats-Unis.* Talence: Centre de Recherches Amér. Anglophone, Maison des Sciences de l'Homme d'Aquitaine, 1986.

Bergreen, Laurence. *As Thousands Cheer: The Life of Irving Berlin.* New York: Viking Penguin, 1990.

Berlin, Normand. *Eugene O'Neill.* (Mod. Dramatists Ser.) 1982. New York: St. Martin's, 1988.

———, ed. *Eugene O'Neill: Three Plays* [*The Iceman Cometh, Long Day's Journey into Night,* and *Mourning Becomes Electra*]. (Casebook Ser.) London: Macmillan Education, 1989.

Berry, Faith. *Langston Hughes: Before and Beyond Harlem*. Westport, CT: Lawrence Hill, 1983.

Berson, Misha, ed. and introd. *Between Worlds: Contemporary Asian-American Plays*. New York: TCG, 1990.

Betsko, Kathleen, and Rachel Koenig. *Interviews with Contemporary Women Playwrights*. New York: Beech Tree-Morrow, 1987.

Bigsby, C. W. E., comp. *Edward Albee: Bibliography, Biography, Playography*. (Theatre Checklist 22.) London: Theatre Quarterly, 1980.

Blau, Herbert. *The Eye of the Prey: Subversions of the Postmodern*. (Theories of Contemp. Culture 9.) Bloomington: Indiana UP, 1987.

Bloom, Harold, ed. *Arthur Miller's* All My Sons. (Mod. Crit. Interps.) New York: Chelsea, 1988.

————, ed. *Arthur Miller's* Death of a Salesman. (Mod. Crit. Interps.) New York: Chelsea, 1988.

————, ed. *Edward Albee*. (Mod. Crit. Views.) New York: Chelsea, 1987.

————, ed. *Eugene O'Neill*. (Mod. Crit. Views.) New York: Chelsea, 1987.

————, ed. *Eugene O'Neill's* The Iceman Cometh. (Mod. Crit. Interps.) New York: Chelsea, 1987.

————, ed. *Eugene O'Neill's* Long Day's Journey into Night. (Mod. Crit. Interps.) New York: Chelsea, 1987.

————, ed. *Ezra Pound*. (Mod. Crit. Views.) New York: Chelsea, 1987.

————, ed. *Joyce Carol Oates*. (Mod. Crit. Views.) New York: Chelsea, 1987.

————, ed. *Richard Wright*. (Mod. Crit. Views.) New York: Chelsea, 1987.

————, ed. *Robert Lowell*. (Mod. Crit. Views.) New York: Chelsea, 1987.

————, ed. *Tennessee Williams*. (Mod. Crit. Views.) New York: Chelsea, 1987.

————, ed. *Tennessee Williams's* The Glass Menagerie. (Mod. Crit. Interps.) New York: Chelsea, 1988.

————, ed. *Tennessee Williams's* A Streetcar Named Desire. (Mod. Crit. Interps.) New York: Chelsea, 1988.

————, ed. *Vladimir Nabokov*. (Mod. Crit. Views.) New York: Chelsea, 1987.

Bogard, Travis. *Contour in Time: The Plays of Eugene O'Neill*. Rev. ed. New York: Oxford UP, 1988.

Bouchard, Larry D. *Tragic Method and Tragic Theology: Evil in Contemporary Drama and Religious Thought*. University Park: Pennsylvania State UP, 1989.

Bower, Martha Gilman, ed. More Stately Mansions: *The Unexpurgated Edition*. New York: Oxford UP, 1988.

Boxill, Roger. *Tennessee Williams*. (Mod. Dramatists Ser.) New York: St. Martin's, 1989.

Brater, Enoch, ed. *Feminine Focus: The New Women Playwrights*. New York: Oxford UP, 1989.

Brater, Enoch, and Ruby Cohn, eds. *Around the Absurd: Essays on Modern and Postmodern Drama*. Ann Arbor: U of Michigan P, 1990.

Braunlich, Phyllis Cole. *Haunted by Home: The Life and Letters of Lynn Riggs*. Norman: U of Oklahoma P, 1988.

Brophy, Robert. *Robinson Jeffers: Poetry and Response: A Centennial Tribute*. Los Angeles: Occidental Coll., 1987.

Brown-Guillory, Elizabeth. *Their Place on the Stage: Black Women Playwrights in America*. (Contribs in Afro-American & African Studies 117.) Westport, CT: Greenwood, 1988; Praeger, 1990.

Emanuel, James A. *Langston Hughes* (TUSAS) 123.) Boston: Twayne-G. K. Hall, 1967.

Estrin, Mark W., ed. *Critical Essays on Lillian Hellman*. (CEAL.) Boston: G. K. Hall, 1989.

Euba, Femi. *Archetypes, Imprecators, and Victims of Fate: Origins and Developments of Satire in Black Drama*. (Contribs. in Afro-American & African Studies 126.) Westport, CT: Greenwood, 1989.

Falk, Signi L. *Tennessee Williams*. 2nd ed. (TUSAS 10.) Boston: Twayne-G. K. Hall, 1978.

Feibleman, Peter S. *Lilly: Reminiscences of Lillian Hellman*. New York: Morrow, 1988.

Felgar, Robert. *Richard Wright*. (TUSAS 386.) Boston: Twayne-G. K. Hall, 1980.

Fensch, Thomas, ed. *Conversations with John Steinbeck*. (Lit. Conversations Ser.) Jackson: U of Mississippi P, 1988.

Fisher, Judith L., and Stephen Watt, eds. *When They Weren't Doing Shakespeare: Essays on Nineteenth-Century British and American Theatre*. Athens: U of Georgia P, 1989.

Flinn, Denny Martin. *What They Did for Love: The Untold Story behind the Making of* A Chorus Line. New York: Bantam, 1989.

Foard, Elisabeth C. *William Saroyan: A Reference Guide*. Boston: G. K. Hall, 1988.

Folsom, Michael, ed. *Mike Gold: A Literary Anthology*. New York: International, 1972.

Forman, Jack Jacob. *Presenting Paul Zindel*. (TUSAS 540.) Boston: Twayne-G. K. Hall, 1988.

*Forry, Steven Earl. *Hideous Progenies: Dramatizations of* Frankenstein *from Mary Shelley to the Present*. Philadelphia: U of Pennsylvania P, 1990.

French, Warren. *John Steinbeck*. 2nd ed. (TUSAS 2.) Boston: Twayne-G. K. Hall, 1975.

Gallup, Donald C. *Pigeons on the Granite: Memories of a Yale Librarian*. New Haven: Yale U Lib., 1988.

Garner, Stanton B., Jr. *The Absent Voice: Narrative Comprehension in the Theater*. Champaign: U of Illinois P, 1989.

Garson, Helen L. *Truman Capote*. (Lit. & Life: Amer. Writers.) New York: Continuum, 1989.

*Gellrich, Michelle. *Tragedy and Theory: The Problem of Conflict since Aristotle*. Princeton, NJ: Princeton UP, 1988.

Gentile, John S. *Cast of One: One-Person Shows from the Chautauqua Platform to Broadway Stage*. Champaign: U of Illinois P, 1989.

George, Diana Hume, ed. *Sexton: Selected Criticism*. Champaign: U of Illinois P, 1988.

Gilbert, Sandra M., and Susan Gubar. *The War of the Words*. New Haven, CT: Yale UP, 1988. Vol. 1 of *No Man's Land: The Place of the Woman Writer in the 20th Century*. 3 vols. 1988– .

Glass, Philip. *Music by Philip Glass*. Ed. Robert T. Jones. New York: Harper, 1988.

Goodwin, Donald W. *Alcohol and the Writer*. Kansas City, MO: Andrews, 1988.

Gordon, Eric A. *Mark the Music: The Life and Works of Marc Blitzstein*. New York: St. Martin's, 1989.

Ilson, Carol. *Harold Prince: From* Pajama Game *to* Phantom of the Opera. Ann Arbor, MI: UMI, 1989.

Inverso, MaryBeth. *The Gothic Impulse in Contemporary Drama.* (Theatre and Dramatic Studies 63.) Ann Arbor, MI: UMI, 1990.

Jacobs, Susan. *On Stage: The Making of a Broadway Play* [Mary Mercier's *Johnny No-Trump*]. New York: Knopf, 1972.

Jenkins, Ron. *Acrobats of the Soul: Comedy and Virtuosity in Contemporary American Theatre.* New York: TCG, 1988.

Jones, Eugene H. *Native Americans as Shown on the Stage, 1753–1916.* Metuchen, NJ: Scarecrow, 1988.

Johnson, Greg. *Understanding Joyce Carol Oates.* (Understanding Contemp. Amer. Lit. Ser.) Columbia: U of South Carolina P, 1987.

Johnson, Paul. *Intellectuals.* New York: Harper, 1988.

Jurak, Mirko, ed. *Cross-Cultural Studies: American, Canadian and European Literatures: 1945–1985.* Ljubljana, Yug.: Eng. Dept., Filozofska Fakulteta, 1988.

Kakutani, Michicko. *The Poet at the Piano: Portraits of Writers, Filmmakers, Playwrights, and Other Artists at Work.* New York: Times, 1988.

Karman, James. *Critical Essays on Robinson Jeffers.* (Crit. Essays. Ser.) Boston: G. K. Hall, 1990.

———. *Robinson Jeffers: Poet of California.* San Francisco: Chronicle, 1987.

*Kase-Polisini, Judith, ed. *Drama as Meaning Maker.* Lanham, MD: UP of America, 1989.

Kawin, Bruce F., ed. *Faulkner's MGM Screenplays.* Knoxville: U of Tennessee P, 1982.

Kazacoff, George. *Dangerous Theatre: The Federal Theatre Project as a Forum for New Plays.* New York: Peter Lang, 1989.

Kazan, Elia. *Elia Kazan: A Life.* New York: Knopf, 1988.

Keller, Gary D., ed. *Chicano Cinema: Research, Reviews, and Resources.* Binghamton, NY: Bilingual, 1985.

Kellner, Bruce. *A Gertrude Stein Companion: Content with the Example.* Westport, CT: Greenwood, 1988.

Kelly, Kevin. *One Singular Sensation: The Michael Bennett Story.* New York: Doubleday, 1990.

Kendall, Alan. *George Gershwin: A Biography.* New York: Universe, 1987.

Kennedy, Adrienne. *Adrienne Kennedy in One Act.* Minneapolis: U of Minnesota P, 1988.

———. *The Deadly Triplets: A Theatre Mystery & Journal.* Minneapolis: U of Minnesota P, 1990.

Kerman, Cynthia Earl, and Richard Eldridge. *The Lives of Jean Toomer: A Hunger for Wholeness.* Baton Rouge: Louisiana State UP, 1989.

Keyssar, Helene. *Feminist Theatre: An Introduction to Plays of Contemporary British and American Women.* London: Macmillan, 1984; New York: Evergreen-Grove, 1985; New York: St. Martin's, 1990.

Kernan, Robert F. *Gore Vidal.* (Lit. & Life: Amer. Writers.) 1982 (Mod. Lit. Ser.) New York: Continuum, 1989.

King, Kimball, ed. *Sam Shepard: A Casebook.* (GRLH 861/Casebook on Mod. Dramatists 2.) New York: Garland, 1988.

———. *Ten Modern American Playwrights: An Annotated Bibliography.* New York: Garland, 1982.

Kinney, Arthur, ed. *Critical Essays on William Faulkner: The Sartoris Family.* (CEAL.) Boston: G. K. Hall, 1985.

Kobernick, Mark. *Semiotics of the Drama and the Style of Eugene O'Neill.* (FoS 19.) Amsterdam: Benjamins, 1989.

Kolin, Philip C., ed. *American Playwrights since 1945: A Guide to Scholarship, Criticism, and Performance.* Westport, CT: Greenwood, 1989.

———, ed. *Conversations with Edward Albee.* (Lit. Conversations Ser.) Jackson: UP of Mississippi, 1988.

———. *David Rabe: A Stage History and a Primary and Secondary Bibliography.* New York: Garland, 1988.

Kramer, Larry. *Reports from the Holocaust: The Making of an AIDS Activist.* New York: St. Martin's, 1989.

Kramer, Victor A., ed. *The Harlem Renaissance Re-Examined.* (Georgia State Lit. Studies 2.) New York: AMS, 1987.

Kretzoi, Charlotte, ed. *High and Low in American Culture.* Budapest: Dept. of Eng., Loránd Eötvös U, 1986.

Kreuger, Miles. Show Boat*: The Story of a Classic American Musical.* 1977. New York: Da Capo, 1990.

Lederer, Katharine. *Lillian Hellman.* (TUSAS 338.) Boston: Twayne-G. K. Hall, 1979.

Lee, Lawrence, and Barry Gifford. *Saroyan: A Biography.* 1984. New York: Paragon, 1987.

Leeming, Glenda. *Poetic Drama.* (Mod. Dramatists Ser.) New York: St. Martin's, 1989.

Lees, Gene. *Inventing Champagne: The Worlds of Lerner and Loewe.* New York: St. Martin's, 1990.

Lenz, Günter H., ed. *History and Tradition in Afro-American Culture.* Frankfurt: Campus, 1984.

Leonard, William Torbert. *Once Was Enough.* Metuchen, NJ: Scarecrow, 1986.

Lerner, Alan Jay. *A Hymn to Him: The Lyrics of Alan Jay Lerner.* Ed. Benny Green. New York: Limelight, 1987.

———. *The Musical Theatre: A Celebration.* 1987. New York: Da Capo, 1989.

Link, Franz, ed. *Paradeigmata: Literarische Typologie des Alten Testaments, II: 20. Jahrhundert.* Berlin: Duncker, 1989.

Londré, Felicia. *Tennessee Williams: Life, Work, and Criticism.* (Authoritative Studies in World Lit.) Fredricton, NB: York, 1989.

Ludlam, Charles. *The Complete Plays of Charles Ludlam.* Ed. Steven Samuels and Everett Quinton. New York: Harper, 1990.

Mamet, David. *Some Freaks.* New York: Viking Penguin, 1989.

———. *Writing in Restaurants.* New York: Viking Penguin, 1986.

Mandelbaum, Ken. A Chorus Line *and the Musicals of Michael Bennett.* 1989. New York: St. Martin's, 1990.

Marcuson, Lewis R. *The Stage Immigrant: The Irish, Italians, and Jews in American Drama, 1920–1960.* New York: Garland, 1990.

Mason, Jeffrey D. *Wise-Cracks: The Farces of George S. Kaufman.* Ann Arbor, MI: UMI, 1988.

Mates, Julian. *America's Musical Stage: 200 Years of Musical Theatre.* 1985. Westport, CT: Praeger, 1987.

Maufort, Marc, ed. *Eugene O'Neill and the Emergence of American Drama.* (Costerus 75.) Amsterdam: Rodopi, 1989.

McClure, Michael. *Scratching the Beat Surface.* Berkeley, CA: North Point, 1982.

McDonough, Edwin J. *Quintero Directs O'Neill.* Ann Arbor, MI: UMI, 1988.

McKay, Nelli Y. *Jean Toomer, Artist: A Study of His Literary Life and Work 1894–1936.* Chapel Hill: U of North Carolina P, 1984.

Mendelson, Edward, ed. *Plays and Other Dramatic Writings, 1928–1938: W. H. Auden and Christopher Isherwood.* Vol. 1 of *The Complete Works of W. H. Auden.* Princeton, NJ: Princeton UP, 1988.

Meyers, Jeffrey, ed. *Robert Lowell: Interviews and Memoirs.* Ann Arbor: U of Michigan P, 1988.

Mikolyzk, Thomas A. *Langston Hughes: A Bio-Bibliography.* (Bio-Bibliographies in Afro-American and African Studies 2.) Westport, CT: Greenwood, 1990.

Miller, Gabriel. *Clifford Odets.* (Lit. & Life: Amer. Writers.) New York: Continuum, 1989.

Mogen, David. *Ray Bradbury.* Boston: Twayne-G. K. Hall, 1986.

Mogen, David, Mark Busby, and Paul Bryant, eds. *The Frontier Experience and the American Dream: Essays on American Literature.* College Station: Texas A&M UP, 1989.

Moyers, Bill. *Bill Moyers' World of Ideas: Conversations with Thoughtful Men and Women about American Life Today and the Ideas Shaping Our Future.* Ed. Betty Sue Flowers. New York: Doubleday, 1989.

Mullen, Edward J. *Langston Hughes.* (CEAL.) Boston: G. K. Hall, 1986.

Murray, Timothy D. *Evolving Texts: The Writing of Tennessee Williams.* Newark: U of Delaware Lib., 1988.

Natalle, Elizabeth J. *Feminist Theatre: A Study in Persuasion.* Metuchen, NJ: Scarecrow, 1985.

Nelson, Emmanuel S., ed. *Connections: Essays on Black Literatures.* Canberra: Aboriginal Studies, 1988.

Nelson, Richard, ed. Strictly Dishonorable *and Other Lost American Plays.* New York: TCG, 1986.

Nelson, T. G. A. *Comedy: An Introduction to Comedy in Literature, Drama, and Cinema.* New York: Oxford UP, 1990.

Neuman, Shirley, and Ira B. Nadel, eds. *Gertrude Stein and the Making of Literature.* Houndsmills, Eng.: Macmillan, 1988.

Neuman, Shirley, and Smaro Kamboureli, eds. *A Mazing Space: Writing Canadian Women Writing.* Edmonton: Longspoon, 1986.

Newlin, Jeanne T., introd. Our Town *On Stage: The Original Promptbook in Facsimile.* (Howard and Mary Bingham Ser. in the Howard Theatre Collection 1.) Cambridge, MA: Harvard UP, 1988.

Newman, Robert P. *The Cold War Romance of Lillian Hellman and John Melby.* Chapel Hill: U of North Carolina P, 1989.

Numbers, Ronald L., and Jonathan M. Butler, eds. *The Disappointed: Millerism and Millenarianism in the Nineteenth Century.* (Religion in North Amer.) Bloomington: Indiana UP, 1987.

O'Daniel, Therman B., ed. *Jean Toomer: A Critical Evaluation.* Washington, D.C.: Howard UP, 1988.

Odets, Clifford. *The Time Is Ripe: The 1940 Journals of Clifford Odets.* Introd. William Gibson. New York: Grove, 1988.

O'Neill, Eugene. *As Ever, Gene: The Letters of Eugene O'Neill to George Jean*

Nathan. Ed. Nancy L. Roberts and Arthur W. Roberts. Madison, NJ: Fairleigh Dickinson UP, 1987.

———. *The Eugene O'Neill Songbook*. Col. and annot. Travis Bogard. (Theatre and Dramatic Ser. 56.) Ann Arbor, MI: UMI, 1990.

———. *O'Neill: Complete Plays*. Ed. Travis Bogard. 3 vols. New York: Library of America, 1988.

———. *Selected Letters of O'Neill*. Ed Travis Bogard and Jackson R. Bryer. New Haven, CT: Yale UP, 1988.

———. *The Unfinished Plays: Notes for* The Visit of Malatesta, The Last Conquest, *and* Blind Alley Guy. Ed. Virginia Floyd. New York: Continuum, 1988.

———. *The Unknown O'Neill: Unpublished and Unfamiliar Writings of Eugene O'Neill*. Ed. Travis Bogard. New Haven, CT: Yale UP, 1988.

Osborn, M. Elizabeth, ed., *On New Ground: Contemporary Hispanic-American Plays*. New York: TCG, 187.

*Packard, William. *The Art of the Playwright: Creating the Magic of Theatre*. New York: Paragon, 1987.

Palumbo, Donald, ed. *Spectrum of the Fantastic*. (Contribs. to the Study of Science Fiction & Fantasy 31.) Westport, CT: Greenwood, 1988.

Parker, Stephen Jan. *Understanding Nabokov*. (Understanding Contemp. Amer. Lit. Ser.) Columbia: U of South Carolina P, 1987.

Pearlman, Mickey, ed. *Mother Puzzles: Daughters and Mothers in Contemporary American Literature*. (Contribs. in Women's Studies 110.) Westport, CT: Greenwood, 1989.

Pearson-Davis, Susan, ed. and introd., with critical essays. *Wish in One Hand, Spit in the Other: A Collection of Plays by Suzan Zeder*. New Orleans: Anchorage, 1990.

Pennington-Jones, Paulette, comp. *Amiri Baraka: Bibliography, Biography, Playography*. (Theatre Checklist 18.) London: Theatre Quarterly, 1978.

Perloff, Marjorie, ed. *Postmodern Genres*. (Okla. Project for Discourse & Theory Ser.) Norman: U of Oklahoma P, 1989.

Peterman, Michael. *Robertson Davies*. (TWAS 780.) Boston: Twayne-G. K. Hall, 1986.

Peters, Jan Eden, and Thomas Michael Stein, eds. *Scholastic Widwifery: Studien zum Satirischen in der englischen Literatur 1600–1800*. Tübingen: Narr, 1989.

*Peterson, Bernard L., Jr. *Contemporary Black American Playwrights and Their Plays: A Biographical Directory and Dramatic Index*. Westport, CT: Greenwood, 1988.

*———. *Early Black American Playwrights and Dramatic Writers: A Biographical Directory and Catalog of Plays, Films, and Broadcasting Scripts*. Westport, CT: Greenwood, 1990.

Phillips, Gene D. *Fiction, Film, and Faulkner: The Art of Adaptation*. Knoxville: U of Tennessee P, 1988.

Pollack, Rhoda-Gale. *George S. Kaufman*. (TUSAS 525.) Boston: Twayne-G. K. Hall, 1988.

Porter, Horace. *Stealing the Fire: The Art and Protest of James Baldwin*. Hanover, NH: Wesleyan UP, 1989.

Porter, Laurin. *The Banished Prince: Time, Memory, and Ritual in the Late Plays of Eugene O'Neill.* (Theater and Dramatic Ser. 54.) Ann Arbor, MI: UMI, 1988.

Prasad, Hari Mohan. *The Dramatic Art of Eugene O'Neill.* New Delhi: Associated Publ. House, 1987. (Distrib. by Advent Books, NY.)

Presley, Delma E. The Glass Menagerie*: An American Memory.* (MWS 43.) Boston: G. K. Hall, 1990.

Price, Reynolds. *Clear Pictures: First Loves, First Guides.* New York: Atheneum, 1989.

Prideaux, Tom. *Love or Nothing: The Life and Times of Ellen Terry.* New York: Limelight, 1988.

*Raben, Estelle Manette. *Major Strategies in Twentieth Century Drama: Apocalyptic Vision, Allegory and Open Form.* (Amer. Univ. Studies 4/Engl. Lang. & Lit. 67.) New York: Peter Lang, 1989.

Radcliff-Umstead, Douglas, ed. *Transformations: From Literature to Film.* Kent, OH: Romance Langs. Dept., Kent State U, 1987.

Rampersad, Arnold. *The Life of Langston Hughes: 1941–1967: I Dream a World.* Vol. 2 of 2 vols. 1988. New York: Oxford UP, 1989.

Redmond, James, ed. *Drama and Philosophy.* (Th D 12.) New York: Cambridge UP, 1990.

*———, ed. *Drama and Religion.* (Th D 5.) New York: Cambridge UP, 1983.

———, ed. *Farce.* (Th D 10.) New York: Cambridge UP, 1988.

———, ed. *The Theatrical Space.* (Th D 9.) New York: Cambridge UP, 1987.

———, ed. *Women in Theatre.* (Th D 11.) New York: Cambridge UP, 1989.

Reid, Richard, ed. Elektra*: A Play by Ezra Pound and Rudd Fleming.* Princeton, NJ: Princeton UP, 1989.

Rollyson, Carl, Jr. *Lillian Hellman: Her Legend and Her Legacy.* New York: St. Martin's, 1988.

Roudané, Matthew C., ed. *Contemporary Authors Bibliographical Series, Vol. 3: American Dramatists.* Detroit: Gale, 1989.

———. *Understanding Edward Albee.* (Understanding Contemp. Amer. Lit.) Columbia: U of South Carolina P, 1987.

———. Who's Afraid of Virginia Woolf?*: Necessary Fictions, Terrifying Realities.* (MWS 34.) Boston: Twayne-G. K. Hall, 1990.

Sanders, Leslie Catherine. *The Development of Black Theatre in America: From Shadows to Selves.* Baton Rouge: Louisiana State UP, 1988.

Savran, David. *Danger: Present Tense Theatre.* Providence, RI: Paradigm, 1988. N. pag.

———. *In Their Own Words: Contemporary American Playwrights.* New York: TCG, 1988.

———. *The Wooster Group, 1975–1985: Breaking the Rules.* Ann Arbor, MI: UMI, 1986. Rptd. as *Breaking the Rules: The Wooster Group,* New York: TCG, 1988.

Schechner, Richard. *The Performance Group:* Dionysus in 69. New York: Farrar, 1970.

———. *Performance Theory.* Rev. and enl. ed. New York: Routledge, 1988.

Schlueter, June, ed. *Feminist Rereadings in Modern American Drama.* Madison, NJ: Fairleigh Dickinson UP, 1989.

———, ed. *Modern American Drama: The Female Canon.* Madison, NJ: Fairleigh Dickinson UP, 1990.

Schmitt, Natalie Crohn. *Actors and Onlookers: Theater and Twentieth-Century Scientific Views of Nature.* Evanston, IL: Northwestern UP, 1990.

Schöne, Albrecht, Wilhelm Vosskamp, and Eberhard Lämmert, eds. *Kontroversen alte und neue, XI: Historische und aktuelle Konzepte der Literaturgeschichtsschreibung; Zwei Königskinder? Zum Verhältnis von Literatur und Literaturwissenschaft.* Tübingen: Niemeyer, 1986.

Schroeder, Patricia Richard. *The Presence of the Past in Modern American Drama.* (Fairleigh Dickinson UP Awards.) Madison, NJ: Fairleigh Dickinson UP, 1989.

*Scolnicov, Hanna, and Peter Holland, eds. *The Play out of Context: Transferring Plays from Culture to Culture.* New York: Cambridge UP, 1989.

Sewall, Richard B. *The Vision of Tragedy.* New ed., rev. New York: Paragon, 1990.

Shank, Theodore. *American Alternative Theatre.* 1982. (Mod. Dramatist Ser.) New York: St. Martin's, 1989.

Shapiro, Adrian M., Jackson R. Bryer, and Kathleen Field. *Carson McCullers: A Descriptive Bibliography of Criticism.* New York: Garland, 1980.

Sharrar, Jack F. *Avery Hopwood: His Life and Plays.* Jefferson, NC: McFarland, 1989.

Shaugnessy, Edward L. *Eugene O'Neill in Ireland: The Critical Reception.* (Contribs. in Drama & Theatre Studies 25.) Westport, CT: Greenwood, 1988.

Sheaffer, Louis. *O'Neill: Son and Playwright,* 1968. New York: Paragon, 1989.

Shnayerson, Michael. *Irwin Shaw: A Biography.* New York: Putnam, 1989.

Shrager, Sidney. *Scatology in Modern Drama.* New York: Irvington, 1982.

Shuman, R. Baird. *William Inge.* Rev. ed. (TUSAS 95.) Boston: Twayne-G .K. Hall, 1989.

Shyer, Laurence. *Robert Wilson and His Collaborators.* New York: TCG, 1989.

Siegle, Robert. *Suburban Ambush: Downtown Writing and the Fiction of Insurgency.* Baltimore: Johns Hopkins UP, 1989.

Simard, Rodney. *Postmodern Drama: Contemporary Playwrights in America and Britain.* Lanham, MD: UP of America, 1984.

Simon, Bennett. *Tragic Drama and the Family: Psychoanalytic Studies from Aeschylus to Beckett.* New Haven, CT: Yale UP, 1988.

Simon, John. *The Sheep from the Goats: Selected Literary Essays of John Simon.* New York: Weidenfeld-Random, 1989.

Singh, Amritjit, William S. Shiver, and Stanley Brodwin, eds. *The Harlem Renaissance: Revaluations.* (GRLH 837/Crit. Studies on Black Life & Culture 17.) New York: Garland, 1989.

Skloot, Robert. *The Darkness We Carry: The Drama of the Holocaust.* Madison: U of Wisconsin P, 1988.

———. *The Theatre of the Holocaust: Four Plays.* Madison: U of Wisconsin P, 1982.

Smilowitz, Erika Sollish, and Roberta Quarles Knowles, eds. *Critical Issues in West Indian Literature.* Parkersburg, IA: Caribbean, 1984.

Smith, Bruce. *Costly Performances: Tennessee Williams: The Last Stage.* New York: Paragon, 1990.

Smith, Madeline, and Richard Eaton. *Eugene O'Neill: An Annotated Bibliography, 1973–1985.* (GRLH 860.) New York: Garland, 1988.

Standley, Fred L., and Louis H. Pratt, eds. *Conversations with James Baldwin.* (Lit. Conversations Ser.) Jackson: UP of Mississippi, 1989.

mentation. Ed. Andrea P. A. Belloli. Introd. Heiner Müller. Los Angeles: Otis Art Institute of Parsons School of Design Exhibition Center, 1984.

Wilt, Judith. *Abortion, Choice, and Contemporary Fiction: The Armageddon of the Maternal Instinct.* Chicago: U of Chicago P, 1990.

Windham, Donald. *Lost Friendships: A Memoir of Truman Capote, Tennessee Williams, and Others.* New York: Paragon, 1989. Rpt. of New York: Morrow, 1987, which combined two earlier privately printed limited editions: *Footnote to a Friendship,* New York: S. Campbell, 1983, and *As If . . . : A Personal View of Tennessee Williams,* New York: S. Campbell, 1985.

Winter, William. *The Life of David Belasco.* 2 vols. 1918. Salem, NH: Ayer, n.d.

Woll, Allen. *Black Musical Theatre: From* Coontown *to* Dreamgirls. Baton Rouge: Louisiana State UP, 1989.

Wood, Audrey, and Max Wilk. *Represented by Audrey Wood.* New York: Doubleday, 1981.

Wright, William. *Lillian Hellman: The Image, the Woman.* New York: Simon, 1986.

Zach, Wolfgang, and Heinz Kosok, eds. *Comparison and Impact* and *National Images and Stereotypes.* Vols. 2 and 3 of *Literary Interrelations: Ireland, England and the World.* (Studies in Engl. and Compar. Lit.) Tübingen: Narr, 1987.

Zadan, Craig. *Sondheim & Co.* 2nd ed., rev. and updated. New York: Harper, 1988.

LIST OF JOURNALS INDEXED

(*ceased publication)

Acta Litteraria Academiae Scientiarum Hungaricae. Budapest, Hungary.
Aevum: Rassegna di Scienze Storiche, Linguistiche e Filologiche. Facolta di Lettere dell' Universita Cattolica del Sacro Cuore, Milan, Italy.
African Literature Association Bulletin.
African Literature Today. Freetown, Sierra Leone.
Agenda. London, England.
America (National Catholic Weekly Review). 106 W. 56th St., New York, NY 10019.
American Film. P.O. Box 2046, Marion, OH 43305.
American Heritage. 60 Fifth Ave., New York, NY 10011.
The American Journal of Psychoanalysis: Journal of the Association for the Advancement of Psychoanalysis. Agathon Press, Albany, NY.
American Literary Realism, 1870–1910. Univ. of New Mexico, Albuquerque.
American Literary Scholarship: An Annual. Indiana Univ., Bloomington.
American Literature: A Journal of Literary History, Criticism, and Bibliography. Duke Univ., Durham, NC.
American Music. Univ. of Illinois P, 54 E. Gregory Dr., Champaign, IL 61820.
American Quarterly. Washington, D.C.
The American Scholar. Washington, D.C.
The American Spectator. P.O. Box 10448, Arlington, VA 22210.
American Theatre. TCG, 355 Lexington Ave., New York, NY 10017.
American Transcendental Quarterly: A Journal of New England Writers. Kingston, RI.
Americana. 205 W. Center St., Marion, OH 43302.
The Americas Review: A Review of Hispanic Literature and Art of the USA. Univ. of Houston, Houston, TX.
Amerikastudien/American Studies. Univ. Würzburg, Würzburg, Germany.
Analytical & Enumerative Bibliography. DeKalb, IL.
Andy Warhol's Interview. 19 E. 32nd. St., New York, NY 10016.
Anglistik & Englischunterricht. Heidelberg, Germany.
Another Chicago Magazine. Chicago, IL.
The Antigonish Review. St. Francis Xavier Univ., Antigonish, NS, Canada.
The Antioch Review. Antioch Coll., Yellow Springs, OH.
Appalachian Journal: A Regional Studies Review. Appalachian State Univ., Boone, NC.
Arcadia: Zeitschrift für Vergleichende Literaturwissenschaft. Berlin, Germany.
Ariel: A Review of International English Literature. Univ. of Calgary, Calgary, AB, Canada.
Armchair Detective: A Quarterly Journal Devoted to the Appreciation of Mystery, Detective, and Suspense Fiction. New York, NY.
Art & Antiques. Box 840, Farmingdale, NY 11737.
Art in America. 542 Pacific Ave., Marion, OH 43306.
Artforum. P.O. Box 3000, Dept. AF, Denville, NJ 07834.
L'Artichaut.
Assaph: Studies in the Theatre. Tel Aviv Univ., Tel Aviv, Israel.

Atenea: Revista de Ciencia, Arte y Literatura de la Universidad de Concepción. Concepción, Chile.

Atlanta. 1360 Peachtree St., Atlanta, GA 30309.

Australasian Drama Studies. Univ. of Queensland, St. Lucia, Australia.

Ball State University Forum. Ball State Univ., Muncie, IN.

Black American Literature Forum. Indiana State Univ., Terre Haute, IN.

BOMB Magazine. P.O. Box 2003, Canal Station, New York, NY 10013.

Boston Magazine. 300 Massachusetts Ave., Boston, MA 02115.

Bulletin de la Société de Stylistique Anglaise.

Bulletin of Bibliography. Westport, CT.

Business Week. P.O. Box 430, Hightstown, NJ 08520.

Cahiers Roumains d'Etudes Littéraires: Revue Trimestrielle de Critique, d'Esthétique, et d'Histoire Littéraires. Bucharest, Romania.

California. P.O. Box 2579, Boulder, CO 80321.

Canadian Literature. Univ. of British Columbia, Vancouver, BC, Canada.

Canadian Review of American Studies. London. ON, Canada.

Canadian Review of Comparative Literature/Revue Canadienne de Littérature Comparée. Edmonton, AB, Canada.

Canadian Theatre Review. Univ. of Guelph, Guelph, ON, Canada.

The Catholic World (now *The New Catholic World*). 545 Island Rd., Ramsey, NJ 07446.

CEA Critic: An Official Journal of the College English Association. Lewisburg, PA.

The Centennial Review. Michigan State Univ., East Lansing, MI.

Chicago. 414 N. Orleans, Chicago, IL 60604.

Children's Literature Association Quarterly. Calgary, AB, Canada.

The Christian Century. 5615 W. Cermak Rd., Cicero, IL 60650.

Christianity Today. 465 Gundersen Dr., Carol Stream, IL 60188.

Chu-Shikoku Studies in American Literature. Hiroshima Univ., Hiroshima, Japan.

Classical and Modern Literature: A Quarterly. Terre Haute, IN.

Cleveland Magazine. 1422 Euclid Ave., Cleveland, OH 44115.

Clio: A Journal of Literature, History, and the Philosophy of History. Indiana Univ.-Purdue Univ. at Fort Wayne, Fort Wayne, IN.

College Language Association Journal. Atlanta, GA.

Columbia Library Columns. Columbia Univ., New York, NY.

Commonweal. 15 Dutch St., New York, NY.

Commonwealth Essays and Studies, Dijon, France.

The Comparatist: Journal of the Southern Comparative Literature Association. Clemson Univ., Clemson, SC.

Comparative Drama. Western Michigan Univ., Kalamazoo, MI.

Conference of College Teachers of English Studies. Univ. of Texas at Arlington, Arlington, TX.

Confluencia: Revista Hispánica de Cultura y Literatura. Univ. of Northern Colorado, Greeley, CO.

Connecticut. 123 West Tryon Ave., Teaneck, NJ 07666.

Connoisseur. P.O. Box 10172, Des Moines, IA 50347.

Contemporary Literature. Univ. of Wisconsin, Madison, WI.

Cristallo: Rassegna di Varia Umanità. Bolzano, Italy.

Critical Texts: A Review of Theory and Criticism. Columbia Univ., New York, NY.

D Magazine. 3988 N. Central Expressway, Suite 1200, Dallas, TX 75204.

Dance Magazine. P.O. Box 2089, Knoxville, IA 50197.

Detroit Monthly. 965 E. Jefferson, Detroit, MI 48207.

Dialog: Miesięcznik Póswięcony Dramaturgii Współczesnej: Teatralnej, Filmowej, Radiowej, Telewizyjnej. Warsaw, Poland.

The Dickensian. London, England.

Documenta.

Drama. London, England.

The Drama Review. See *TDR: The Drama Review.*

The Dramatist Guild Quarterly. 234 W. 44th St., New York, NY 10036.

Durham University Journal. Univ. of Durham, Durham, England.

Early American Literature. Univ. of North Carolina, Chapel Hill, NC.

Eigo Seinen. Tokyo, Japan.

Elle. P.O. Box 10934, Des Moines, IA 50347.

Encounter. London, England.

English Studies: A Journal of English Language and Literature. Nijmegen, Netherlands.

English Studies in Canada. Edmonton, AB, Canada.

Esquire. P.O. Box 7146, Red Oak, IA 51591.

Essays in Arts and Sciences. Univ. of New Haven, West Haven, CT.

Essays in Literature. Western Illinois Univ., Macomb, IL.

Essays in Theatre. Univ. of Guelph, Guelph, ON, Canada.

Essence. P.O. Box 53400, Boulder, CO 80322.

Estreno: Cuardernos del Teatro Español Contemporáneo. Cincinnati, OH.

Estudos Anglo-Americanos. São Paulo, Brazil.

Etudes Anglaises: Grand-Bretagne, Etats-Unis. Montesson, France.

Etudes Littéraires. Quebec, PQ, Canada.

The Eugene O'Neill Newsletter. See *The Eugene O'Neill Review.*

The Eugene O'Neill Review. (Formerly *The Eugene O'Neill Newsletter.*) Suffolk Univ., Boston, MA.

*Evergreen Review.

Explicación de Textos Literarios. California State Univ., Sacramento, CA.

Explicator. Washington, D.C.

Explorations in Ethnic Studies: The Journal of the National Association for Ethnic Studies. Claremont, CA.

Fame. P.O. Box 51048, Boulder, CO 80321.

Film Comment. 140 W. 65th St., New York, NY 10023.

Filologischeski Nauki. Moscow, Russia.

Finsk Tidskrift. Åbo, Finland.

Foreign Literature Studies. China.

Foreign Literatures. Beijing Foreign Studies Univ., Beijing, People's Republic of China.

Forum Modernes Theater. Tübingen, Germany.

Gentlemen's Quarterly. P.O. Box 53816, Boulder, CO 80322.

The Georgia Review. Univ. of Georgia, Athens, GA.

Gestos: Teoria y practica del Teatro Hispanico. Irvine, CA.

The Gettysburg Review. Gettysburg Coll., Gettysburg, PA.

Griot: Official Journal of the Southern Conference on Afro-American Studies, Inc. Lafayette, LA.

Harper's. P.O. Box 1937, Marion, OH 43305.

Harper's Bazaar. P.O. Box 7178, Red Oak, IA 51591.

The Hemingway Review. Ohio Northern Univ., Ada, OH.

*High Fidelity.

House & Garden. P.O. Box 53916, Boulder, CO 80322.

*Houston City Magazine.

Horizon. Tuscaloosa, AL.

The Hudson Review. New York, NY.

Ilha do Desterro: A Journal of Language and Literature. Univ. Federal de Santa Catarina, Florianópolis-S.C., Brazil.

Imagine: International Chicano Poetry Journal. Boston, MA.

Index on Censorship. London, England.

Intellect. (Now *USA Today.*) Society for the Advancement of Education, Valley Stream, NY.

The Iowa Review. Univ. of Iowa, Iowa City, IA.

Ironwood. Tucson, AZ.

Jet. 820 S. Michigan Ave., Chicago, IL 60605.

Journal: College of Arts & Essays. Hankuk Univ. of Foreign Studies, Seoul, Republic of Korea.

Journal of American Culture. Bowling Green State Univ., Bowling Green, OH.

Journal of American Studies. Brighton, England.

Journal of Canadian Fiction. Montreal, PQ, Canada.

Journal of Canadian Poetry. Nepean, ON, Canada.

Journal of Canadian Studies/Revue d'Etudes Canadiennes. Trent Univ., Peterborough, ON, Canada.

Journal of Dramatic Theory and Criticism. Univ. of Kansas, Lawrence, KS.

The Journal of Ethnic Studies. Western Washington Univ., Bellingham, WA.

Journal of Evolutionary Psychology. Pittsburgh, PA.

The Journal of Indian Writing in English. Karnatak, India.

Journal of Literature and Criticism.

Journal of Popular Culture. Bowling Green, OH.

Journal of the American Musicological Society. 201 S. 34th St., Philadelphia, PA 19104.

Journal of the American Name Society. See *Names.*

Journal of the Department of English. Calcutta Univ., Calcutta, India.

Kodikas/Code/Ars semeiotica: International Journal of Semiotic, Amsterdam, Netherlands.

Kaleidoscope: International Magazine of Literature, Fine Arts, & Disability.

*Kansas City Monthly.

Kunapipi. Århus, Denmark.

Kyushu American Literature. Fukuoka, Japan.

The Langston Hughes Review. Providence, RI.

Language and Culture. Hokkaido Univ., Kitaku, Japan.

Latin American Theatre Review. Univ. of Kansas, Lawrence, KS.

Library Chronicle of the University of Texas. Austin, TX.

*Life (1883–1936).

Literary Half-Yearly. Univ. of Mysore, Mysore, India.

Literatur in Wissenschaft und Unterricht. Kiel, Germany.

Literature/Film Quarterly. Salisbury State Coll., Salisbury, MD.
Literaturna Misŭl. Sofia, Bulgaria.
Literaturnaia Armeniia: Ezhemesiachnyĭ Literaturno-Khudozhestvennyĭ i Ob-schchestvenno-Politicheskiĭ Zhurnal. Yerevan, Armenia.
Los Angeles. P.O. Box 10726, Des Moines, IA 50349.
Maclean's. P.O. Box 1600, Postal Station A, Toronto, ON, Ontario.
Mademoiselle. P.O. Box 4348, Boulder, CO 80322.
Manhattan, inc. (merged with *M* into *M Inc.*) P.O. Box 57099, Boulder, CO 80322.
Massachusetts Review: A Quarterly of Literature, the Arts and Public Affairs. Amherst, MA.
Meerut Journal of Comparative Literature and Language. Meerut Univ., Meerut, India.
MELUS: The Journal of the Society for the Study of Multi-Ethnic Literature of the United States. Amherst, MA.
Meta: Journal des Traducteurs/Translators' Journal. Univ. of Montréal, Montreal, PQ, Canada.
Miami. (Merged with *South Florida Magazine,* which see.)
Michigan Quarterly Review. Univ. of Michigan, Ann Arbor, MI.
Midamerica: The Yearbook of the Society for the Study of Midwestern Literature. East Lansing, MI.
Mid-America Review. Bowling Green State Univ., Bowling Green, OH.
Mid-Hudson Language Studies. Poughkeepsie, NY.
Midwest Quarterly: A Journal of Contemporary Thought. Pittsburg State Univ., Pittsburg, KS.
Milwaukee. 312 E. Buffalo, Milwaukee, WI 53202.
Mirabella. P.O. Box 7105, Red Oak, IA 51591.
Mississippi: A View of the Magnolia State. (Now just *Mississippi.*) Highland Village, Suite 261, Jackson, MS 39211.
Mississippi Folklore Register. Univ. of Southern Mississippi, Hattiesburg, MS.
Mississippi Philological Association.
The Missouri Review. Univ. of Missouri, Columbia, MO.
Modern Austrian Literature: Journal of the International Arthur Schnitzler Research Association. California State Coll, San Bernardino, CA.
Modern Drama. Univ. of Toronto, Toronto, ON, Canada.
Money. P.O. Box 30607, Tampa, FL 33630.
Mosaic: A Journal for the Interdisciplinary Study of Literature. Univ. of Manitoba, Winnipeg, MB, Canada.
Mother Jones. P.O. Box 58249, Boulder, CO 80322.
Mpls/St Paul. 12 S. 6th St., Suite 1030, Minneapolis, MN 55402.
Ms. P.O. Box 57132, Boulder, CO 80322.
The Musical Quarterly. 16-00 Pollitt Dr., Fair Lawn, NJ 07410.
Names: Journal of the American Name Society. Vermillion, SD.
The Nathaniel Hawthorne Review. Clemson, SC.
The Nation. P.O. Box 1953, Marion, OH 43305.
National Review. P.O. Box 96639, Washington, D.C., 20077.
Neohelicon: Acta Comparationis Litterarum Universarum. Budapest, Hungary.
Neophilogus. Groningen, Netherlands.
Die Neueren Sprachen. Frankfurt, Germany.
New England Monthly.

New Hampshire Profiles. P.O. Box 7649, Teaneck, NJ 07666.
New Jersey Monthly. P.O. Box Call 120, Morristown, NJ 07960.
The New Leader. 275 Seventh Ave., New York, NY 10001.
New Mexico Magazine. P.O. Box 409, Mount Morris, IL 61054.
New Orleans Review. Loyola Univ., New Orleans, LA.
The New Republic. P.O. Box 56515, Boulder, CO 80322.
*New Statesman.
New Theatre Quarterly. Cambridge Univ. Pr., New York, NY.
New York. P.O. Box 54661, Boulder, CO 80322.
New Yorker. 20 W. 43rd St., New York, NY 10036.
The New York Review of Books. P.O. Box 2094, Knoxville, TN 50197.
The New York Times Magazine. 229 W. 43rd St., New York, NY 10036.
New York Woman. P.O. Box 2063, Harlan, IA 51593.
Newsweek. Livingston, NJ 07039.
NMAL: Notes on Modern American Literature. Jamaica, NY.
Notes and Queries. Oxford, England.
Notes on Contemporary Literature. Carrollton, GA.
Notes on Mississippi Writers. Univ. of Southern Mississippi, Hattiesburg, MS.
Obsidian II: Black Literature in Review. North Carolina State Univ., Raleigh, NC.
Oklahoma Observer. P.O. Box 53371, Oklahoma City, OK 73152.
The Old Northwest: A Journal of Regional Life and Letters. Miami Univ., Oxford, OH.
Opera News. 1865 Broadway, New York, NY 10023.
Orbis Litterarum: International Review of Literary Studies. Copenhagen, Denmark.
*Ovation.
Pacific Northwest. P.O. Box 34666, Seattle, WA 98124.
Paideuma: A Journal Devoted to Ezra Pound Scholarship. Univ. of Maine, Orono, ME.
Panjab University Research Bulletin (Arts). Panjab Univ., Chandigarh, India.
La Palabra y el Hombre: Revista de la Universidad Veracruzana. Univ. Veracruzana, Veracruz, Mexico.
Papers on Language and Literature: A Journal for Scholars and Critics of Language and Literature. Southern Illinois Univ., Edwardsville, IL.
The Paris Review. 45-39 171 Place, Flushing, NY 11358.
Parnass: Kunst, Architektur, Fotografie, Musik, Theater, Literatur. Austria.
Pembroke Magazine. Pembroke State Univ., Pembroke, NC.
People Weekly. P.O. Box 30603, Tampa, FL 33630.
Performing Arts Journal. New York, NY.
Perspectives in Biology and Medicine. Univ. of Chicago Pr., Chicago, IL.
Perspectives on Contemporary Literature. Univ. of Louisville, Univ. Pr. of Kentucky, Lexington, KY.
Philadelphia Magazine. 1500 Walnut St., Philadelphia, PA 19102.
Philippine Studies. Ateneo de Manila Univ., Manila, Philippines.
The Philosophical Forum: A Quarterly. Boston Univ. Pr., Boston, MA.
Phoenix. 4707 N. 12th St., Phoenix, AZ 85014.
Phylon: The Atlanta University Review of Race and Culture. Atlanta Univ., Atlanta, GA.
Pittsburgh Magazine. 4802 Fifth Ave., Pittsburgh, PA 15213.

Playbill: The National Theatre Magazine. 71 Vanderbilt Ave., New York, NY 10169.
PMLA: Publications of the Modern Language Association of America. New York, NY.
Il Ponte: Rivista Mensile de Politica e Letteratura Fondata da Piero Calamandrei. Florence, Italy.
Praxis Des Neusprachlichen Unterrichts. Dortmund, Germany.
Premiere. P.O. Box 11395, Des Moines, IA 50347.
Présence Africaine: Revue Culturelle du Monde Noir/Cultural Review of the Negro World. Paris, France.
The Progressive. P.O. Box 421, Mount Morris, IL 61054.
Publications of the Arkansas Philological Association. Univ. of Central Arkansas, Conway, AR.
Publications of the Mississippi Philological Association. Jackson, MS.
Publishers Weekly. P.O. Box 1979, Marion, OH 43302.
Quaderni di Lingue e Letterature. Verona, Italy.
Queen's Quarterly: A Canadian Review. Queen's Univ., Kingston, ON, Canada.
Quimera: Revista de Literatura. Barcelona, Spain.
Renascence: Essays on Value in Literature. Marquette Univ., Milwaukee, WI.
Rendezvous: Journal of Arts and Letters. Idaho State Univ., Pocatello, ID.
Resources for American Literary Study. College Park, MD.
Restoration and 18th Century Theatre Research. Loyola Univ. of Chicago, Chicago, IL.
Revista Alicantina de Estudios Ingleses.
Revista Canaria de Estudios Ingleses. Univ. de La Laguna, Tenerife, Spain.
Review. Blacksburg, VA.
Review of Contemporary Fiction. Elmwood Park, IL.
Revue Belge de Philologie et d'Histoire/Belgisch Tÿdschrift voor Filologie en Geschiedenis. Brussels, Belgium.
Revue Française d'Etudes Américaines. Paris, France.
Rolling Stone. 745 Fifth Ave., New York, NY 10151.
SAGE: A Scholarly Journal on Black Women. Atlanta, GA.
Sagetrieb: A Journal Devoted to Poets in the Imagist/Objectivist Tradition. (Formerly *Sagetrieb: A Journal Devoted to Poets in the Pound-H. D.-Williams Tradition.*) Univ. of Maine at Orono, Orono, ME.
San Diego Magazine. P.O. Box 85049. San Diego, CA 92138.
San Jose Studies. San Jose State Univ., San Jose, CA.
*Saturday Review.
Saul Bellow Journal. West Bloomfield, MI.
Savvy Woman. P.O. Box 359029, Palm Coast, FL 32035.
Scripsi. Parkville, Australia.
The Short Story Review. 450 Irving St., #4, San Francisco, CA 94122.
Sipario: Il Mensile Italiano dello Spettacolo. Milan, Italy.
Slavic and East European Arts. SUNY at Stony Brook, Stony Brook, NY.
Sophia English Studies.
South Atlantic Quarterly. Duke Univ., Durham, NC.
South Carolina Review. Clemson Univ., Clemson, SC.
South Florida Magazine. (Formerly *Miami/South Florida Magazine.*) P.O. Box 140008, Miami, FL 33114.

Southern Accents: The Magazine of Fine Southern Interiors and Gardens. 2100
    Lakeshore Dr., Birmingham, AL 35209.
Southern Humanities Review. Auburn Univ., Auburn, AL.
Southern Literary Journal. Univ. of North Carolina, Chapel Hill, NC.
The Southern Quarterly: A Journal of the Arts in the South. Univ. of Southern
    Mississippi, Hattiesburg, MS.
The Southern Review. Louisiana State Univ., Baton Rouge, LA.
Southpoint.
Southwest Review. Southern Methodist Univ., Dallas, TX.
Soviet Literature. Moscow, Russia.
Sports Illustrated. P.O. Box 30602, Tampa, FL 33630.
Stanford Literature Review. Stanford Univ., Stanford, CA.
Steaua. Bucharest, Romania.
*Studia Neophilologica: A Journal of Germanic and Romance Languages and
    Literature.* Stockholm, Sweden.
Studies in American Drama, 1945–Present. Ohio State Univ. Pr., Columbus,
    OH.
Studies in American Fiction. Northeastern Univ., Boston, MA.
Studies in American Humor. Southwest Texas State Univ., San Marcos, TX.
Studies in Contemporary Satire: A Creative and Critical Journal. Clarion Univ.,
    Clarion, PA.
Studies in the Humanities. Indiana Univ. of Pennsylvania, Indiana, PA.
Studies in the Literary Imagination. Georgia State Univ., Atlanta, GA.
Studium. Rome, Italy.
Sunset. P.O. Box 2040, Harlan, IA 51537.
Suplemento Lit. La Nación. Buenos Aires, Argentina.
Tamarack: Journal of the Edna St. Vincent Millay Society. Cambridge, MA.
*Tamkang Review: A Quarterly of Comparative Studies between Chinese and For-
    eign Literatures.* Tamkang Univ., Taipei, Taiwan, Republic of China.
TDR: The Drama Review: A Journal of Performance Studies. (Formerly *The
    Drama Review.*) New York, NY.
Tennessee Williams Literary Journal. Metairie, LA.
Texas Books in Review. Center for Texas Studies, Univ. of North Texas, Denton,
    TX.
The Texas Techsan. Texas Tech Univ. Ex-Students Association, Lubbock, TX.
Text and Performance Quarterly. (Formerly *Literature in Performance: A Journal
    of Literary and Performing Arts.*) Taos, NM.
Textual Practice. Andover, Hants., England.
The Drama Review. See *TDR.*
Theater. Yale School of Drama, New Haven, CT.
TheaterWeek. 28 W. 25th St., 4th Floor, New York, NY 10010.
Theatre Annual. Univ. of Akron, Akron, OH.
Theatre Arts.
Theatre Crafts. P.O. Box 470, Mount Morris, IL 61054.
Theatre History in Canada/Histoire du Théâtre au Canada. Toronto, ON, Can-
    ada.
Theatre History Studies. Univ. of North Dakota, Grand Forks, ND.
Theatre Journal. Johns Hopkins Univ. Pr., Baltimore, MD.
Theatre Magazine.
Theatre News. Washington, D.C.

Theatre Southwest: Journal of the Southwest Theatre Conference.
Theatre Survey: The American Journal of Theatre History. Indiana Univ., Bloomington, IN.
Theatrefacts. London, England.
Third Rail: A Review of International Arts & Literature. Los Angeles, CA.
Time. Time & Life Bldg., Rockefeller Center, New York, NY 10020.
Town & Country. P.O. Box 2093, Harlan, IA 51593.
Travel Holiday. 28 W. 23rd St., New York, NY 10010.
Triveni: Journal of Indian Renaissance. Machilipatnam, India.
TV Guide, P.O. Box 400, Radnor, PA 19088.
Twentieth Century Literature: A Scholarly and Critical Journal. Hofstra Univ., Hempstead, NY.
The USF Language Quarterly. Univ. of South Florida, Tampa, FL.
U.S. News & World Report. P.O. Box 55929, Boulder, CO 80323.
Unisa English Studies: Journal of the Department of English. Pretoria, South Africa.
University of Dayton Review. Univ. of Dayton, Dayton, OH.
Vanity Fair. P.O. Box 53515, Boulder, CO 80321.
Village Voice. P.O. Box 1905, Marion, OH 43302.
Vogue. P.O. Box 55980. Boulder, CO 80322.
Vsesvit: Literaturno-Mystets'kyi̇ ta Hromads'ko-Politychnyi̇ Zhurnal. Kiev, Ukraine.
W. P.O. Box 2601, Boulder, CO 80321.
Waiguoyu. Shanghai International Studies Univ., Shanghai, People's Republic of China.
Wascana Review. Univ of Regina, Regina, SK, Canada.
Washingtonian. 1828 L St., NW, Washington, D.C. 20036.
West Georgia College Review. West Georgia Coll., Carrollton, GA.
Western American Literature. Logan, UT.
Westways. P.O. Box 8574, Boulder, CO 80328.
Whole Earth Review. 27 Gate Five Rd., Sausalito, CA 94965.
Wide Angle: A Film Quarterly of Theory, Criticism, and Practice. Ohio Univ., Athens, OH.
*Wigwag. Box 823, Farmingdale, NY 11737.
William Carlos Williams Review. Swarthmore Coll., Swarthmore, PA.
Women & Performance: A Journal of Feminist Theory. New York, NY.
Women's Studies: An Interdisciplinary Journal. New York, NY.
World Literature Today: A Literary Quarterly of the University of Oklahoma. Norman, OK.
World Literature Written in English. Univ. of Guelph, Guelph, ON, Canada.
Writer's Digest. P.O. Box 1952, Marion, OH 43306.
Xavier Review. Xavier Univ., New Orleans, LA.
The Yale Review. Yale Univ., New Haven, CT.
Yankee. Depot Square, Peterborough, NH 03458.
Zeitschrift für Anglistik und Amerikanistic. Leipzig, Germany.
The Zora Neale Hurston Forum. Baltimore, MD.

INDEX OF CRITICS

(the numbers in parentheses indicate the times a name appears on a page if
more than once)

LIST OF ADAPTED AUTHORS AND WORKS

(for unchanged titles, see Index of Titles)

INDEX OF TITLES

INDEX OF PLAYWRIGHTS

(dates noted when available)